Visual Engine
The Selected Works of 18 Top Designers

VISUAL ENGINE

The selected works of 18 top designers

PAGE ONE

Foreword

VISUAL ENGINE
Copyright © 2009 Liaoning Science and Technology Publishing House

Asian edition published in 2009 by
Page One Publishing Pte Ltd
20 Kaki Bukit View
Kaki Bukit Techpark II
Singapore 415956
Tel: (65) 6742-2088
Fax: (65) 6744-2088
enquiries@pageonegroup.com
www.pageonegroup.com

First published in 2009 by Liaoning Science and Technology Publishing House

Writers Ken Cato, Leonardo Sonnoli, Marion Deuchars, Martin Woodtli, Michel de Boer, Park Kum jun, Patrick Thomas, Pekka Loiri, Reza Abedini, Russell Warren-fisher, Sabina Oberholzer&Ranto Tagli, Saed Meshki, Seymour Chwast, Stefan Sagmeister, Toni Traglia, U.G.Sato, Vince Frost, Woody Pirtle, Wout De Vringer, Yarom Vardimon.

Editor & designer Xu Guiying

ISBN 978-981-245-757-8

All rights reserved. No part of this publication may be reproduced, stored in any retrieval system or transmitted, in any form or by any means, electronic, mechanical, photocopying, recording or otherwise, without prior permission in writing from the publisher. For information, contact Page One Publishing Pte Ltd.

Printed and bound in China

As leaders in various fields of art design, many respectable designers have striking similarities in experience, design concept, technical performance, and achievement. The 18 designers selected in this book come from different parts of the world, and they are very active in the contemporary art stage. This valuable volume contains works of these excellent designers, which will be a visual feast for its readers for they can appreciate the wonderful works and at the same time feel like they are at the frontiers of global design. Above all, the book also includes what the designers have to say about their most important work and readers will get an all-round understanding of the designers. To seek similarity in distinctiveness is one essential feature of this book.

008-029 Ken Cato, Australia

AS a long-standing member of AGI and its past president, Ken Cato has won numerous international
and Australian design awards, and his work is presented in museums and galleries throughout the world.

030-049 Leonardo Sonnoli, Italy

Leonardo Sonnoli is a member of the AGI International Executive Committee. His
award-winning poster designs have been widely exhibited and published.

050-075 Marion Deuchars, UK

Marion Deuchars' work has been described as having a "deeply
attuned spatial Gestalt that has a refreshing effortless quality". Her strengths are to be able to
visually articulate a broad range of subjects and clients with her distinctive works.

076-109 Martin Woodtli, Switzerland

Photo by Daniel Sutter

Martin Woodtli is one of the most accomplished representatives of the
new design scene in Switzerland. He is well known for his proficiency in various programs — he sketches
with the keyboard as quickly as with pencil and paper.

110-127 Michel de Boer, Netherlands

Michel de Boer has more than 25 years' experience
in the field of corporate identity and brand design. He has received many honorary positions and awards,
including two prestigious D&AD Golden Awards and seven D&AD Silver Awards.

128-157 Park Kum-jun, Korea

Kum-jun Park is president/creative director of 601BISANG, adjunct professor of Hongik University, and vice president of the Publication Department of VIDAK. He has received literally hundreds of international design awards. He believes that a living design comes from reality and is based on politics, society and culture.

158-177 Pekka Loiri, Finland

As president of the Lahti Poster Biennial in Finland, he has received many awards for his posters in Finland's Best Posters competitions. Pekka Loiri has also been involved in education, for instance, as a lecturer at a number of universities of art and design. In addition, he has taught for longer periods of time in Reykjavik and as a visiting professor at the Cracow Academy of Art and the Art Academy in Usti and Labem.

178-209 Reza Abedini, Iran

As a member of Iranian Graphic Designers Society and AGI, the supervisor of the cultural committee of I.G.D.S, writer and critic in the field of visual arts since 1990, and managing director and editor-in-chief of *Manzar*, Occasional Pictorial magazine, Abedini has received many awards for his work and he has had many solo exhibitions worldwide.

210-227 Russell Warren-Fisher, UK

An LA nomination by Gert Dumbar for the "Creative Futures" award helped him launch Warren-Fisher's independent career directly after he graduated from the RCA. In 2004 he became head of research for Print Digital (an experimental digital printing facility) at the Royal College of Art, London.

228-245 Saed Meshki, Iran

He is now teaching at the same university where he graduated. At the same time, as an art director and graphic designer of several publication houses, Saed has focused his efforts on book design, and founded Meshki publication house in 2003. Numerous books on illustration and literature are to appear soon.

246-263 Seymour Chwast, USA

He is a founding partner of the celebrated Push Pin Studios, whose distinct style has had a worldwide influence on contemporary visual communications. His works are in a variety of styles and media. His work has been exhibited in major galleries and museums in the United States, Europe, Japan, Brazil and Russia.

264-295 Stefan Sagmeister, USA

Stefan Sagmeister is among today's most important graphic designers. His creative world is marked by his innovative way of merging the unmergeable. A profound understanding of the creative process is evident in his work. He uses technical solutions and instruments as tools for creating beautiful "hybrids", which level the conventional boundaries between categories.

296-307 Toni Traglia, Italy

Since 1987 he has worked in the advertising field for the first five years of his career and then he specialised in the art direction, working for agencies located in Switzerland and in Milan. He has been entrusted with corporate design and packaging works.

308-327 U.G.Sato, Japan

As a member of AGI, JAGDA, and TIS, he has held numerous solo exhibitions in Tokyo, Finland, Amsterdam, Osaka, Kawasaki, Nagoya, etc. and has also participated in many joint exhibitions. He has won numerous awards including Gold Prize at International Biennale of Graphic Design Brno , etc.

328-345 Vince Frost, Australia

As a member of CSD, D&AD, ISTD, AGDA and AGI, Vince plays an active role in the world design community, lecturing at colleges and conferences. After graduating from the design industry's best finishing school, he set up Frost Design in 1994. Since then, many awards have come his way.

346-353 Woody Pirtle, USA

Woody Pirtle has served on the board of *HOW* magazine, Sustainable Hudson Valley, and the American Institute of Graphic Arts. In October 2003 he was awarded the prestigious AIGA Medal for his career contribution to the design profession. His work has been exhibited worldwide.

354-377 Wout De Vringer, Netherlands

He has been a member of the AGI since 2002. Together with Ben Faydherbe, he formed his own studio in the Hague (1986) to work more for cultural institutions. He gave guest lectures at Yale University (New Haven), SUNY Purchase (New York State), CalArts (Los Angeles) etc. and taught graphics at the Evening Academy in Rotterdam.

378-399 Yarom Vardimon, Israel

He has been a professor of Visual Communications since 1980. He was in charge of the submission of the undergraduate program and Master program in Israel, and presently, he is the vice president for Academic Affairs and Dean of the Faculty of Design at the Shenkar College of Engineering and Design, Ramat Gan.

Ken Cato

Ken Cato is an Australian designer with international reputation. He is the chairman of Cato Purnell Partners, which was established in Melbourne in 1970 and with offices in Sydney, Brisbane, Perth, Wellington, Buenos Aires, Barcelona, Santiago, Guadalajara, Mexico City and representative offices in London, Mumbai, New York, Singapore, Tokyo, Taipei, Dubai and Guangzhou. Cato Purnell Partners is the largest design company in the Southern Hemisphere.

Cato's work encompasses all facets of corporate identity, brand management and design. His philosophy of design is dynamically holistic which provides synergistic solutions. As a graphic designer, his work has earned him international reputation. He has won numerous international and Australian design awards, and his work is presented in museums and galleries throughout the world. He is a long-standing member of AGI and is past AGI President. The world's largest student design conference was founded by Ken Cato in 1991. Now approaching its 17th year, AGIdeas attracts annually over 2000 young designers from the world.

In 1995, Ken was awarded the first Australian Honorary Doctorate of Design from Swinburne University and was inducted into the Hall of Fame of the Inaugural Victorian Design Awards. Ken is a foundational member of the Australian Writers and Art Directors Association, a member of the American Institute of Graphic Arts, ICOGRADA, Design Institute of Australia, Australian Marketing Institute, Industrial Design Council of Australia, and patron of the Australian Academy of Design.

Ken is also an acclaimed author and has written numerous books.

PROJECT: SEVENTY-FIFTH ANNIVERSARY
TYPE: BRAND IDENTITY
CLIENT: THE SYDNEY STORE

"The idea was to wrap the entire building as a very large present. The timeframe, building regulations, permits and approvals all provided barriers. The theme for the street front windows was to deal with their 75-year-old fashion and extend them in a large scale. All that seemed insurmountable became possible eventually, even the time frame." – Ken Cato

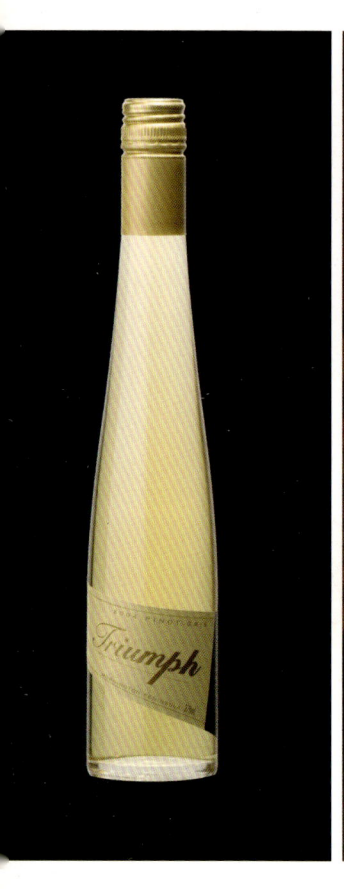

Top Left: Packaging for T'Gallant
Top Right: Packaging for T'Gallant
Bottom Left: Packaging for Peerick Vineyard
Bottom Right: Packaging for De Bortoli

Corporate identity and packaging system for Poppy cosmetic products

Packaging for Victoria Bitter from Foster's Group Limited

Left: Packaging for Empire Lager from Foster's Group Limited
Middle: Packaging for Light Ice from Foster's Group Limited
Right: packaging for Aquana, a new water product developed by Coca Cola, New Zealand

Top Left: Corporate identity for IAG
Top Right: Corporate identity for the NorthStar bus company in Auckland, New Zealand
Middle Left: Corporate identity for Southern Cross Broadcasting
Middle Right: Corporate identity for the Collie Print Trust
Bottom: Corporate identity for Metasource

014

Top: Corporate identity for the Royal Guide Dogs Association
Bottom: Corporate identity for Epiderm Research and Education

EPIDERM
RESEARCH & EDUCATION

016

Opposite: Corporate identity program for the Supply Chain
Corporate identity for Energy Australia

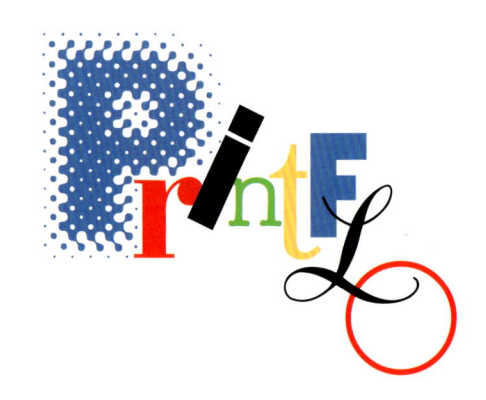

Top: Identity for Melbourne's bid for the 1996 Olympic Games
Middle Left: Corporate identity for the Hospital of Hope Timor-Leste,
a foundation set up to help raise capital to build the hospital in East Timor
Middle Right: Corporate identity for Printflo
Bottom Left: Corporate identity for iVistra
Bottom Right: Corporate identity for Energex

SYDNEY
Super Dome

Corporate identity for Sydney SuperDome, the gymnastics venue for the 2000 Olympic Games

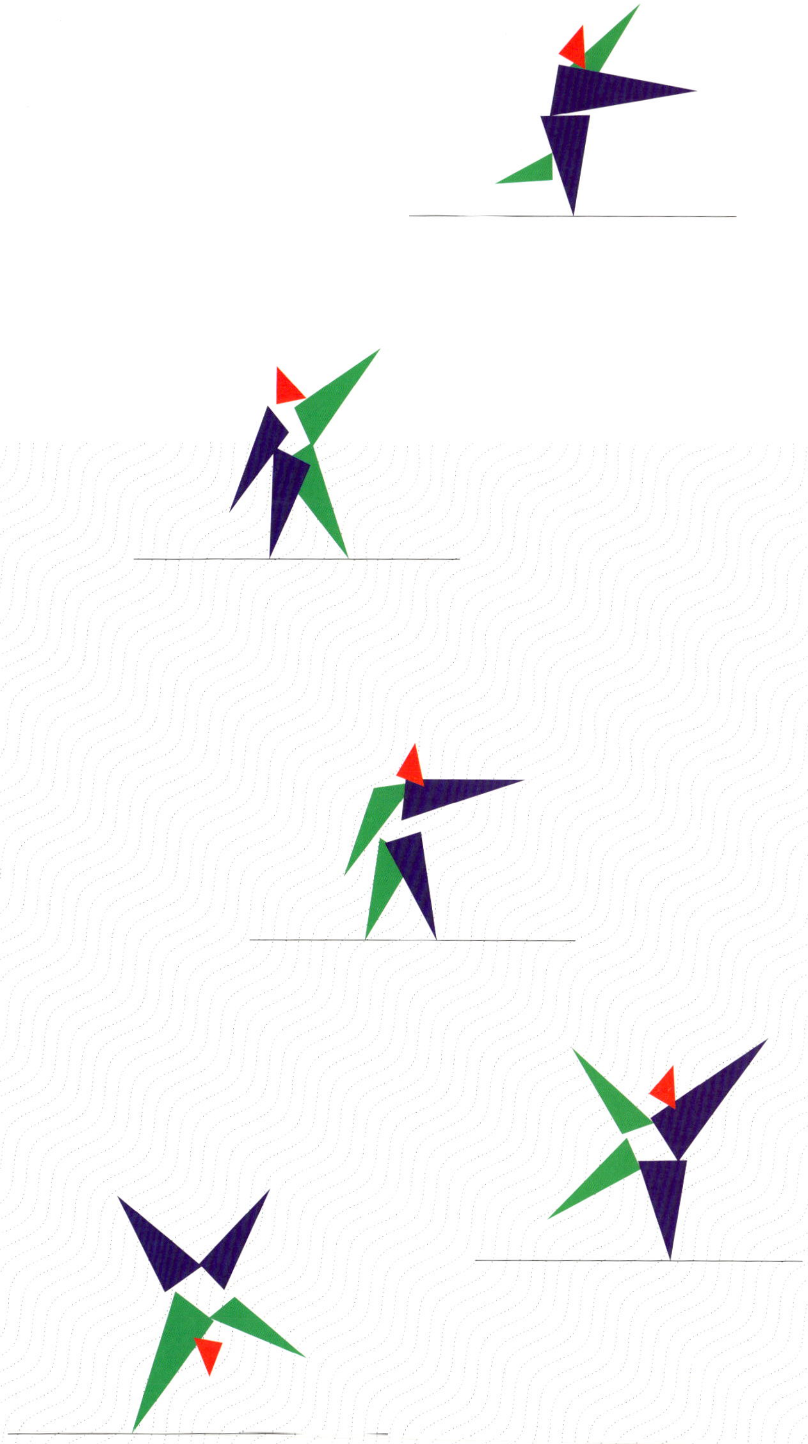

019

Top: Identity campaign for the National University of Singapore
Bottom: Corporate identity for Roxburgh Park

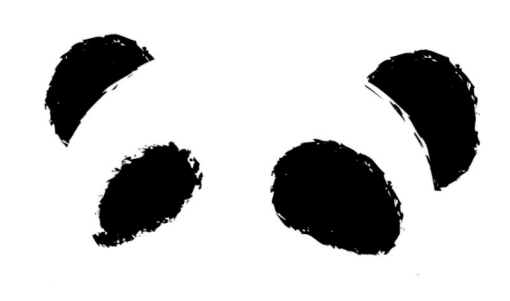

Identity program poster for
AGIdeas 2005 International Design Week

Top: Corporate identity for Myfuture, an internet-based career and training exploration
Bottom: Brand identity for Hidden Creek

Top and middle: Name, corporate identity for Myki, the Victorian State Government's public transport smart card ticketing system
Bottom: Corporate identity for Link, a New Zealand bus company

Corporate identity for Medibank Private

Hospitals & Extras

medibank

Package Plus

Combined hospital and extras packages

medibank

feel better

PackageBonus No matter which PackagePlus option you choose, you'll be rewarded with a PackageBonus. This enables you to claim, each Calendar Year, a Benefit to use towards a range of approved Membership and health-related expenses.

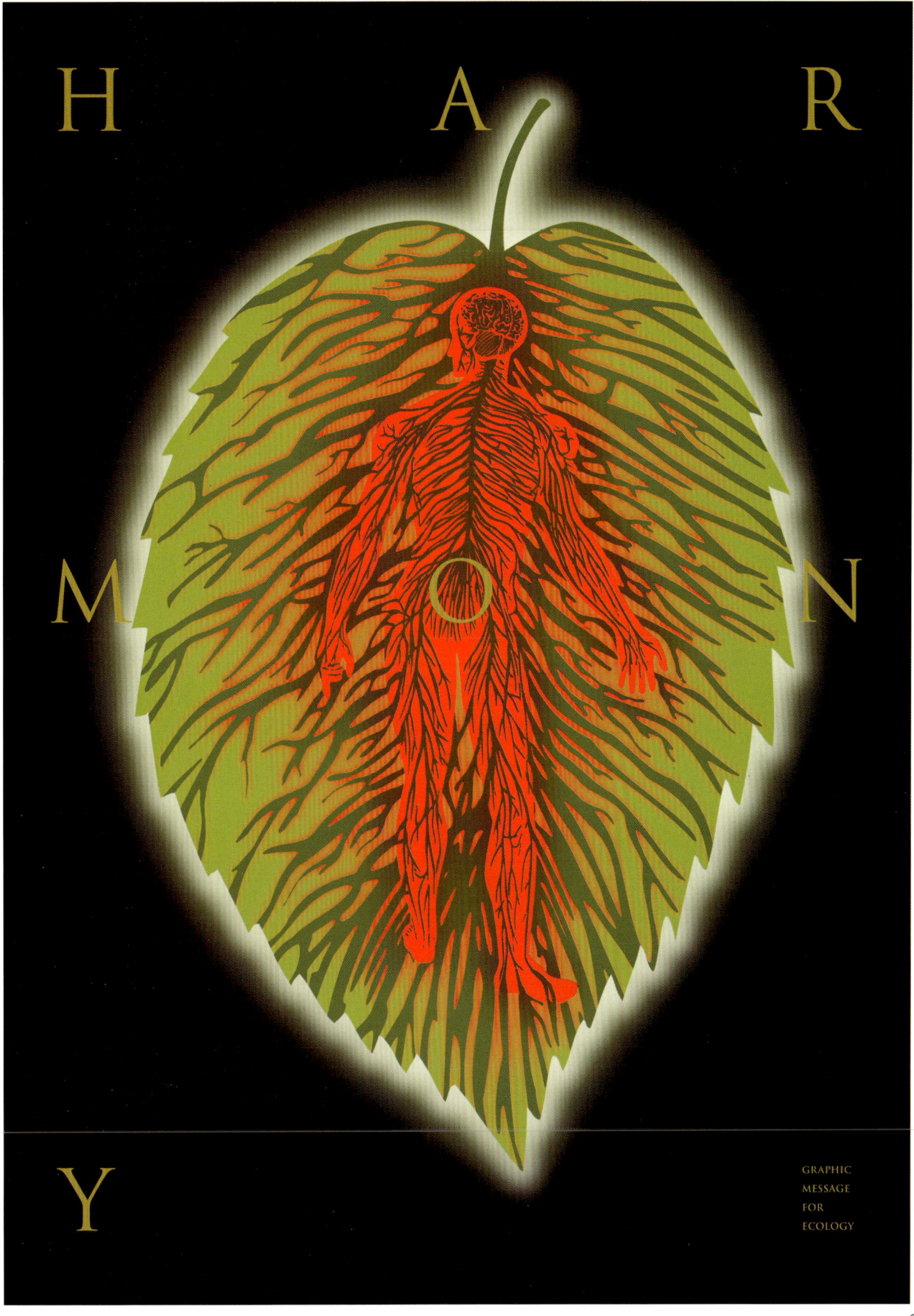

Poster for an international exhibit at the Ginza Graphic Gallery in Japan

HARMONY

GRAPHIC MESSAGE FOR ECOLOGY

025

026

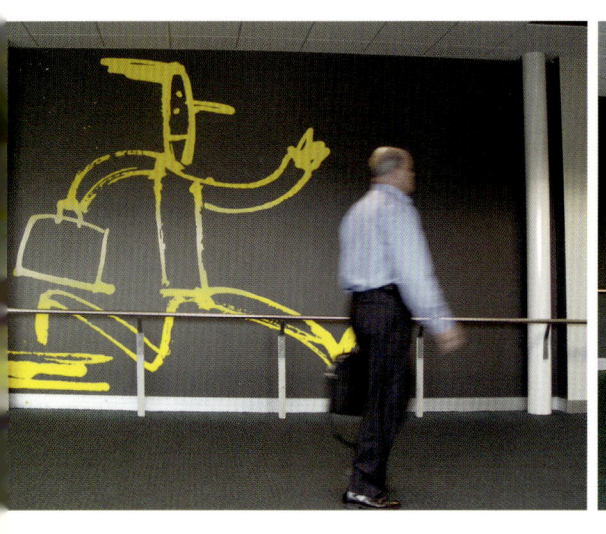

The corporate identity and positioning, 'Wild at Heart' captures what is unique about Wellington's wild weather and coastline as well as the spirit of its people

Packaging for Pura Milk products from National Dairies
Opposite: Name and corporate identity for the world's largest purpose-built Airport City, World Central in Dubai and its related developments World Central Science and Technology Park, World Central Golf Resort, World Central Logistics City, World Central International Airport and World Central Commercial City

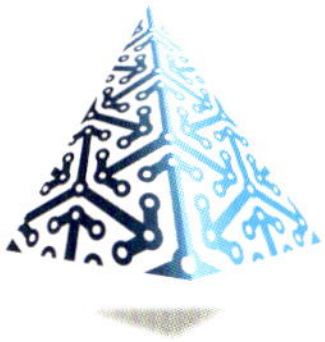
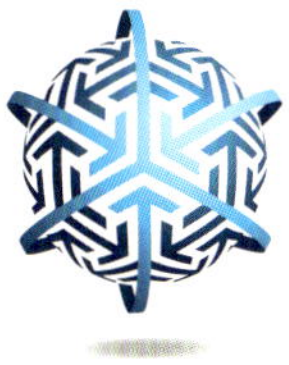
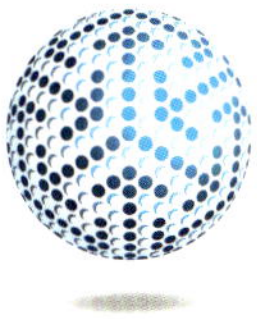
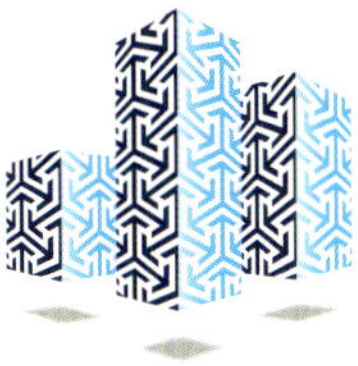
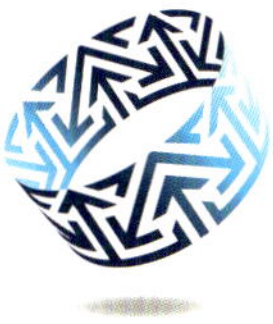
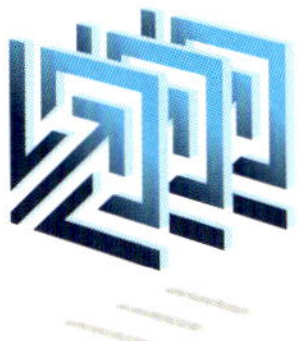
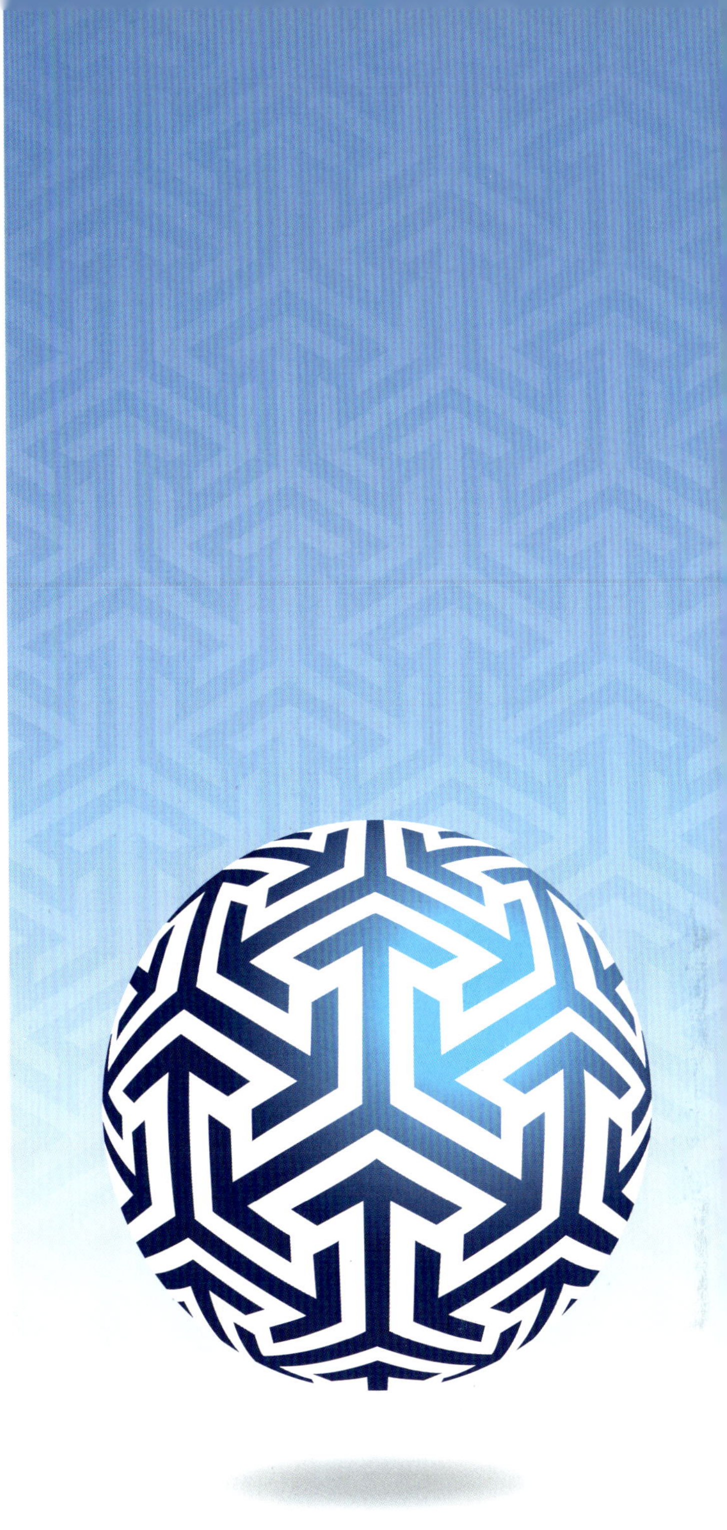
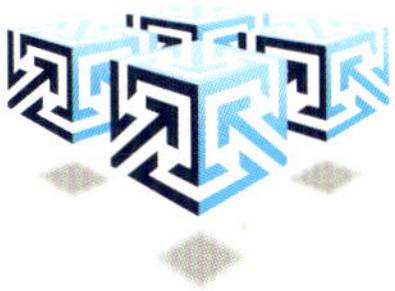
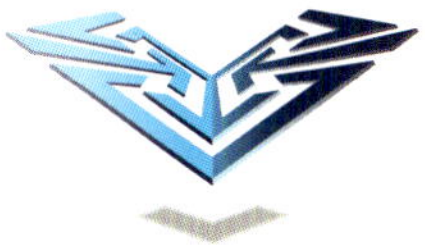

Leonardo Sonnoli

Leonardo Sonnoli was awarded a diploma from the High Institute of Industrial Arts of Urbino in 1962, and received his professional instruction and training at the Tassinari/Vetta Studio of Trieste. In 2002, along with Paolo Tassinari and Pierpaolo Vetta, he founded CODEsign. He is involved with the visual identity of private and public companies, the communication of cultural events, editorial design, signal systems and graphic exhibitions.

His posters are held in major international public collections (National Library of France in Paris, Museum of Decorative Arts in Zurich). His works have been presented in several exhibitions such as 4:3; 50 Years of Italian and German Design in Bonn; Leonardo Sonnoli, in the town of Pesaro in Chaumont; 8 Graphic Designers in Ningbo (China); the 5th Colour+Leonardo Sonnoli, in Tehran. Moreover, he has published his works in the respective catalogues, international journals both in Italy and abroad, including the reviews *Area*; *Black and White*; *La grafica in Italia*; *Red, Wine and Green*; *Leonardo Sonnoli*. He was awarded silver medal by the Art Exhibition of Toyama (Japan), and received the "Mention of Honour" recognition at the XIX Premio Compasso d'oro/Adi, the Merit Award of the Art Directors Club of New York, the Special Prize at the First China International Poster Biennial and the Golden Bee Award in Moscow.

Sonnoli is a member of the AGI International Executive Committee, and a member of the AGI (2000). Now he is teaching at the Faculty of Design and Arts of the Iuav University of Venice, living and working between Rimini and Trieste.

PROJECT: RIGHTS AND DUTIES
TYPE: POSTER
CLIENT: DON GAUDIANO FOUNDATION

"National conference, on the rights and duties of people in the metropolitan areas, organised by the Don Gaudiano Foundation. The two words 'rights' and 'duties' in Italian (diritti e doveri) start with the same 'd' and are two opposite sides of the same face." – Leonardo Sonnoli

dirittidoveri

Poster made for a series of lectures on children books
Opposite: Graphic work for Australian Academy of Design, Melbourne, Australia

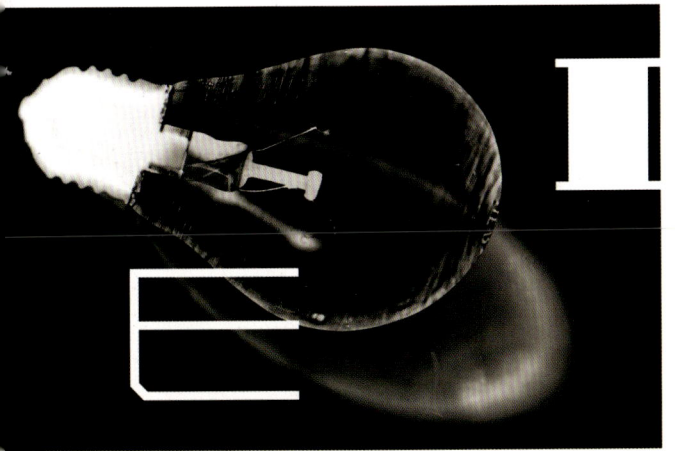

ideas come from history

tribute
to
laszlo
moholy-nagy
designed
by
leonardo
sonnoli

A reverse motion to the future

The expression "genius loci" has often been generalized because of brief and concise analysis. Exception: the typo/graphical work of Leonardo Sonnoli, where coincidences and historic-geographical returns may lead us to summarize the complexity of "spirit of places" and of time, we would add. The author is perfectly aware of this and while he is designing posters, he is used to scattering clues and indications on the tangled composition of signs and images.
He was born in Trieste in the early sixties of last century, of csaric tuscan descent he has an hybrid origin like many people in that region. LS attended a technical school, which could be seen as a direct derivation of the Hapsburg "Industrials". At the beginning of the twentieth century, in the class of heads of art at the "Industrials", there were students such as Urbano Corva, Giorgio Dabovich, Nino Ferenzi, Giovanni Giordani, Piero Lucano, Guido Marussig, Argio Orell, Antonio Quaiatti, Pollione Sigon, Vito Timmel, Giulio Toffoli: they were a specialized group working within solid typolithographic local worlds (Modiano and Salto above all), they were the artists of Trieste of the poster movement, who along with the more famous Leopoldo Metlicovitz and Marcello Dudovich, held a very persistent position within the history of the Italian and European poster. Grown up in the border town par excellence, at the intersection between the Mediterranean and the Northern Europe, LS has breathed present times which were hanging between past and future, along with many broadminded people and also with many contradictions. During the Eighties he was in Urbino, as a student of the Superior Institute for artistic industries, the school of Albe Steiner; among his teachers there were Michele Provinciali from Parma and Alfred Hoenegger, from Dachau in Germany; as it is easy to imagine, from the South he learns a free and creative approach to his projects and from the North he learns especially the methodology. For his graduation essay he went back to his home town, he was in Trieste to register, record and study the work of Urbano Corva. While he was there he also had a short but intense professional experience. He then started a series of study trips to countries of deep typographic traditions such as the Netherlands and Germany. He has been on tracks of Jan Tschichold, Herbert Bayer, Laszlo Moholy Nagy, he could improve his knowledge about the immense but unsolved liaison between artistic avant-guardes and possible technical reproducibility. From people like Theo Van Doesburg, El Lissitzky, Kurt Schwitters he borrowed the planning approach and often the formal repertoire. So, while living in Northern Europe, he started to install that sort of rear-view mirror on the modernity which will allow him to safely follow an independent research route in the future years: although in an apparently reckless cadence, quotations and remixings of his works are arranged in a logical evolution and not simply reproduced. He then moved to the South: in 1990 he started his business as an art director at the studio of Massimo Dolcini in Pesaro; he was working in the Marche, the region of Seneca and Pannaggi but he lived in Rimini on the coast, so beloved by Dudovich who worked there in 1922 and in 1946. The overall result of the intersection between the international language of European graphic work and the provincial vernacular is still to be verified: LS who has recently become a member of the Alliance Graphique Internationale, has received many reviews, too many to be listed here, especially from international critics.
Before closing, two questions and two temporal attempts to give an answer:
is it considered to be anachronistic the decision of LS to propose the poster as a preferred sector of his professional activity? It is true that the new media, after radio and television, have pushed the placard to the edge of communication, but the exceptions of Oliviero Toscani for the Benetton company and the waxy posters of our latest Italian general election should make us think over it, positively and negatively. Considering the word "manifesto", is it correct to make a distinction among its political meaning (i.e. Manifesto of the Communist Party), its artistic meaning (i.e. Manifesto of the Futurists), its persuasive meaning (i.e. commercial posters) or its institutional meaning (i.e. the posters announcing cultural and public events)? Historically it seems to be correct but in reality it is anachronistic: the upsetting movements of this end/beginning millennium make ambiguity one of the principal driving-force of communication. For this reason the work of LS is important: because he is able to overlap, hybridize, cut and dim those techniques and languages that the tradition has transmitted to us as well defined and shaped ones but only apparently.
Pierpaolo Vetta, 2001

Predmeti brez duše
Omara z rdečimi šipami.
Dolgčas spi v kotu.
Avtomobil je senzacija.
Kozmičini dih: potres.
Na razžarjeni zarji
rdeči ATOM
Nenapisana moja beseda
odsev
odsev.
ATOM
Smeh kralja Dade
na lesenem konjičku.
Hi, hi.
Pum.
Srečko Kosovel

Poster printed front and back for a lecture in Ljubljana (Slovenia) on history and with letters as method to design

034

Left: Presentation of the novel book *La Discarica*
Right: Poster designed in occasion of the AGI Congress in Berlin in September 2005

035

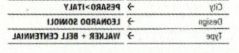

Poster-tribute to Matthew Carter made in occasion of his lecture in Italy.
Opposite: Typographic poster for the International Ningbo Poster Exhibition

EMPTYNESS

emptypeness è la fuga dalla composizione tipografica
che rappresenta solo se stessa, è la volontà di stare in silenzio
pur usando il nostro alfabeto fonetico.

emptypeness is an escape from a typographical composition
that represents only itself; it is the desire to remain silent
whilst using our phonetic alphabet.

A B C D E
F G H I J
K L M N O P Q
R S T U
V W X Y Z

una lettera è fatta del significato della parola che compone,
del contenuto che trasporta; tipografare senza contenuti non è nemmeno
esercizio di stile: è solamente esercizio anestetico.

meglio allora usare un tipo vuoto, non esistente, ana/grafico dichiaratamente,
per mettere in rilievo, togliendo spessore, la vuotezza di senso
e l'inutilità di esistere di questo poster solo contenitore.

emptypeness è la fuga dalla composizione tipografica
che rappresenta solo se stessa, è la volontà di stare in silenzio
pur usando il nostro alfabeto fonetico.

a letter takes on the meaning of the word it composes
and the content it relays. typography without content is not even
an exercise in style; it is simply an "unaesthetic" exercise.

far better therefore, to use an empty, non-existent and declaredly
non-graphic type in order to highlight, by removing depth,
the emptiness of sense and the futility of this poster that is merely a container.

emptypeness is an escape from a typographical composition
that represents only itself; it is the desire to remain silent
whilst using our phonetic alphabet.

leonardo sonnoli
codesign 2004

038

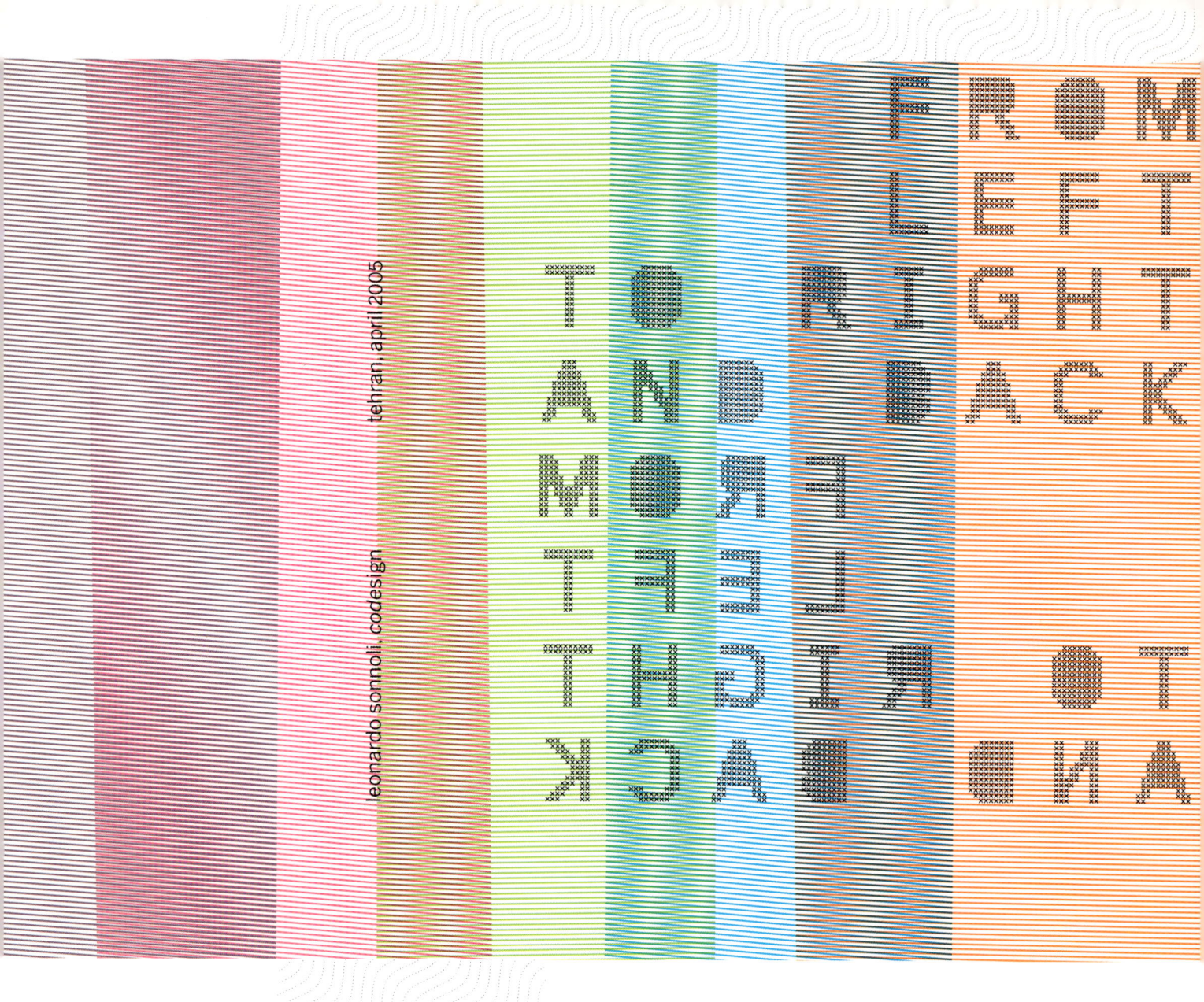

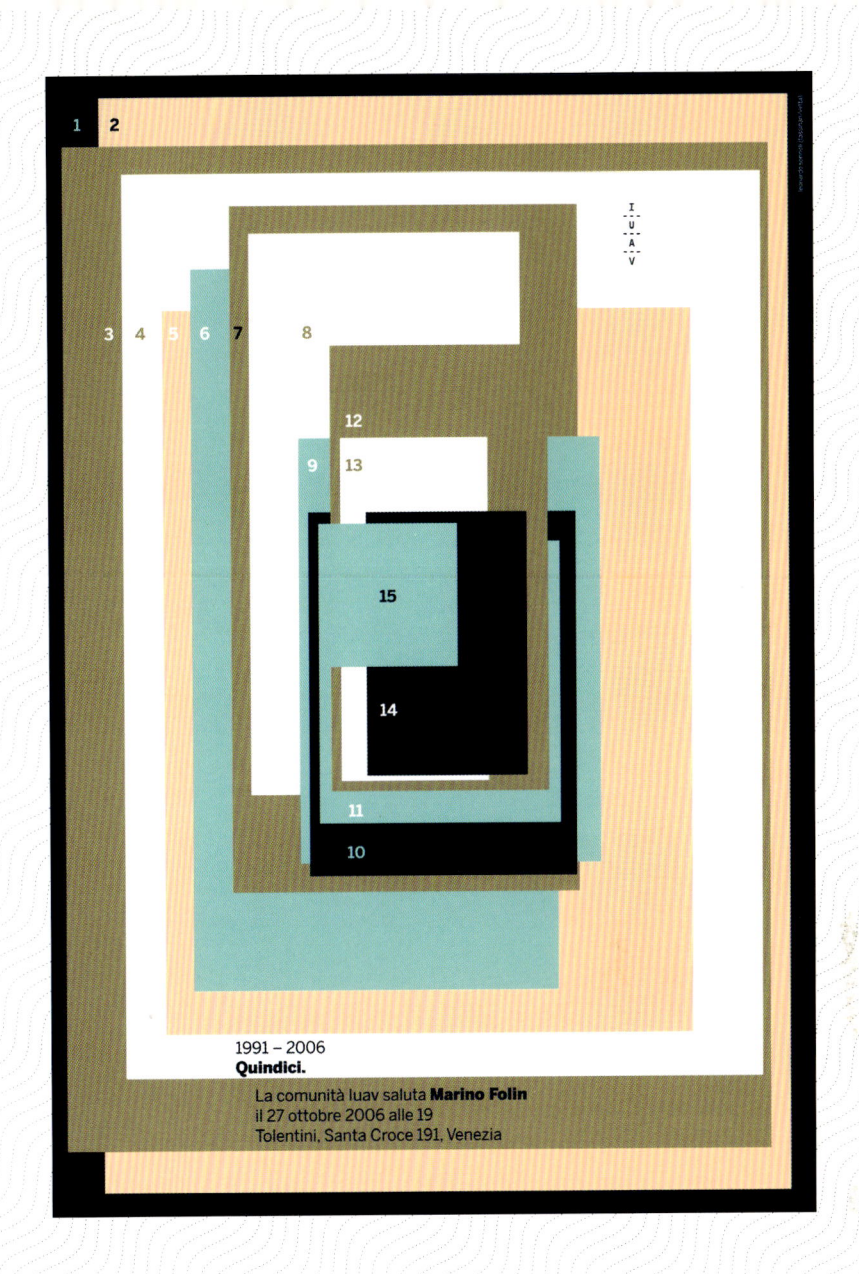

Opposite: Poster designed for his personal lecture and exhibition in Tehran, titled "From Left to Right and Back"
Poster for celebrating 15 years of Mr. Folin's direction in University Iuav of Venice

KAZUYO SEJIMA
+
RYUE NISHIZAWA
SANAA

BASILICA PALLADIANA DI VICENZA
30 OTTOBRE 2005 - 29 GENNAIO 2006
ORARIO 10.00 > 18.00 CHIUSO LUNEDÌ
APERTO 31.10 26.12 2.1
INGRESSO: INTERO 8,00 € RIDOTTO 5,00 €

-> PROMOTORI
•COMUNE DI VICENZA
•PROVINCIA DI VICENZA
•REGIONE DEL VENETO

-> PATROCINIO
•ASSOCIAZIONE
INDUSTRIALI
DI VICENZA -
SEZIONE
COSTRUTTORI EDILI
•ORDINE DEGLI
ARCHITETTI
PIANIFICATORI
PAESAGGISTI
E CONSERVATORI
DELLA PROVINCIA
DI VICENZA
•FONDAZIONE
DEGLI ARCHITETTI
DI VICENZA
•CAMERA DI COMMERCIO
I.A.A. DI VICENZA
•UNIVERSITÀ DELLA
SVIZZERA ITALIANA -
ACCADEMIA DI
ARCHITETTURA,
MENDRISIO
•UNIVERSITÀ IUAV
DI VENEZIA

-> ORGANIZZAZIONE
•ABACOARCHITETTURA
•COMUNE DI VICENZA - ASSESSORATO
ALLE ATTIVITÀ CULTURALI
-> INFORMAZIONI
BASILICA PALLADIANA +39.0444322196
WWW.ABACOARCHITETTURA.ORG
-> INFORMAZIONI TURISTICHE
CONSORZIO VICENZAÉ +39.0444320854
WWW.VICENZAE.ORG

TRENITALIA
INGRESSO RIDOTTO
AI POSSESSORI
DI BIGLIETTO
FERROVIARIO
CON DESTINAZIONE
VICENZA

Poster designed in occasion of the exhibition in Vicenza (Italy) of the architects Kazuyo Sejima and Ryue Nishizawa - Sanaa

The corporate identity for the Insiel company, a mark could condense the two main principles of the company: simple and complex, simple solutions for complex problems

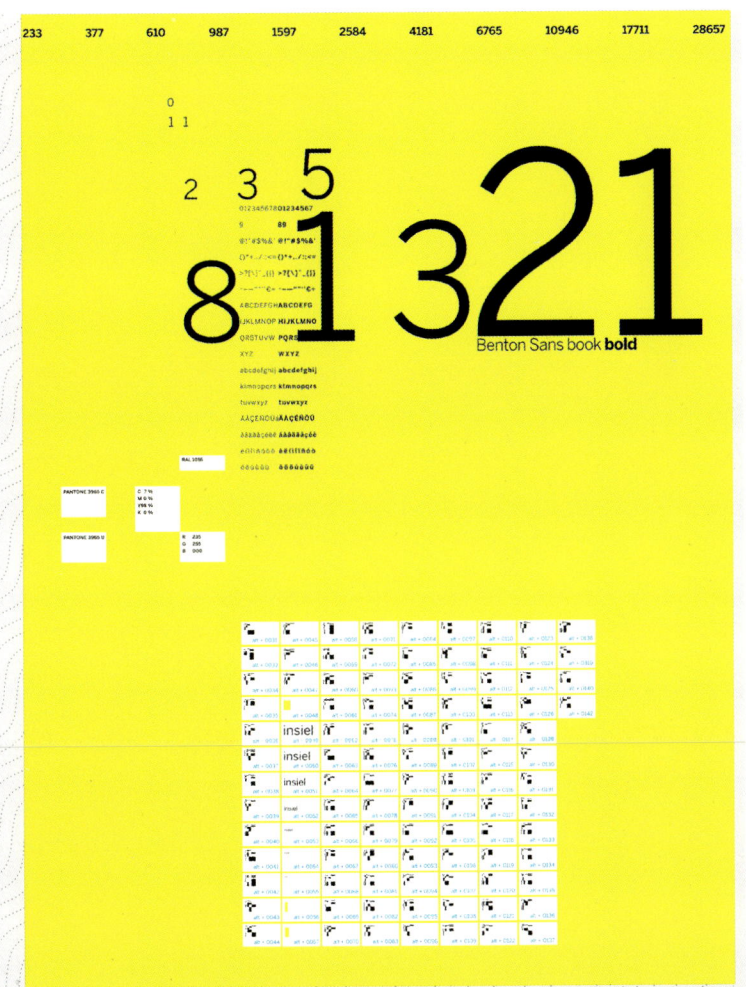

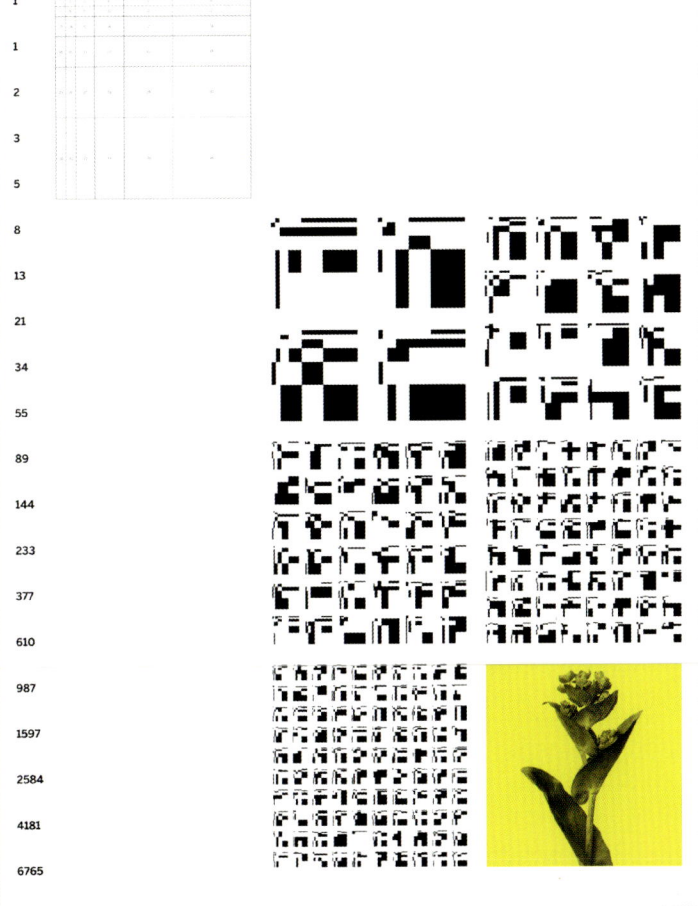

041

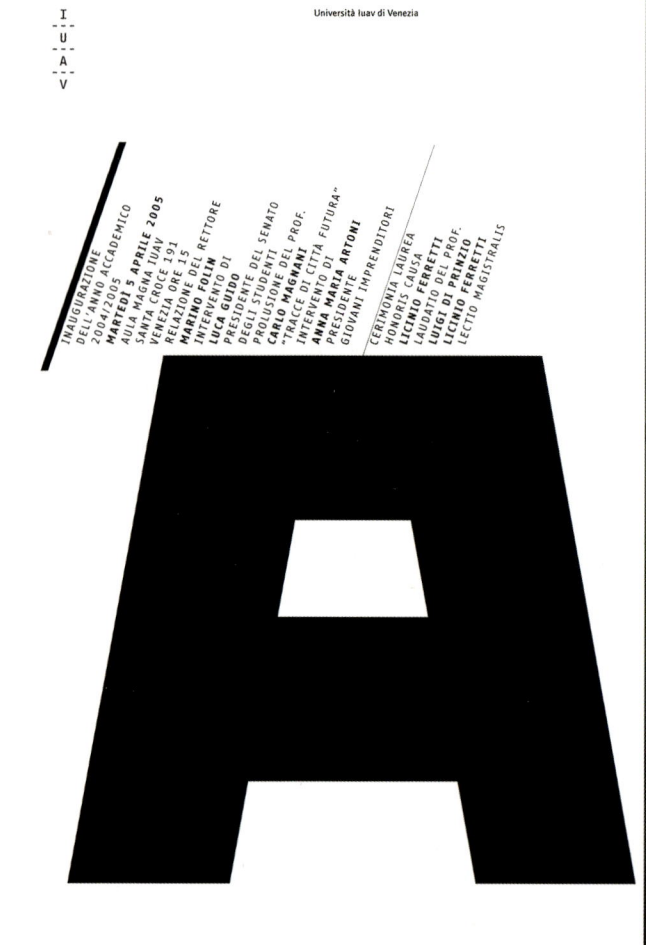

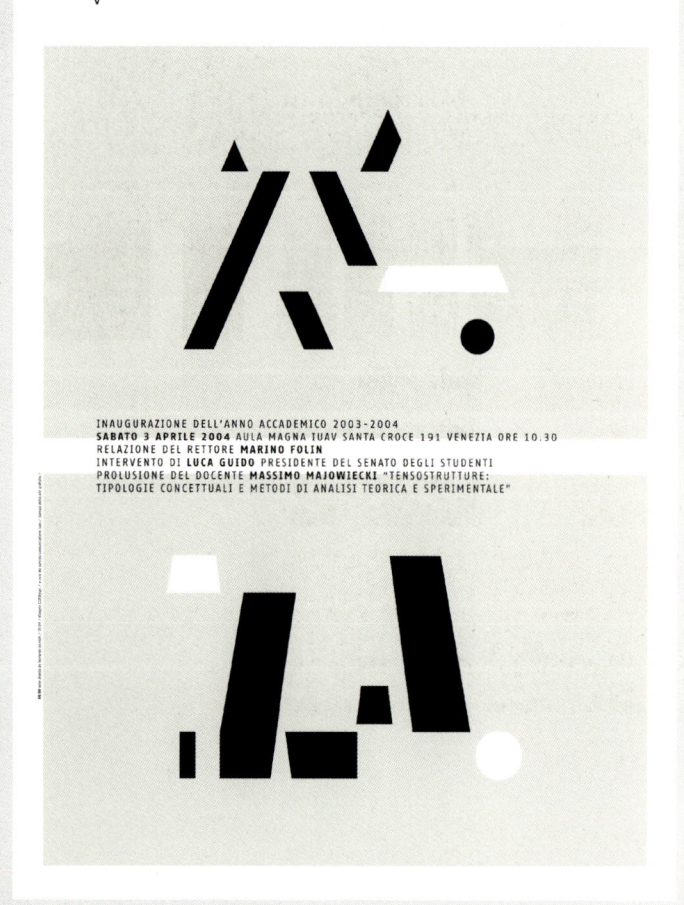

Top: Double poster (two posters 70x100 posted together) for the University Iuav of Venice Academic Year opening in 2005
Bottom: Single poster (printed in offset two colours + drycut) for the University Iuav of Venice Academic Year opening in 2003

WHEN I'VE NOTH- ING TO SAY I WRITE IT IN BOLD.

kakejiku by leonardo sonnoli
congress in kyoto agi 2006 to to

"Kakejiku" for an exhibition at the Ginza Graphic Gallery in Tokyo

044

Spreads: Competition for the corporate identity of the Kieler Woche, an international regatta in North Germany (not realised)

045

tartini font

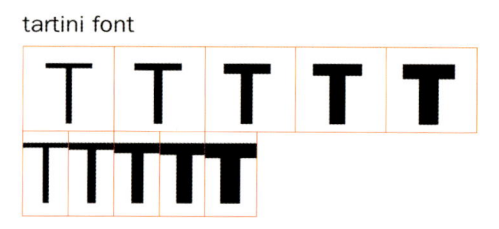

identità visiva
per il **conservatorio
giuseppe tartini**

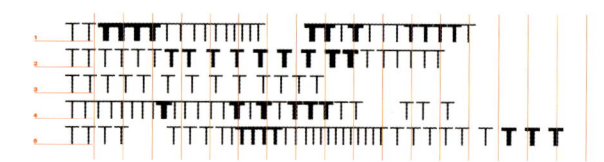

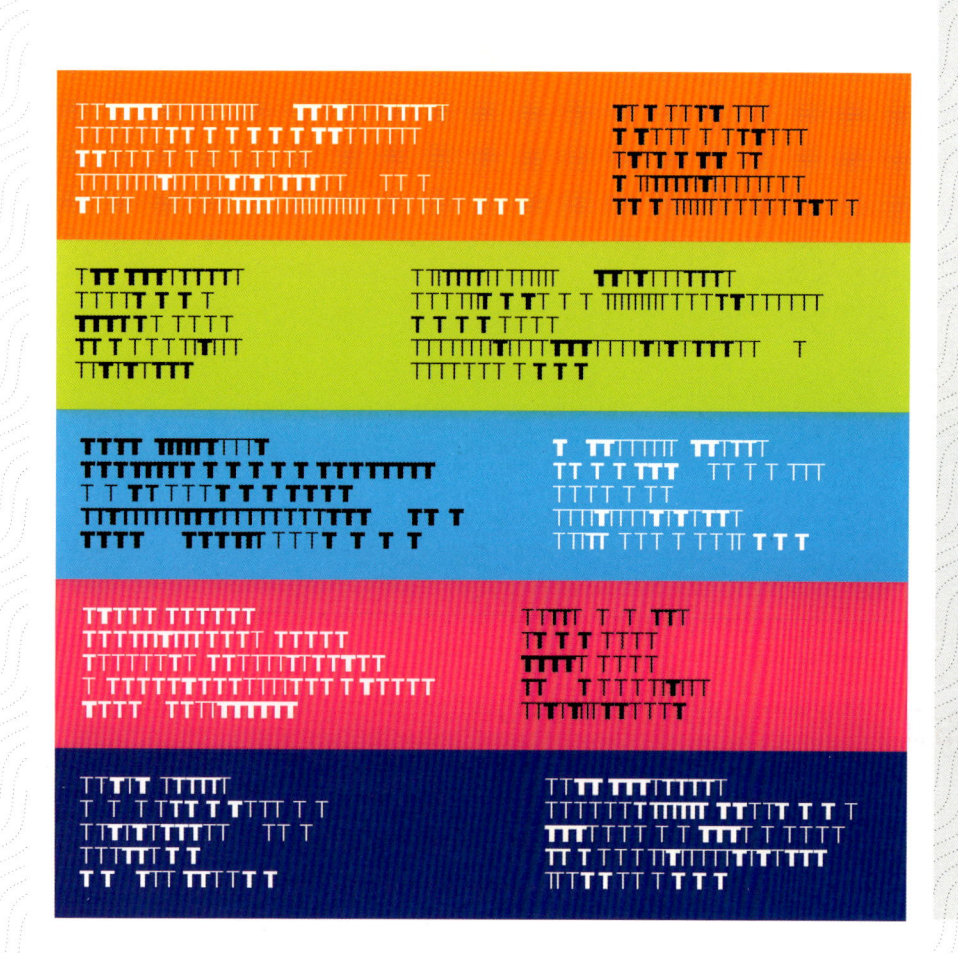

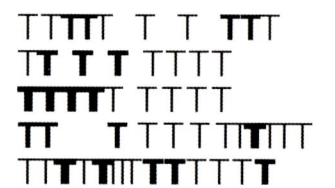

**Conservatorio
statale
di musica
Giuseppe
Tartini**

Opposite: Moving logotype made for the Tartini Music Conservatoire
Poster for an exhibition on Sonnoli's work, located in Palermo, Sicily

Poster printed on both sides, it is a tribute to the Italian graphic designer Pino Tovaglia, one in a series dedicated to the milestones of the Italian graphic design

Poster-tribute to Gianfranco Grignani, one of the most influential Italian graphic designers of the post war, made in occasion of a lecture on his work

Marion Deuchars

Born in Scotland, Marion Deuchars is a London based illustrator/artist. She studied illustration and printmaking at Duncan of Jordanstone College of Art in Dundee, Scotland and illustration at the Royal College of Art, London in 1989. Along with fellow RCA students, she formed an art and design studio and continues today to work in a multi-disciplinary studio in North London. Deuchars has been voted amongst the 100 top designers in the UK.

Since graduating, Deuchars has worked with major design and advertising agencies worldwide. Her commercial work has covered a varied range of illustration and design, including corporate literature, publishing, editorial, packaging, retail, advertising, design for web, brand development, craft, and architecture.

Deuchars has a distinct graphic language that utilises everything from pencils, paint, to photography and photoshop. Her work has been described as having a "deeply attuned spatial Gestalt" and has a refreshing effortless quality. Her strengths are to be able to visually articulate a broad range of subjects and clients with her distinctive artworks. Her clients are many and vary from FIA Formula One, Levi's, Volkswagen, Adidas, to *Time Magazine*. Recent projects include a regular series of weekly political illustrations for the *Guardian Newspaper*, producing the Design and Art Directors' annual report with Vince Frost which involved handwriting all the text of over 6000 words, and collaborating with Fernando Gutierrez to create a strong identity for the Spanish Publisher Losada's back catalogue of 3000 titles.

Presently she is producing a limited edition set of silkscreen prints from her Cuba and other reportage projects and working on a children's book.

Member of AGI since 2001

PROJECT: GEORGE ORWELL BOOK COVERS
TYPE: ILLUSTRATION
CLIENT: PENGUIN BOOKS

"My aim with producing imagery for the series was to provide very simple, striking covers that captured the spirit of Orwell and that translated each book in a distinct and contemporary way. The big challenge (because he has been interpreted by nearly every generation) was how to find a unique but relevant voice that would encourage someone who had never picked up Orwell to do so, and those who had, pick up again." – Marion Deuchars

Spreads: Self promotional work produced from a two-month stay in Havana, Cuba

052

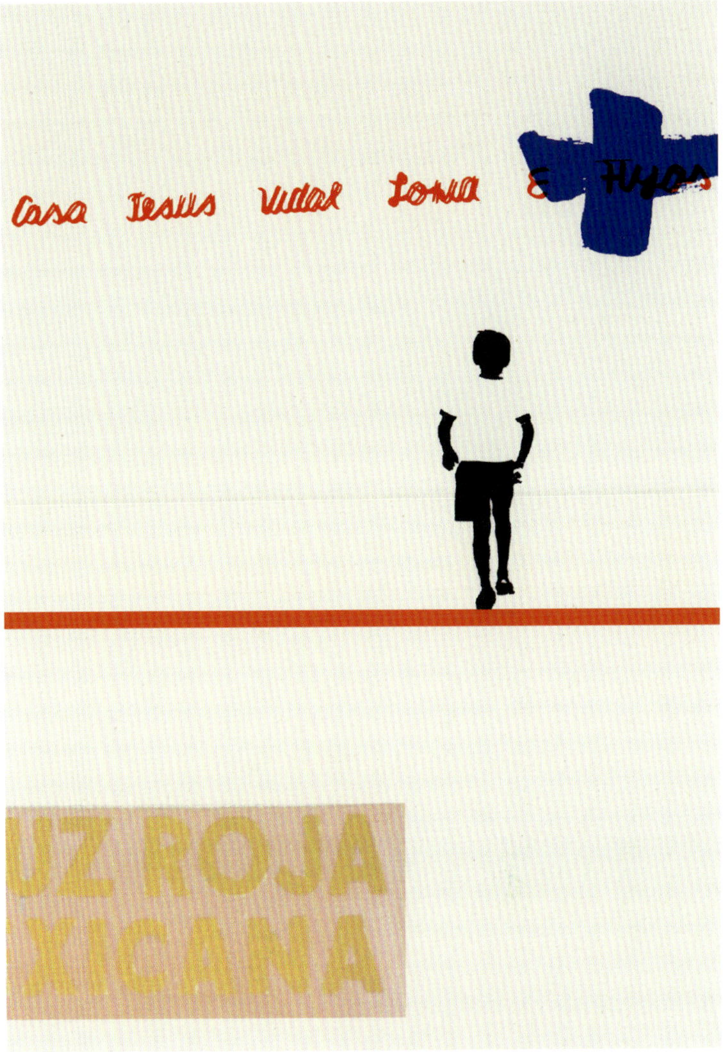
UZ ROJA
XICANA

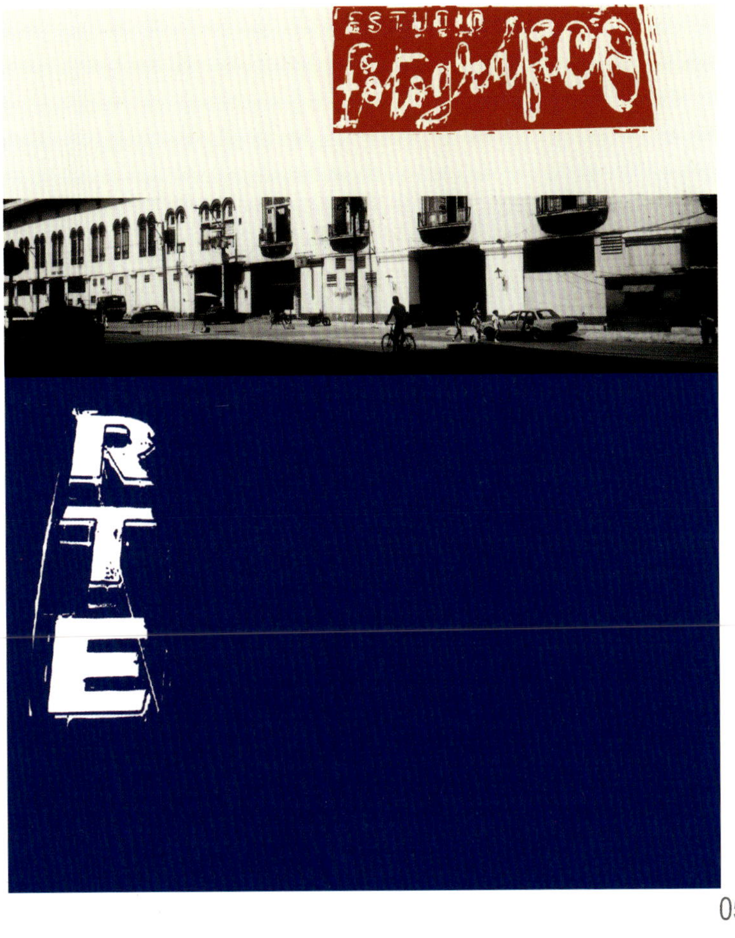
ESTUDIO
fotografico
RTE

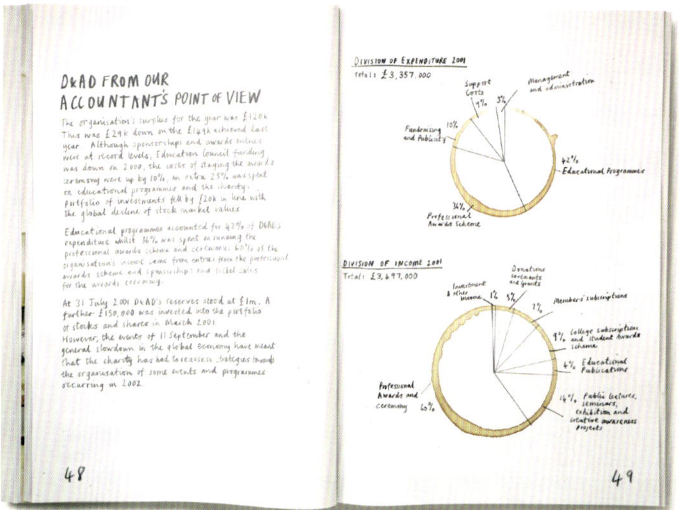

Spreads: Illustration and design for D&AD Annual Report

Fourth Estate Publishing Catalogue 2003

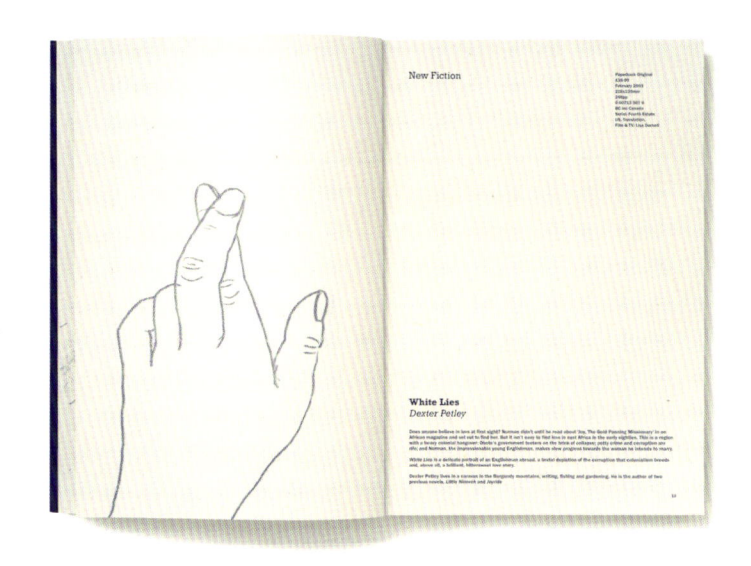

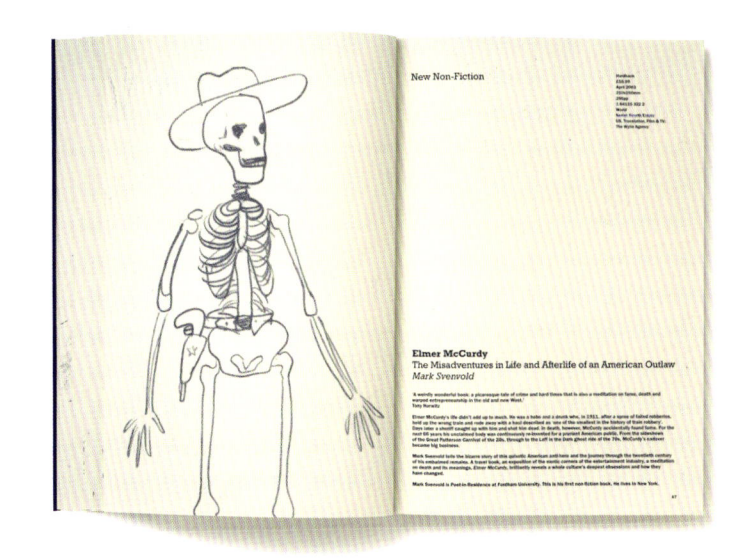

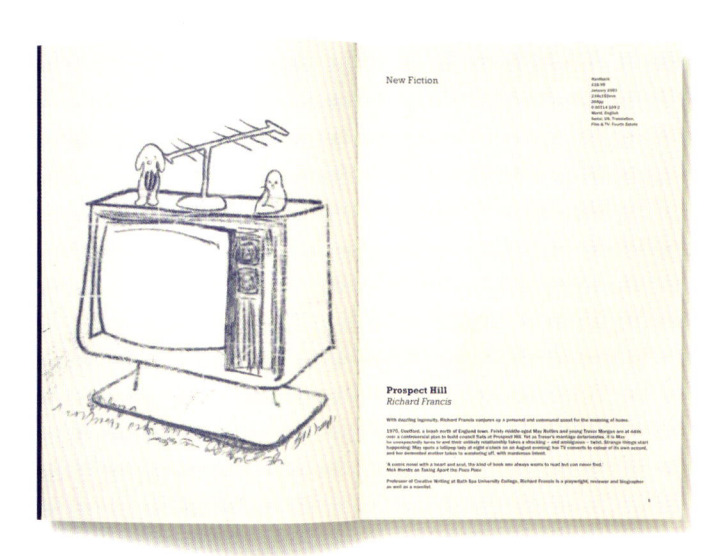

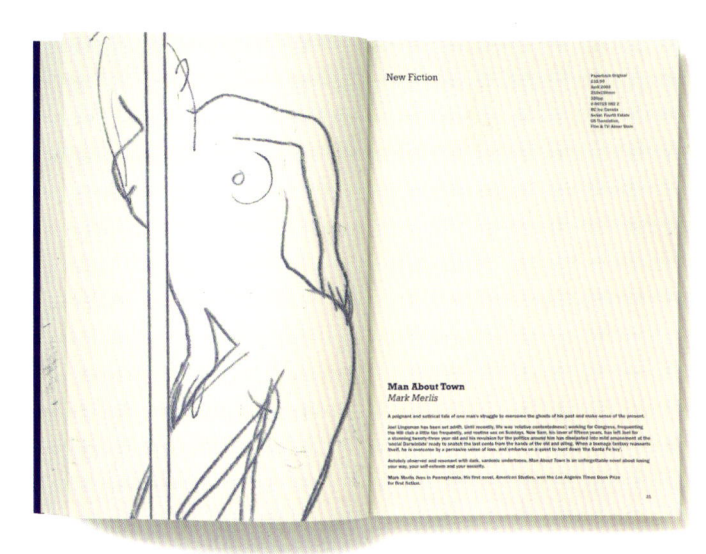

Debbie de Coo
Eenvoud

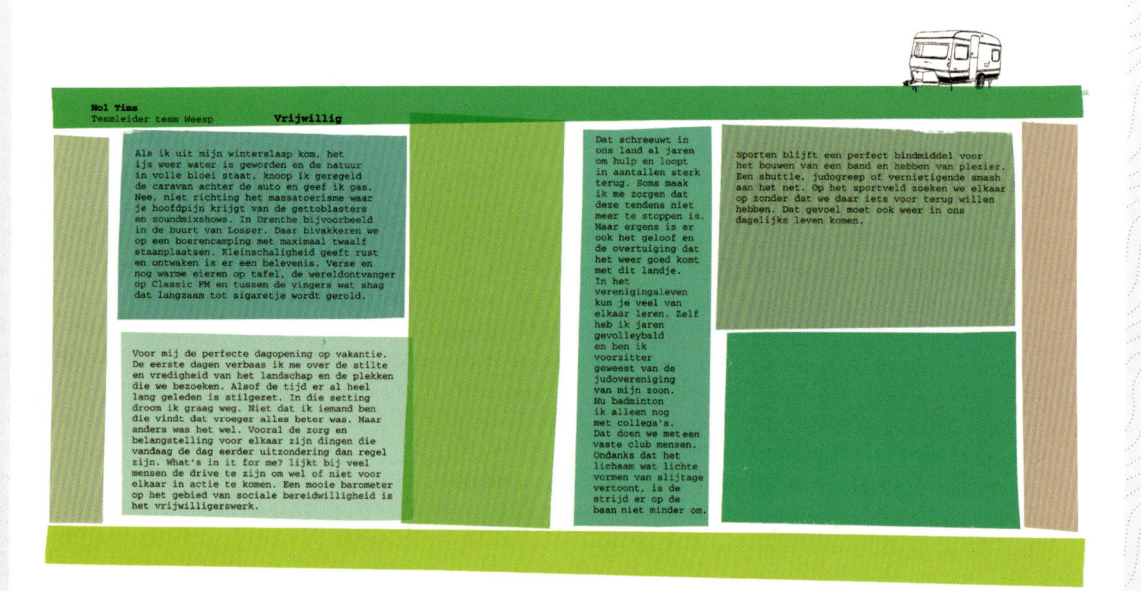

'Ik zie veel drukte om me heen.
Veel gehaast, mensen
die van alles willen en moeten
en de lat ontzettend hoog leggen.
Ik zorg er bewust voor dat mijn
leventje overzichtelijk en niet
te complex wordt. Onthaasten
is een modewoord dat bij mij zijn
juiste betekenis vindt.

Na het werk vind je me vaak samen met mijn
maatje en man Richard in de keuken. Daar staan we,
met een wijntje in de hand, heerlijk te kletsen over
de dag en de dingen die ons interesseren. Ik hecht
veel waarde aan eten en de sociale functie ervan.
Al jaren ben ik idolaat van Italië en La Dolce Vita.
We hebben vrienden in Bergamo waar ik eigenlijk ieder
jaar een paar weken naar toe moet. De taal, die
rollende r, de handgebaren, emoties en openheid.
Ik kan er geen genoeg van krijgen.

Net als het landschap dat zo heerlijk glooit
en je een sprookjesachtig gevoel geeft. Ook
daar vind ik een soort eenvoud in het leven.

Aandacht voor de familie, respect voor de
natuur en de ongekende passie voor koken en het
leven. Wij zijn hier zo van de regeltjes en de
structuur. Daar is het meer improviseren en iets
positiefs doen met de situatie, in plaats van
deze te veranderen. Italianen zijn zo heerlijk
makkelijk en bijna altijd gezellig. Hoewel mijn
leven redelijk gestructureerd is, ben ik ook
makkelijk en flexibel.

Mijn deur en ijskast staan altijd voor iedereen
open. Ik hoop dat die zo blijft. Ik ben
nu al een paar maanden in verwachting.
Een magisch en heel intens gevoel. Ik heb al een
ontzettende band met die kleine. Een klein mensje
in je buik doet mooie dingen met je. Hoewel ik de
babykamer al bijna klaar heb, neem ik bewuster rust
en tijd voor mezelf. Heerlijk met een boek 's avonds
op de bank met Richard naast me.

Simpel maar mooi geluk waar
ik veel kracht en energie uit haal.'

FEDERICO FE
ADOLCE

Nol Tims
Teamleider team Weesp **Vrijwillig**

Als ik uit mijn winterslaap kom, het
ijs weer water is geworden en de natuur
in volle bloei staat, knoop ik geregeld
de caravan achter de auto en geef ik gas.
Nee, niet richting het massatoerisme waar
je hoofdpijn krijgt van de gettoblasters
en soundmixshows. In Drenthe bijvoorbeeld
in de buurt van Losser. Daar bivakkeren we
op een boerencamping met maximaal twaalf
staanplaatsen. Kleinschaligheid geeft rust
en ontwaken is er een belevenis. Verse en
nog warme eieren op tafel, de wereldontvanger
op Classic FM en tussen de vingers wat shag
dat langzaam tot sigaretje wordt gerold.

Voor mij de perfecte dagopening op vakantie.
De eerste dagen verbaas ik me over de stilte
en vredigheid van het landschap en de plekken
die we bezoeken. Alsof de tijd er al heel
lang geleden is stilgezet. In die setting
droom ik graag weg. Niet dat ik iemand ben
die vindt dat vroeger alles beter was. Maar
anders was het wel. Vooral de zorg en
belangstelling voor elkaar zijn dingen die
vandaag de dag eerder uitzondering dan regel
zijn. What's in it for me? lijkt bij veel
mensen de drive te zijn om wel of niet voor
elkaar in actie te komen. Een mooie barometer
op het gebied van sociale bereidwilligheid is
het vrijwilligerswerk.

Dat schreeuwt in
ons land al jaren
om hulp en loopt
in aantallen sterk
terug. Soms maak
ik me zorgen dat
deze tendens niet
meer te stoppen is.
Maar ergens is er
ook het geloof en
de overtuiging dat
het weer goed komt
met dit landje.
In het
verenigingsleven
kun je veel van
elkaar leren. Zelf
heb ik jaren
gevolleybald
en ben ik
voorzitter
geweest van de
judovereniging
van mijn zoon.
Nu badminton
ik alleen nog
met collega's.
Dat doen we met een
vaste club mensen.
Ondanks dat het
lichaam wat lichte
vormen van slijtage
vertoont, is de
strijd er op de
baan niet minder om.

Sporten blijft een perfect bindmiddel voor
het bouwen van een band en hebben veel plezier.
Een shuttle, judogreep of vernietigende smash
aan het net. Op het sportveld zoeken we elkaar
op zonder dat we daar iets voor terug willen
hebben. Dat gevoel moet ook weer in ons
dagelijks leven komen.

Marja Visser

Meditatie

Spreads: Dutch Police Annual Report 2003

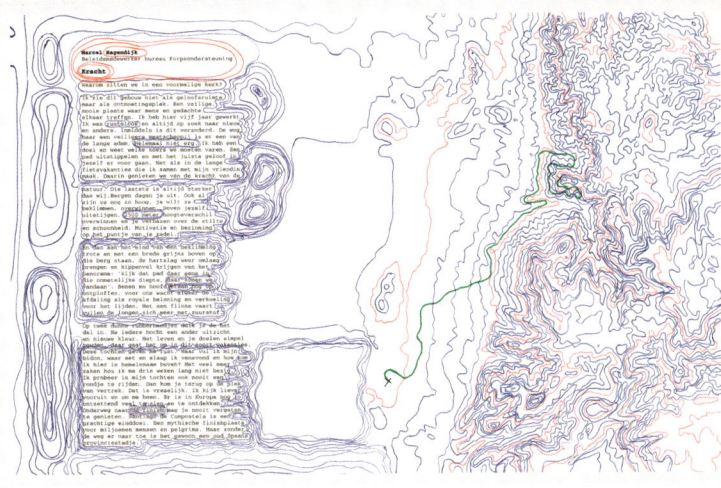

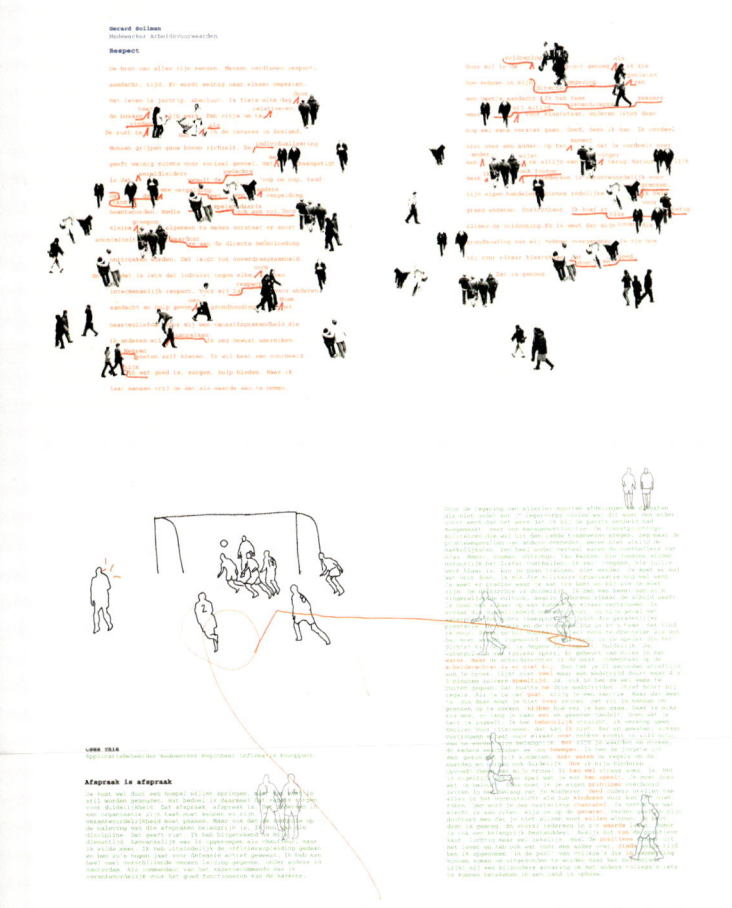

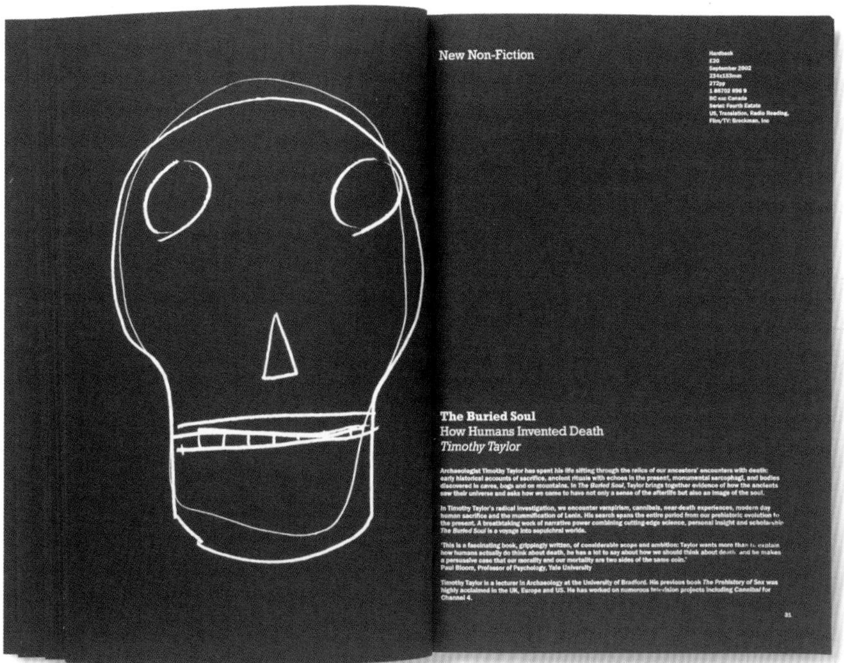
New Non-Fiction
The Buried Soul
How Humans Invented Death
Timothy Taylor

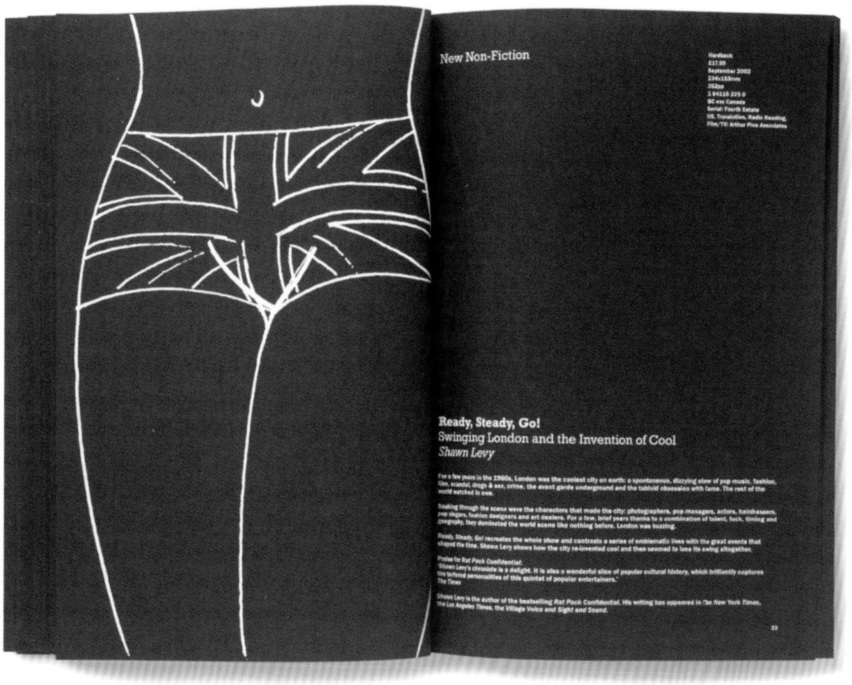
New Non-Fiction
Ready, Steady, Go!
Swinging London and the Invention of Cool
Shawn Levy

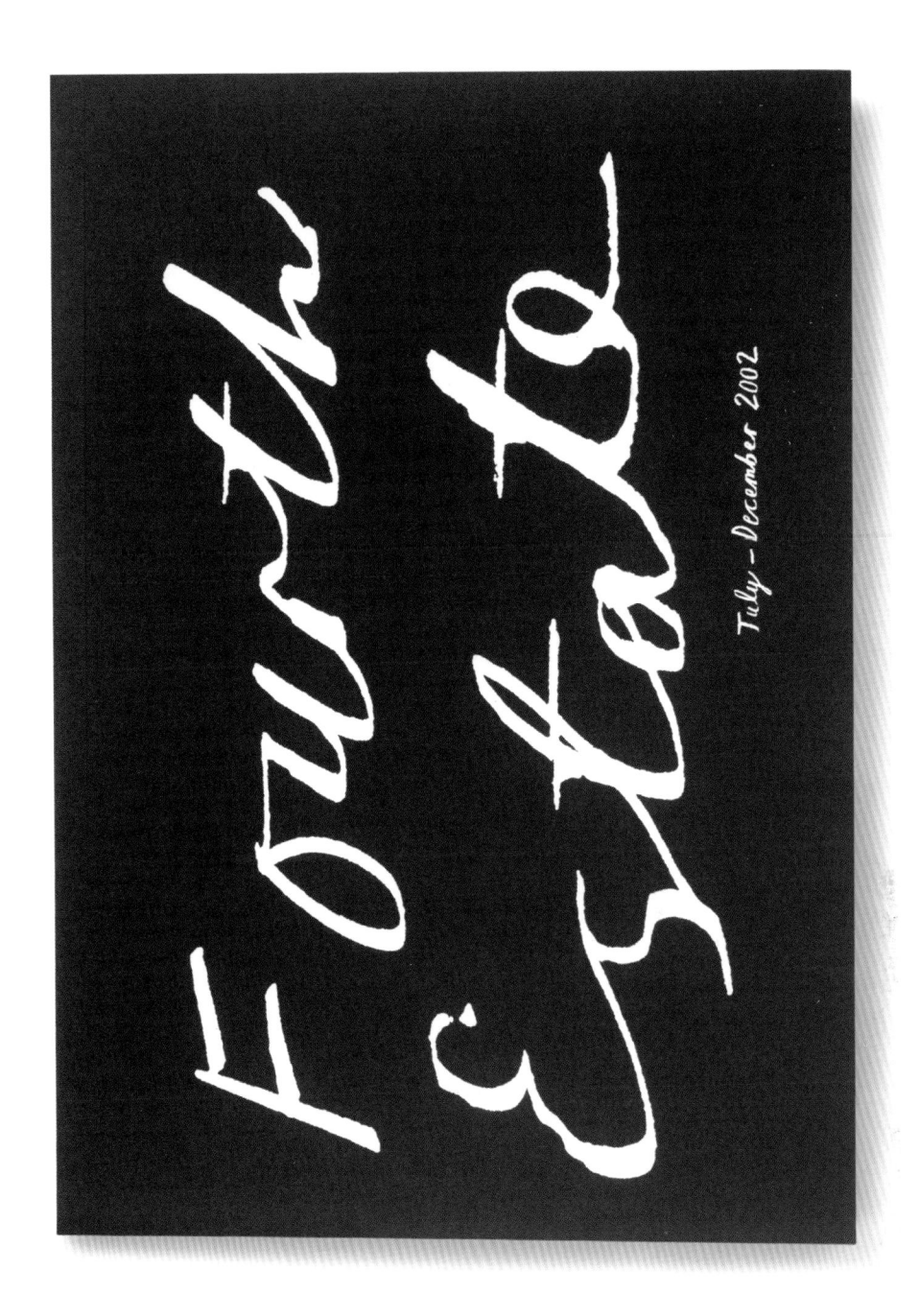

Spreads: Fourth Estate Publishing Catalogue 2002

Guardian Newspaper "the decline of McDonalds"

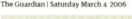

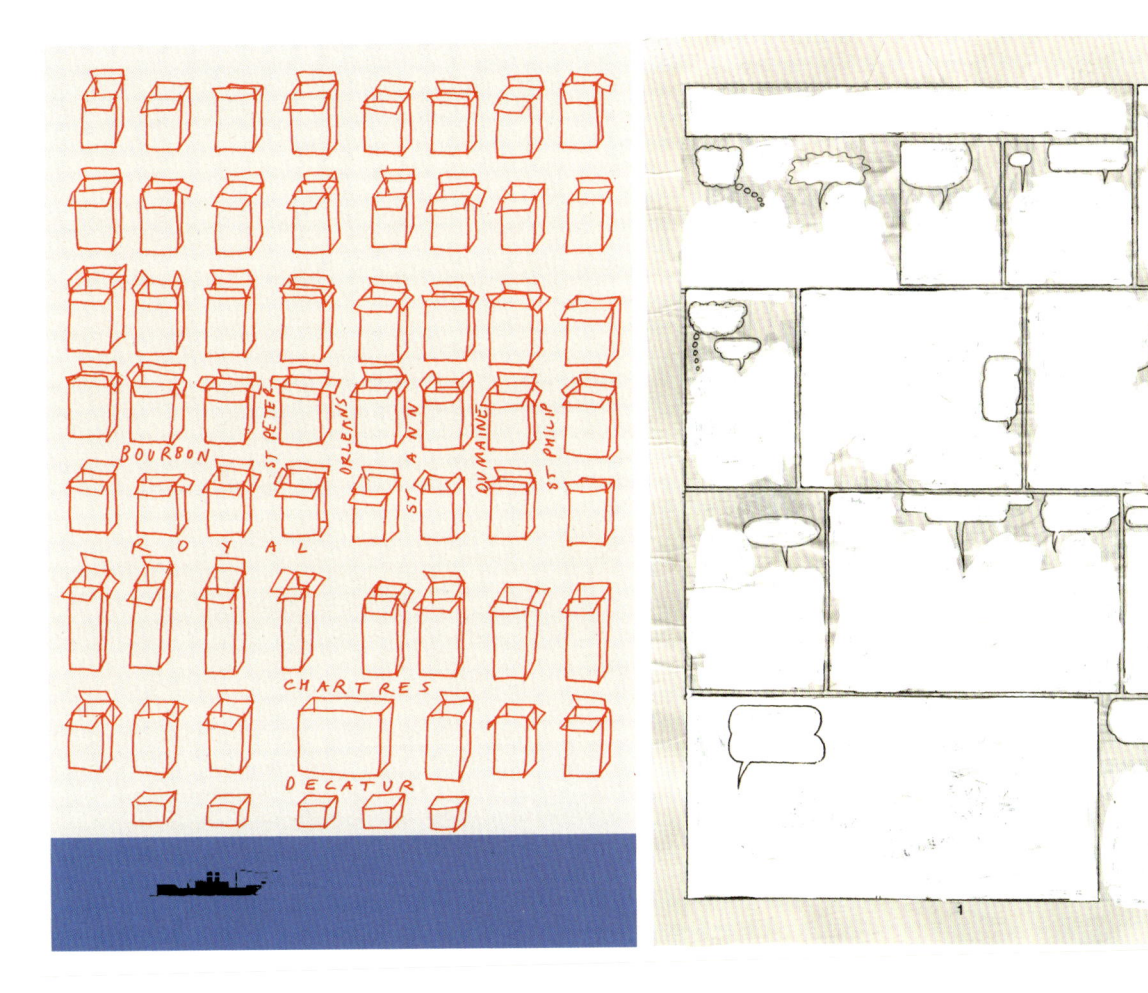

Editorial illustrations produced for the *Saturday Guardian Newspaper*

Spreads: *Guardian Newspaper*, selection of main essay pages

| Marina Hyde on celebrity divorce 29 | Ulrich Beck: facing up to a world of risk 31 | Jonathan Steele on Islam and Europe 32 | Norman Johnson in praise of older dads 33 |

Hearts and minds

What is this thing called love? Poetry, biology, or the essence of being alive?

Essay by Mark Vernon Illustrations by Marion Deuchars

Brokeback Mountain is inevitably called a gay cowboy movie. Ang Lee's film of what happened when two guys fell in love during the summer of 1963 while tending sheep in homophobic Wyoming was bound to get that label. This is a shame. It detracts from what I take to be a core theme, namely that these men did not expect to fall in love. In Annie Proulx's short story upon which the film is based the suggestion is that they are bewitched by the mountain itself. It is not as if they would have gone to a gay bar looking for a good time if it weren't for the fact that they had to eke out a living on harsh high pastures.

Rather, love overwhelms them – like a creeper, slowly but surely. That it was same-sex love is only a detail, though one that serves to underline the way that love steals up on them unawares. They have no understanding of how it works, or why. "This thing", "a hold", "I swear..." – these are the inarticulate words the characters use to refer to the love that is a mystery and a gift. It comes to them out of nowhere, just given. Though, once received, it becomes the given of their lives.

Which, ultimately, is what love is like – gay or straight. Why should it be that one person gets under the skin of another? Why is it that one day life is fine lived alone and the next it is unbearable? What is this thing called love? Whatever else it is, it is big business. No sooner does the silver tinsel of Christmas come down than the red hearts of Saint Valentine's Day go up. Perhaps we get the celebration we deserve: for contemporary notions of love are dominated by two strands of thought – the sentimental and the scientific.

The sentimental stems from the ideal that fires romantic love. It has a long pedigree, going back at least as far as Aristophanes' myth in Plato's Symposium. Aristophanes said that originally human beings were hermaphrodite wholes. Then, in punishment for hubris, Zeus cut each in two. Thereafter, men and women were condemned to spend their lives looking for their lost halves – erotic desire manifesting the horror of not being whole. If found, the two rejoin in sexual congress: an ecstatic annihilation of their separate selves.

The sentimental appropriation of Aristophanes' myth today conveniently forgets its dark undercurrents. Industries that promote February's annual love-fest adopt only the upside. "There is someone out there for you." The "guess who?" of the Valentine's card signifies the life-changing potential of the right romantic discovery. The romance seems irresistible (I feel like a cold fish objecting to it) but really this has little to do with love. Mostly, it is about the fear of being lonely and unlovable. Which is why it is eminently marketable and not just deployed on February 14, but used to sell everything from movies to makeovers.

The second strand is the scientific. It speaks on the matter of love, as opposed to just sex, on the basis of evolutionary psychology. This is easy to caricature, not least because of those proponents who talk so easily as if love were no more than genetically advantageous appeal. This is manifest, according to which account you read, as child-bearing hips in women or potent seed in men (however you detect that). The reason love lasts, or at least aspires to last, they say, is an evolutionary product of the advantages that its longevity brings to love's issue – namely, gene-bearing offspring.

To be fair, some scientists say that love is not adaptive in this crude fashion. It is, perhaps, a complex of emotions that stem from original joint activity that leads to people valuing each other. However, scientists such as the neurobiologist Steven Rose point out that even this line of reasoning is an impoverishment of thought. It reduces love to cost benefit analysis. It turns an economic theory of cooperation into a high status, scientific theory of love. Again, one can understand the appeal of that to the love industries. Love as a science can be used to sell everything from pills to personal ads.

Put the sentimental and the scientific together and the modern Saint Valentine's Day is the result. Love is an experience that stands or falls on emotional intensity and sexual performance.

The question that presses, then, is how to find a way out of this commercial mawkishness. Vowing not to send a card or buy roses at an inflated price is an option. But perhaps one can steal a page out of the marketeer's handbook, seize the opportunity more positively, and use the day to ask again, what is love? A little philosophy of love offers some hard words but rich suggestions that might help recover something deeper. Let me suggest three of the big hitters: Plato, Nietzsche and Augustine.

In Plato's Symposium, at which Aristophanes speaks, Socrates makes a substantial contribution, too. He recounts a conversation he once had with a priestess, Diotima. She told him a story of Love's birth. When Aphrodite was born, the gods held a party. Two of the guests were Poros and Penia. Poros got drunk on nectar and retired to the garden to sleep it off. Penia passed by and, wanting him, slept with him. Love – Eros – was the result.

Poros means "way" in Greek, as in a means or a resource. He is also the son of Metis, which means "cunning". Penia means "poverty" or "lack". Love is what happens when lack combines with cunning means. So, the first thing to say about love is that it is the desire to have and to hold. At base, to say I love you, is to say I want you (and hope you want me). This is the ground even of happy and contented relationships. Is it not the periods apart in which the heart grows fonder again? Do not people text, "I miss you", because it is synonymous with saying, "I love you"? Is it not the fear of losing the beloved, in death or to someone else, that rekindles the flames of love's early passion?

Desiring love is a theme also explored by Nietzsche. In what he called the most personal of his books, The Gay Science, he writes of "the things people call love". His observation is blunt. Many of the things that people call love are actually its opposite: avarice, the obsession with possession. Think of the ideal of romance, he says – the proverbial sailing off into the sunset, the couple together, alone, forever. And then think again. Is it not the wish for unconditional and sole possession of the beloved? Is it not the demand, in return, that the beloved will exclude the whole world as a source of happiness and enjoyment, and turn only to the lover for the satisfaction of their needs? The same language of possession is reflected in the way people ask whether lust has been consummated: "Have you had him (or her)?" they inquire. Avaricious feelings also lie behind the uncomfortable awareness that one's uglier tendencies are exposed by being in love.

This cupidity (from the name for the Roman god of love) also reveals its colours in the lover who tires of relationships, perhaps after a few weeks or short months, only to nurture the desire for someone new. Why does this happen? Because once someone has been possessed, "been had", that lover's goal has been fulfilled. The novelty wore off, they say; the relationship became dull.

It is for the same reason that a relationship that started out as an affair can die, almost overnight, should the illicit liaison lead to a new marriage. Marriage, at least in part, feels like ownership. Some rejoice in that. But if the thing that fired the affair was the impossible desire to own the beloved, then if that ownership is achieved, the desire, by definition, ceases.

Augustine issues another warning about love. When he was young he had a great friend, someone who was sweeter to him than all the other joys of life, he said. They belonged to each other; were another self to each other. But then, when still in their teens, his friend became sick. He developed a fever. He lost consciousness. He rallied **» page 28**

> CONTEMPORARY NOTIONS OF LOVE ARE DOMINATED BY THE SENTIMENTAL AND THE SCIENTIFIC

PASTA

SALADS

Spreads: Spreads from Jamie Oliver *"Jamie's Dinners"*, Penguin Books

NARRATIVA

Cuentos completos
ROBERTO ARLT

LOSADA

NARRATIVA

La mujer moderna más
grande del mundo
ANNA SWAN

LOSADA

NARRATIVA

Huida a las tinieblas
ARTHUR SCHNITZLER

LOSADA

Spreads: Selection of book cover designs for Losada Publishing, Spain

La Confesión de Agustín
JEAN-FRANÇOIS LYOTARD

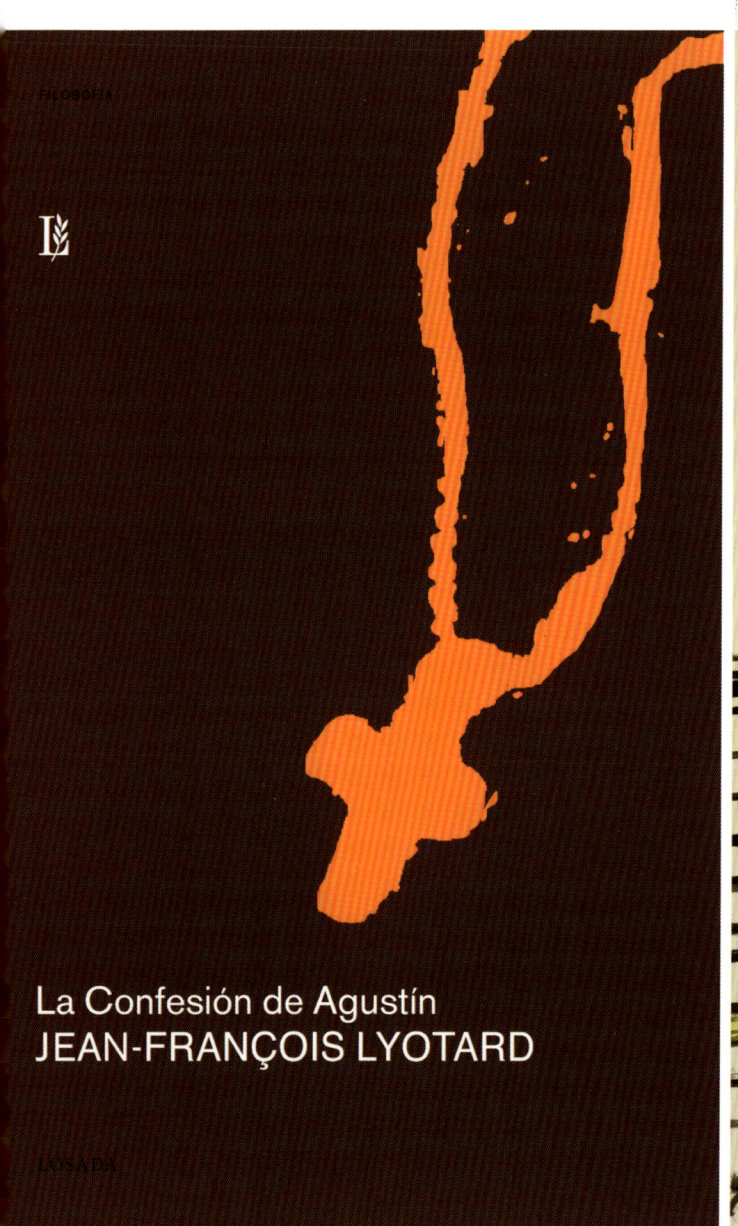

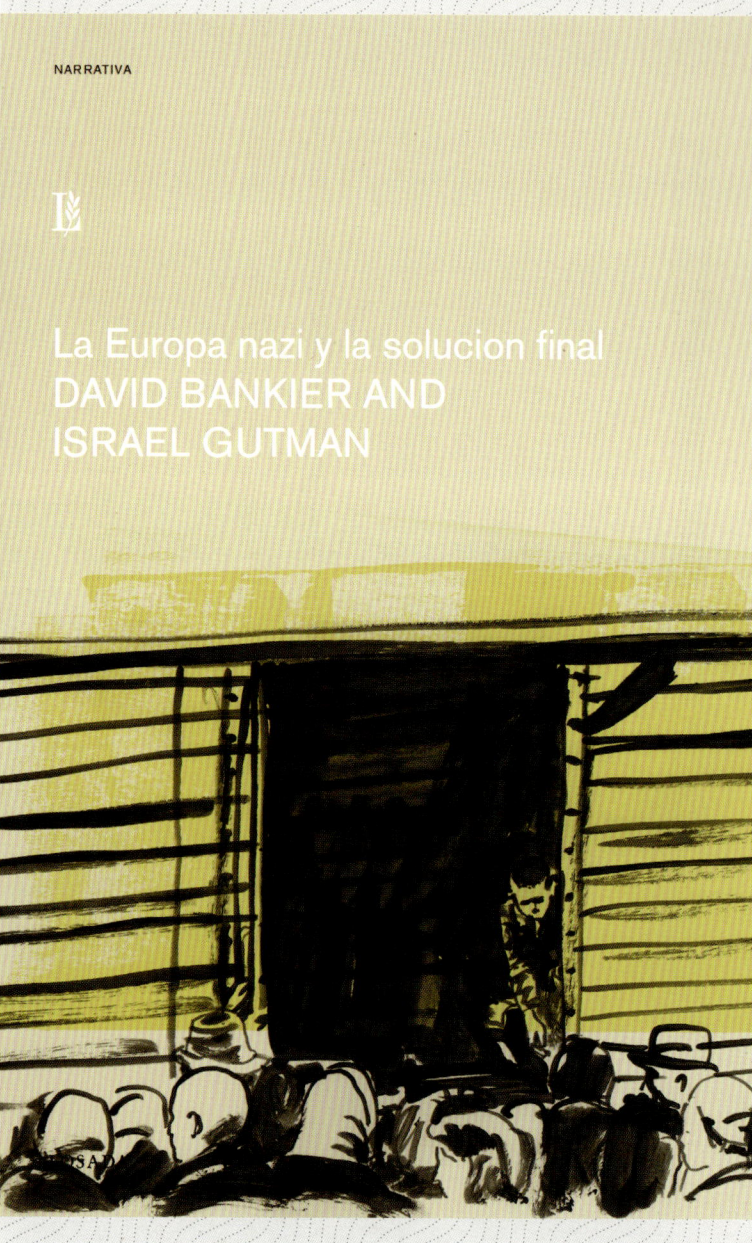

La Europa nazi y la solucion final
DAVID BANKIER AND ISRAEL GUTMAN

Spreads: Selection of book cover designs for Losada Publishing, Spain

NARRATIVA

Teresa
ARTHUR SCHNITZLER

LOSADA

NARRATIVA

Recuerdos
HANS JONAS

LOSADA

AUTOBIOGRAFÍA

Las palabras
JEAN-PAUL SARTRE

LOSADA

069

NARRATIVA

De espaldas a nosotros
MIGUEL BERMEJO

LOSADA

NARRATIVA

La cuestión humana
FRANÇOIS EMMANUEL

LOSADA

FILOSOFÍA

Escepticismo y fe animal
GEORGE SANTAYANA

LOSADA

NARRATIVA

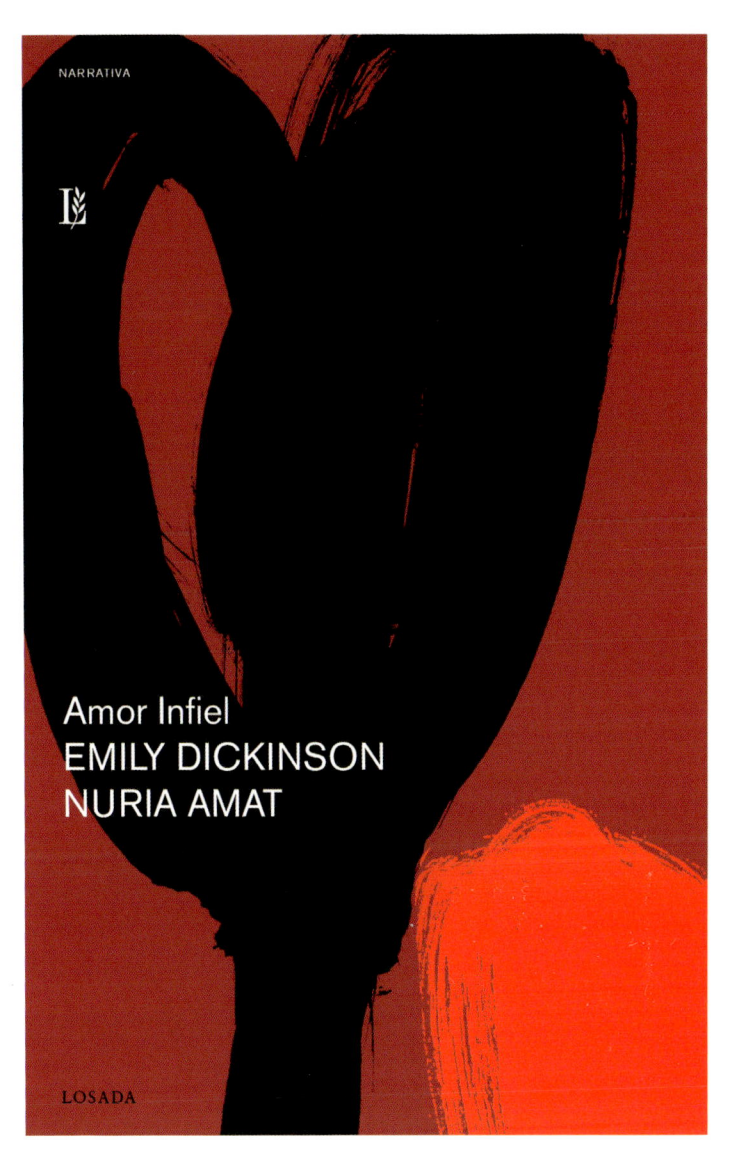

Amor Infiel
EMILY DICKINSON
NURIA AMAT

LOSADA

NARRATIVA

La eternidad no está de más
FRANCOIS CHENG

LOSADA

Spreads: Selection of book cover designs for Losada Publishing, Spain

071

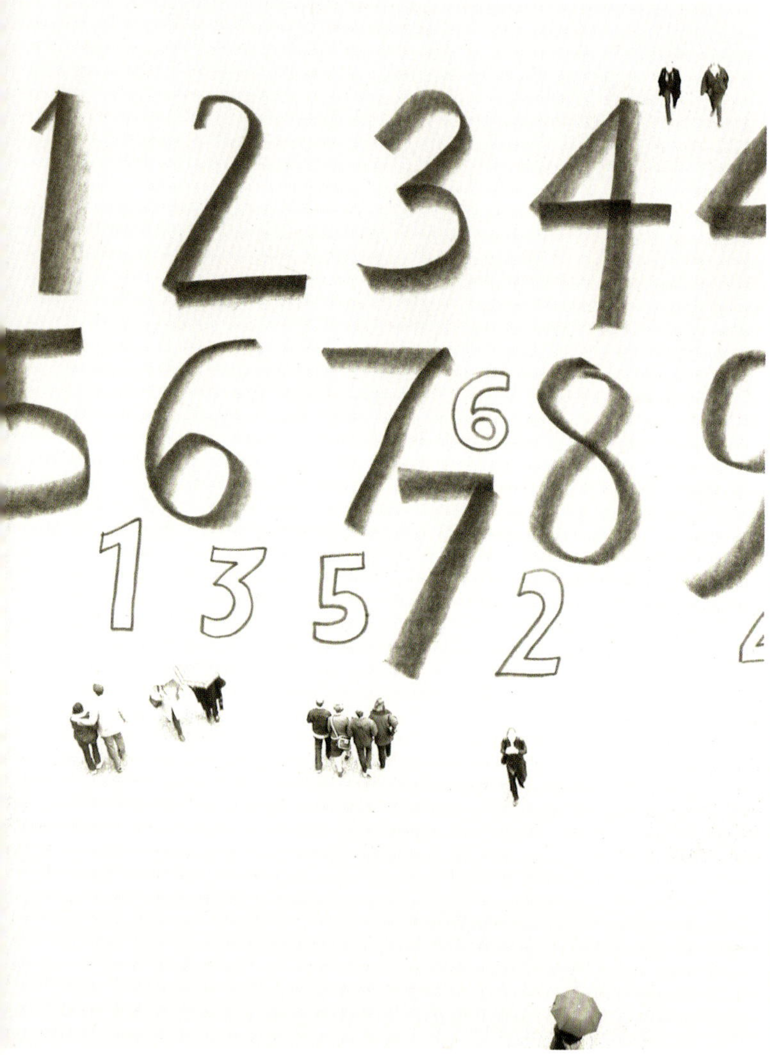

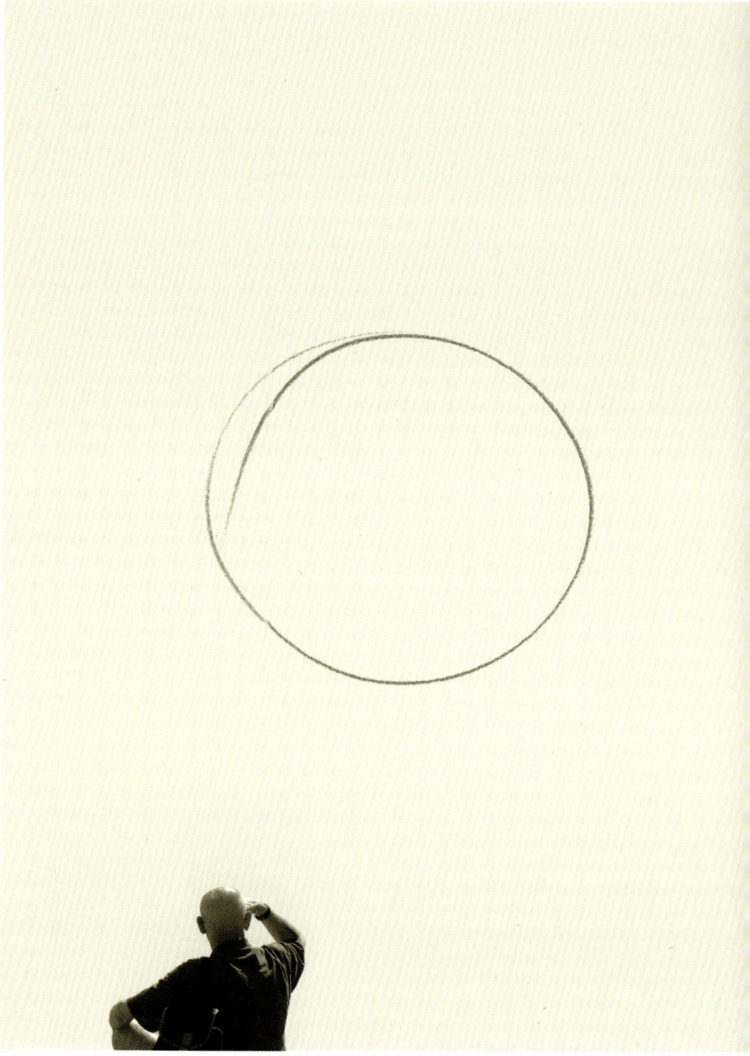

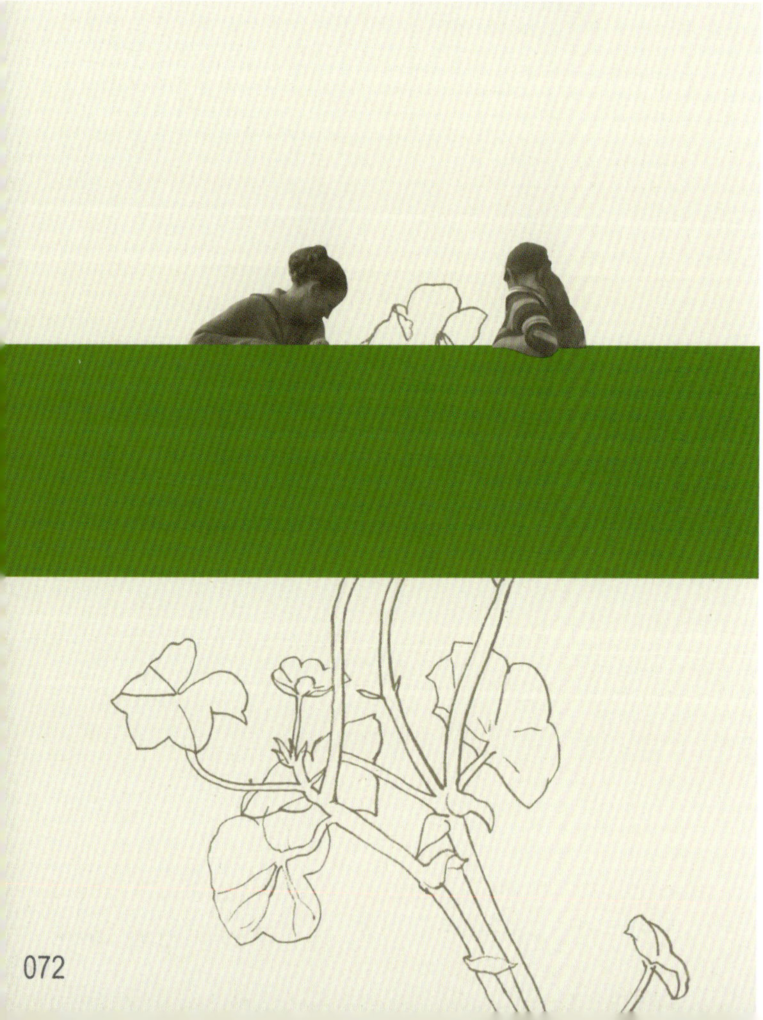

Spreads: Spreads from Planeta Annual Report, Spain

Spreads: Spreads from Planeta Annual Report, Spain

Poster for British Council "Picture This", contemporary illustration from London

074

YOU'RE AN ANIMAL VISKOVITZ!

Alessandro Boffa

"A CHEEKY LITTLE MASTERPIECE THAT DESERVES ITS OWN PLAQUE IN THE PANTHEON OF COMIC LITERATURE... THINK JAMES THURBER CROSSED WITH FRANZ KAFKA" *San Francisco Chronicle*

"IRRESISTIBLE... PROOF THAT SOMETIMES THE BEST WAY TO ILLUMINATE THE HUMAN CONDITION IS TO LET ANOTHER SPECIES DO THE TALKING." *New York Times Book Review*

Translated by John Casey with Maria Sanminiatelli

ISBN 1-84195-414-4

Illustrations for book, *You're an Animal Viskovitch*, published by Canongate

Martin Woodtli

Martin Woodtli is perhaps the most accomplished representative of the new design scene in Switzerland, where the joy of the design process (as opposed to monetary reward) seems to determine the direction of the studios. Swiss designers would rather work for small cultural projects to which they are often connected personally than to fall into the trap of large advertising conglomerates. While at first glance this may seem to be a complete break with all traditions of the famed Swiss international style, the roots of the new generation are still firmly grounded in the world of Brockmann and Bill.

Woodtli does not subscribe to the silly adage circulated by many of his colleagues about the computer being just a tool; he considers it simply as a process. His proficiency in various programs is that he sketches with the keyboard as quickly as with pencil and paper.

Having worked with many artists within the art market, he has no interest in following them but happily remains in the design world. He considers graphic design as a "wonderful medium in which you can create friction within the existing world".

Woodtli is obsessive. He applauds the line from Brian Eno's diary and a good way to create something original is to do something so incredibly painstaking and time-consuming. Woodtli notes, "Sixteen-square-foot black painting made with a very fine (6H) pencil would qualify".

PROJECT: SPORT DESIGN
TYPE: POSTER
CLIENT: MUSEUM FÜR GESTALTUNG ZÜRICH

"The poster 'sport design' contains a number of elements which characterise the entire world of sport. The running track, the seats of the tribune, the separation in active and passive and as well the hidden Dollar sign as the big S, all these perhaps can be seen as the one-dimensionality of the achievement principles and possibility to see the entire thing as a part of reality as well as a kind of bizarre nonsense." – Martin Woodtli

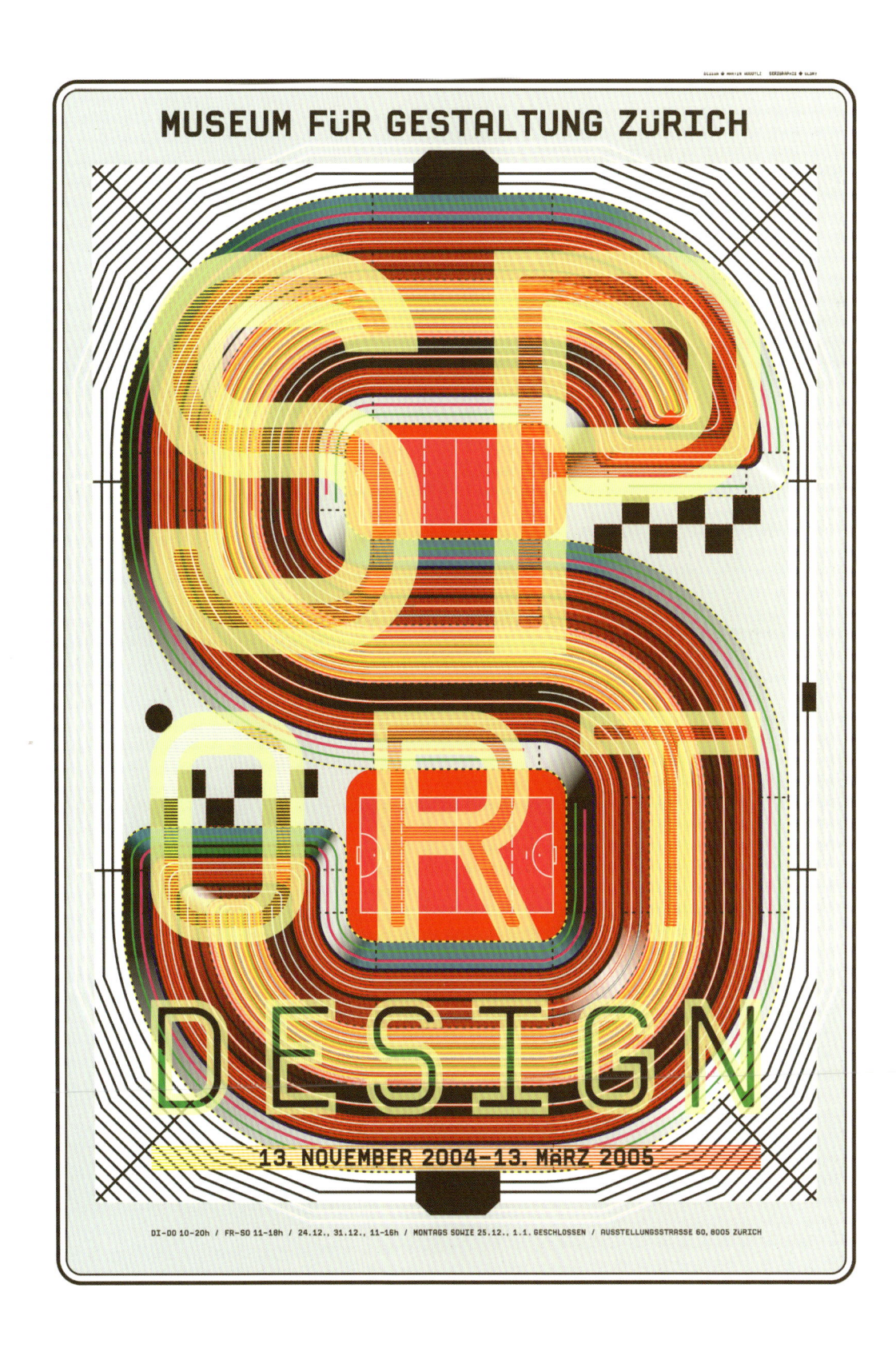

PUBLIKATION
Zur Ausstellung erscheint der erste Band in der Reihe
'Design Collection':
Take away - Design der mobilen Esskultur
Hg. von Museum für Gestaltung Zürich,
Designsammlung: Norbert Wild
Mit einem Essay von Walter Leimgruber
avedition Verlag für Architektur und Design
24 x 16,5 cm, 96 Seiten, 120 Farbabbildungen, D / E
ISBN 3-89986-064-0 / Verkaufspreis CHF 39.80

Bitte frankieren

Ich bestelle ..... Ex. **'Take away'** zu CHF 39.80
(exkl. Versandkosten)

Vorname / Name
Strasse
PLZ / Ort
Datum
Unterschrift

MUSEUM FÜR GESTALTUNG ZÜRICH
VERLAG
POSTFACH
CH-8031 ZÜRICH

E-Mail: verlag@museum-gestaltung.ch
Fax: ++41 / 43 / 446 45 67

TAKE AWAY

DESIGN DER MOBILEN ESSKULTUR
14. DEZEMBER 2005 BIS 19. MÄRZ 2006
MUSEUM FÜR GESTALTUNG ZÜRICH

Take away ist die passende kulinarische Formel zum modernen Lebensstil. Die Wurzeln der mobilen Verpflegung liegen jedoch im frühen 19. Jahrhundert und damit am Anfang der Industrialisierung. Sie forderte und förderte Alternativen zum Essen am Familientisch. Effizienz und Praktikabilität waren gefragt. Take away und seine engen Verwandten Systemgastronomie und Convenience Food funktionieren noch heute nach dieser Regel. Weiterentwickelt hat sich was wir Essen, vor allem aber wie, womit und wo wir es tun. Der funktionale und ästhetische Anspruch steigt, Toleranzwerte bei den Essmanieren sinken: Anything goes - anywhere and anytime, heisst die Devise. Gestalterischer Innovationsgeist bekommt eine neue gesellschaftliche Relevanz. 'Take-away' öffnet mit Charme, Brisanz und Dynamik den Zugang zu diesem wenig untersuchten Designuniversum. Mit dabei sind Geräte wie Picknick-Koffer und Pappbecher, sowie Dokumente vom Foto zum Film und kritische Kommentare. Zusammen präsentieren sie aktuelle Trends im Spiegel ihrer historischen Vorläufer und projizieren die Zukunft anhand modellhafter Visionen.

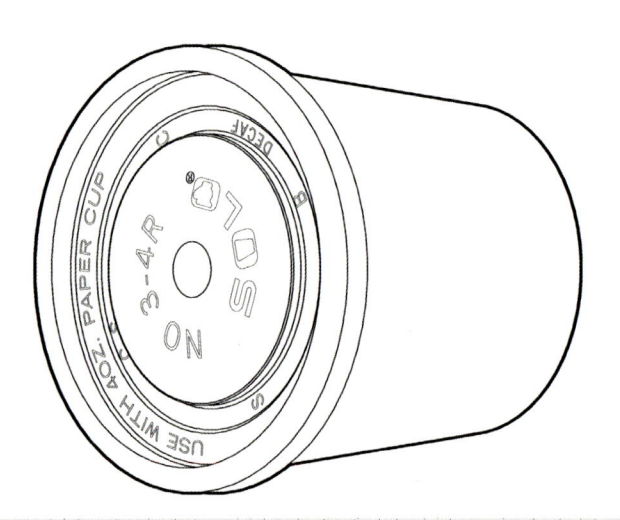

Spreads: Poster and card for design exhibition of Museum für Gestaltung Zürich

079

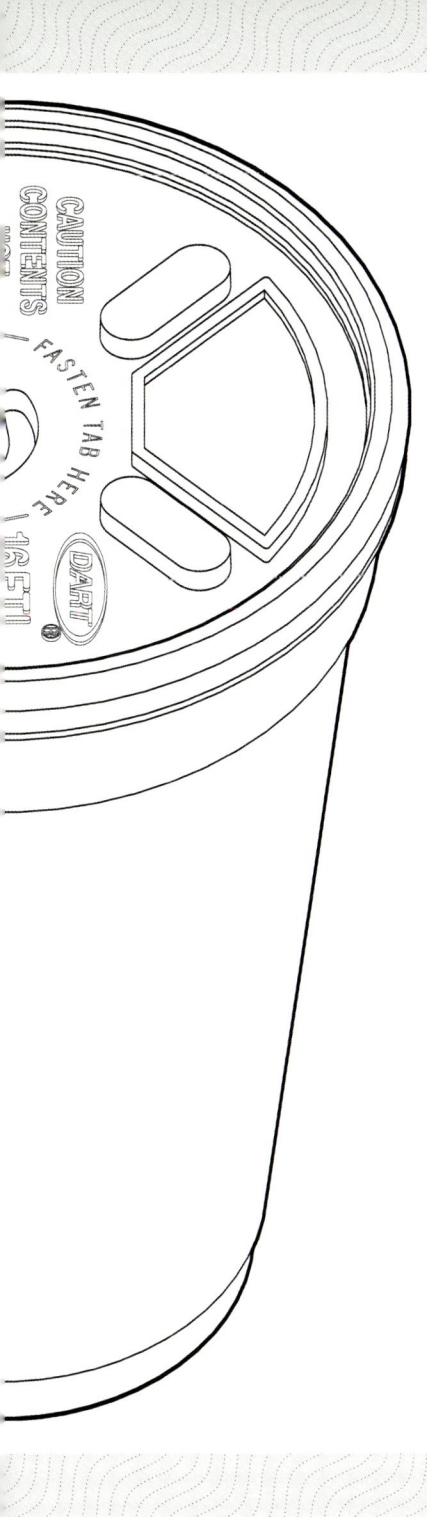

Museum für Gestaltung Zürich

9. Februar bis 5. Juni 2005

Spreads: Poster and card for design exhibition of Museum für Gestaltung Zürich

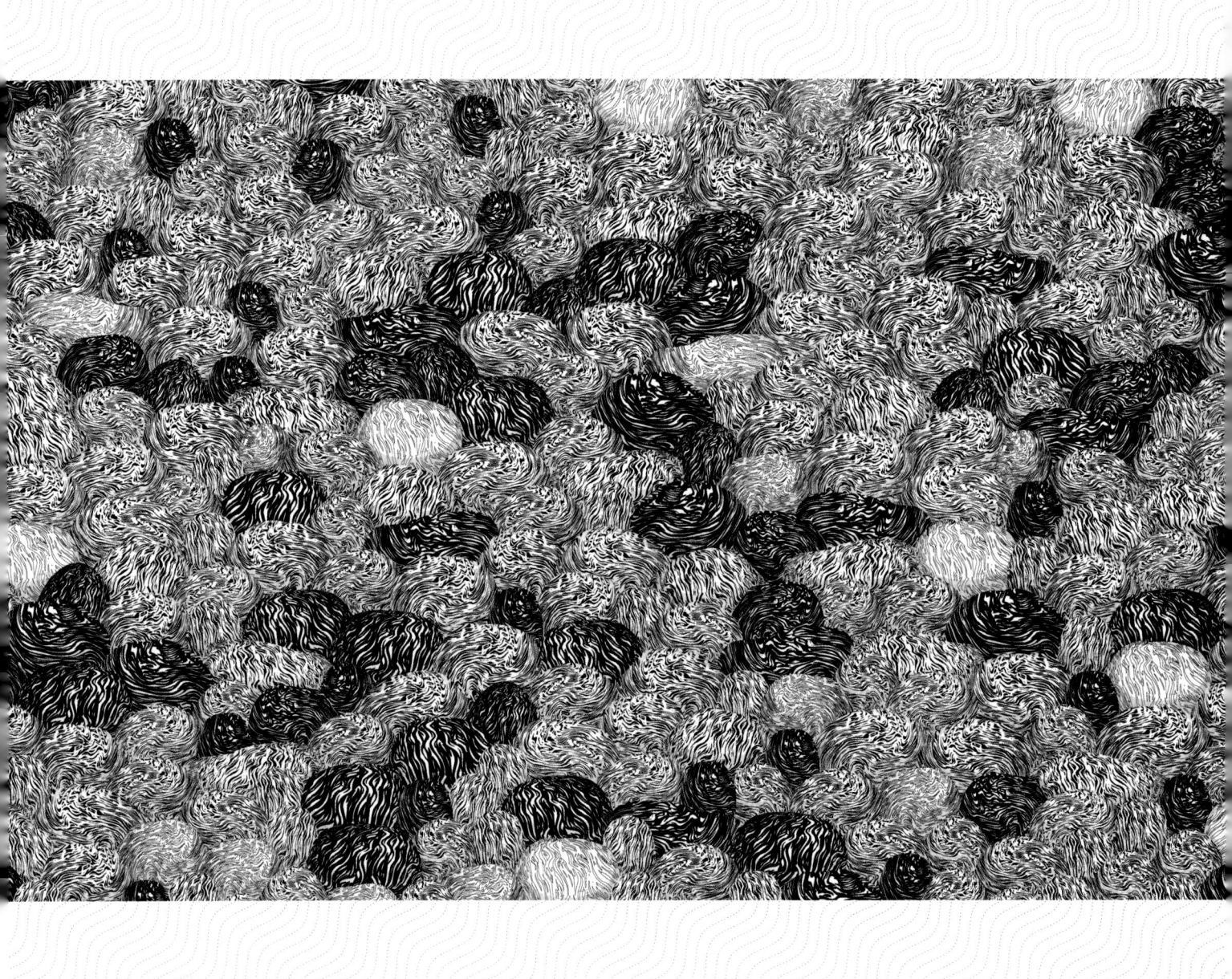

Spreads: Editorial for a life style magazine, *soDA* Magazine

083

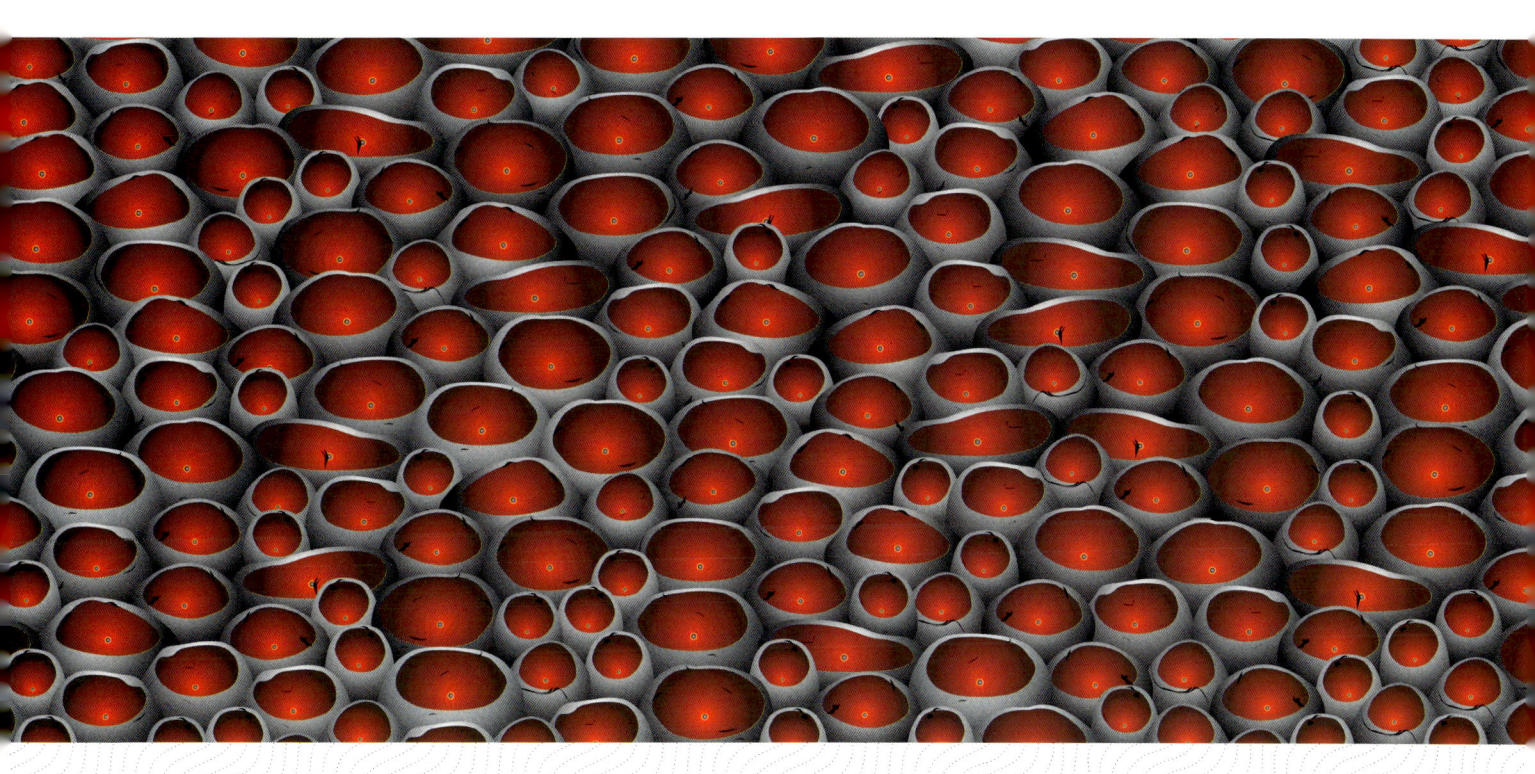

084

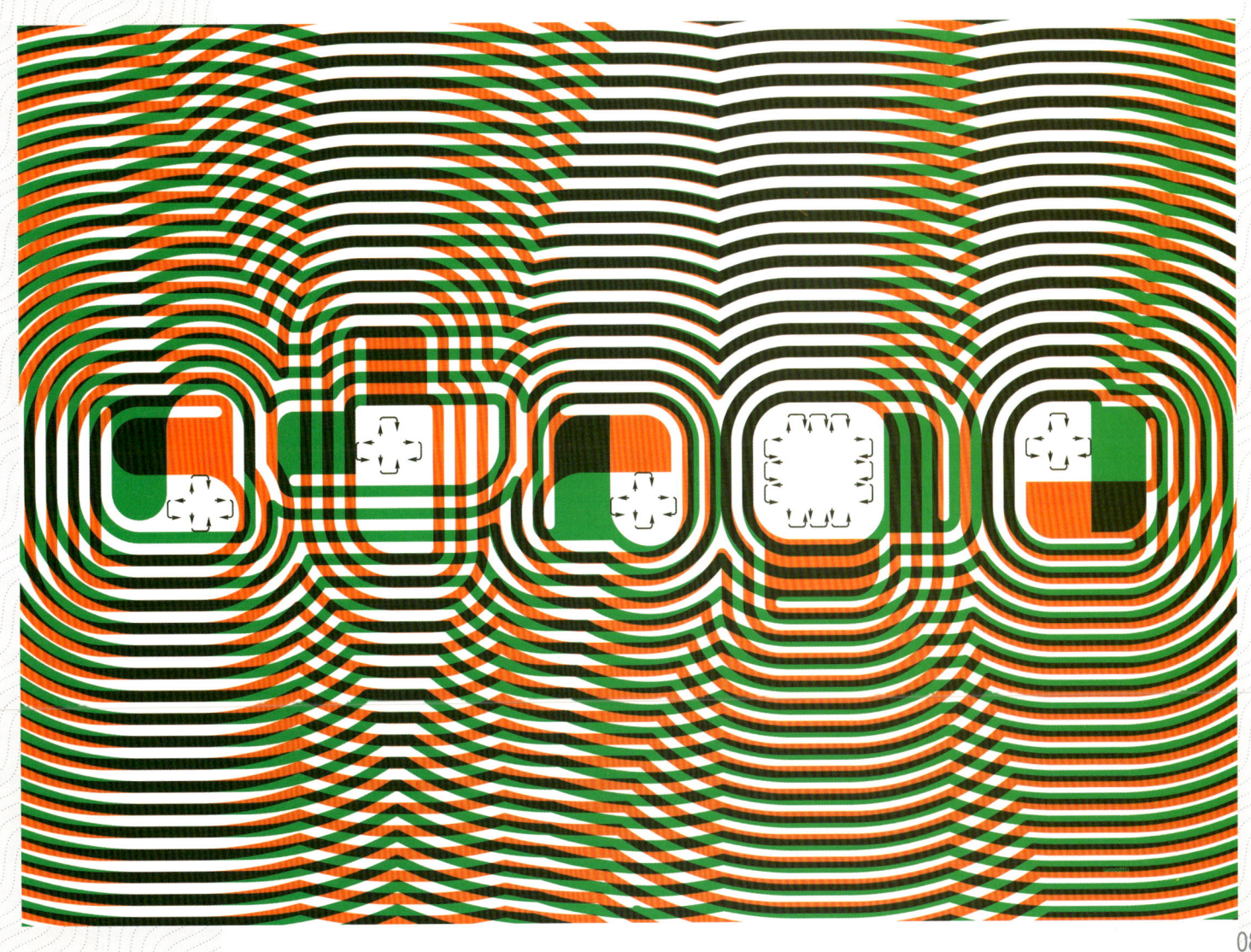

Spreads: Invitation cards titled "Stage" for an art gallery of Stadtgalerie Bern

Spreads: Invitation cards for an art gallery of Stadtgalerie Bern

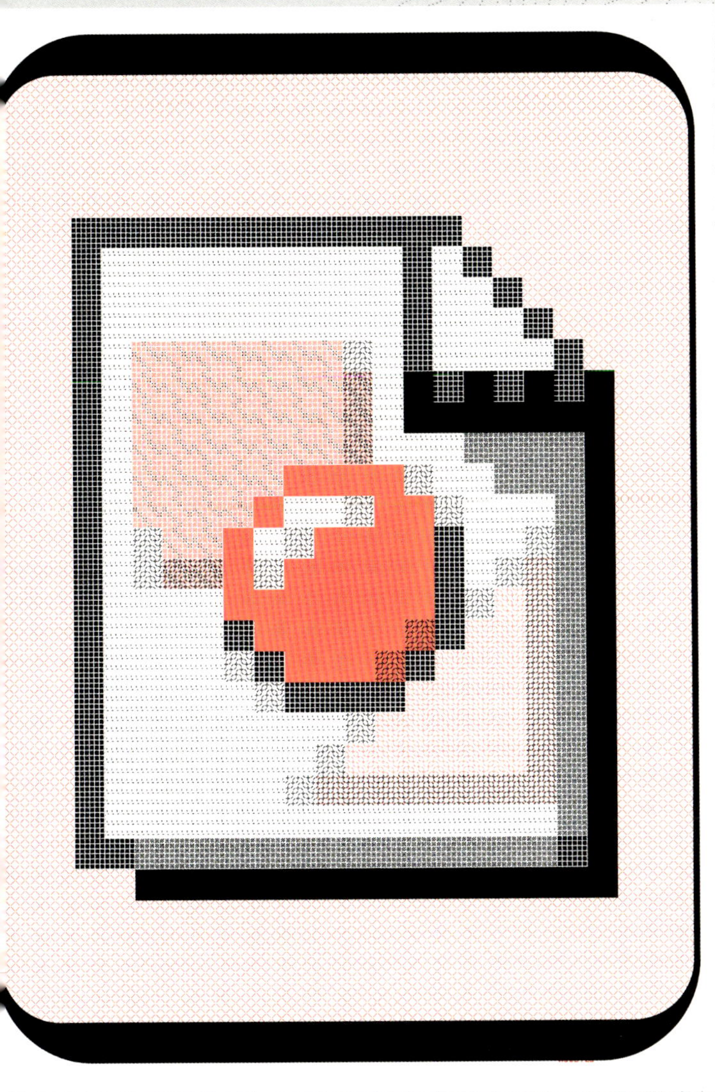

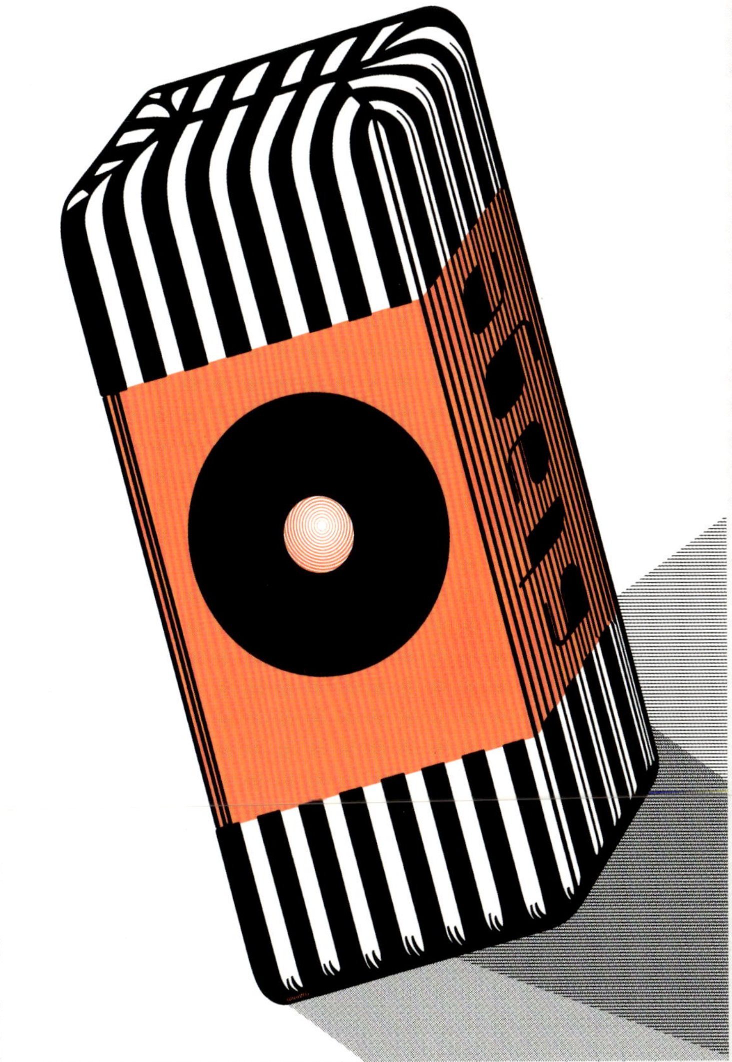

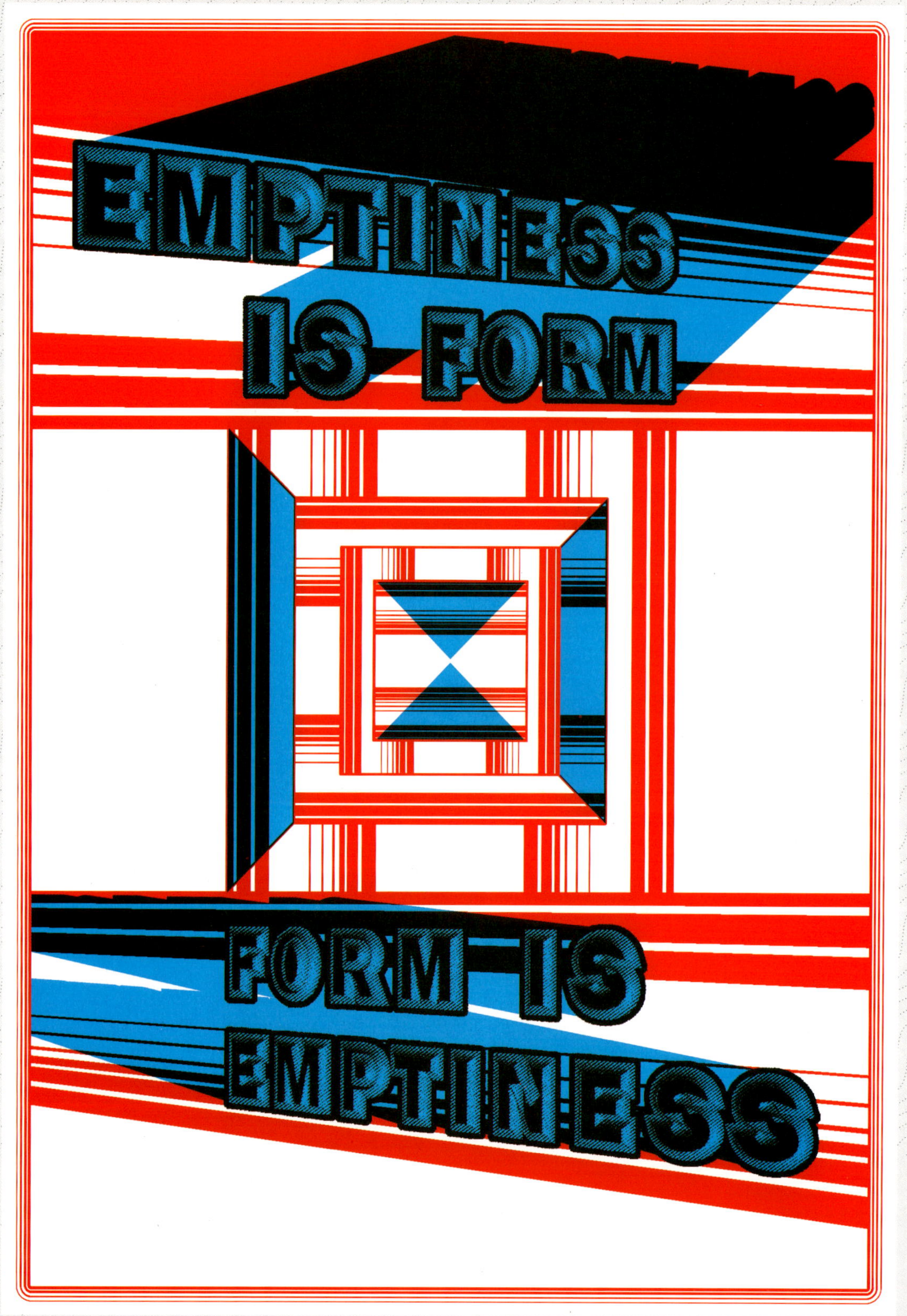
EMPTINESS
IS FORM
FORM IS
EMPTINESS

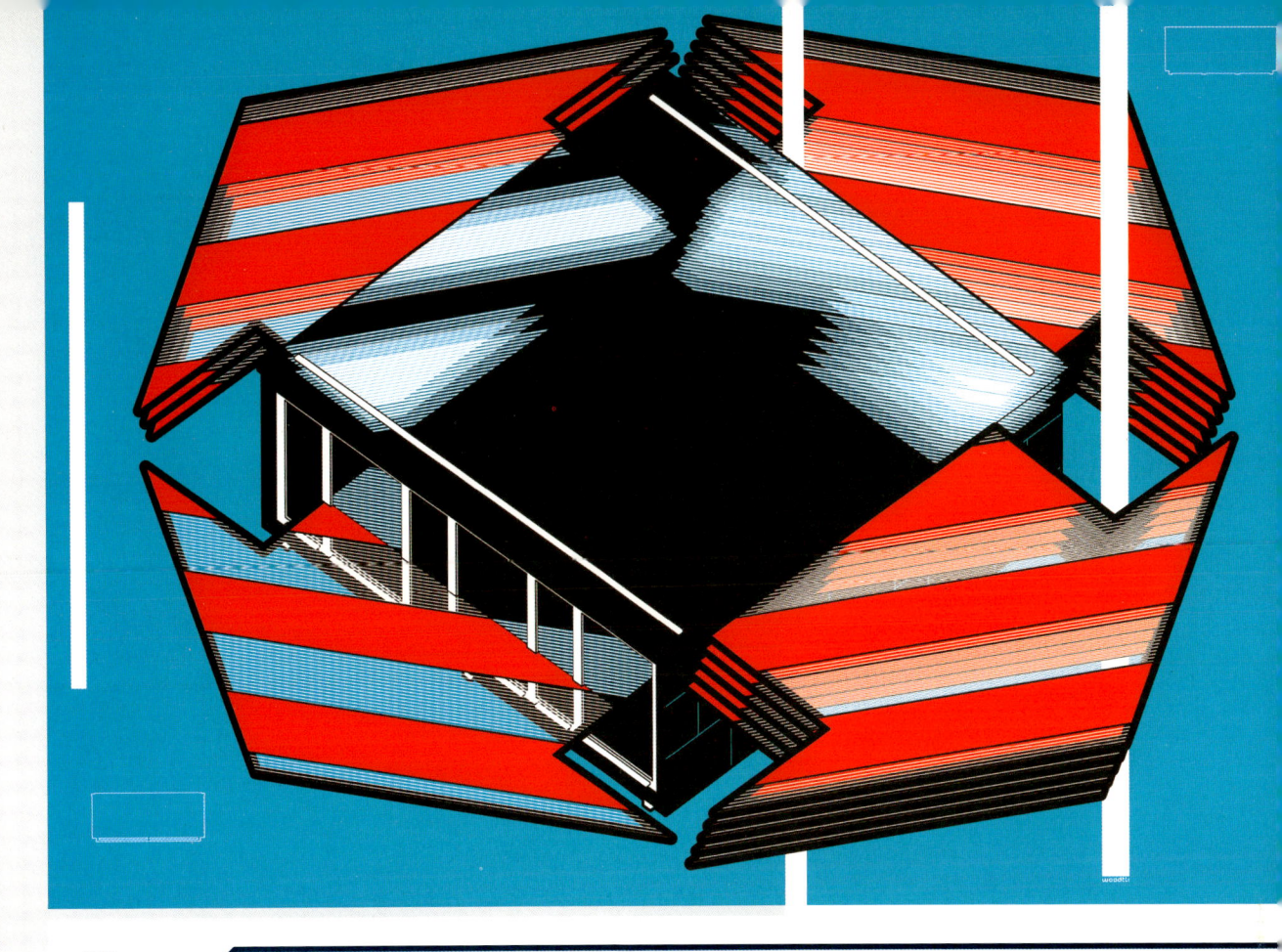

Spreads: Invitation cards for an art gallery
of Stadtgalerie Bern

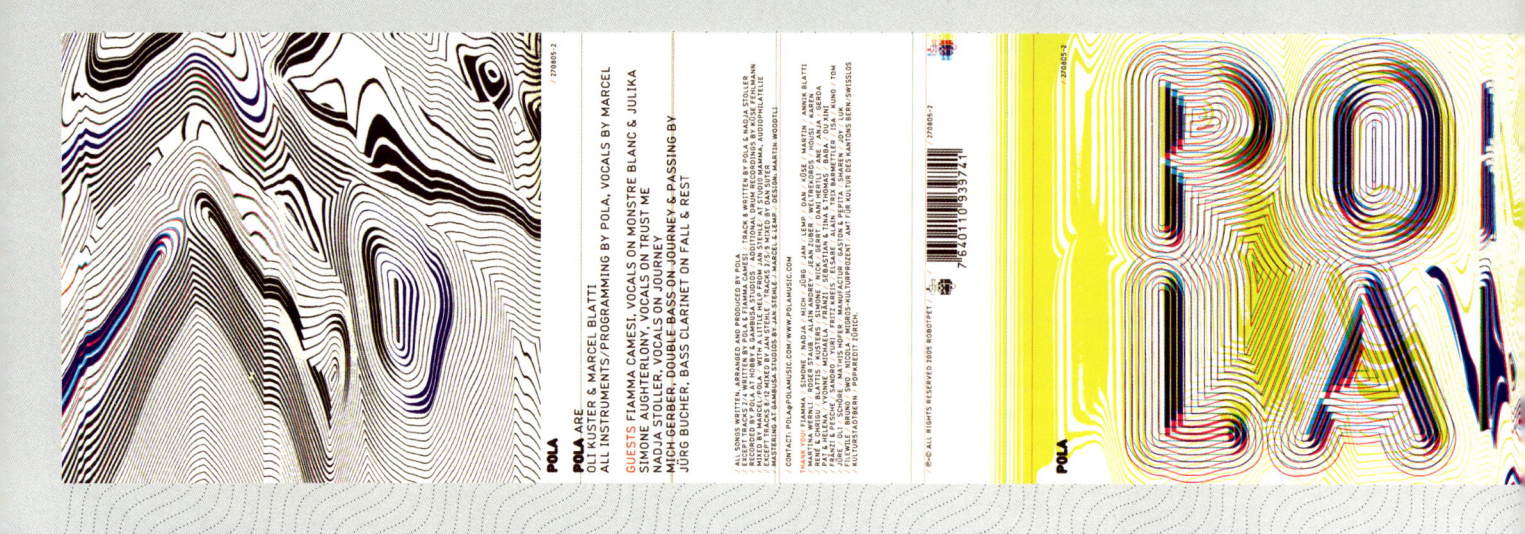

Time	Track		#	Track
4:45	BREATHE	BREATHE	1.	BREATHE
3:01	MONSTRE BLANC	MONSTRE BLANC	2.	MONSTRE BLANC
3:49	TRUST ME	TRUST ME	3.	TRUST ME
4:26	JULIKA	JULIKA	4.	JULIKA
5:05	REMOTE CONTROL	REMOTE CONTROL	5.	REMOTE CONTROL
3:34	FALL	FALL	6.	FALL
4:44	CIRCLES	CIRCLES	7.	CIRCLES
3:50	JOURNEY	JOURNEY	8.	JOURNEY
5:05	HYPER HYPER KILL KILL	HYPER HYPER KILL KILL	9.	HYPER HYPER KILL KILL
3:51	MOUSEDRUM	MOUSEDRUM	10.	MOUSEDRUM
4:00	PUSHING THE PROFITS	PUSHING THE PROFITS	11.	PUSHING THE PROFITS
5:05	PASSING BY	PASSING BY	12.	PASSING BY
3:49	REST	REST	13.	REST

Spreads: CD cover and poster for a music band, Pola, Oli Kuster und Marcel Blatti

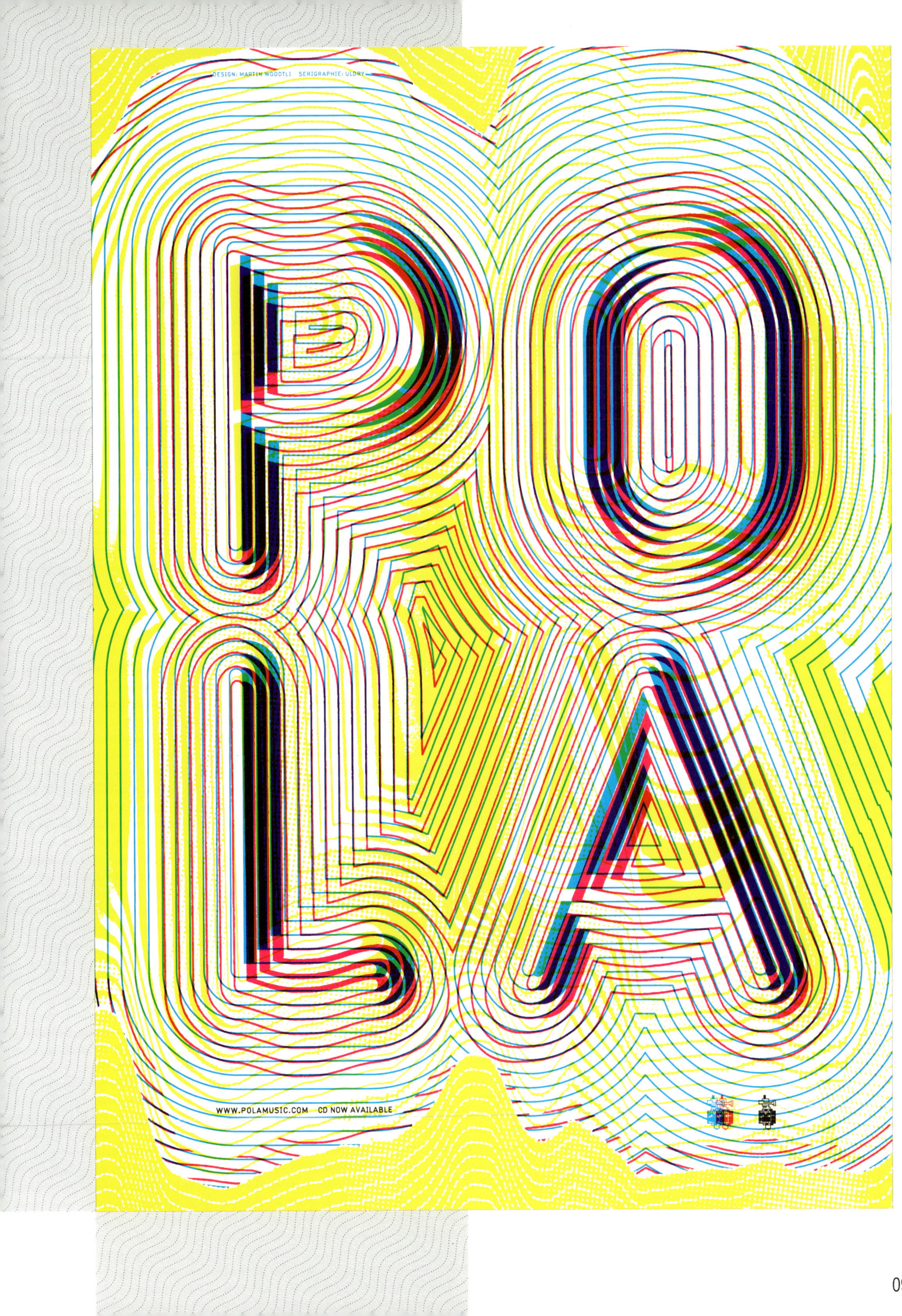
DESIGN: MARTIN WOODTLI SERIGRAPHIE: ULDRY
POLA
WWW.POLAMUSIC.COM CD NOW AVAILABLE

Poster for an art event by Marcel Henry & Beate Engel, Stadtgalerie Bern
Opposite: Poster for a life style magazine, soDA Magazine

SODA *21
JETZT*
IM
PRESSEHANDEL
ERHÆLTLICH*
25:00
AKTION
START
24:00

Poster for an experimental movie and video festival by Patrick Huber, Kunstraum Walcheturm
Opposite: Poster for a jazz festival by Urs Rollin, Hausi Naef

Schöne Töne
Design: Martin Woodtli   Serigraphie: Uldry
14.
SCHAFFHAUSER
KAMMGARN
16. MAI – 17. MAI
JAZZFESTIVAL
2003

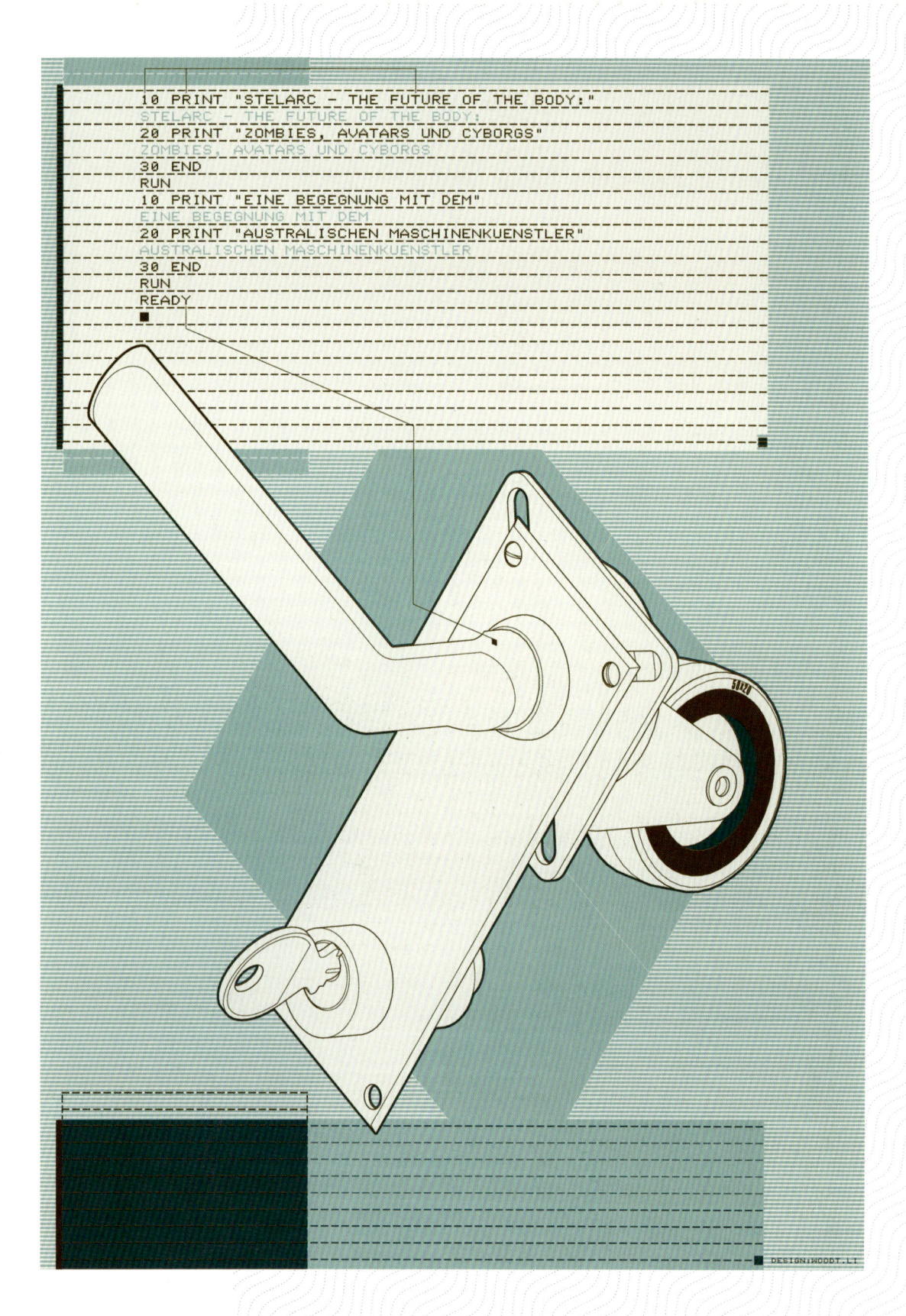

```
10 PRINT "STELARC - THE FUTURE OF THE BODY:"
STELARC - THE FUTURE OF THE BODY:
20 PRINT "ZOMBIES, AVATARS UND CYBORGS"
ZOMBIES, AVATARS UND CYBORGS
30 END
RUN
10 PRINT "EINE BEGEGNUNG MIT DEM"
EINE BEGEGNUNG MIT DEM
20 PRINT "AUSTRALISCHEN MASCHINENKUENSTLER"
AUSTRALISCHEN MASCHINENKUENSTLER
30 END
RUN
READY
■
```

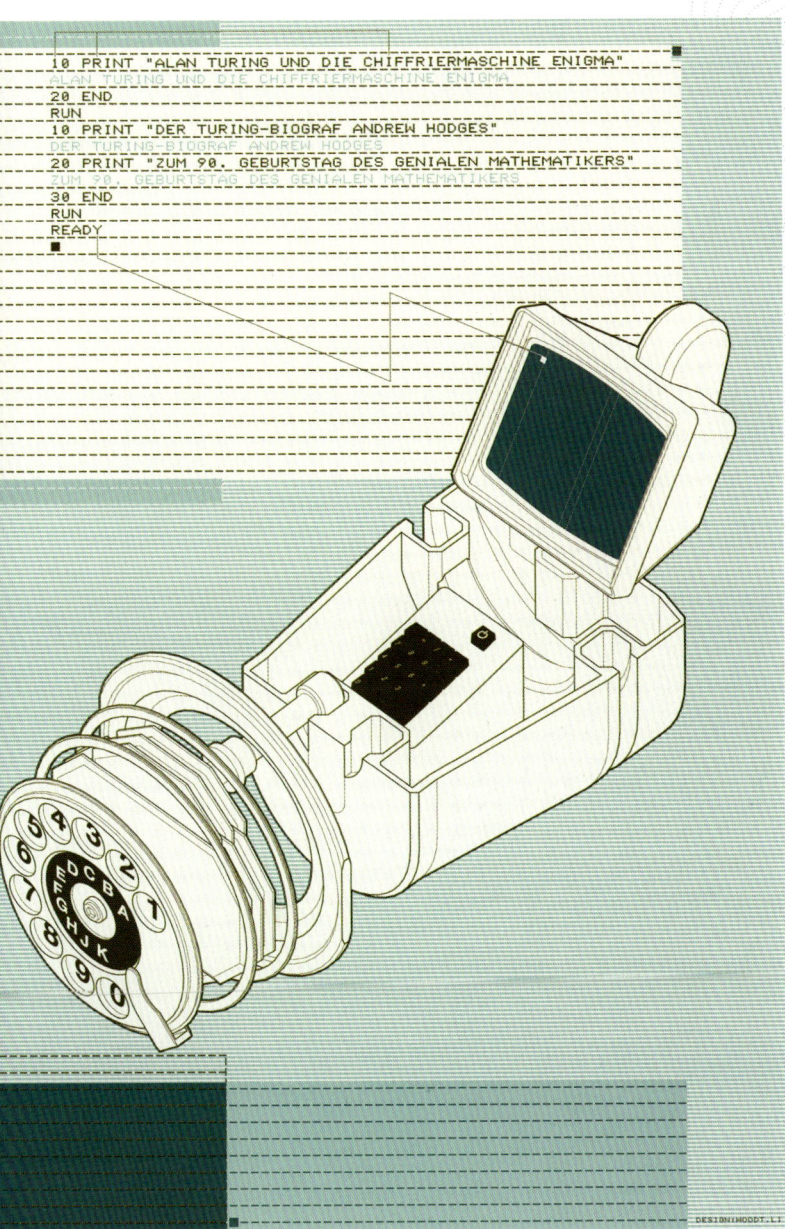

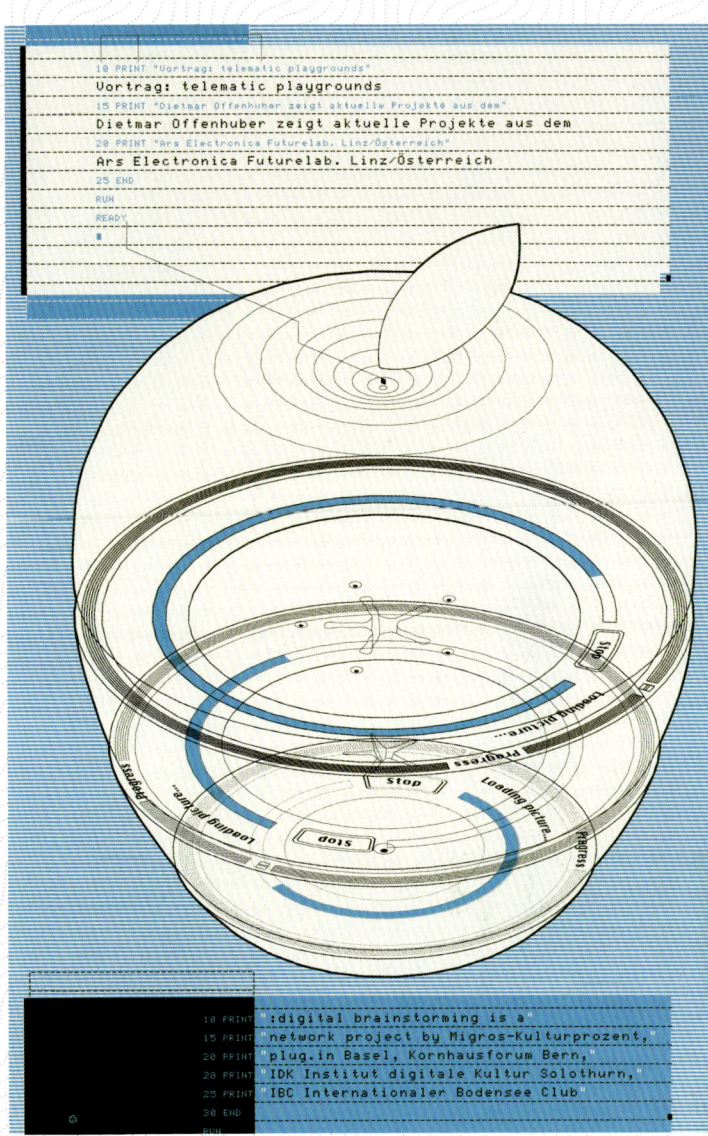

Invitation cards for lecture events

098

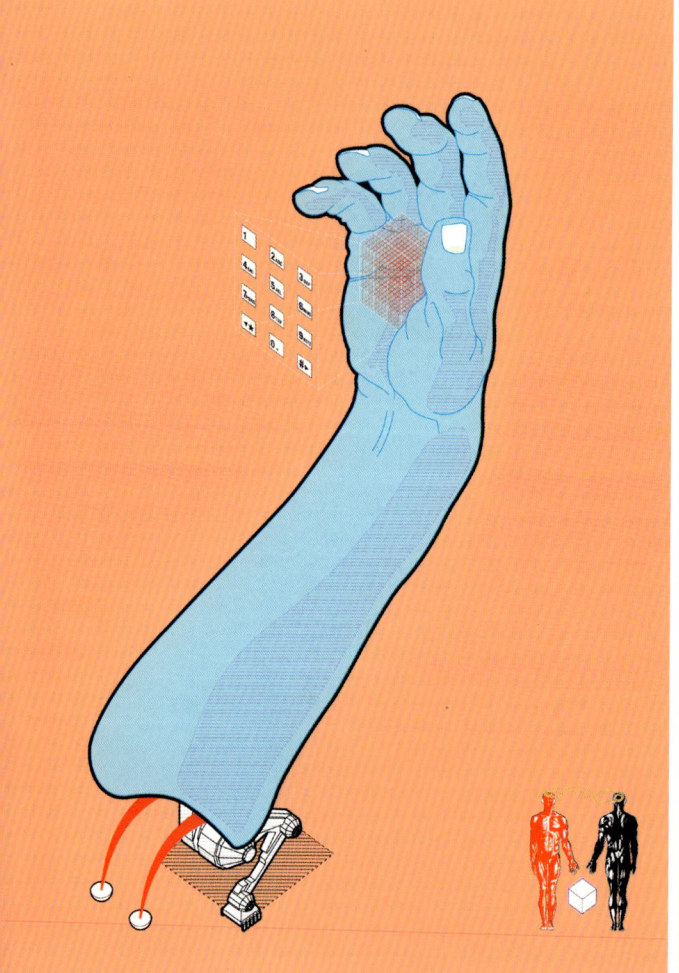

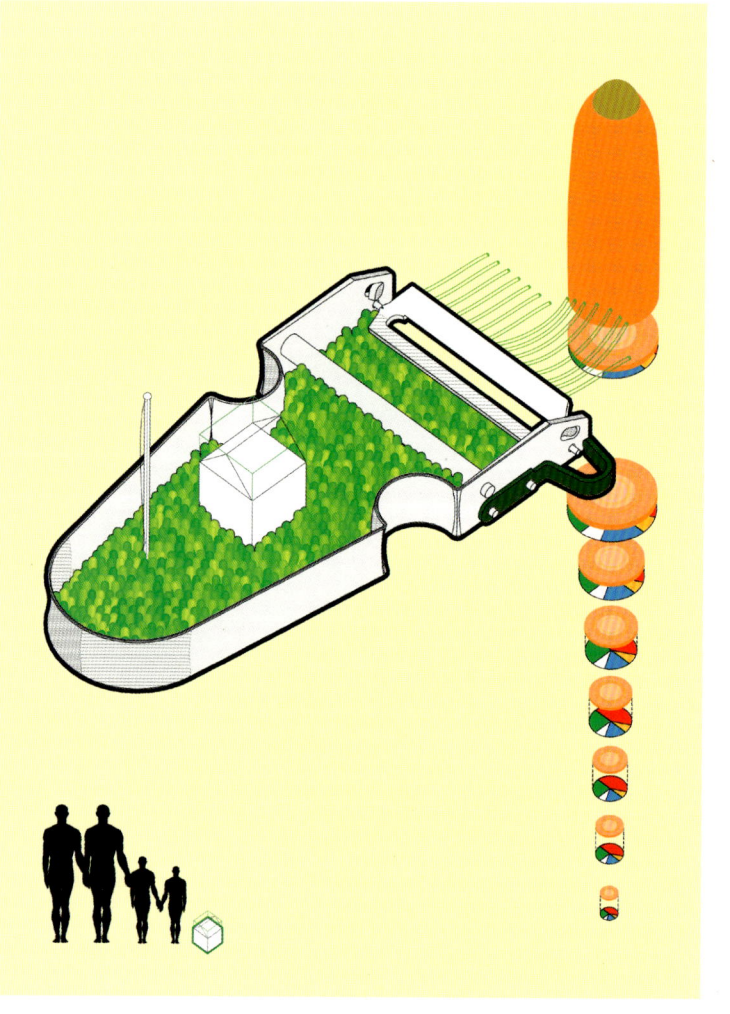

Spreads: Editorials titled "Redefining Retail Relations" for Gottlieb Duttweiler Institution

099

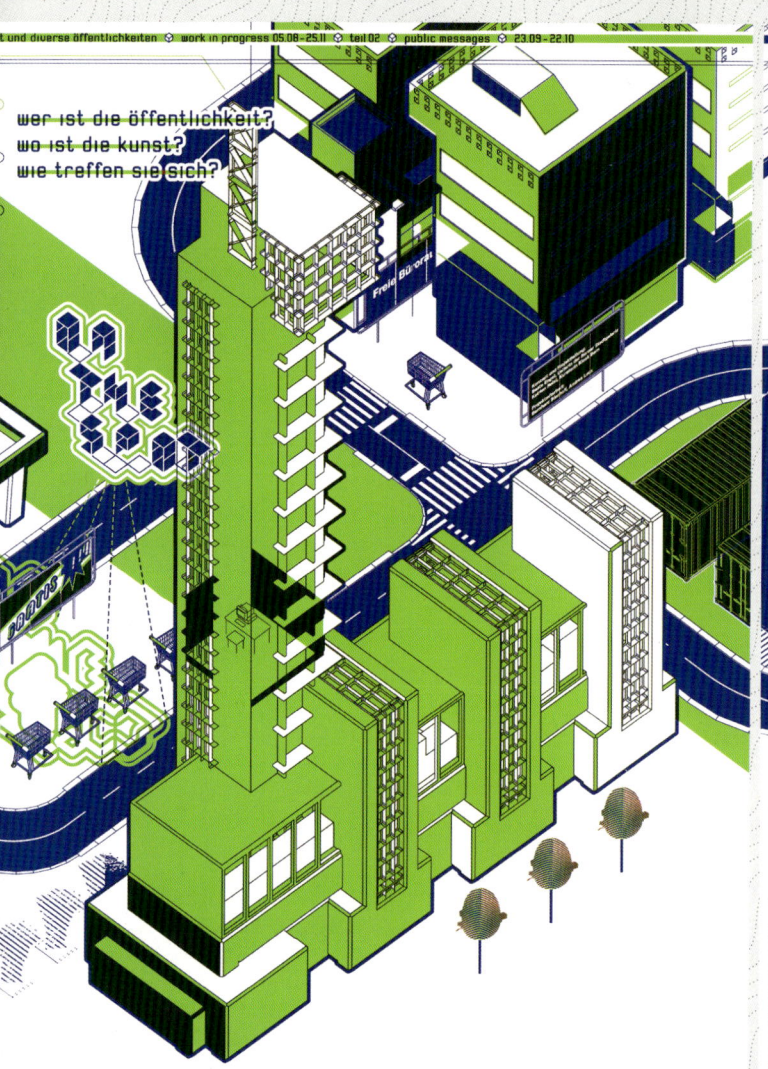

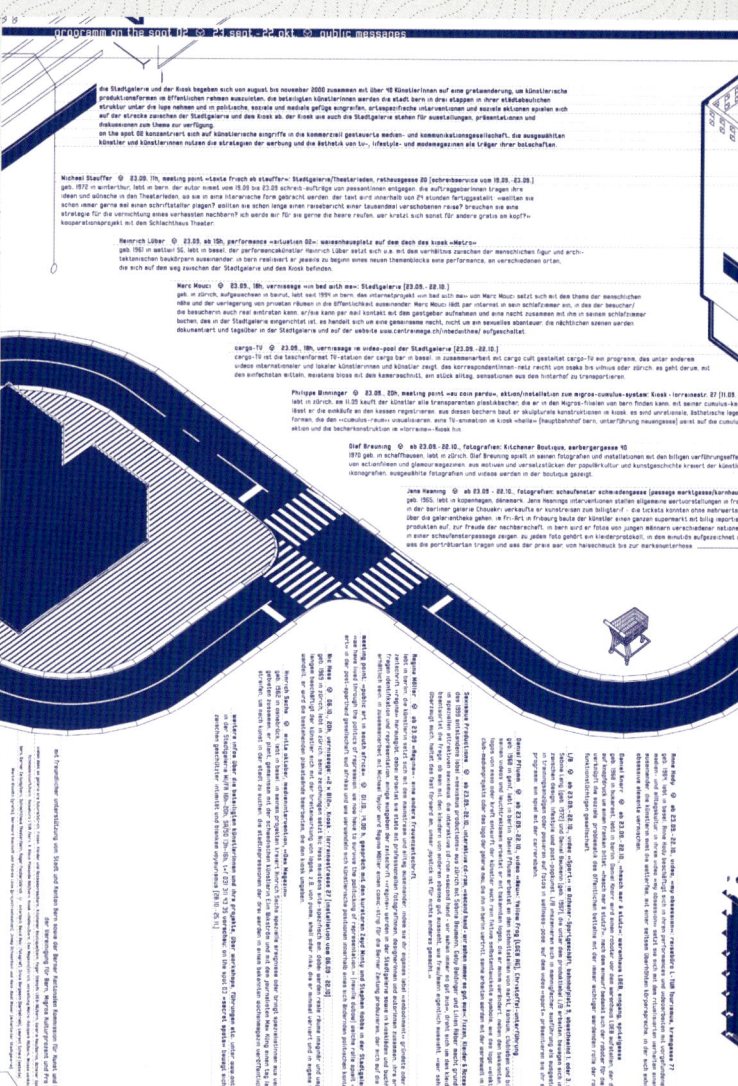

wer ist die öffentlichkeit?
wo ist die kunst?
wie treffen sie sich?

Spreads: Invitation cards and info-papers for an art event for On the Spot

FINDE DEIN RAUMSCHIFF

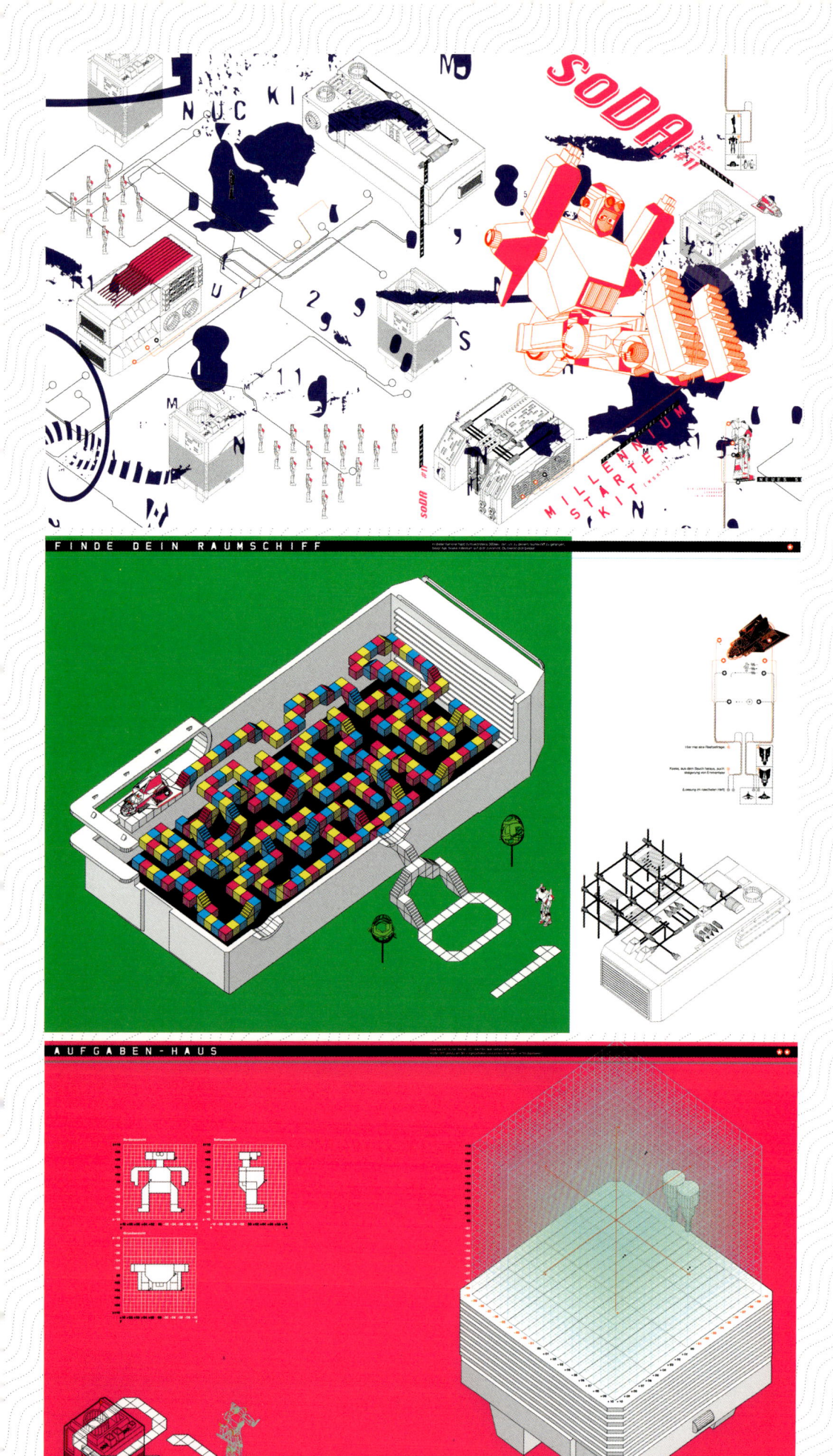

AUFGABEN-HAUS

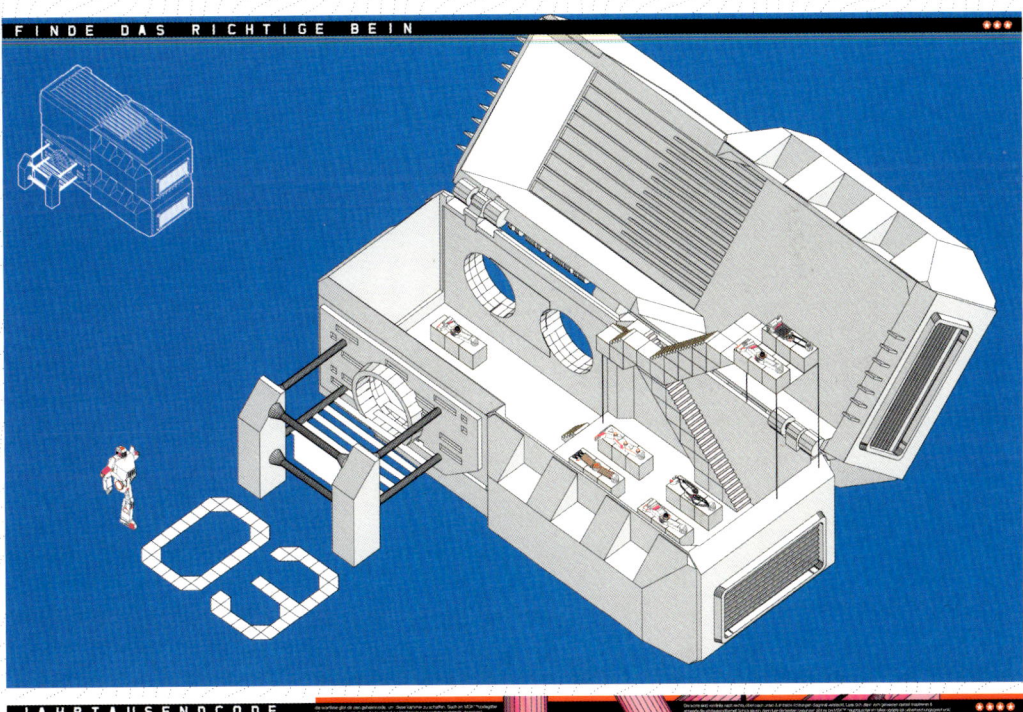

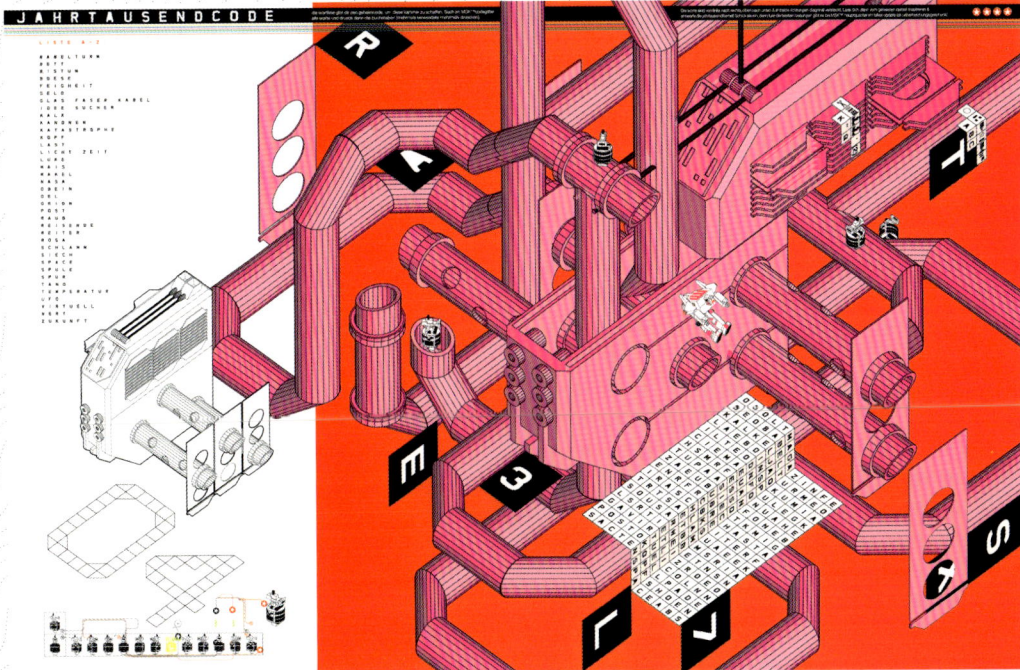

Spreads: Editorials, Millennium Starter Kit™ for *soDA*

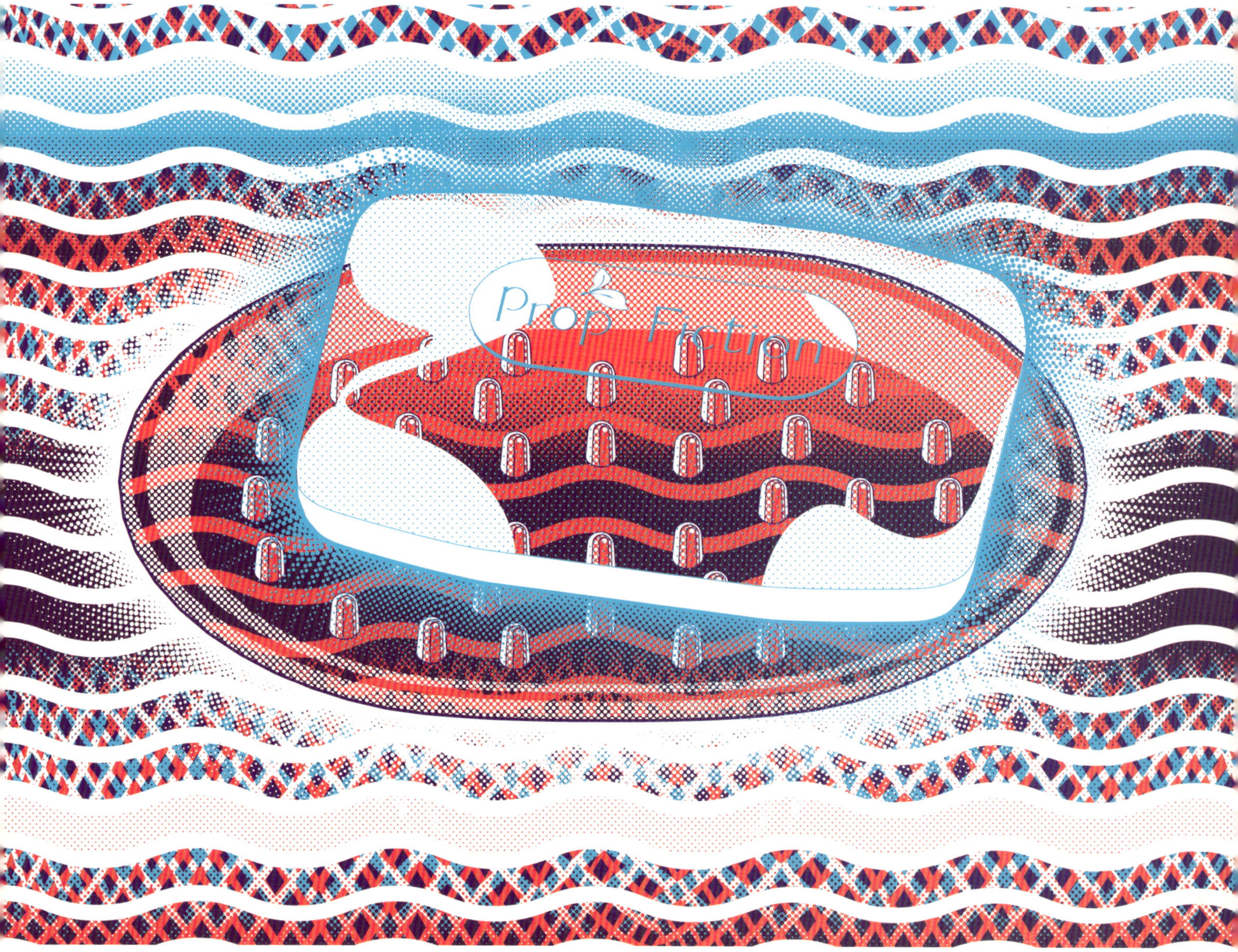

Spreads: Invitation cards for an art gallery of Stadtgalerie Bern

STILL REALITY

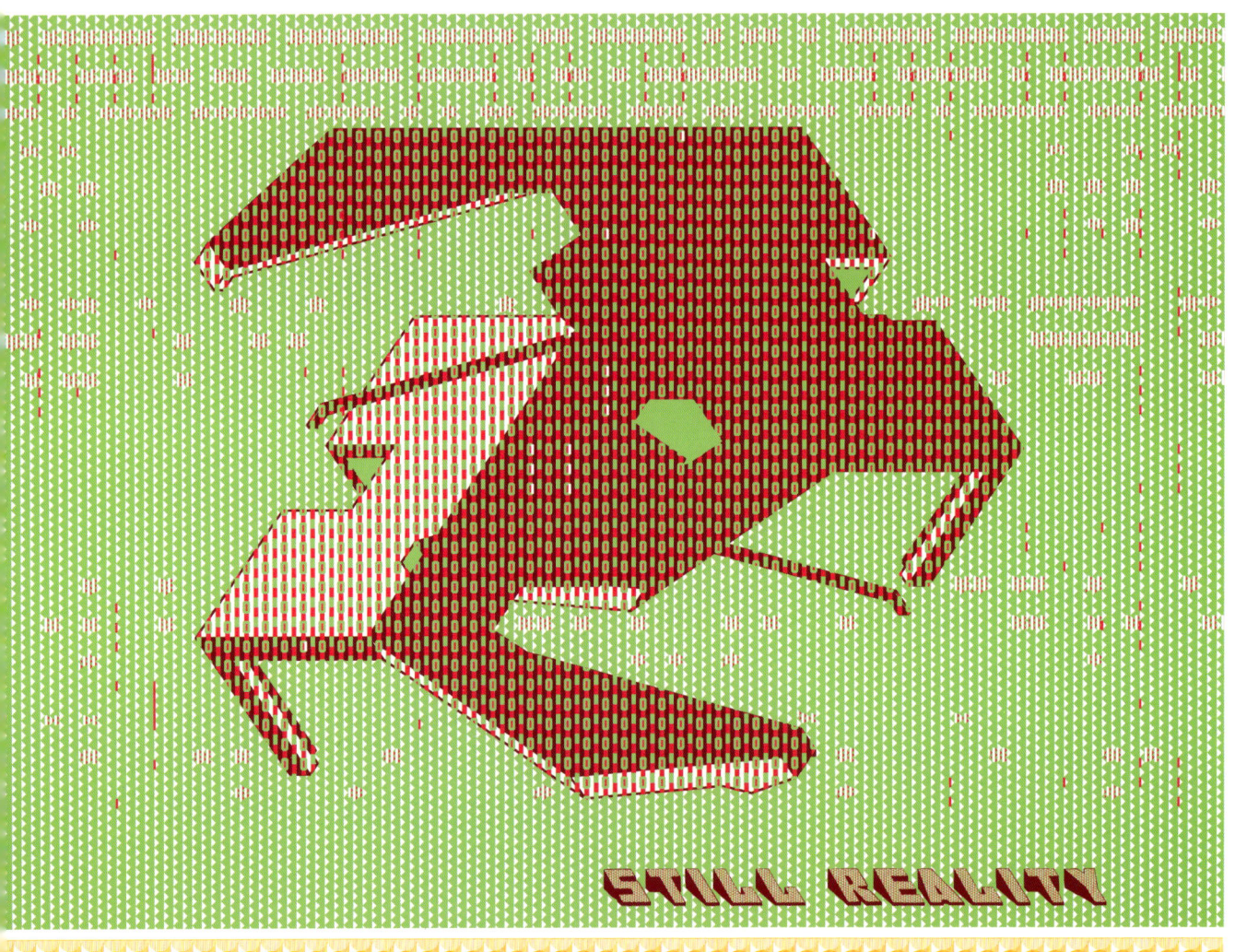

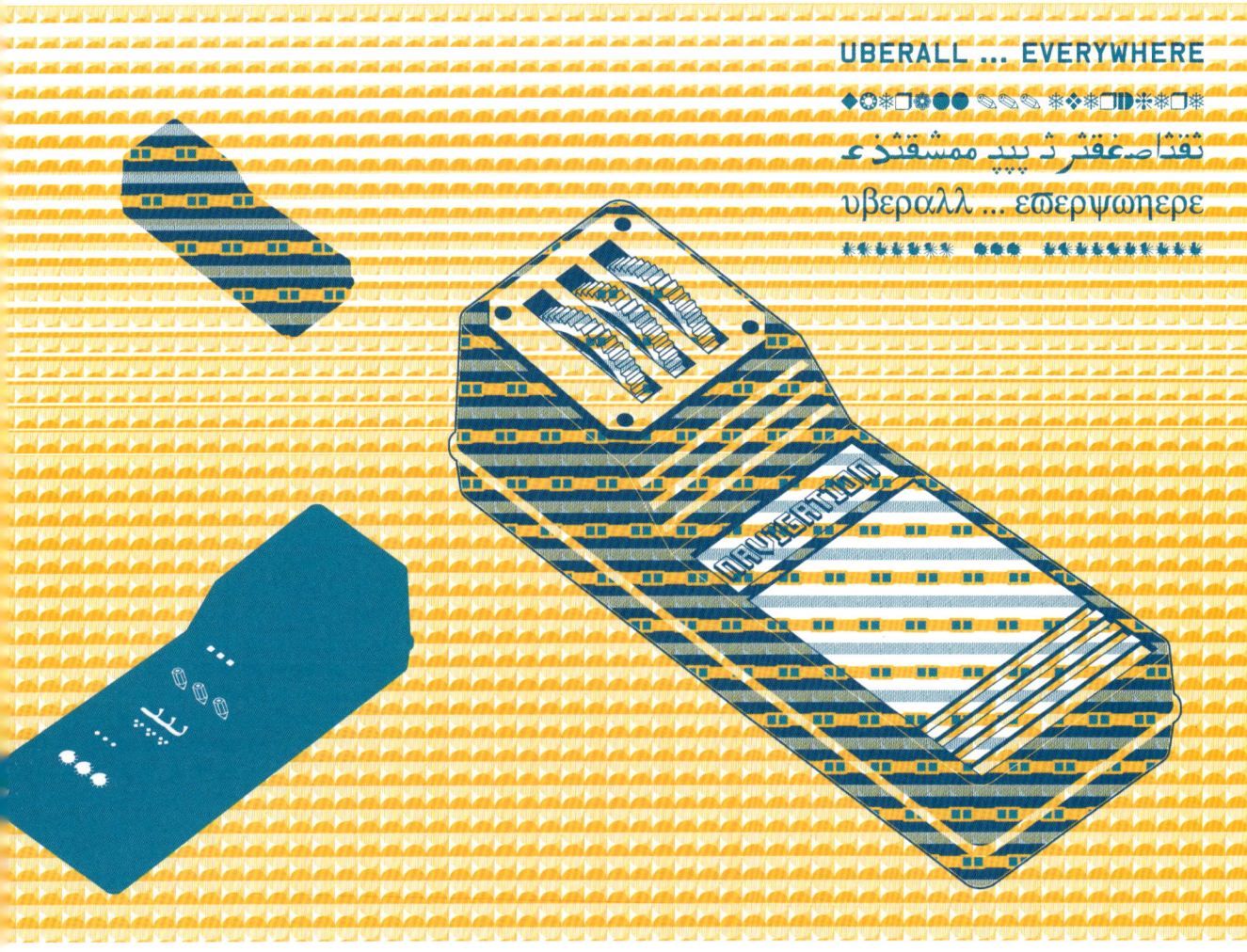

UBERALL ... EVERYWHERE
تقذا صغقثر ث پیډ ممشقثذع
υβεραλλ ... εωερψωηερε

Spreads: Invitation cards for an art gallery of Stadtgalerie Bern

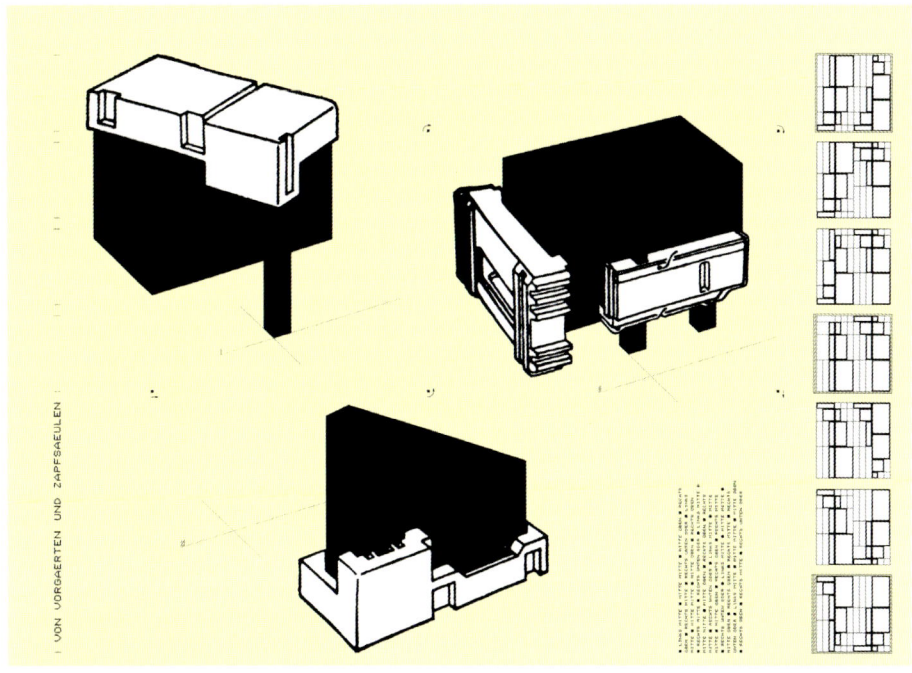

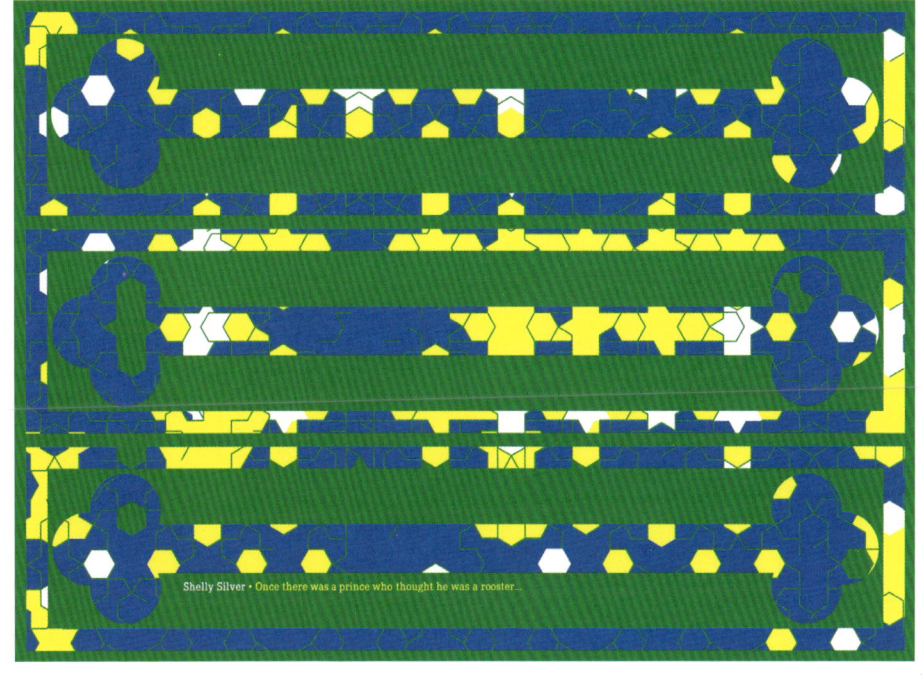

108

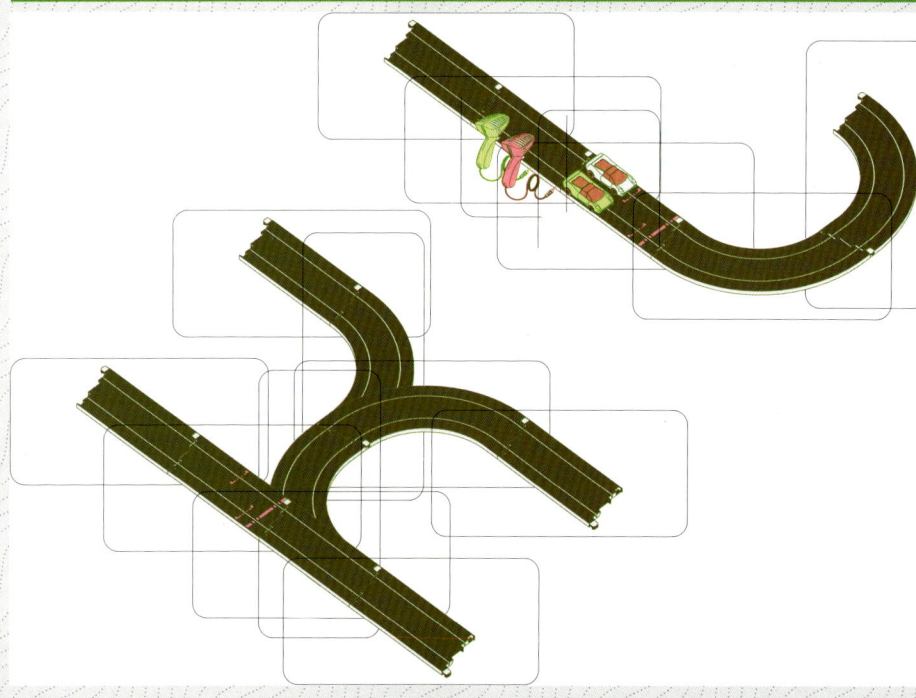

Opposite: Business card for a Photographer, Katharina Lütscher
Invitation cards and poster for a theatre, Der Vogelfänger

Michel de Boer

Michel de Boer graduated from the Academy of Fine Arts and Higher Technologies in Rotterdam. He has worked for two years as an independent designer. In 1980 he became a fulltime member of the Studio Dumbar team of designers and in 1989 he became creative managing partner.

Within Studio Dumbar, Michel de Boer is fully responsible for the creative output. He has more than twenty-five years' experience in corporate identity, brand and design. He worked for many clients around the world on projects that require international implementation in the commercial service sector, non-profit organisations and the public sector.

Michel de Boer has won many awards, especially for D&AD Golden Awards and seven D&AD Silver Awards. He has taken part in many international design conferences and has lectured frequently for colleagues and students all over the world. He has been a tutor to the design department of the Academy of Fine Arts in Den Bosch and professor in design at the I.U.A.V. University in Venice, Italy, since September 2004.

He is the driving-force of the start-up of Dumbar Branding, a new joint venture in Shanghai, which was established in 2005.

PROJECT: PROMOTIONAL POSTER FOR CLASSICAL MUSIC PROGRAM
TYPE: POSTER
CLIENT: AMSTERDAM SINFONIETTA, AMSTERDAM

"Amsterdam Sinfonietta is an independent music ensemble with mainly young musicians. Its image was old fashioned, introvert and distant. The purpose of the new poster series is to direct attention to Amsterdam Sinfonietta in the 'grey' existing mass of classical music programs and to position the brand 'Amsterdam Sinfonietta' in a modern and unique way, geared more to the perception of a younger target group." – Michel de Boer

Spreads: Brochure designs for City of Rotterdam, the Netherlands

GGD
Rotterdam en omstreken

Wat kunt u van onze dienstverlening verwachten

Servicenormen

Dienst Stedelijk Onderwijs
Gemeente Rotterdam

Wat kunt u van onze dienstverlening verwachten

Servicenormen
juli 2001

Form designs for various departments of City of Rotterdam, the Netherlands

Various versions of main and sub logo for City of Rotterdam, the Netherlands

City of Rotterdam

Roteb
Gemeente Rotterdam

OBR
City Development Corporation
City of Rotterdam

Sociale Zaken en Werkgelegenheid
Gemeente Rotterdam

Sport en Recreatie
Gemeente Rotterdam

Bibliotheek
Gemeente Rotterdam

115

Spread: Visual language used as supplement to the logos of the various departments of the City of Rotterdam, the Netherlands

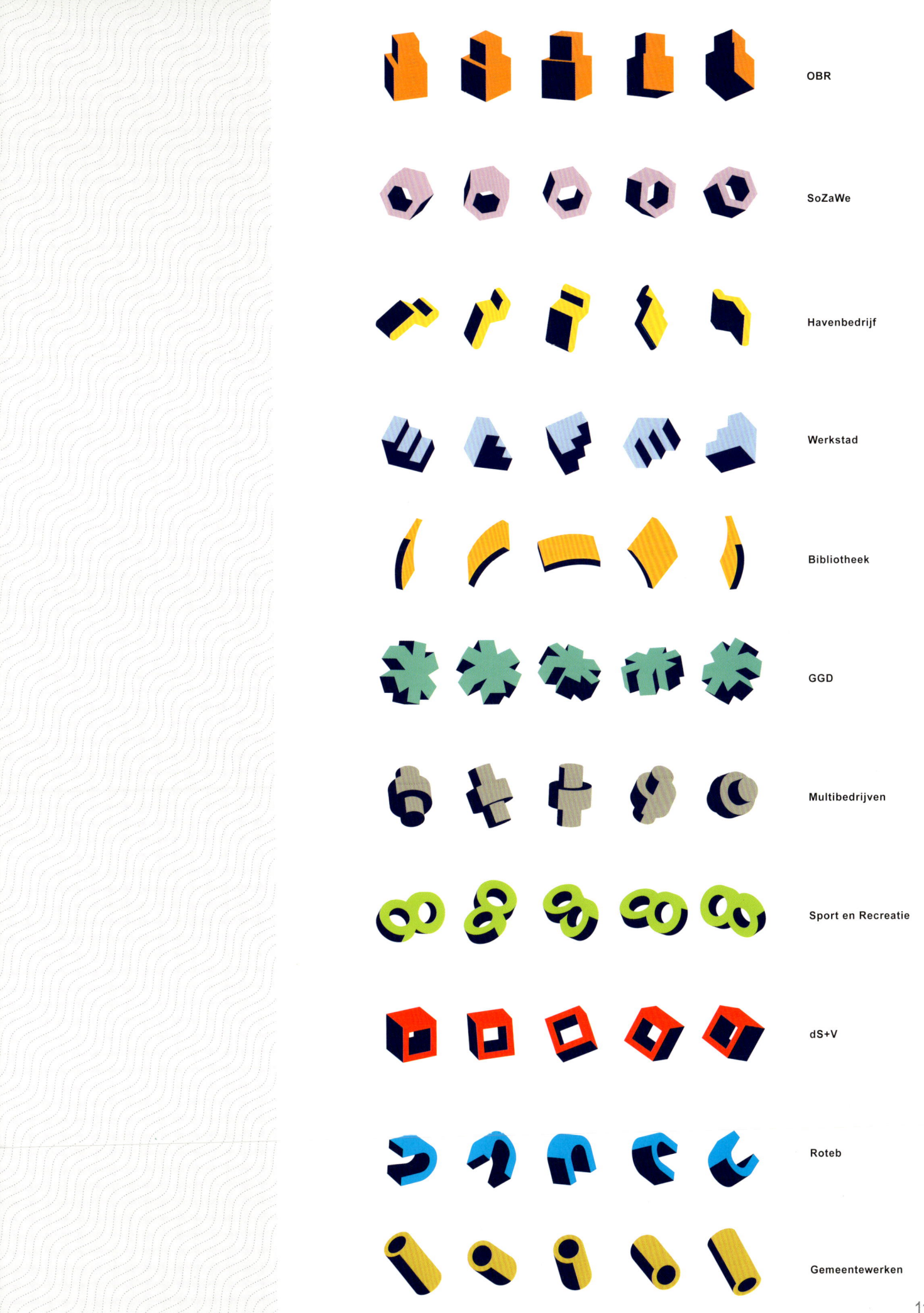

OBR

SoZaWe

Havenbedrijf

Werkstad

Bibliotheek

GGD

Multibedrijven

Sport en Recreatie

dS+V

Roteb

Gemeentewerken

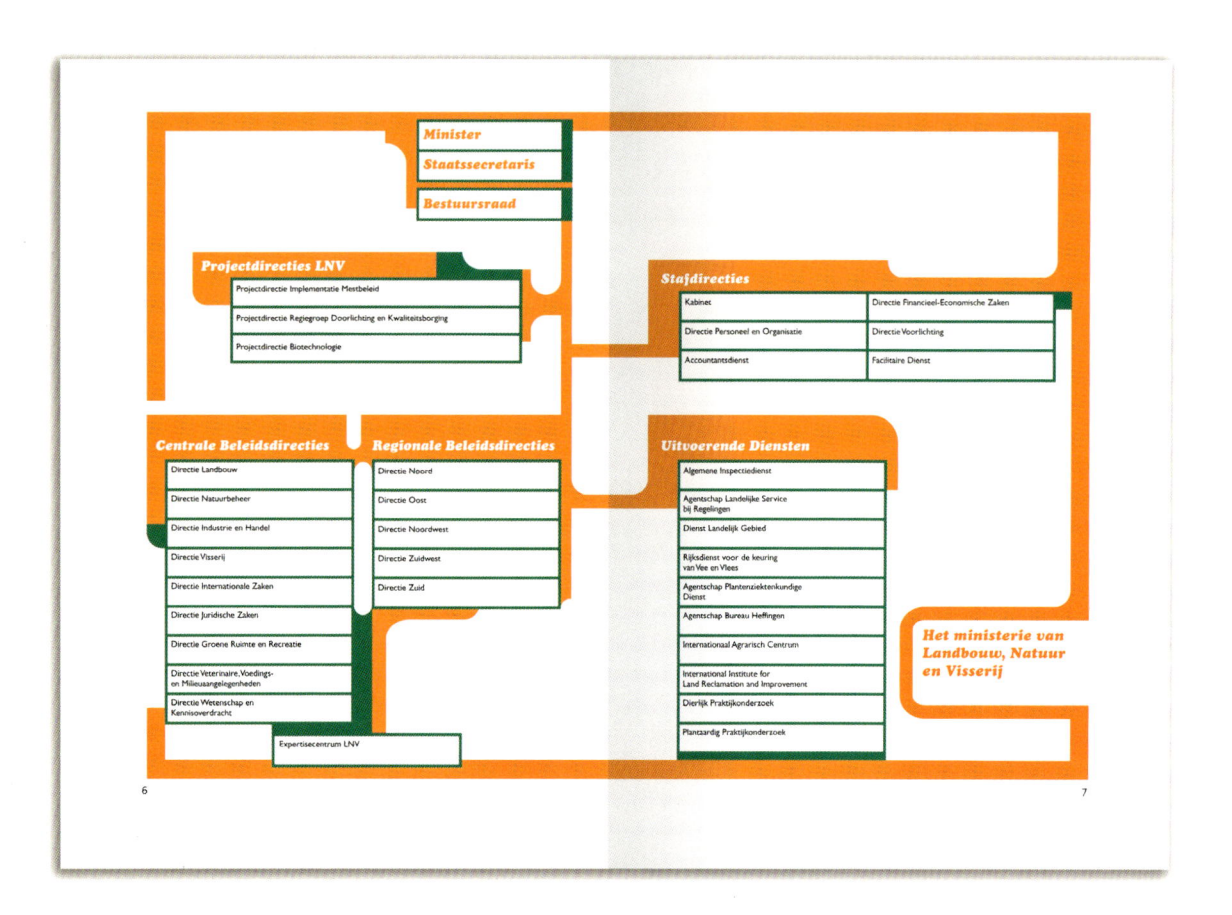

Layouts from *Facts & Figures* publication for Ministry of Agriculture, Nature and Food Quality, the Netherlands

Label series created to support thematic communication of the Ministry of Agriculture, Nature and Food Quality, the Netherlands

Vertrouwd **platteland**,
verrassend perspectief

Veilig **voedsel**,
bewuste keus

Groen **ondernemen**,
innovatieve kracht

Nieuwe paden,
vitale **natuur**

voedsel en groen
van internationale klasse

119

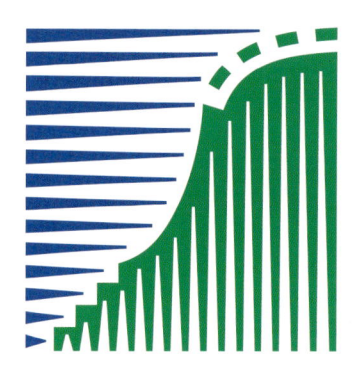

agriculture, nature and food quality

Spreads: Main logo design and logo series created for the various departments for Ministry of Agriculture, Nature and Food Quality, the Netherlands

121

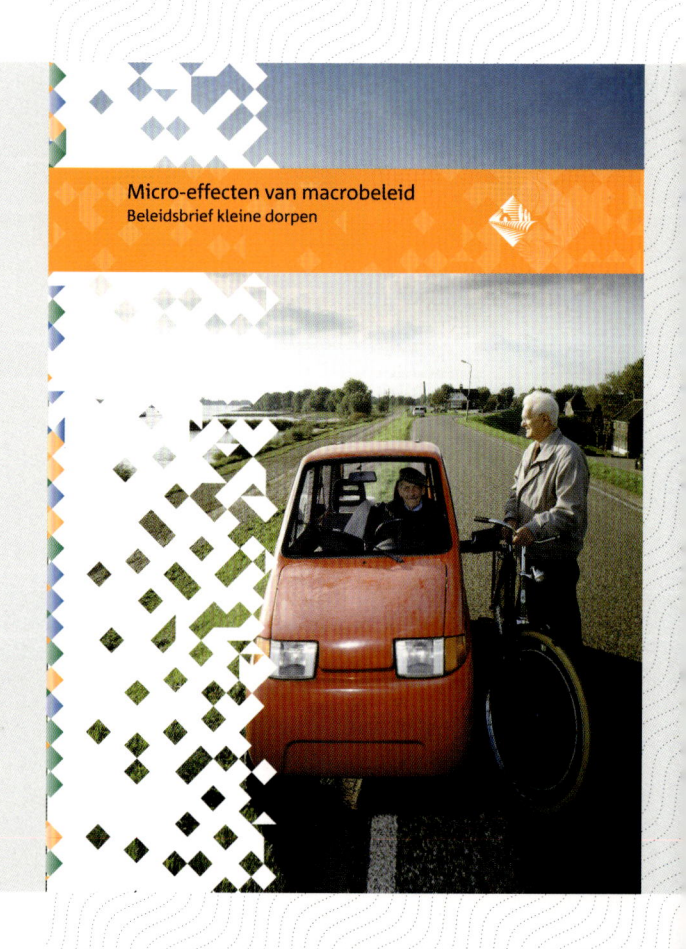

Structuurschema Groene Ruimte 2
Samen werken aan groen Nederland

Ministerie van Landbouw,
Natuurbeheer en Visserij

Micro-effecten van macrobeleid
Beleidsbrief kleine dorpen

Spreads: Cover and layouts from a policy document "SGR2" for Ministry of Agriculture, Nature and Food Quality, the Netherlands

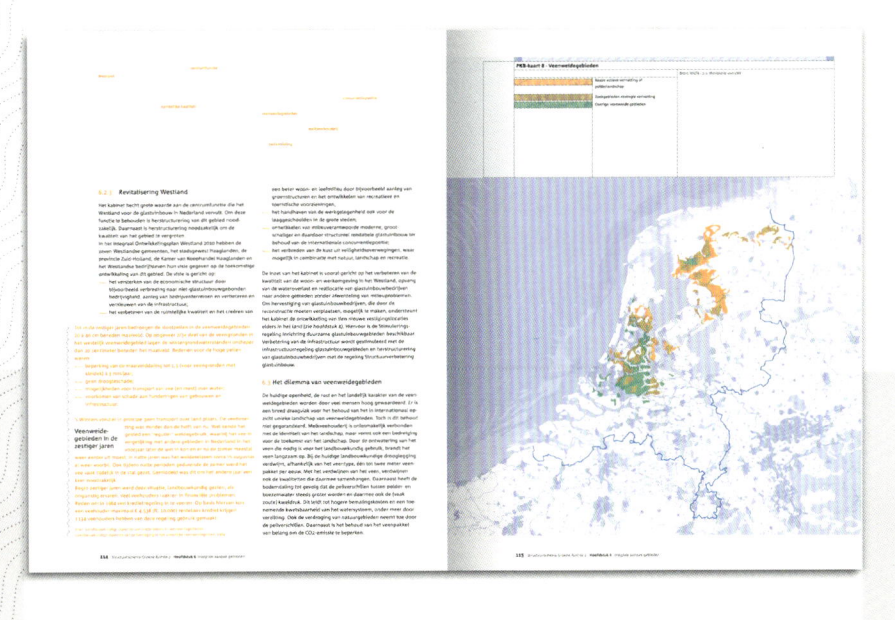

Spreads: Annual report and annual brochure for
Ministry of Economic Affairs, the Netherlands

124

125

Spreads: Corporate identity for Ministry of General Affairs, the Netherlands

Ministerie van Algemene Zaken

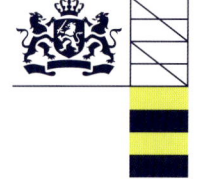

Kabinet van de Minister-President
Ministerie van Algemene Zaken

Minister-President
Ministerie van Algemene Zaken

Rijksvoorlichtingsdienst
Ministerie van Algemene Zaken

Ministerie van Algemene Zaken

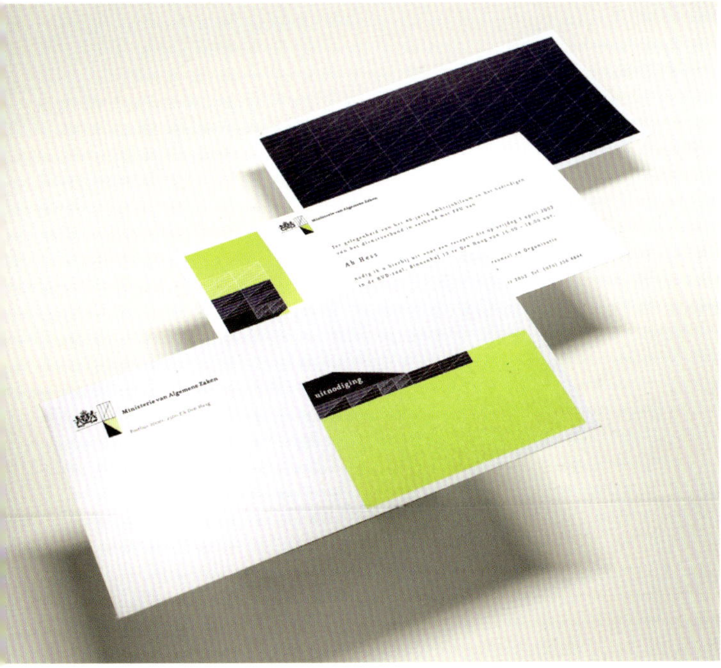
Ministerie van Algemene Zaken
uitnodiging

Eureka
Eureka
Eureka
Eureka
Eureka
Eureka

Ministerie van Algemene Zaken
B
BEZOEKER BINNENHOF 19
ZICHTBAAR DRAGEN
PASNUMMER
10
Ministerie van Algemene Zaken
BEZOEKER BINNENHOF 19
ZICHTBAAR DRAGEN
PASNUMMER
18

Kabinet van de Minister-President
Ministerie van Algemene Zaken
Enny Soons
Stafmedewerker beheer
Binnenhof 19
Postbus 20001
2500 EA Den Haag

Park Kum-jun

Park Kum-jun was born in Korea in 1962. In 1988, he graduated from Hongik University's Department of Communication Design, and received his Master's degree in advertising and public relations from the same university in 1999. After leaving university, he worked for ten years at two top Korean companies, first as a designer at the Ssangyong Group and later as an art director at an advertising agency, Cheil Communications. He founded 601 bisang, a design company, in 1998, and has been its president and creative director ever since. He lectured on visual communication design at Hongik University from 1999 to 2005.

He has won several awards in Korea and many international design competitions, including the Red Dot Best of the best in 2007; the New York ADC Gold Medal in 2002; the 2004 Korea International Poster Biennale; the One Show's Silver Pencil award in 2005; the New York Festival's Gold Medal and Silver Medal in 2007. In addition, his artwork has been chosen for various international design and poster competitions, such as the Graphics Poster Annual, the Graphics Brochure Gold Medal, TDC, *I.D.*, as well as exhibitions and festivals in Chaumont, Toyama, Brno and Warsaw.

He has participated in joint exhibitions throughout the world and held two private exhibitions (Japan and Korea). He has planned and designed a variety of art books, including *Calendars Are Culture*, *601 SPACE PROJECT*, and *Eoureum-the Uniting of Two*. He also worked as vice president for the Visual Information Design Association of Korea (VIDAK) from 2002 to 2005. During the same period, he planned and designed the *VIDAK 2003* and *VIDAK 2005-VIDAK Annuals*, documenting the history of Korea's visual design field as editor-in-chief. Since 2003, he has organised and hosted the "601 ARTBOOK PROJECT" competition in an effort to play an active role in design education while expanding the genre of art books. At the same time, he has developed a line of designer items, "601STREET" through which he communicates with the public at the art shops located within museums all over the Korea.

PROJECT: MY FRIEND FROM MARS- JOY, ANGER, SORROW, PLEASURE
TYPE: SERIES POSTERS
CLIENT: GWANGJU DESIGN BIENNALE

"The theme of the 2005 Gwangju Design Biennale was 'Future Life'. This poster series is based on the imagination and an intellectual quest to discover life on Mars. Joy, anger, sorrow and pleasure, the four major emotions in Eastern thinking, are depicted on lacquered Korean 'hanji', reminiscent of the rough planetary surface of Mars. 1500 X 1090mm, Silk Printing" –- Park Kum-jun

Spreads: The three posters set commemorating the 10th anniversary of 601bisang, each with a theme: what design should do, the design beyond design, and the inside and the outside of design.

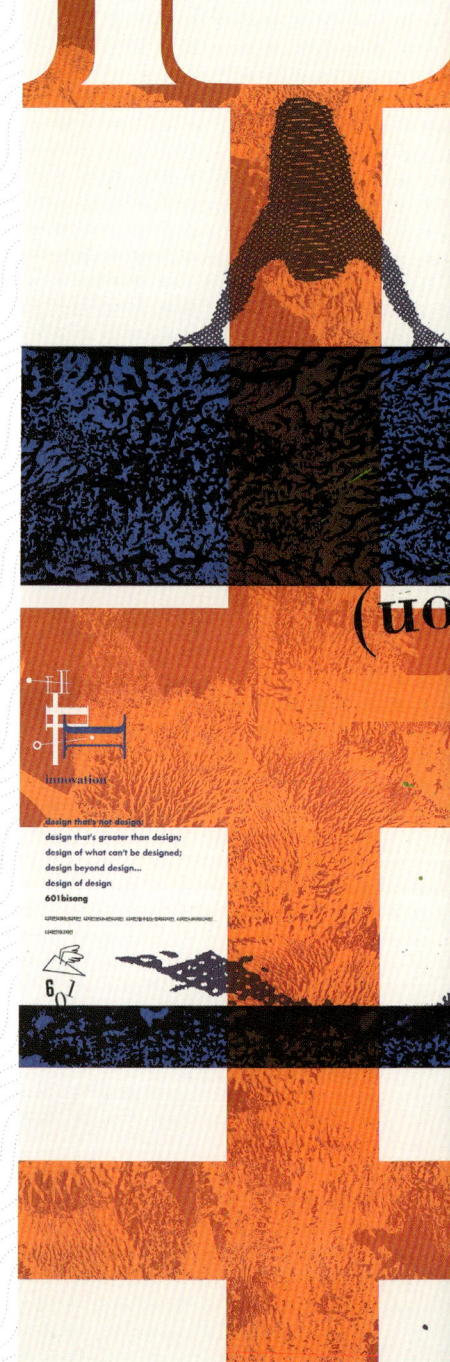

601BISANG
1998-2008

intercommunication
design and non-design;
the past and the future of design;
the beginning and the end of design;
the inside and the outside of design...
601bisang
(intercommunication)
601BISANG
1998-2008

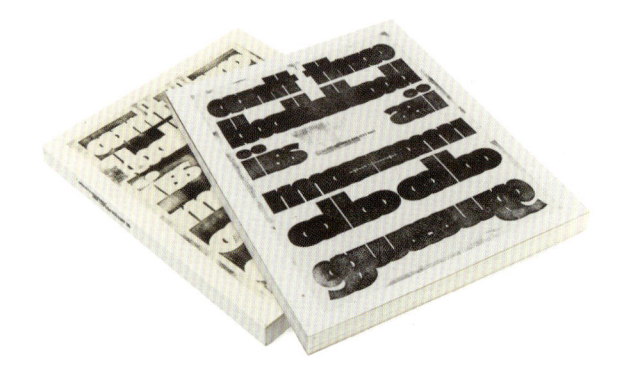

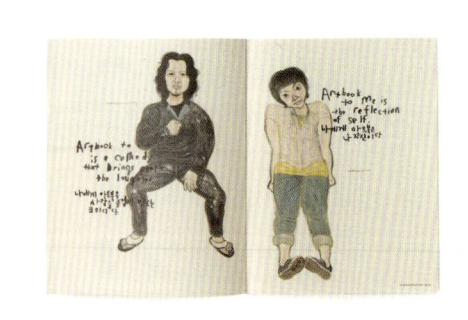

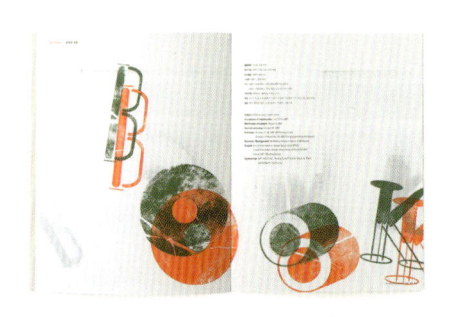

Catalogue compiles the works of award winners from the
5th Art Book Project held by 601Bisang 2007
Opposite: Series posters titled "601 Art Book Project
2007" for 601Bisang

132

133

Left: Poster for the "601 Art Book Project 2006" competition conveys excitement, anticipation, and festivity.
Right: The poster for the "601 Art Book Project 2006" exhibition reused the first poster. Rectangular boxes symbolic of the Art Book Project concept were placed over the original design.
Opposite: Catalogue design for 601 Art Book Project 2006, the winners of the event made this book together, so readers are exposed to their gestures and dialogues with originality and a strong appeal.

134

135

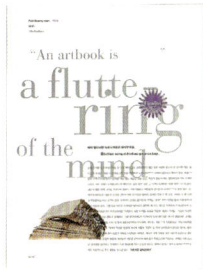

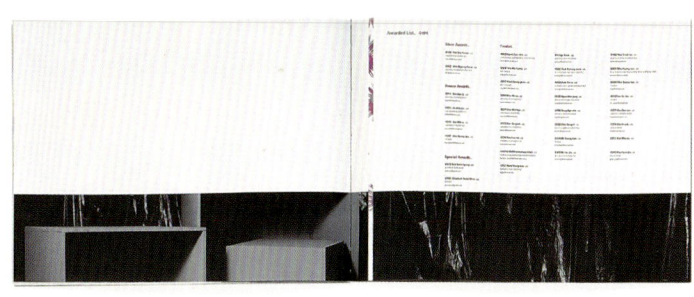

136

Spreads: Book design titled *"EOUREUM-the uniting of two"*, attempts to rediscover the meaning of togetherness ("eoureum") through photo images of communication and rapport for 601bisang.

138

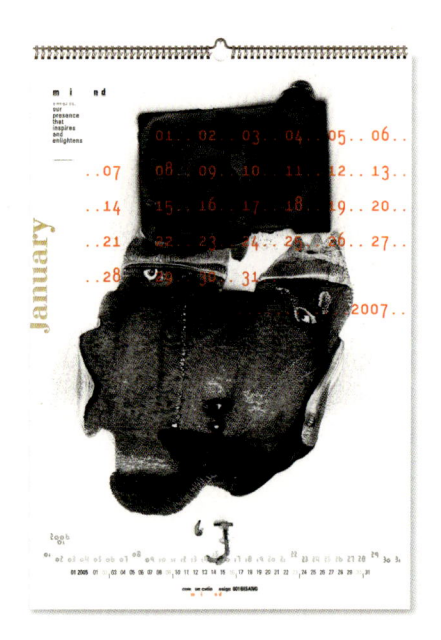

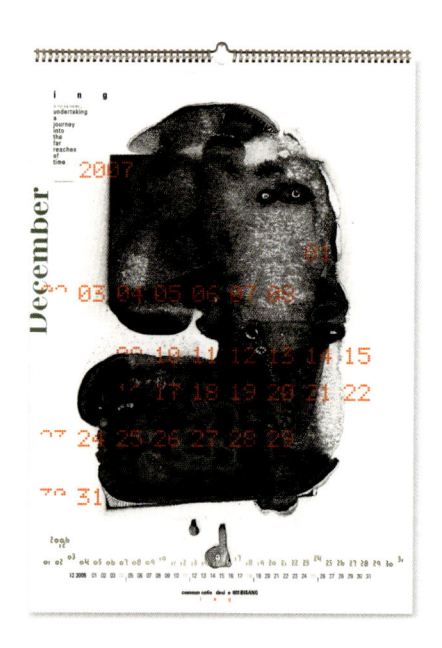

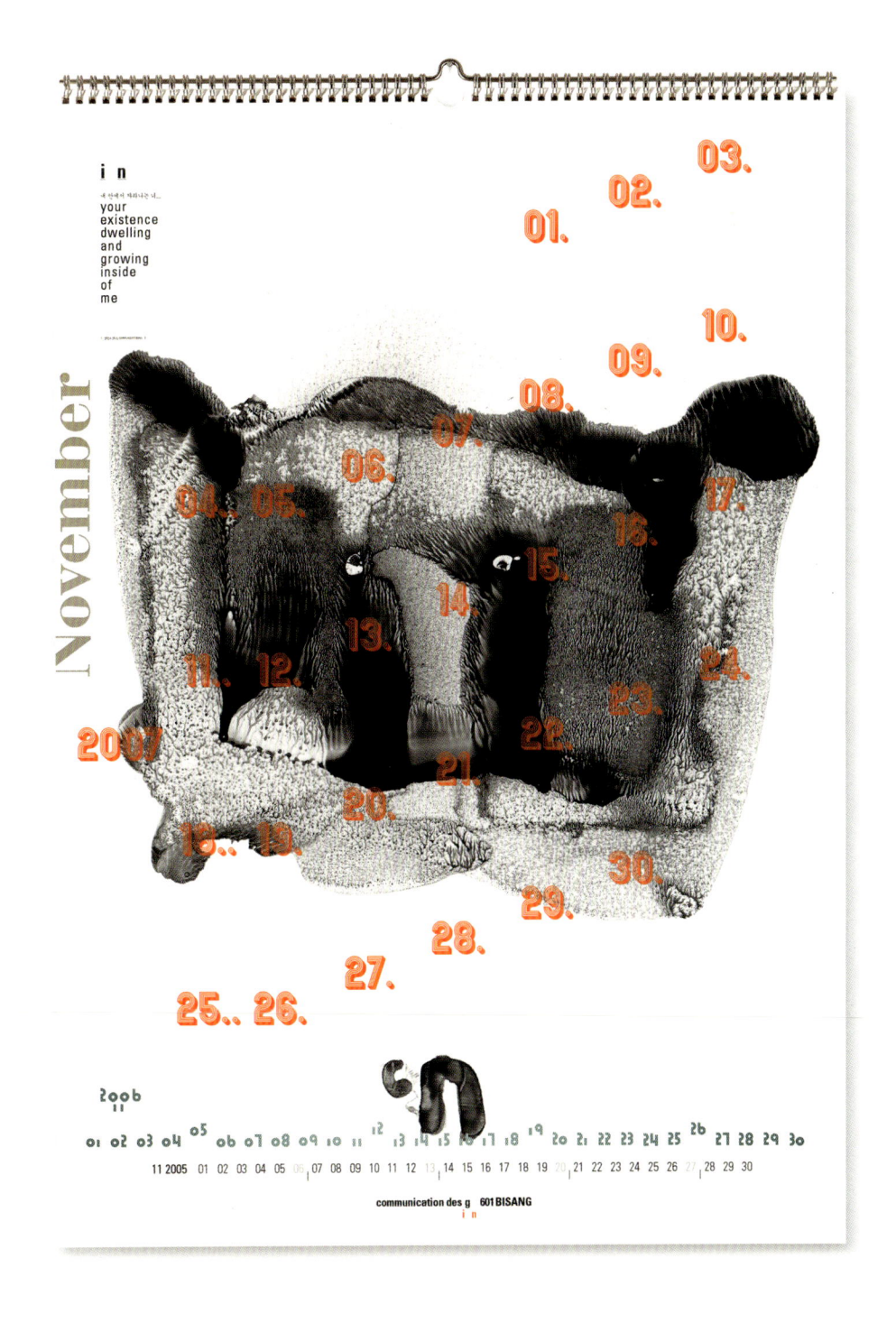

Spreads: This work, which began under the theme of a Calendar Tracking 5 Years, uses twelve keywords to frame the identity of communication design.

Spreads: A poster series for the 2004 Korea Visual Communication Design Festival commemorating the 10th anniversary of the founding of VIDAK (Visual Information Design Association of Korea)

141

142

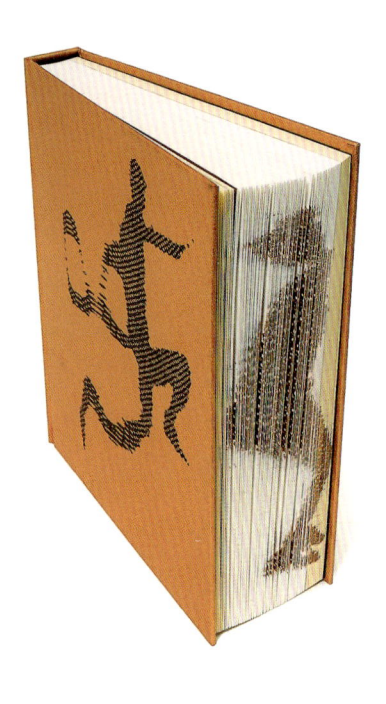

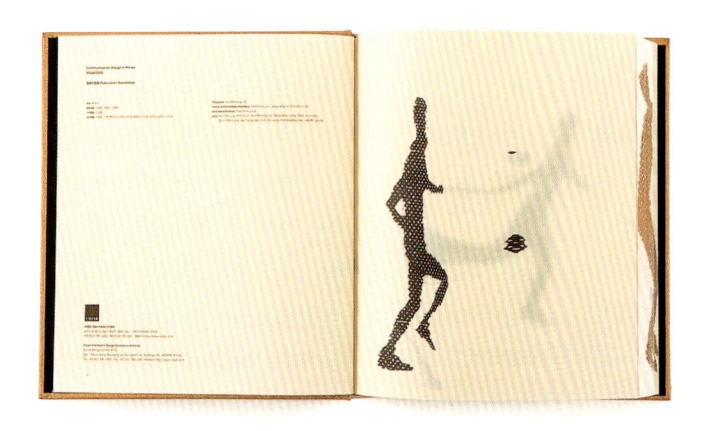

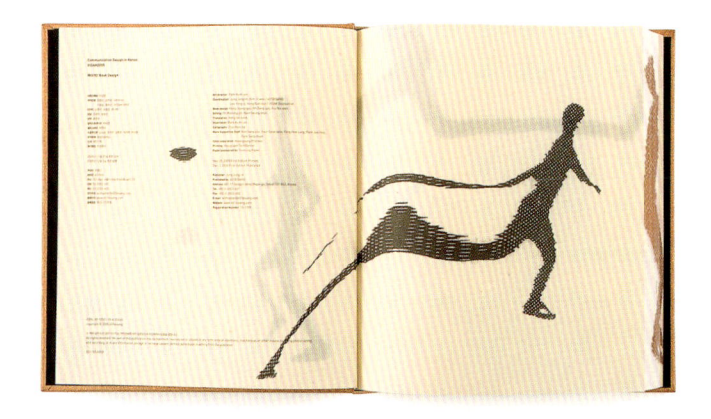

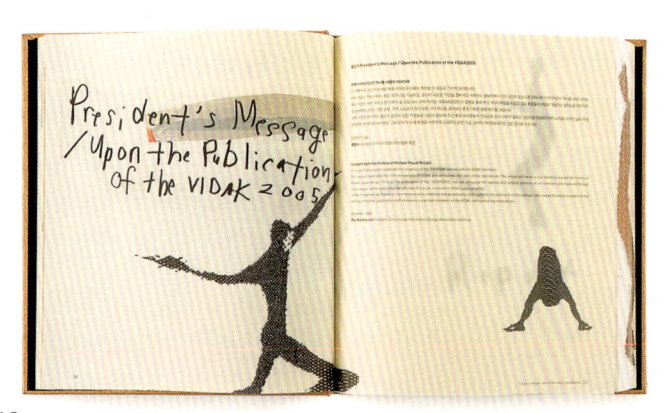

Spreads: This book, in addition to being an annual collection of works by the members of VIDAK, a leading organisation representing Korea's visual design community, also seeks to illustrate the harmony ("oullim") between VIDAK members and other Korean designers.

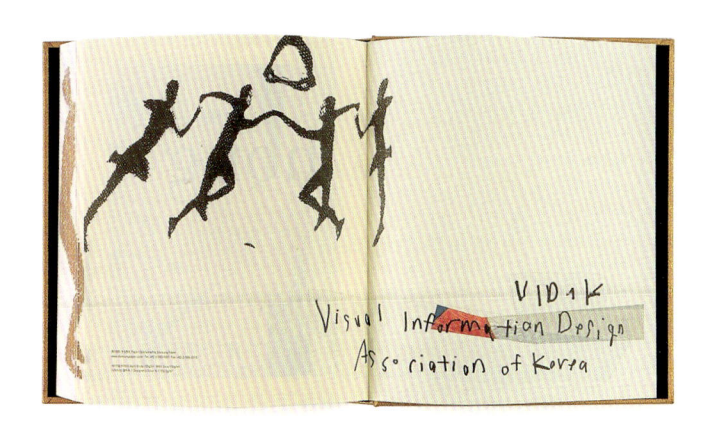

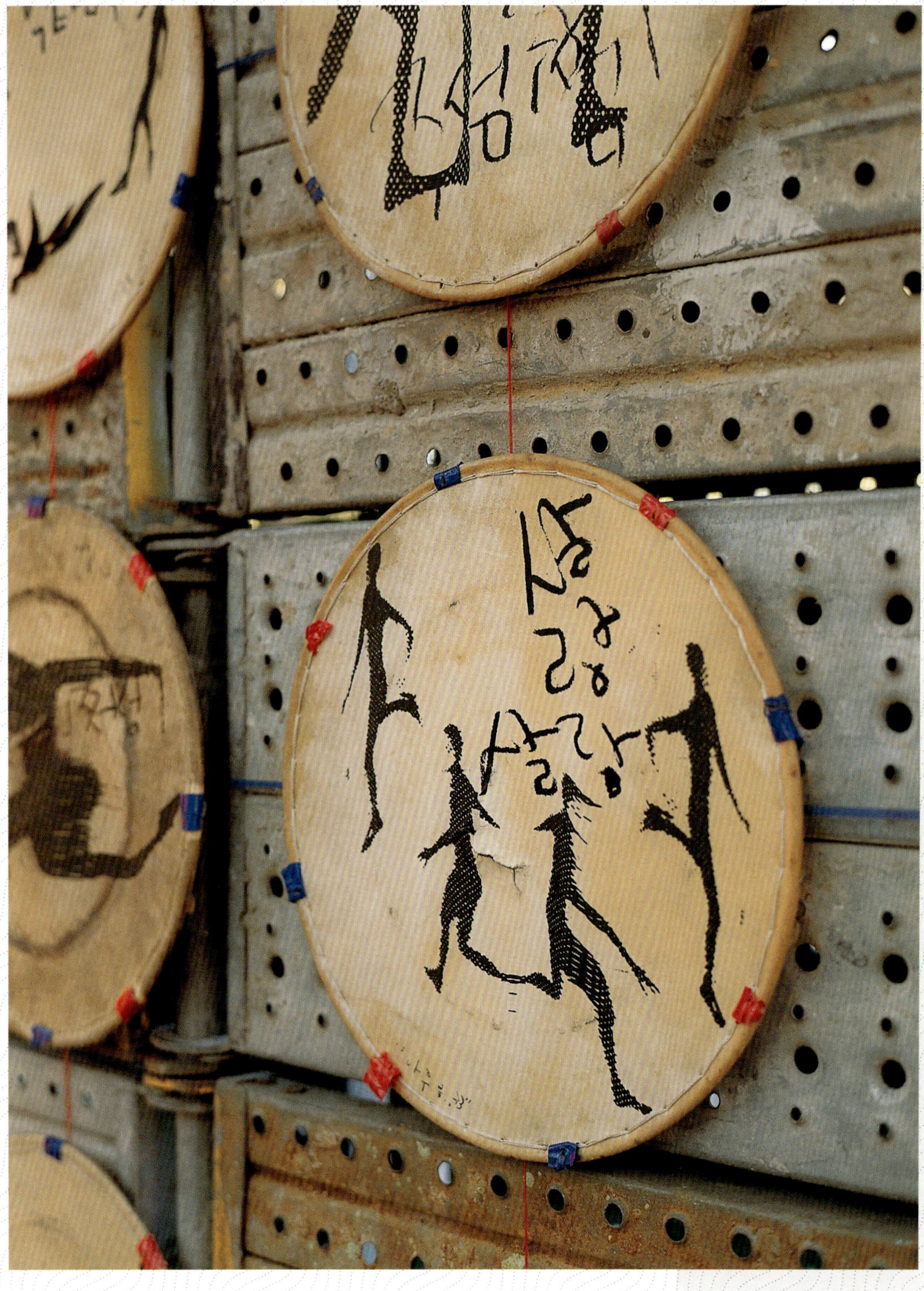

Spreads: Scenes design titled "Aureum-joining together", in people's lives are presented in 33 onomatopoeia and mimetic words.

"PEACE"

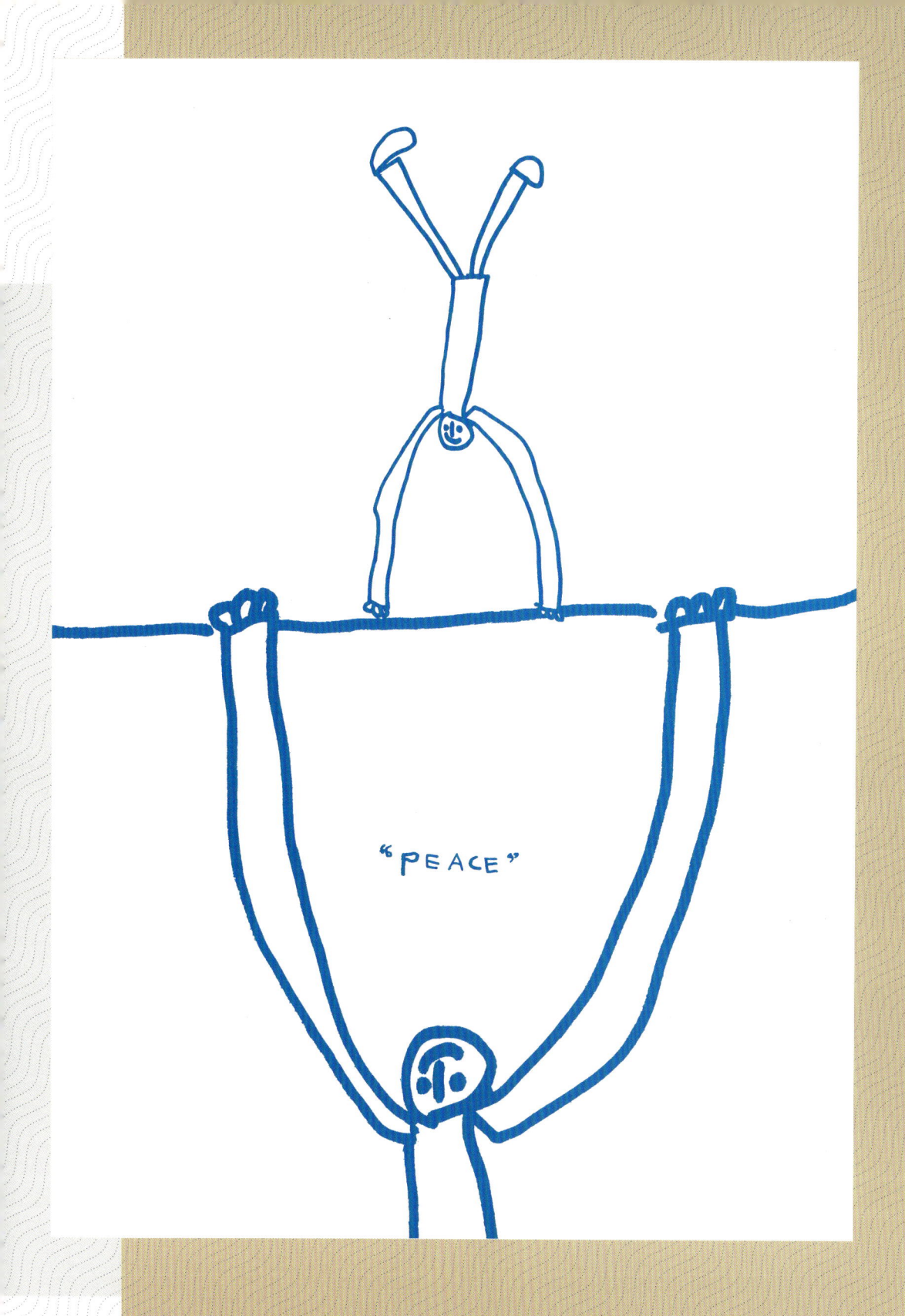

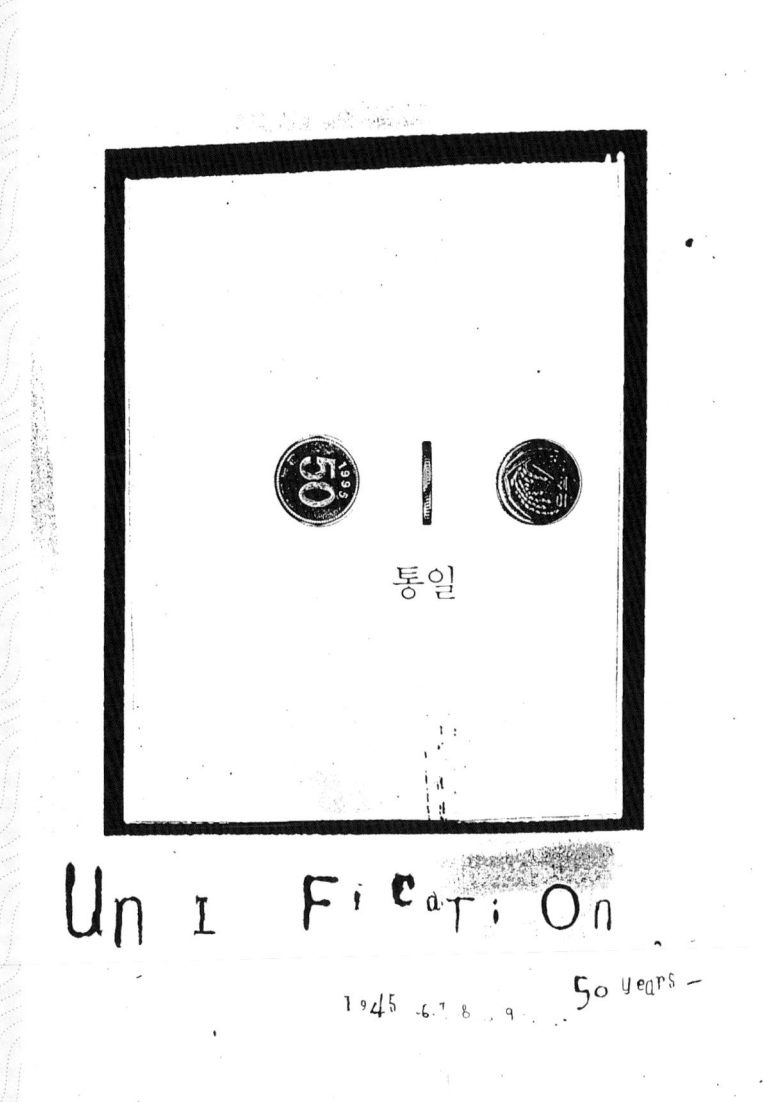

Opposite: Poster titled "Peace" for Gallery Kyo, Tokyo
Poster titled "Unification" for Ministry of National Unification

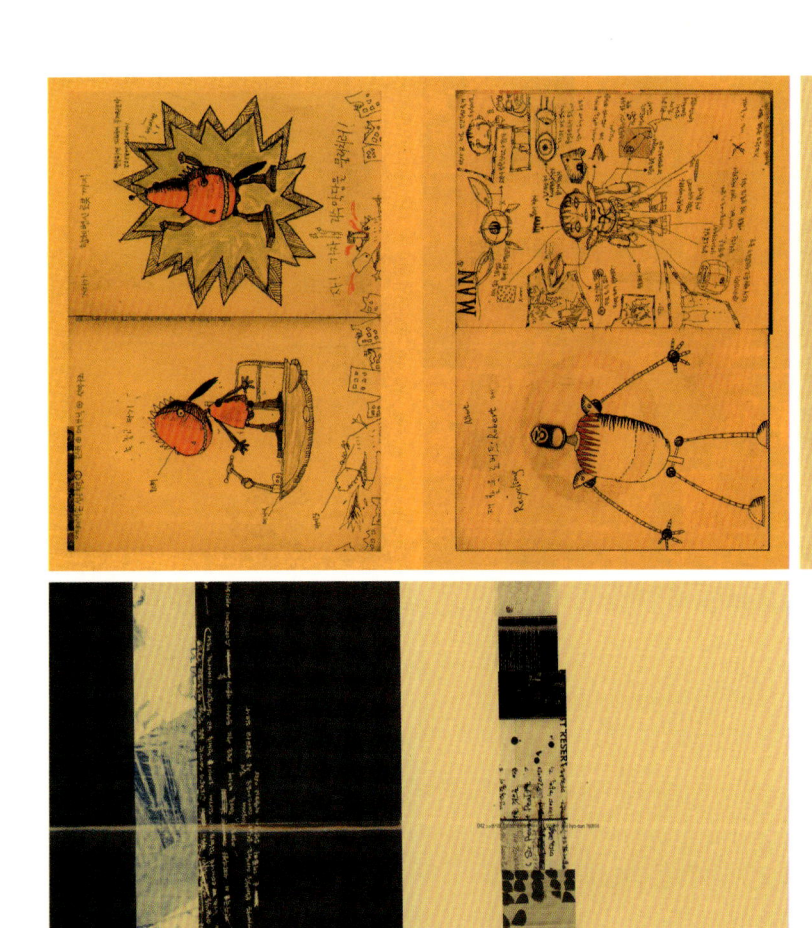

Spreads: Book titled *"2note: time.space"* for 601bisang

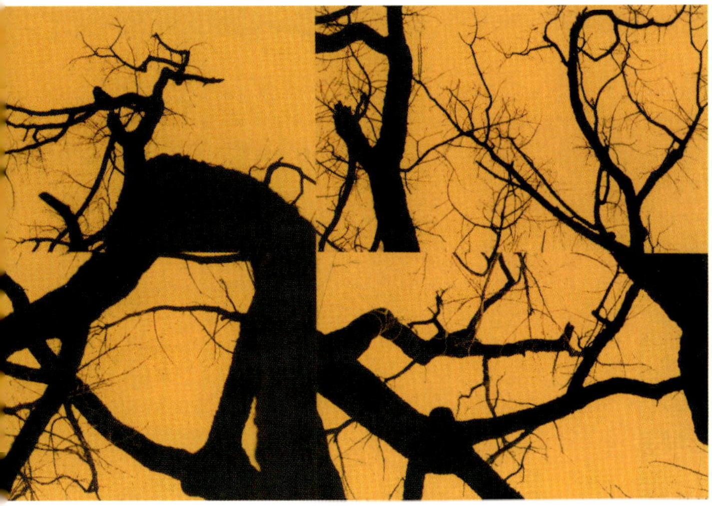

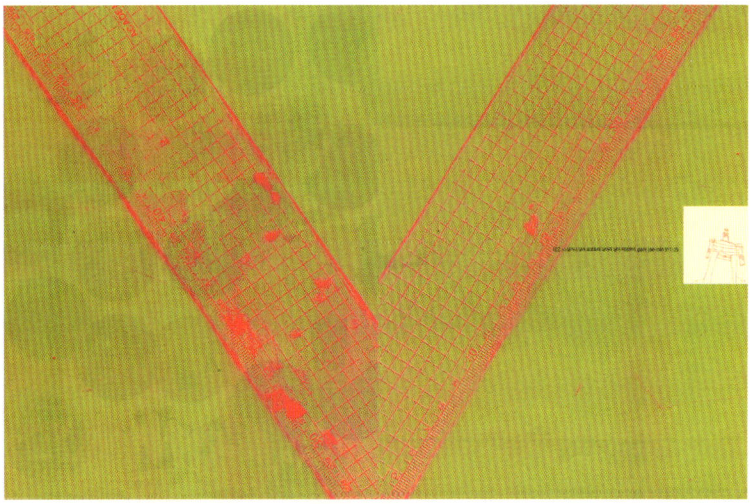

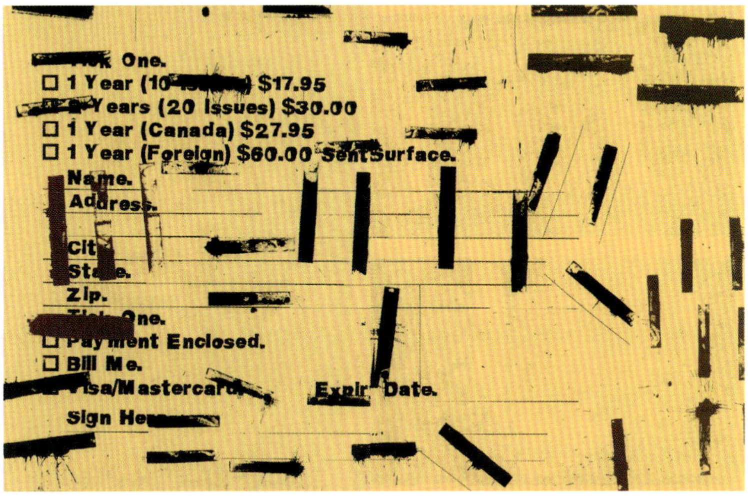

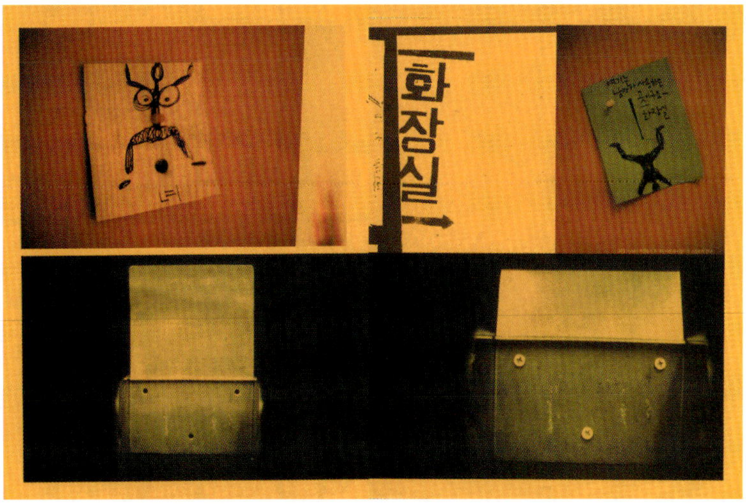

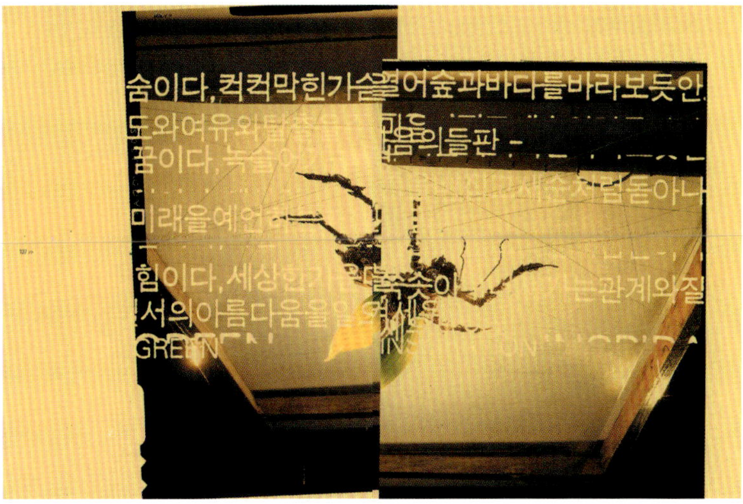

Spreads: *601 Space Project* for 601bisang

150

151

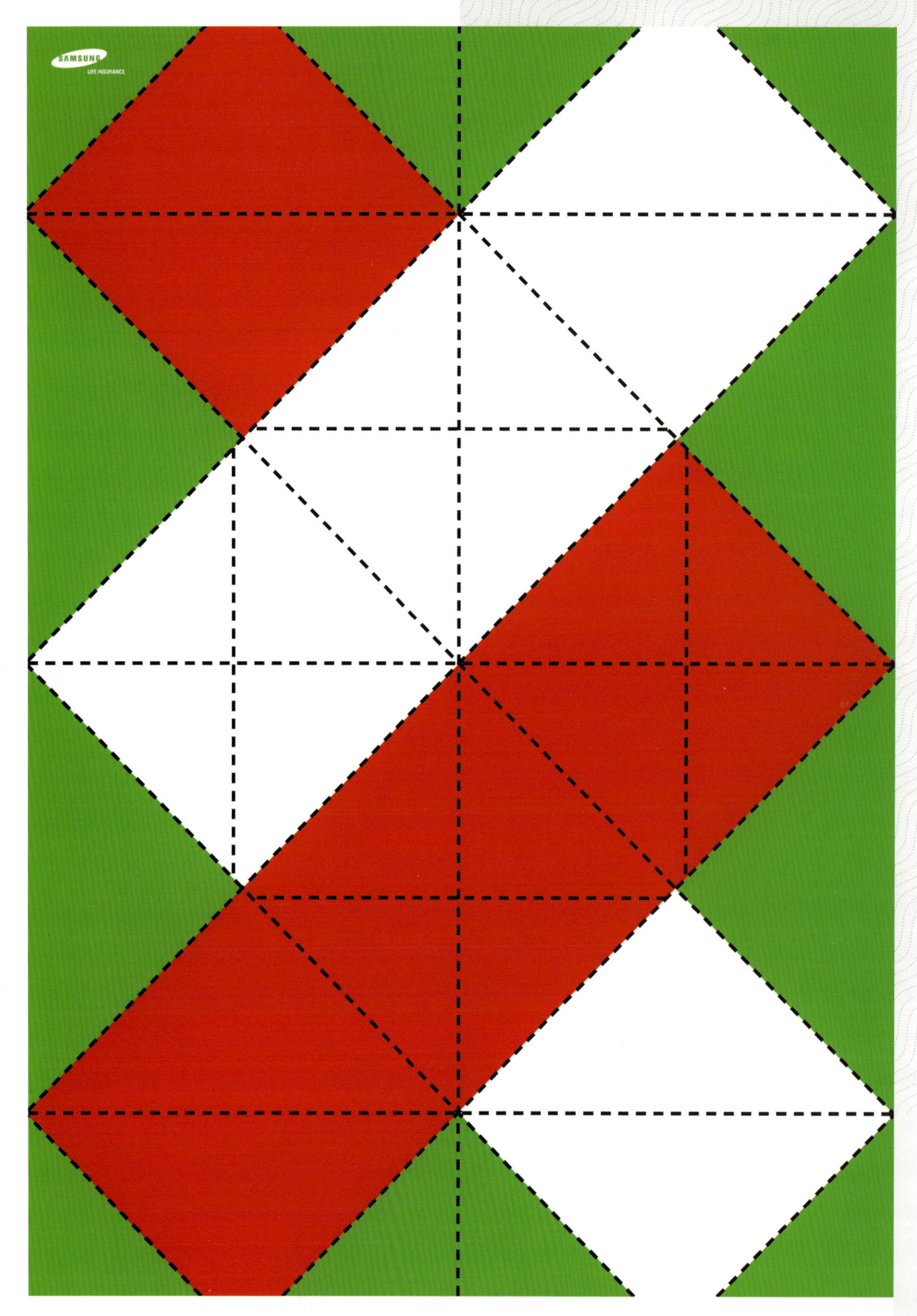

Boat *Knowing what to do and not to do... Insurance gives your life directions.*

Air plane *Higher, futher... get closer to your desire... Insurance helps your dreams come true.*

Spreads: Paper folding of Air plane and
Boat for Samsung Life Insurance

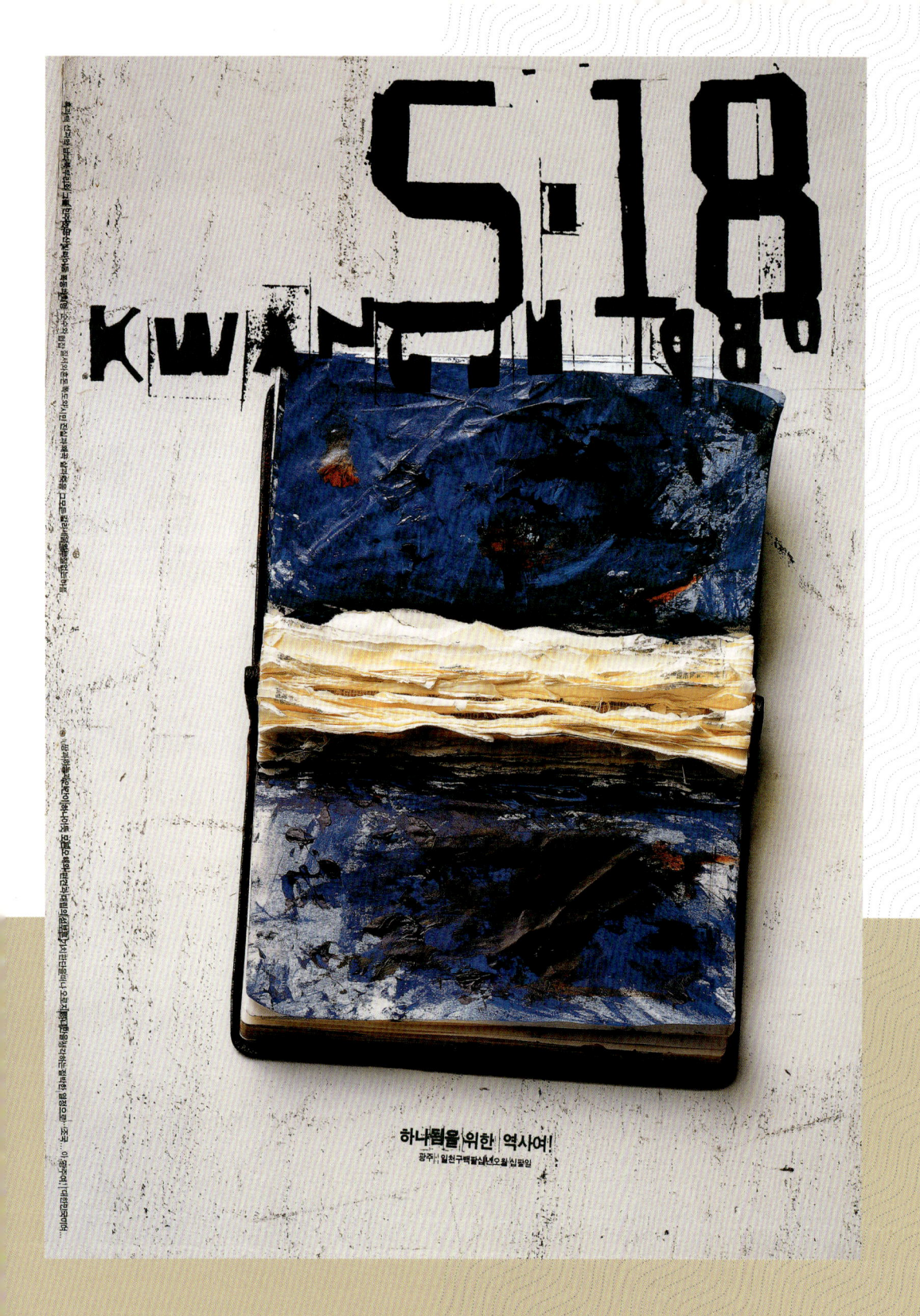

A poster marking the 20th anniversary of the May 18 Gwangju Civil Uprising of May 18th, 1980, Gwangju, Korea

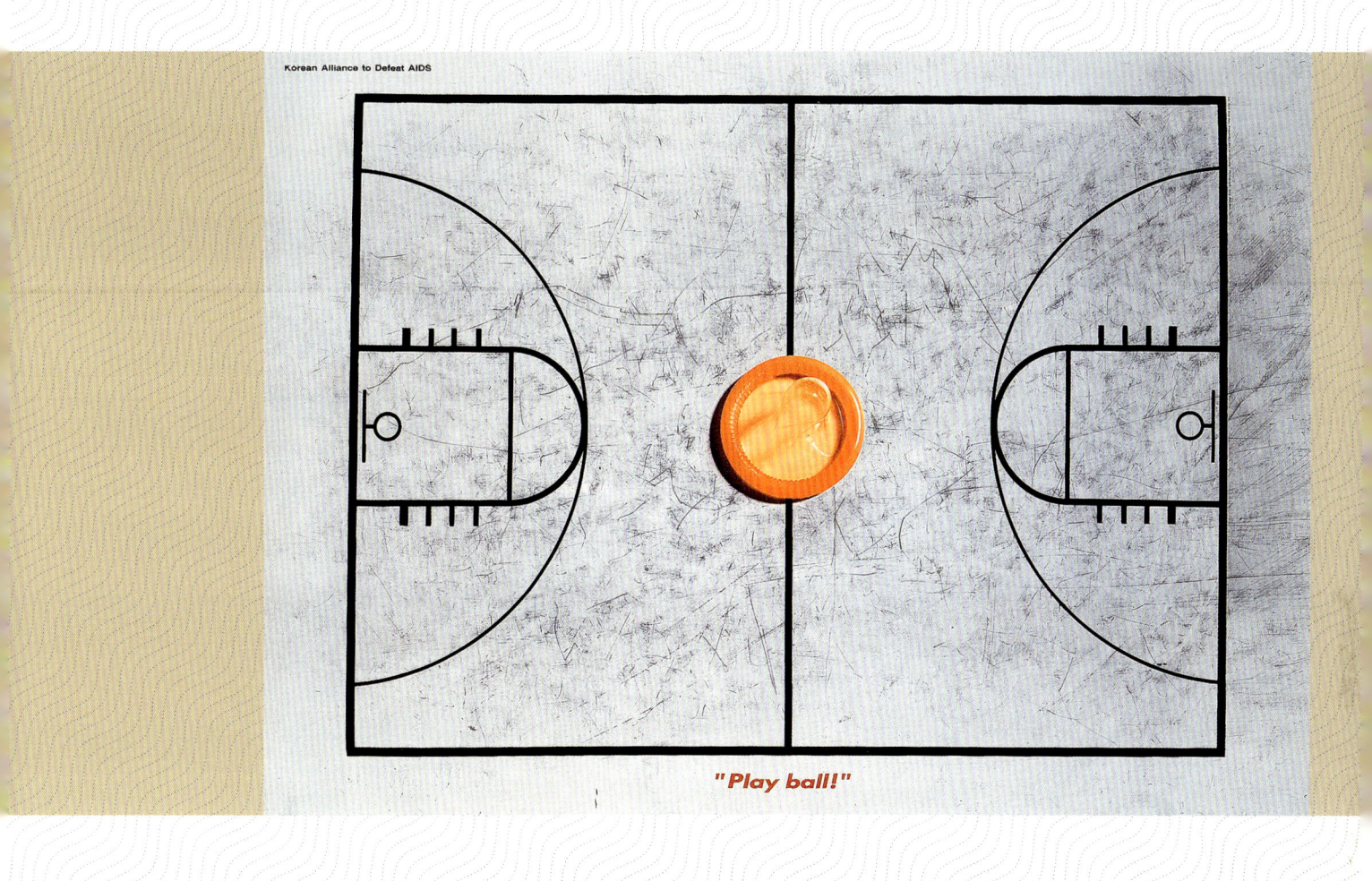

Top: An Aids prevention campaign poster titled "Play Ball!" for Korean Alliance to Defeat AIDS
Bottom: poster titled "SEXIT" for Korean Alliance to Defeat AIDS

The poster that suggestively depicts the meaning of Fever Variations, the theme of the 6th Gwangju Biennale

156

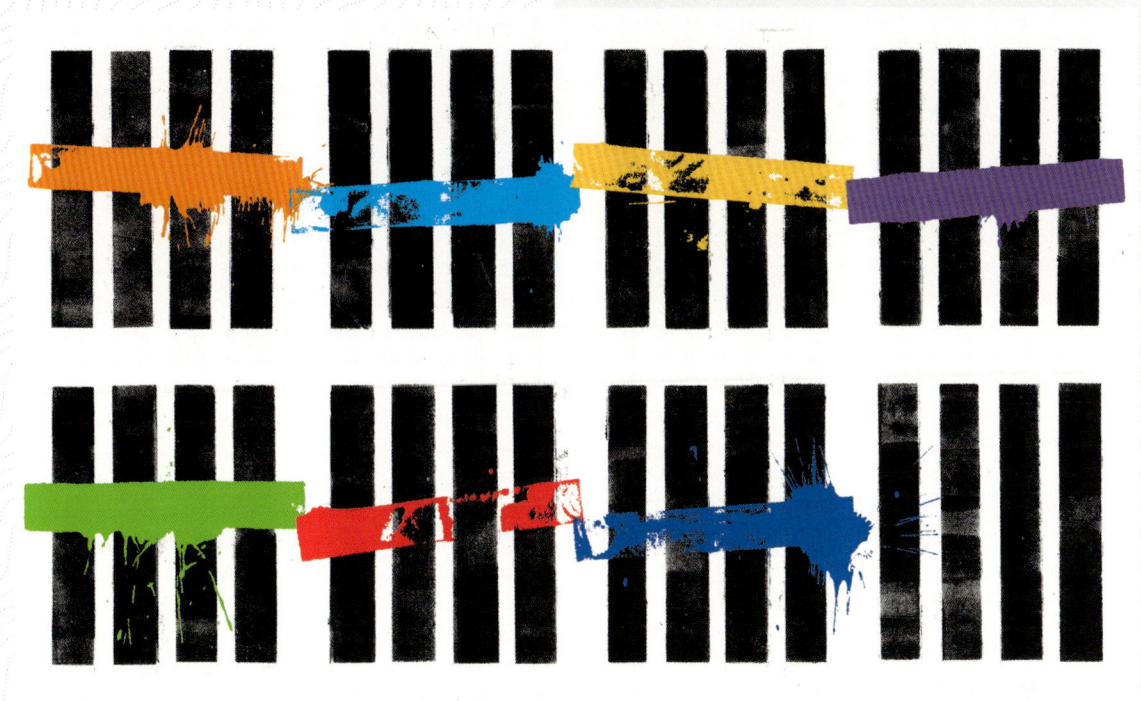

Poster for the 39th Korea Industrial Design Exhibition

The 39th Korea Industrial Design Exhibition

Pekka Loiri

Pekka Loiri's career began in an advertising agency. He then took up work as a freelance graphic designer, specializing in book design. Later, he became the art director of the book studio of WSOY. In addition to book design, his responsibilities involved designing posters.

Alongside his work as a graphic designer, Pekka Loiri has also been involved in education, for instance, as a lecturer at the University of Art and Design in Helsinki (83-97), and has held the chancellor's position at the MG school. He has also lectured at a number of universities of art and design, for instance in Stockholm, Copenhagen, Paris, Beijing and Seoul, Xalapa, Bogota and has taught at the European Poster School in Turin. In addition, he has taught for longer periods of time in Reykjavik and as a visiting professor at the Cracow Academy of Art and the Art Academy in Usti and Labem.

Pekka Loiri's works have been published in many graphic design books and magazines. He also has an entry as a graphic designer in the reference book *Who's Who in Graphic Design in the World*. He has been involved in the production of the several graphic design publications. And his works have been widely shown at leading poster exhibitions all over the world. He has regularly been invited to take part in the Colorado Poster Biennial in the USA, the Ogaki Poster Biennial in Japan, and the Plakatok exhibition in Hungary. His posters have also been included in a number of poster collections in various parts of the world.

He has received many awards for his posters in the Finland's Best Posters competitions. He has twice won the GM (Graafistet Muotoilijat / Graphic Designers Association in Finland) annual poster competition. Loiri's international awards include the first prize in Gabrovo (IBHSA) Poster Biennial 2005 and the Bronze Award in Ningbo Poster Biennial 2007, and so on. Loiri is a member of the Pilot Group and Grafia. He is also the president of the Lahti Poster Biennial in Finland.

PROJECT: TYPOGRAPHY TOOLS
TYPE: POSTER
CLIENT: TYPOMEDIA

"An effective poster is a simple way to capture attention. It opens up straight away and sparks more questions. Its job is to give pleasure and at the same time to spread information. These were my points of departure in designing the poster for the Typography Seminar Typo tools." – Pekka Loiri

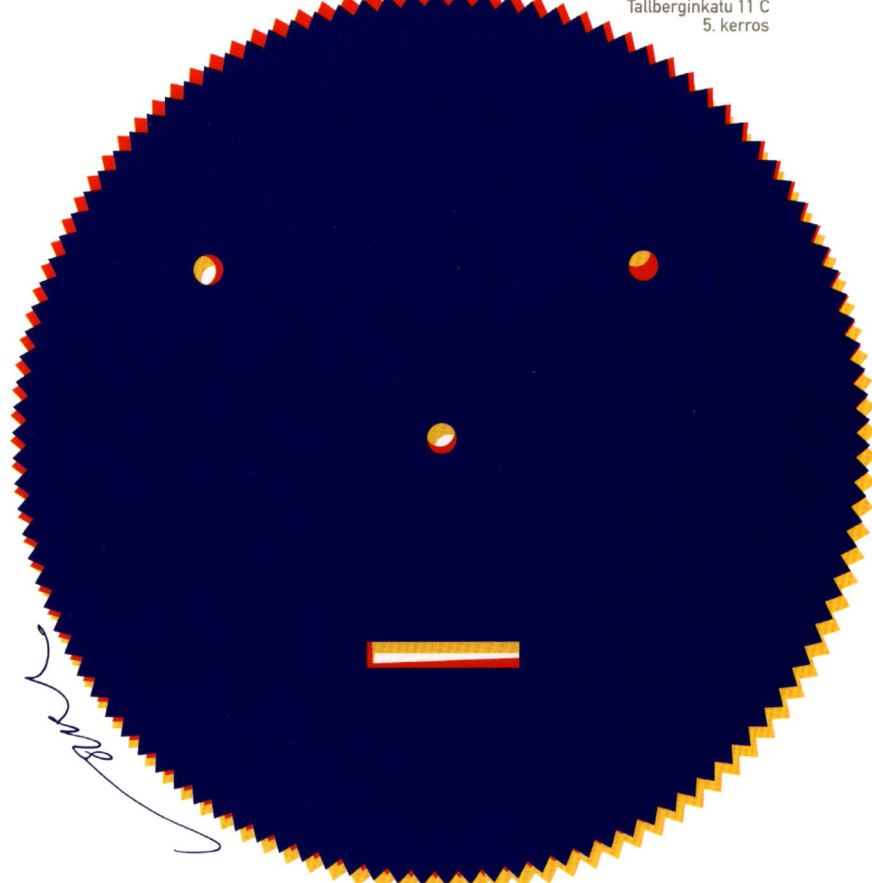

" So far...", exhibition poster for Pekka Loiri´s Poster Exhibition
Opposite: Indicators, an environment poster against air pollution

160

indicators

polluted air heats the climate and affects the **coloration of butterflies,** ultimately turning them black

Theatre poster titled "la Locanderia"
Opposite: "Loiri in Gabrovo", exhibition poster for Pekka Loiri´s Poster Exhibition

LOIRI IN GABROVO ЛОИРИ В ГАБРОВО

ФИНСКИ ПЛАКАТИ НА ПЕКА ЛОИРИ
В ДОМА НА ХУМОРА И САТИРАТА
ГАБРОВО
14 септември–31 декември, 2006
9.00–18.00 ч., всеки ден

Theatre poster titled "Chamber Theatre for all people present"

Jean Siegler
présente: Chambre pour une personne
La Guillotine
Les Misérables
Guillaume Tell
Un Américain à Paris

Jean Siegler presenteert: Theater Kamer voor één persoon De Guillotine, Les Misérables, Wilhelm Tell, An American in Paris

164

"The Beauty of Letters / The Didot family", poster for a typography seminar event

Left: "Infor Visual Educations", poster for visual training
Right: Theatre poster titled "Lady in the Van"
Opposite: "Ideal Husband", theatre poster

IHANNE-AVIOMIES

Lappeenrannan kaupunginteatteri esittää Oscar Wilden näytelmän Ideal Husband. Ohjaus Cilla Back, lavastus Riitta Ukkonen, suomennos Kersti Juva. Ensi-ilta Jukola salissa 3. 2. 2001

nothing to declare?

Käsikirjoitus Bernard Kops, Musiikki David Burman, Ohjaus Eeva Salminen, Lavastus Tarja Jaatine
Pohjoismainen kantaesitys 28. 9.1996 Lappeenrannan kaupunginteatterissa.

Anne Frankin unet

Left: "Nothing To Declare", an invitational poster for an exhibition in the Jerusalem Art Museum
Right: Theatre poster titled "The Dreams of Anne Frank"

168

Left: "Aguante", an environment poster for the International Water Symposium in Mexico City
Right: "Solidarity", poster for solidarity of the victims of the water floods in the Central Europe

169

Poster for Lahti Poster Biennial Exhibition
Opposite: Theatre poster titled "Clown"

170

CLOWN
TheGruppe

Exhibition poster for Tapani Aartomaa and Pekka Loiri Poster exhibition in Warsaw

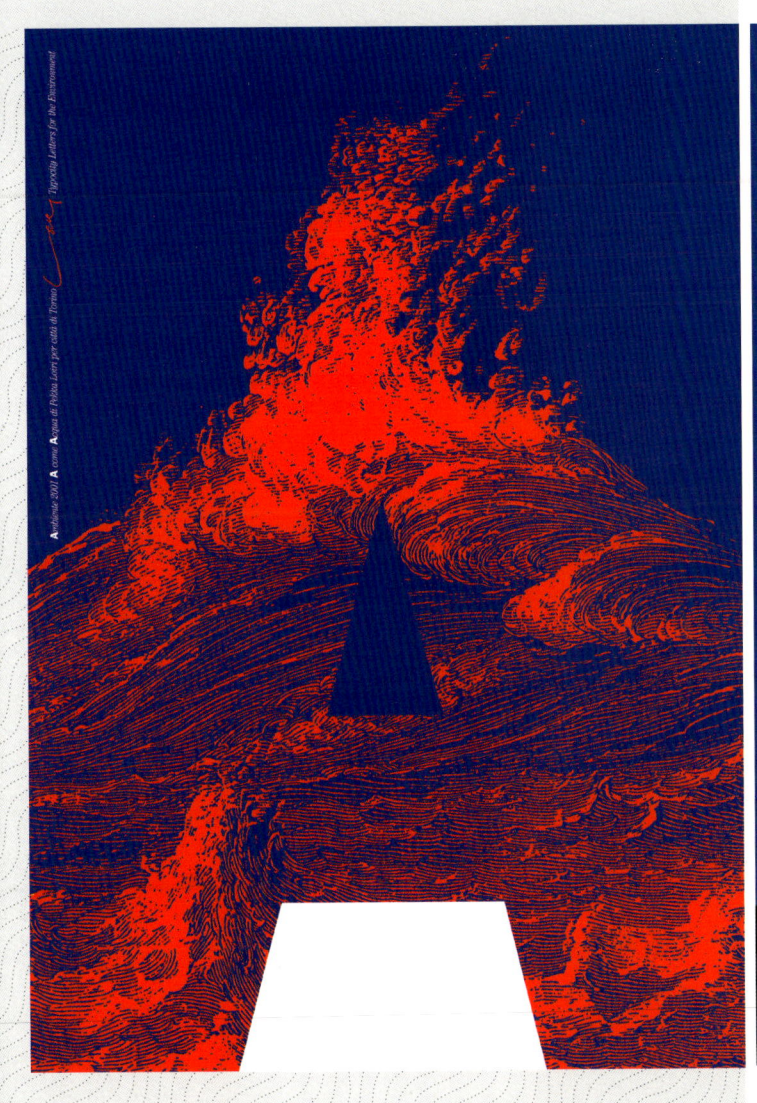

Left: Poster titled "Ambiente"
Right: Theatre poster titled "the Chairs"

Opera poster titled "Nixon in China"
Opposite: Theatre poster titled "The Steamy"

175

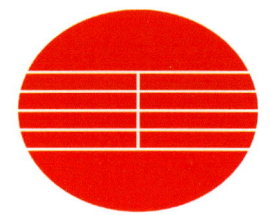

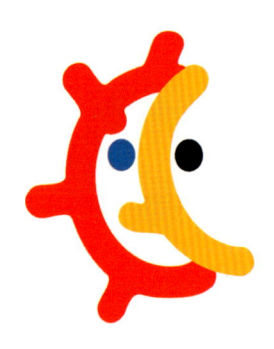

Left: Logo for the Concert Centre; logo for the City Theatre of Lappeenranta; logo for Sclzo Catering (top to bottom)
Middle: Logos for Who´s Who in Finnish media
Right: Symbols for Infor New Ideas Education

176

Left: Symbol for the TAT Group; Symbol for the Finnish Industry and Economy Institution; Logo for Ideabank; Logo for Research and Report books of the Finnish Insurance Institution (top to bottom)
Middle: Logo for Tech Film Archive; Logo for Photo Studio Ateljeekuva; Logo for Research and Report books of the Finnish Insurance Institution (top to bottom)
Right: Logo for Labsystems; Logo for Pekka Loiri's Simply Graphic Exhibitions; Logo for Lads; Logo for Singing Competition in Lappeenranta; Education symbol for Prof. Treining (top to bottom)

Reza Abedini

In 1967, Reza Abedini was born in Tehran, Iran. Graduated in graphic design from the school of Fine Arts in 1985, he got B. A in painting from Tehran Art University in 1992, and got professional career as a graphic designer since 1989. He founded Reza Abedini Studio in 1993.

He has had many one-man exhibitions of his works worldwide: in the Opposite Direction, Iran, 2001; in The Beginning, Iran, 2001; Return, Iran, 2002; Answer?, Iran, 2002; LookBook, Paris, 2005; Native Language, Taiwan, 2005; the Visual Language of REZA ABEDINI, Amsterdam, 2006; Wordless, Iran, 2007.

He has received many awards for his work: Special Award includes Creativity from Iranian Graphic Designers Society, Tehran 1999; Special Prize in China International Poster Biennale, China 2003; Honorable Mention in 13 Colorado International Poster Exhibitions, USA 2003; the Union of Visual Artists of the Czech Republic Award, Brno 2004; Second Prize in the 15th Festival d'affiches de Chaumont France 2004; Gold Prize in Hong Kong International Poster Triennial, Hong Kong 2004; First Prize and Gold Medal in the 8th International Biennial of the Poster in Mexico 2004; Silver Prize in the Second International Poster Biennale Korea 2004; First Prize in the First International Biennale of the Islamic World Poster Iran 2004; Bronze Medal in the 2nd China International Poster Biennia (CIPB) China 2005; First Prize in the 9th Press Festival of Children & Young Adults Iran 2005; Silver Medal in the 20th International Poster Biennale Warsaw Poland 2006; Principal Prince Claus Foundation Laureate, Netherlands 2006; etc.

He was made a member of Iranian Graphic Designers Society in 1997, a member of AGI in 2001, the supervisor of the Cultural Committee of I.G.D.S in 1999, writer and critic in the field of Visual Arts since 1990, managing director and editor-in-chief of of *Manzar*, Occasional Pictorial magazine.

PROJECT: DREAM OF DUST
TYPE: POSTER
CLIENT: REVE D'EAU 2003

"A Poster for an Iranian film whose maker lives in France. The characters speak a few words in the whole film. The compositions, Colour, positive and negative spaces of this poster are inspired by Iranian art and architecture. There is a game between types, shapes and context and all together they make a figure (A woman)." – Reza Abedini

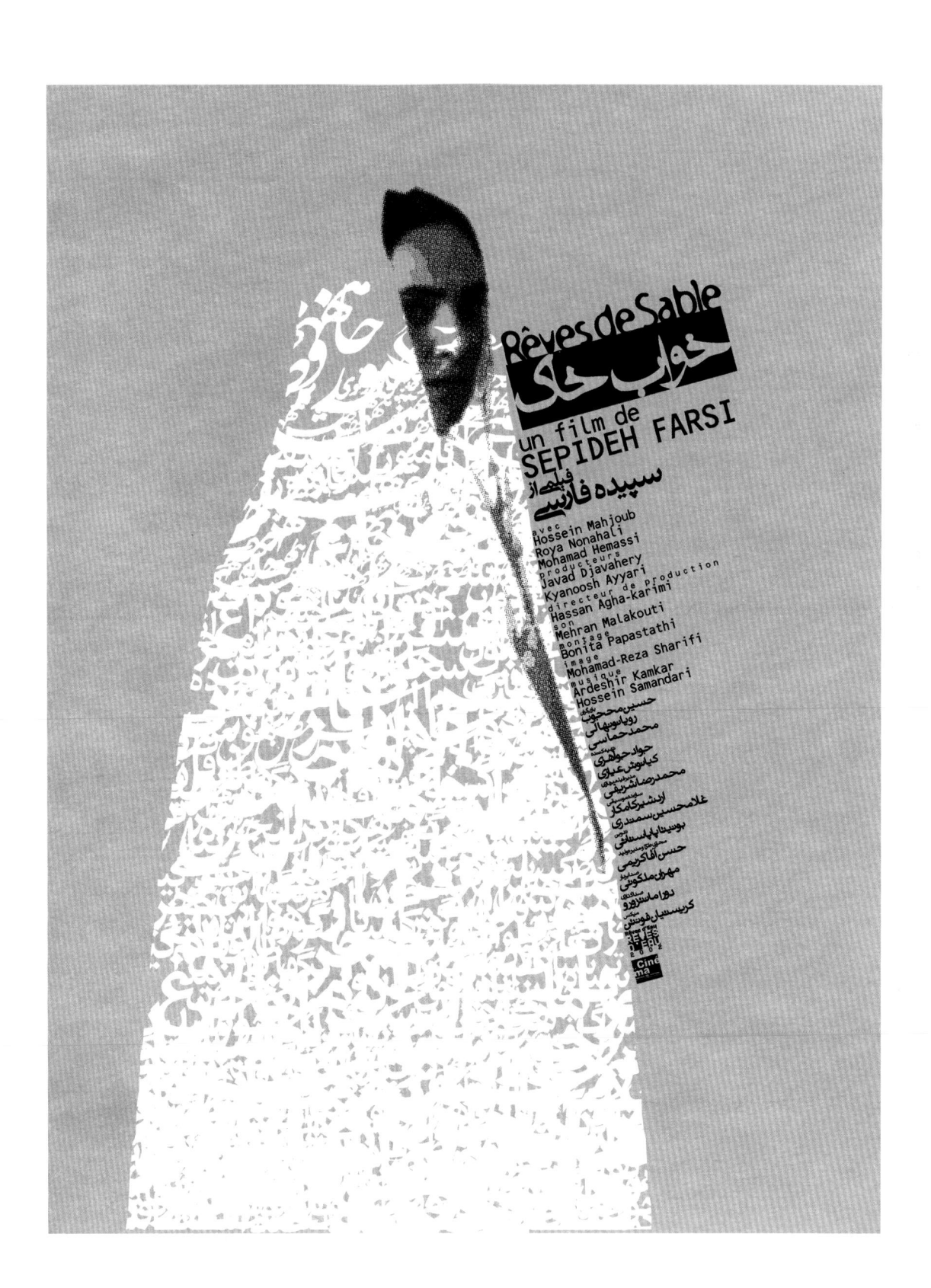

Spreads: Corporate Design for Ati Center 2000

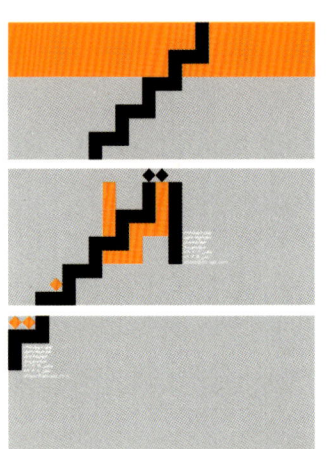

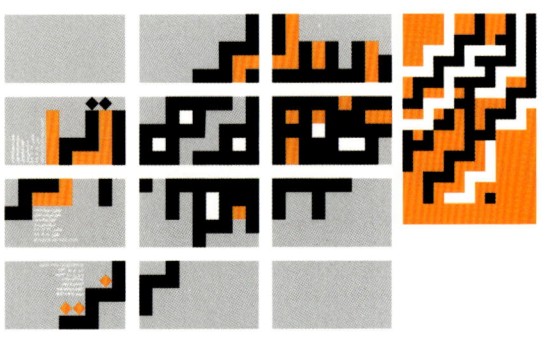

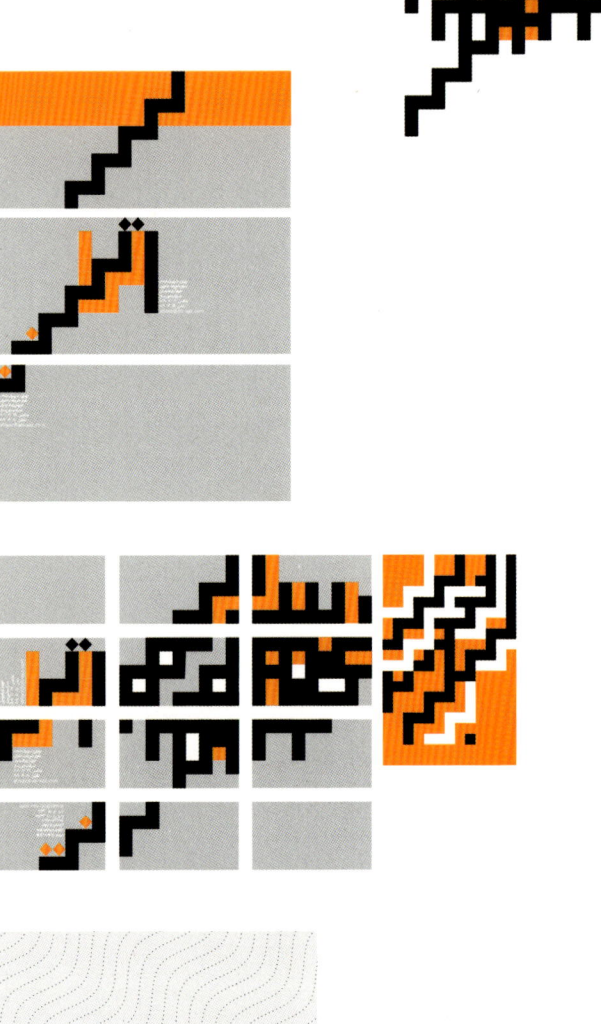

181

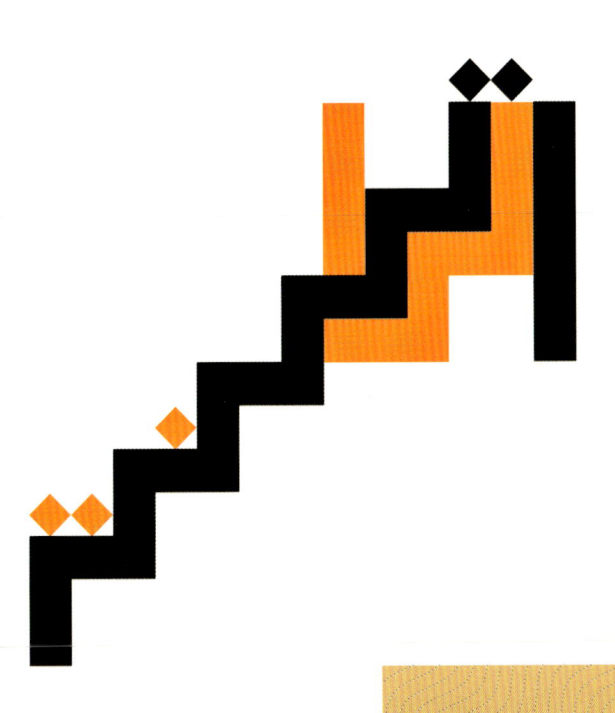

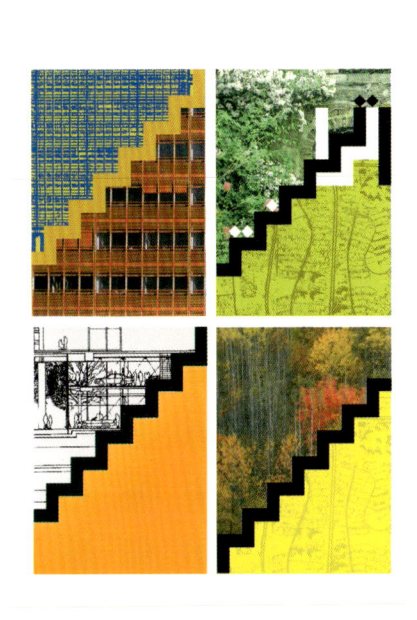

Spreads: Book named *A tail of Dwarfs and Lankier* for Nai publications

کوتوله‌ها و دانه‌ها

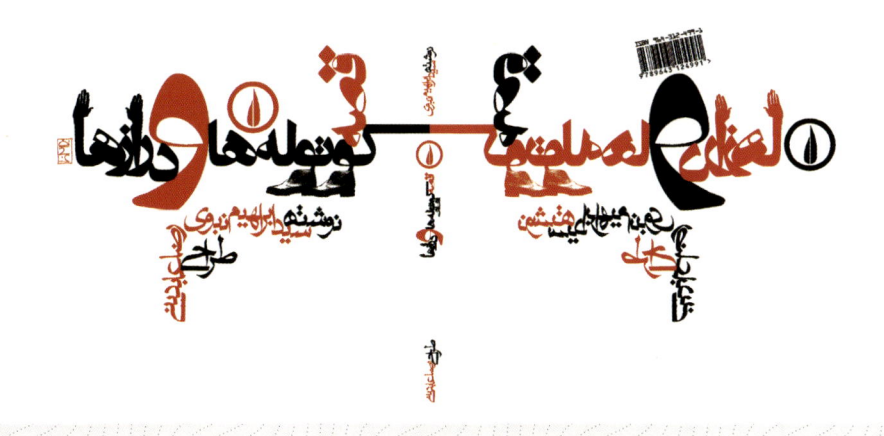

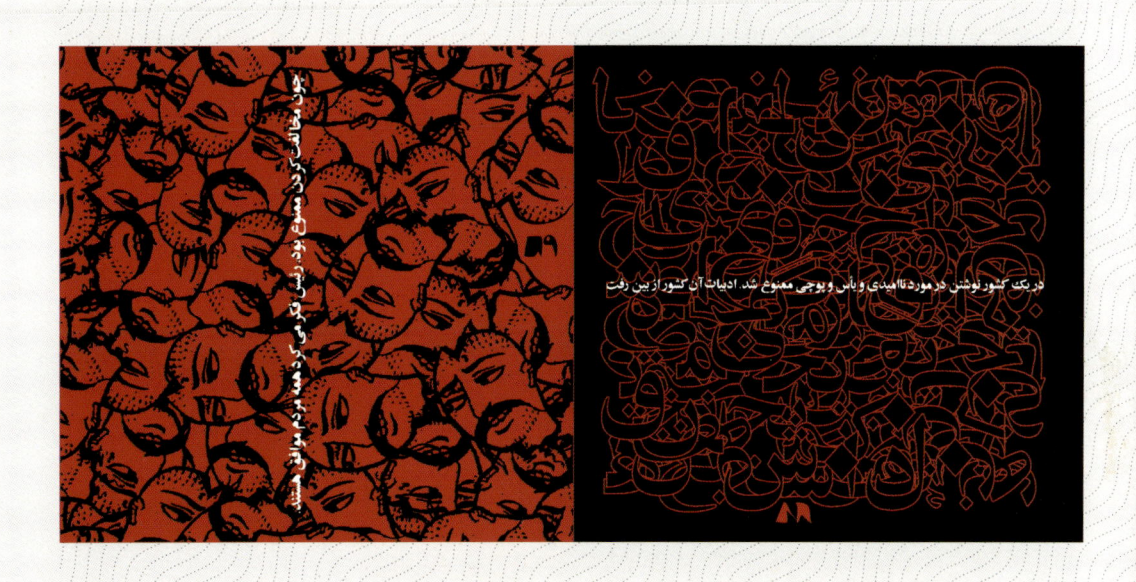

Spreads: Visual language of Reza Abedini, retrospective of R. A in Platform21, Amsterdam

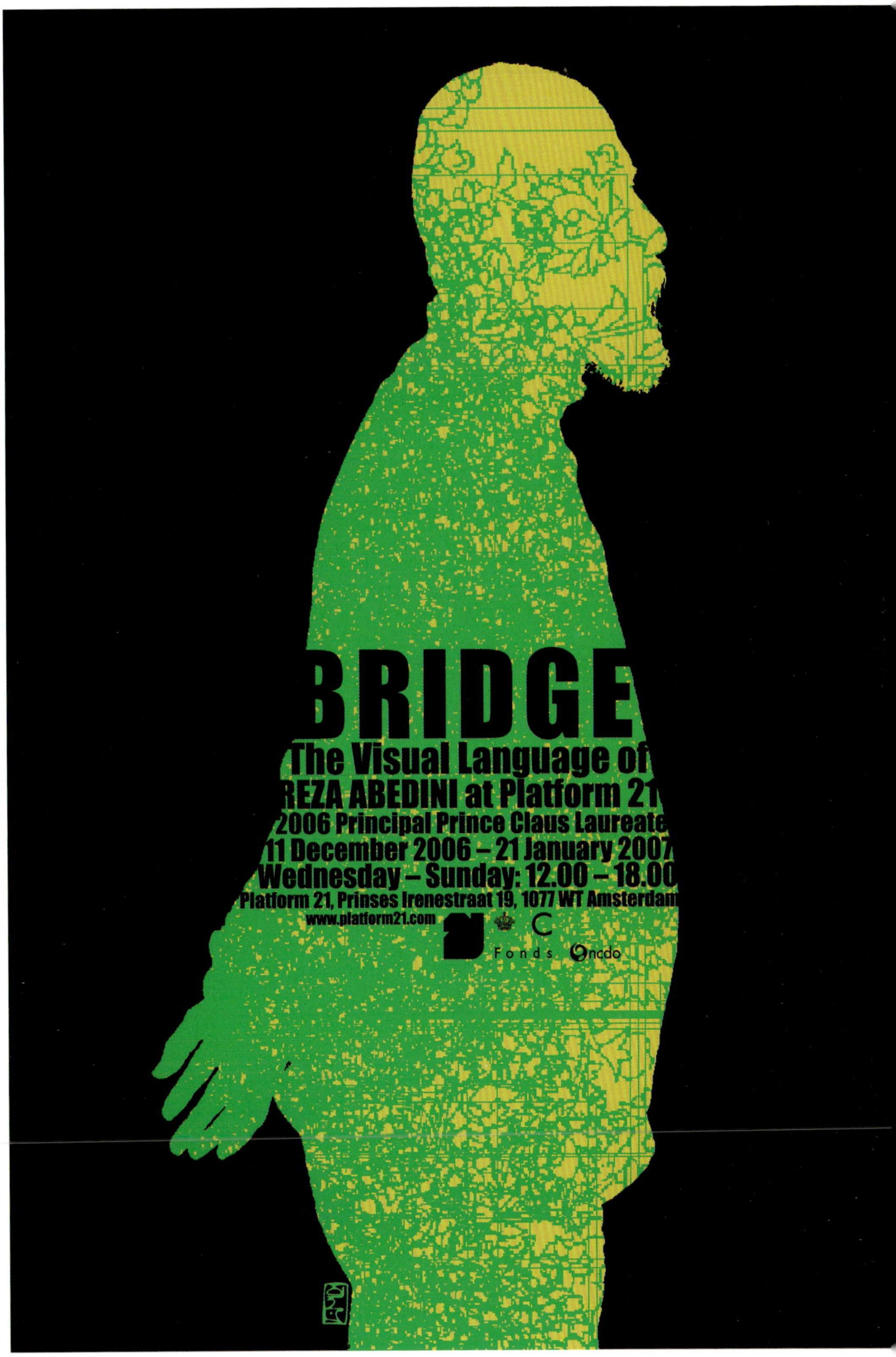
BRIDGE
The Visual Language of
REZA ABEDINI at Platform 21
2006 Principal Prince Claus Laureate
11 December 2006 – 21 January 2007
Wednesday – Sunday: 12.00 – 18.00
Platform 21, Prinses Irenestraat 19, 1077 WT Amsterdam
www.platform21.com
Fonds
ncdo

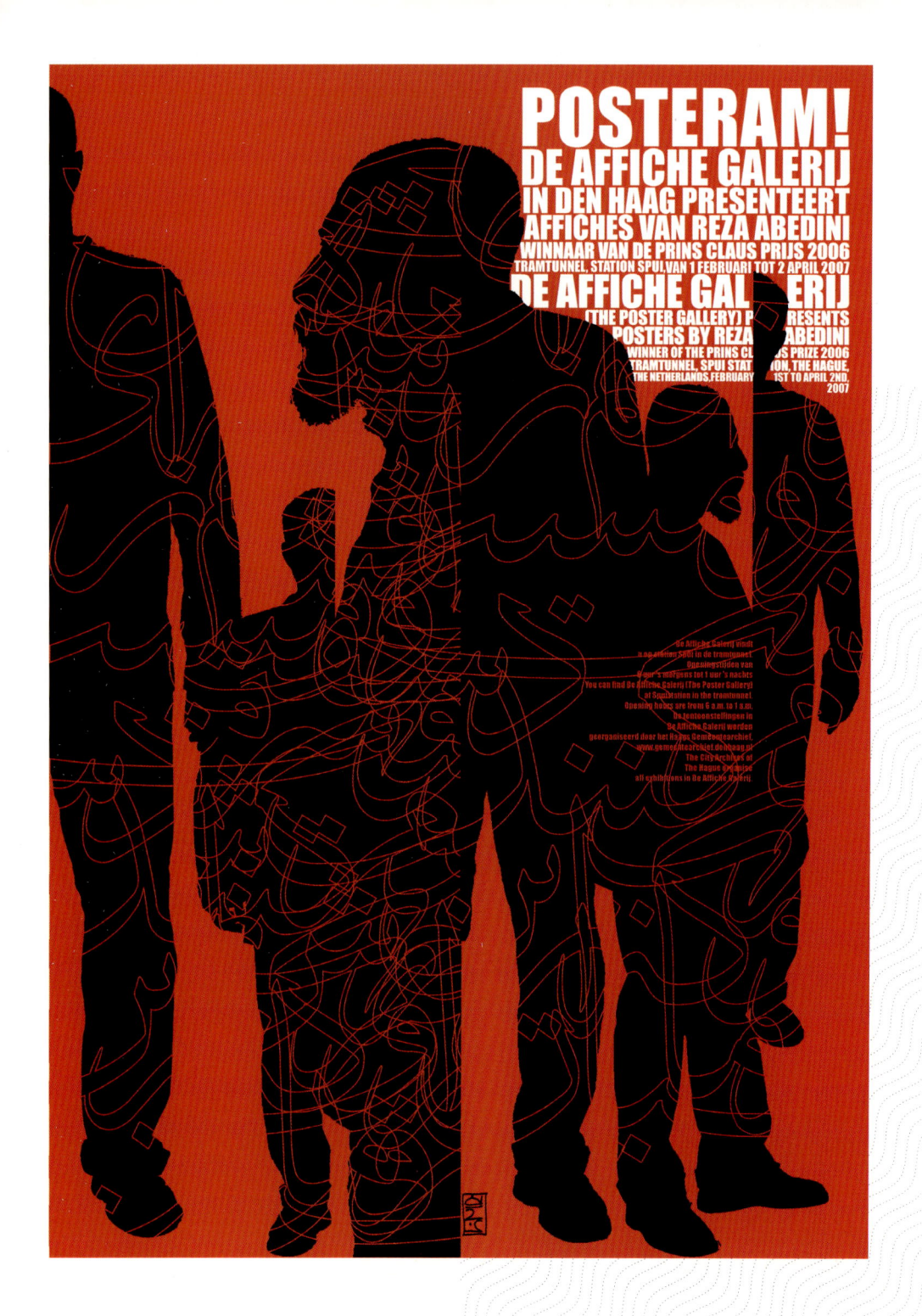

Poster for Reza Abedini Poster Exhibition,
"POSTRAM! Poster Gallery",
the Netherlands 2006

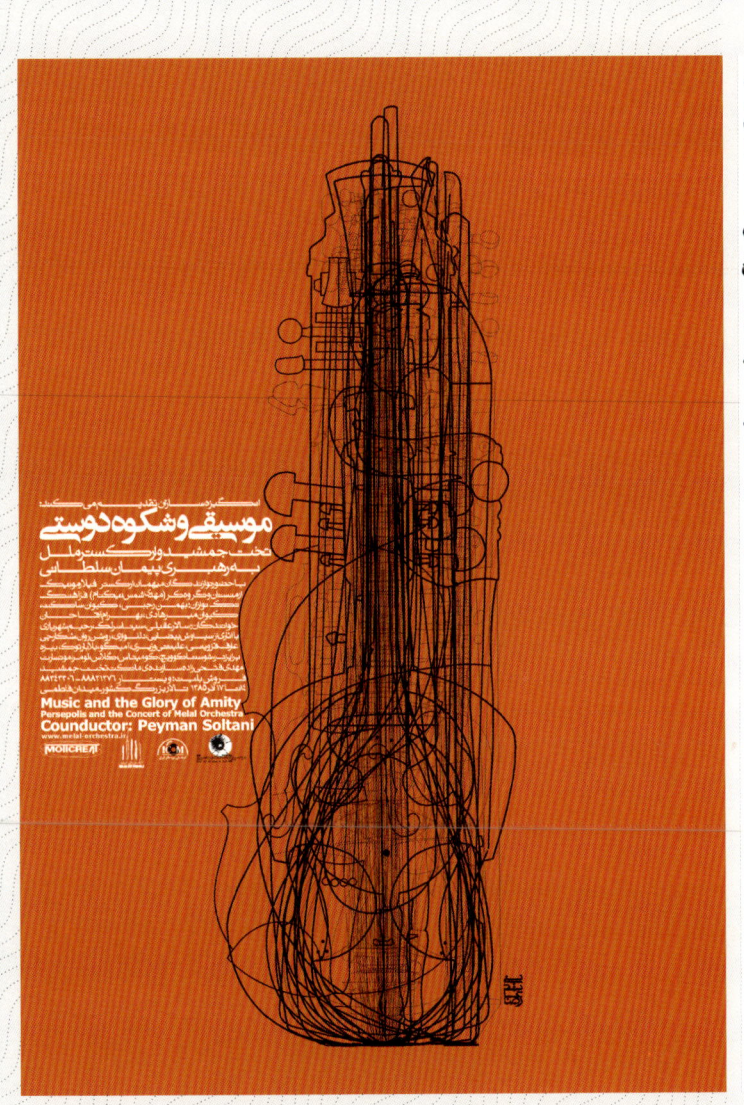

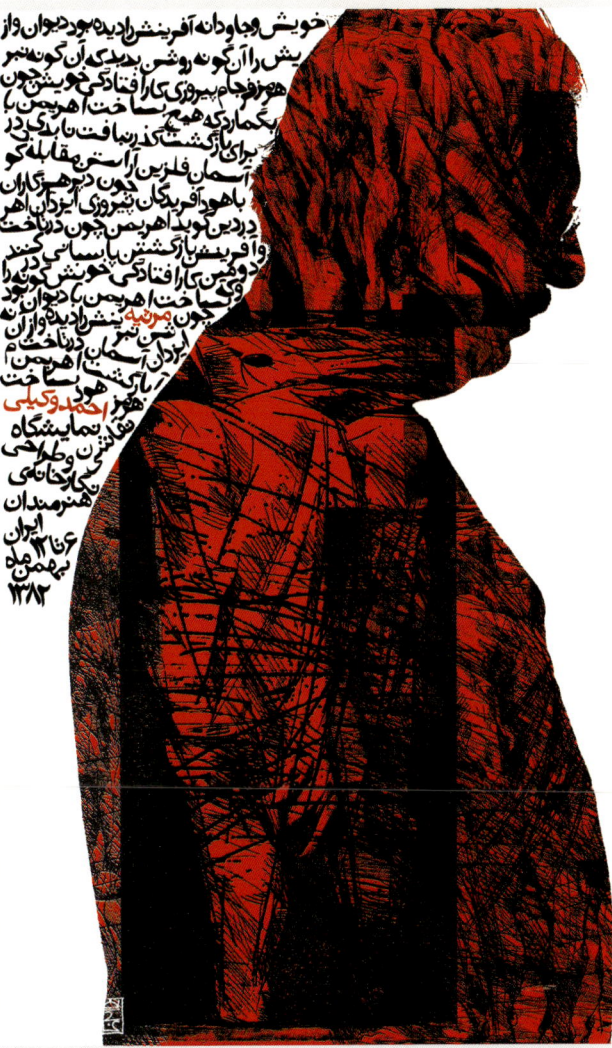

Left: Poster titled "Music and Glory of Amity"
Right: Poster for Ahmad Vakili's painting exhibition

187

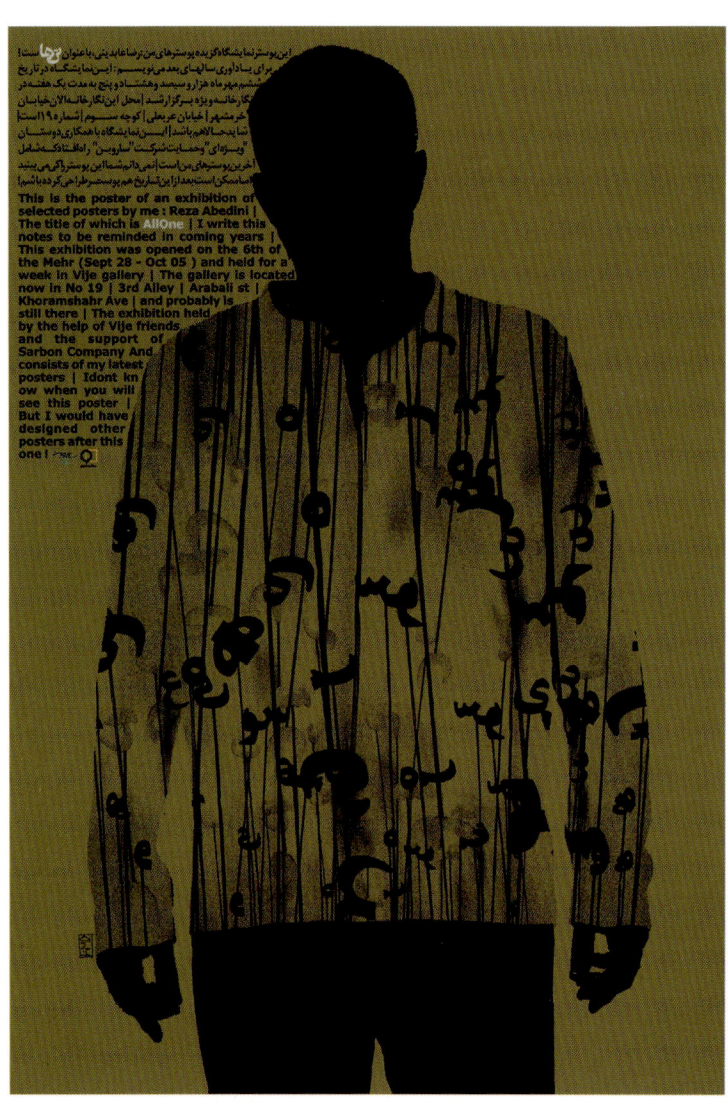

Left: Poster titled "AllOne" for Reza Abedini Poster Exhibition
Right: Poster titled "Draw" for Group Drawing Exhibition

Left: Poster titled "Look Book" for Reza Abedini Book Design Exhibition
Right: Poster titled "Children of Work"

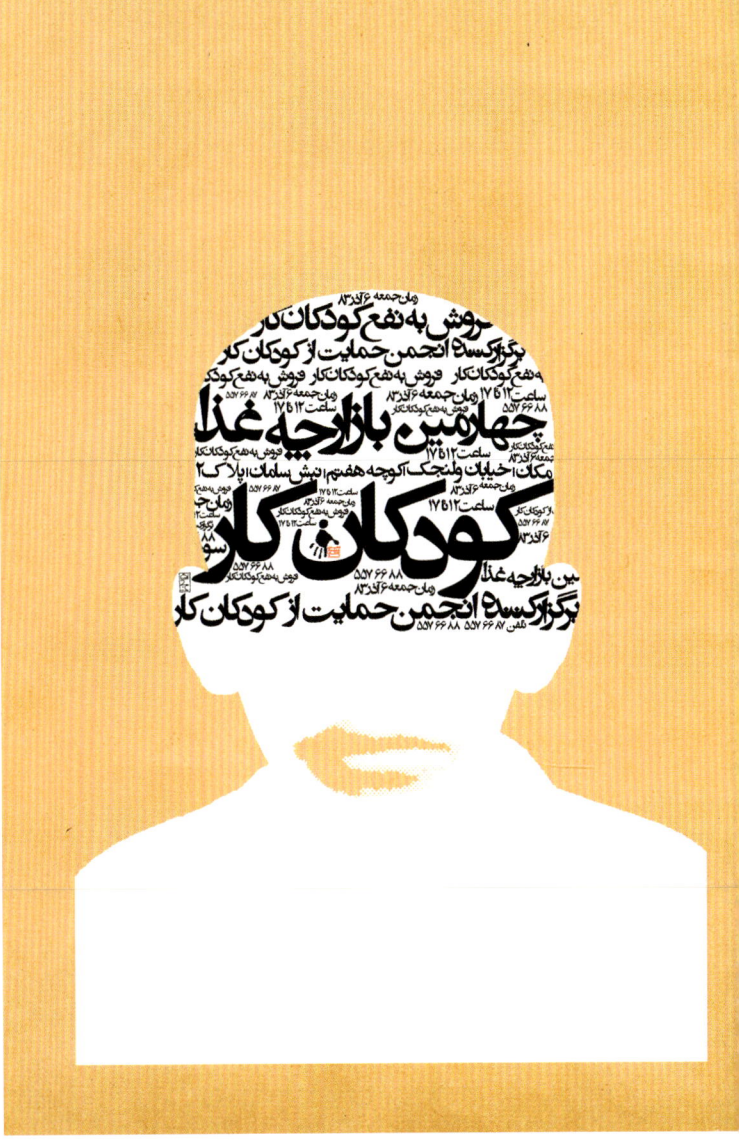

Poster titled "The Third Line" for Reza Abedini Poster Exhibition

Top: Poster titled "Kamal Odin Behzad" for tribute of Iranian Traditional Painter
Bottom Left: Poster titled "In the Beginning..." for Reza Abedini Exhibition
Bottom Right: Poster for Installation Group Exhibition

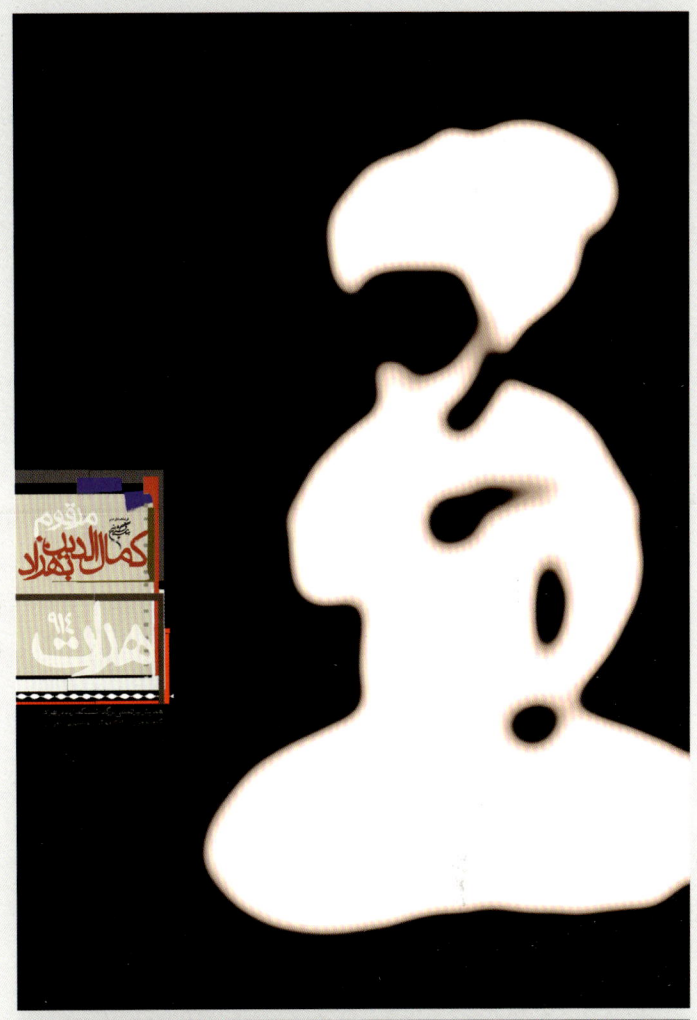

Top: Promotional Poster titled "Cinema Haqiqat" for magazine
Bottom Left: Poster titled "Iranian Imagination" for Iranian France Resident Painters Exhibition
Bottom Right: Poster titled "Complexion" for Virtual Poster Exhibition of Reza Abedini

Poster titled "Jann" for Flute Concert

Spreads: Corporate design including type design, corporate colour, corporate image, logo, posters, stationery, tickets, bags, cards, banners, presents, main catalogue, brochures, gifts and billboards for Fajr International Theatre Festival

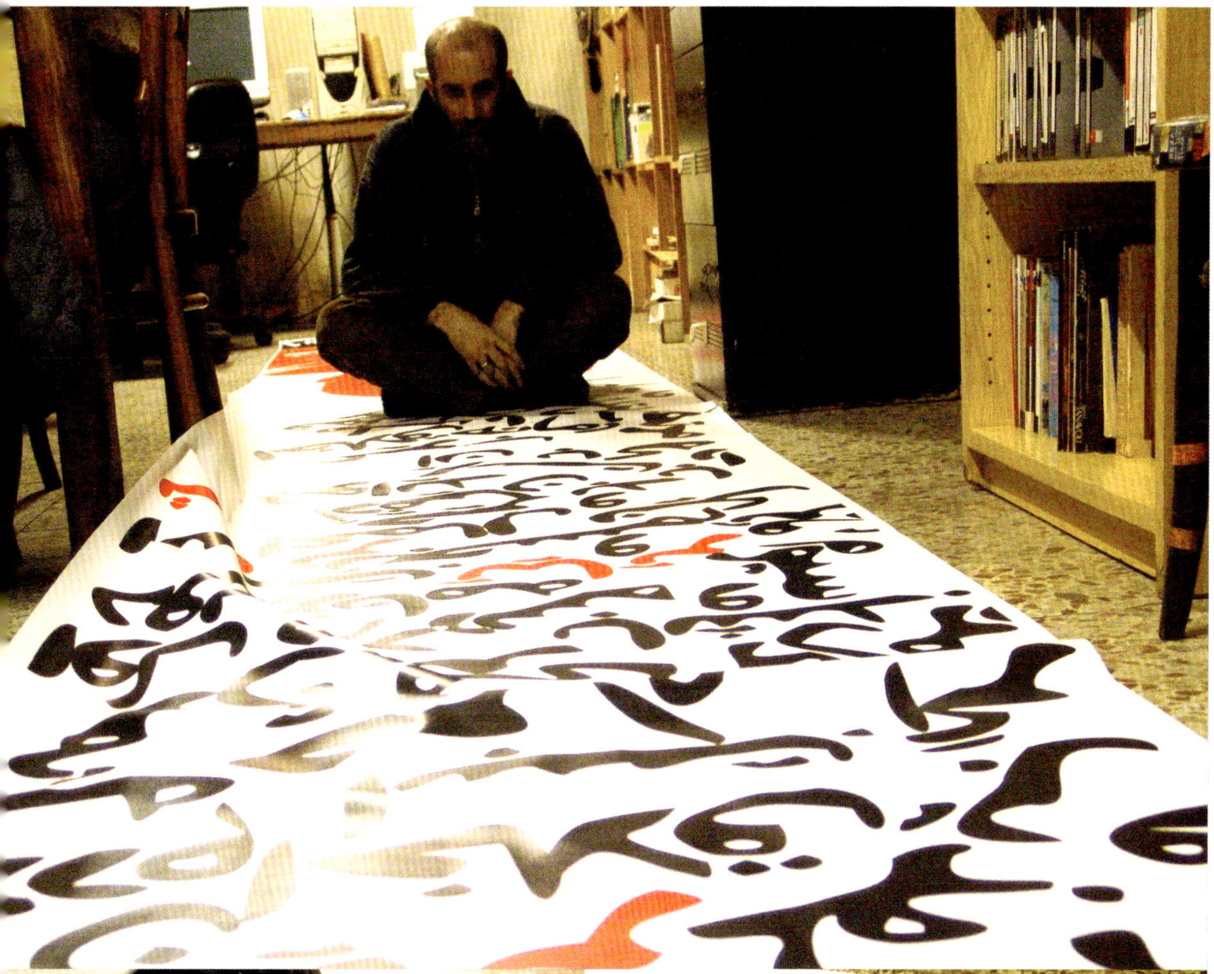

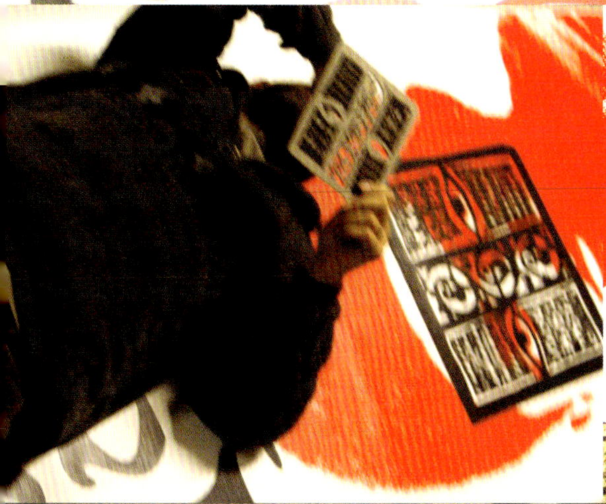

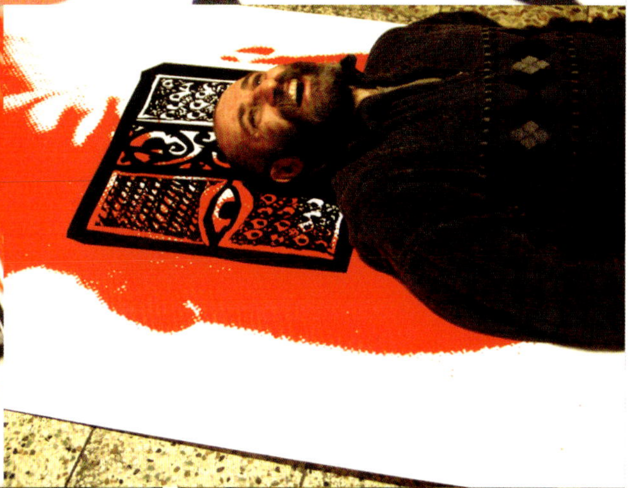

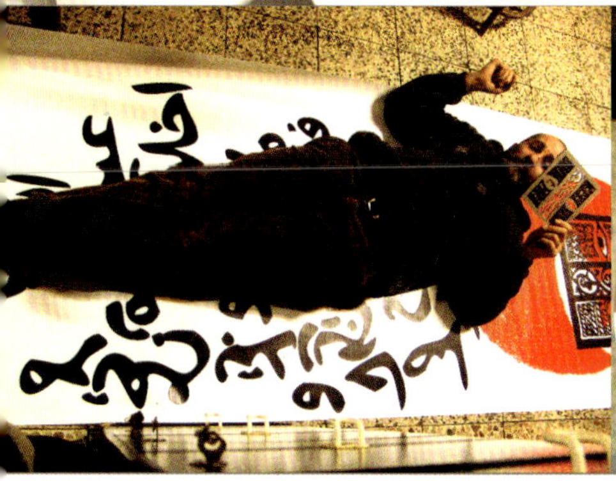

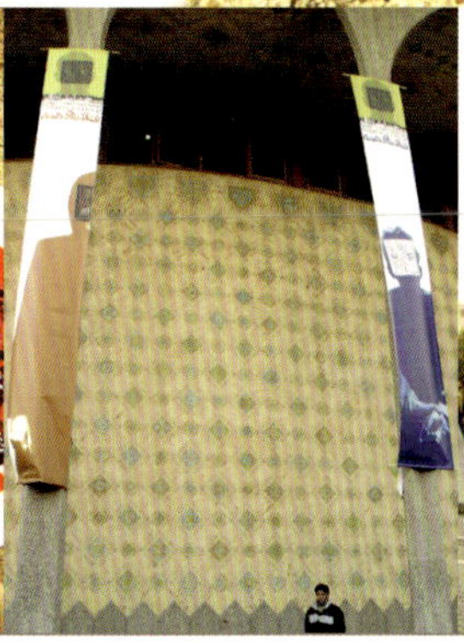

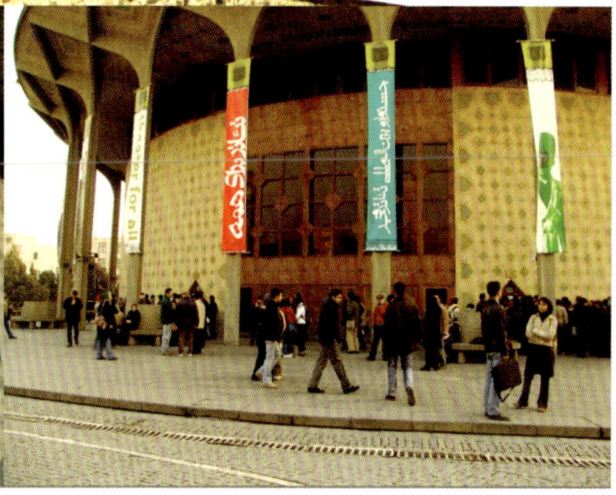

Spreads: Corporate design including type design, corporate colour, corporate image, logo, posters, stationery, tickets, bags, cards, banners, presents, main catalogue, brochures, gifts and billboards for Fajr International Theatre Festival

197

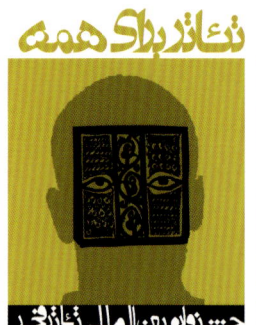

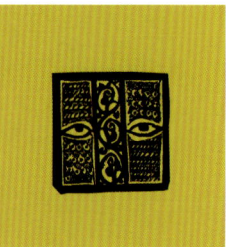

Spreads: Corporate design including type design, corporate colour, corporate image, logo, posters, stationery, tickets, bags, cards, banners, presents, main catalogue, brochures, gifts and billboards for Fajr International Theatre Festival

Fadjr International Theater Festival

theater for all

جشنواره بین ال

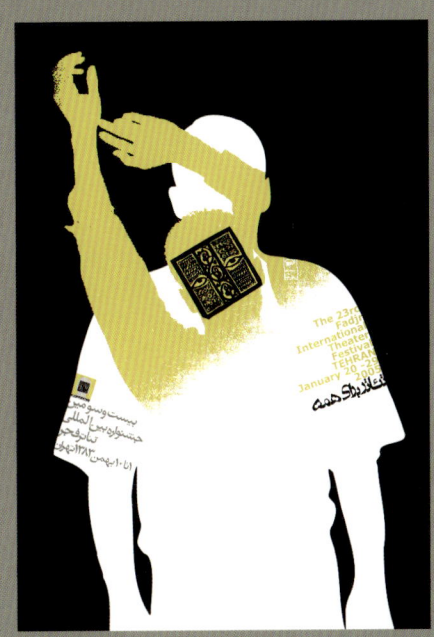

Spreads: Corporate design including type design, corporate colour, corporate image, logo, posters, stationery, tickets, bags, cards, banners, presents, main catalogue, brochures, gifts and billboards for Fajr International Theatre Festival

201

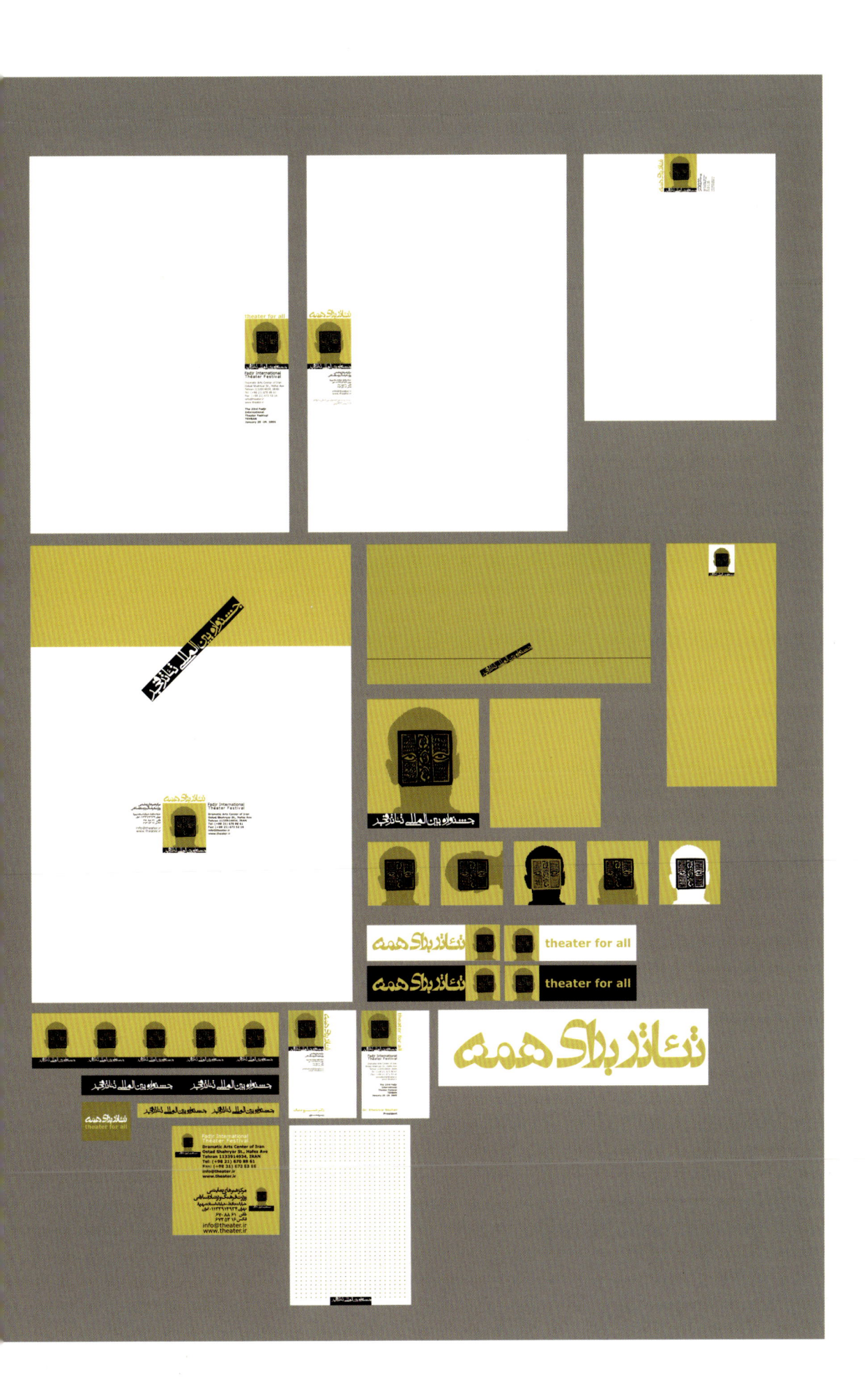

Spreads: Corporate design including type design, corporate colour, corporate image, logo, posters, stationery, tickets, bags, cards, banners, presents, main catalogue, brochures, gifts and billboards for Fajr International Theatre Festival

203

Spreads: Corporate design including type design, corporate colour, corporate image, logo, posters, stationery, tickets, bags, cards, banners, presents, main catalogue, brochures, gifts and billboards for Fajr International Theatre Festival

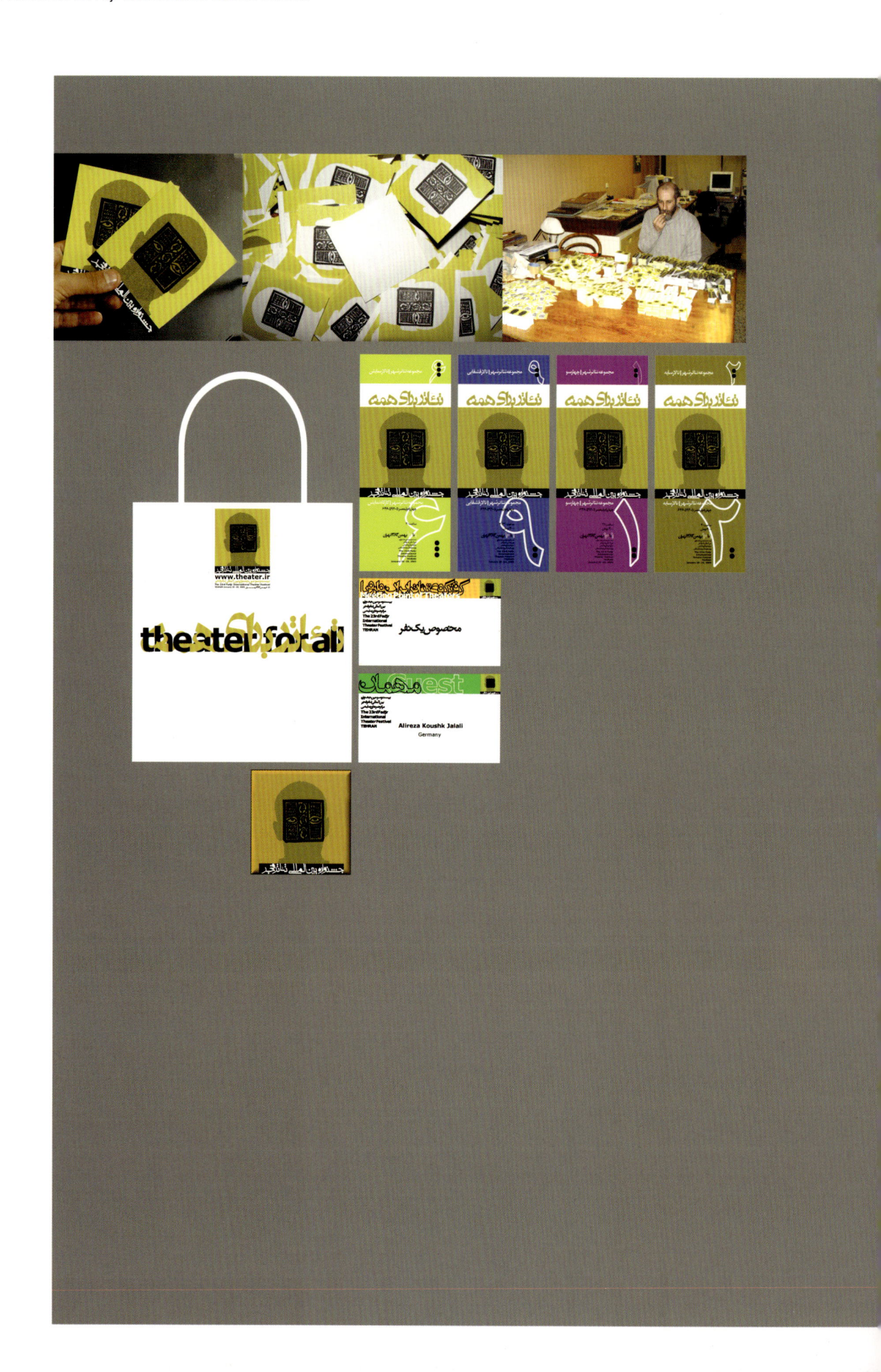

204

205

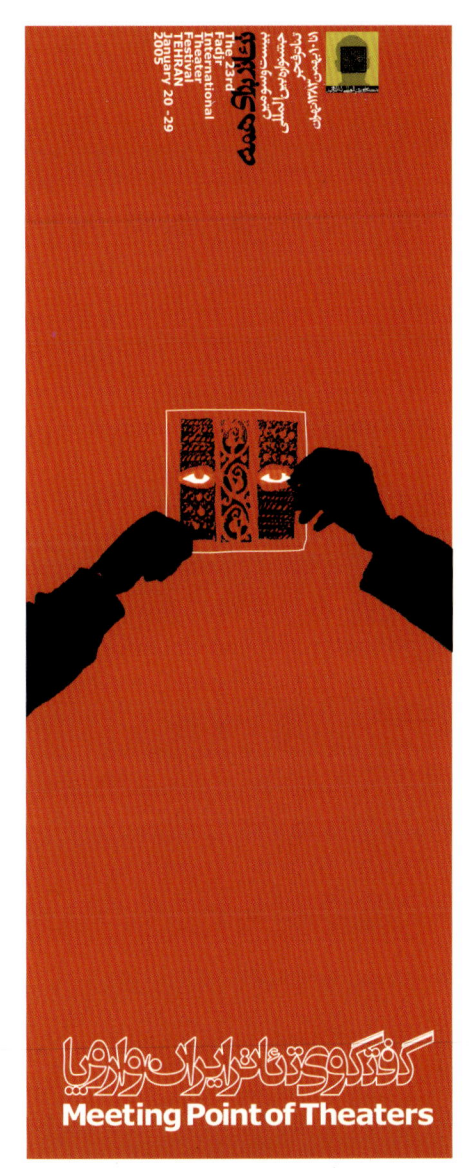

Spreads: Corporate design including type design, corporate colour, corporate image, logo, posters, stationery, tickets, bags, cards, banners, presents, main catalogue, brochures, gifts and billboards for Fajr International Theatre Festival

207

Spreads: Corporate design including type design, corporate colour, corporate image, logo, posters, stationery, tickets, bags, cards, banners, presents, main catalogue, brochures, gifts and billboards for Fajr International Theatre Festival

209

Russell Warren-Fisher

Born in 1964, Russell Warren-Fisher studied graphic design at the London College of Printing from 1983 to 1986, and subsequently at the Royal College of Art from 1986 to 1988. Under the professorial guidance of Gert Dumbar and Derek Birdsall, he was invited to join AGI in 2004.

A nomination by Gert Dumbar for the Creative Futures award helped him launch an independent career directly after graduating from the RCA. He has been working directly with clients such as the British Film Institute, Theatre de Complicite, Hong Kong Telecom and Decca Records, and numerous teaching positions to help China and the Far East to generate new works for 'one man' shows in Tokyo and Osaka.

The space between commercial graphic design and print making, continues to be the area that he enjoys working in the most and currently he distributes his time in the experimental print projects, print research, teaching and applied graphic design.

In 2004, he became the head of research for "Print Digital" (an experimental digital printing facility) at the Royal College of Art, London.

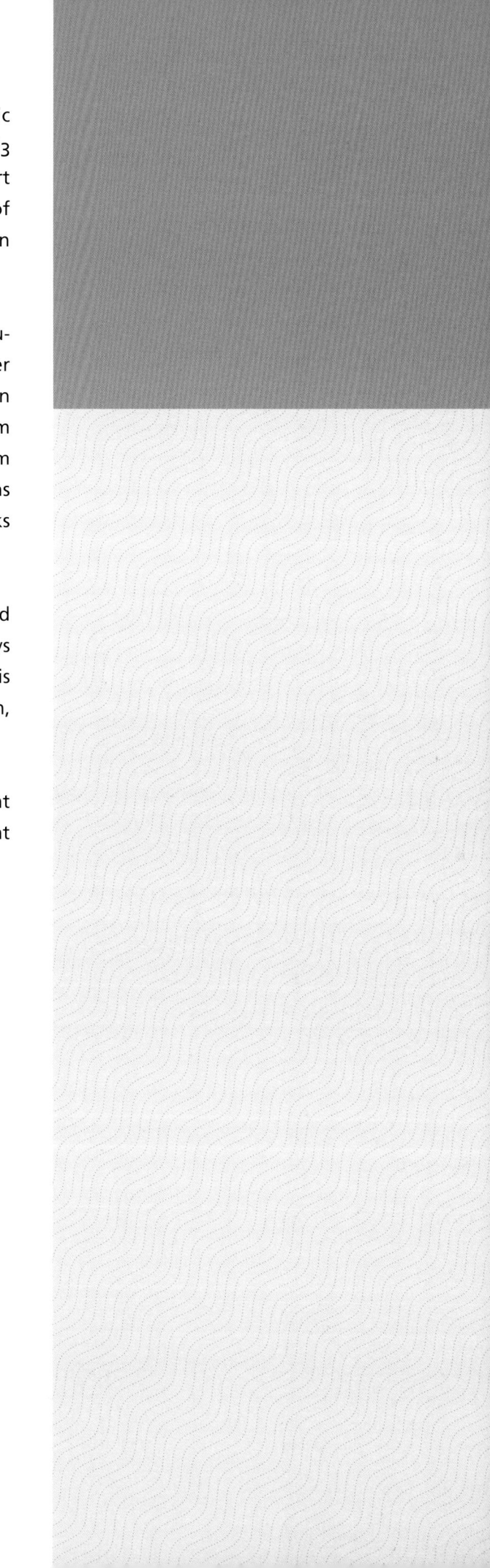

PROJECT: PRINTED MATTER NO.1
TYPE: ILLUSTRATION
CLIENT: RIPE DIGITAL, PARK LANE PRESS, RWF

"This is a page from an experimental print project entitled 'Printed Matter No.1'. In order to illustrate the potential of high quality reprographic and lithographic production processes, deceased creatures were scanned and given a new life as objects of beauty, re-incarnating them as ink on paper." – Russell Warren-Fisher

PRINTED MATTER /
NO.1
THE LIFE AFTER DEATH ISSUE
POSTAGE PAID
MADE IN ENGLAND

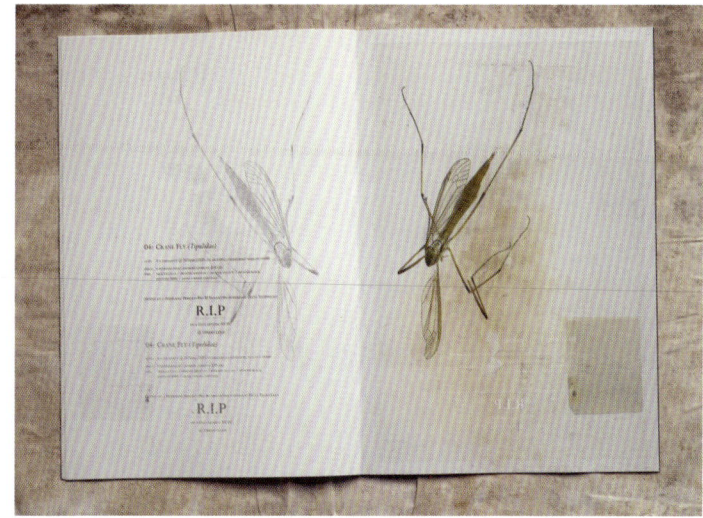

Pages from an experimental print project titled "Printed Matter No.1"

213

Simon McBurney
is moving

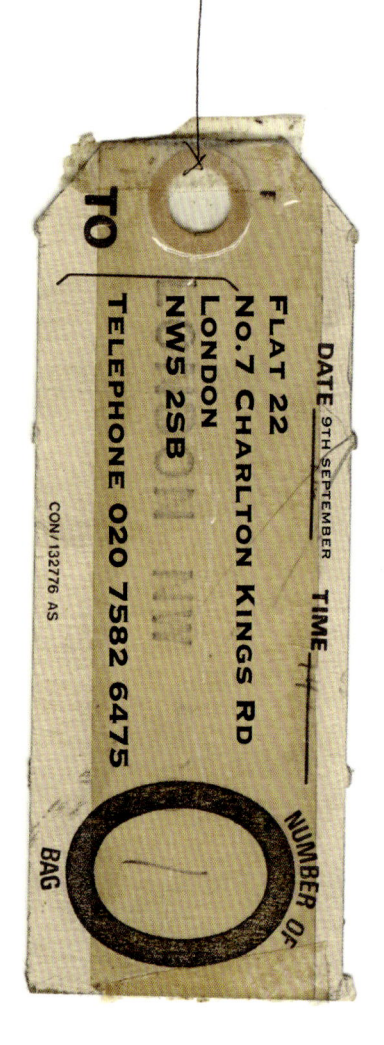

TO
FLAT 22
No.7 CHARLTON KINGS RD
LONDON
NW5 2SB
TELEPHONE 020 7582 6475
CON/132776 AS
DATE 9TH SEPTEMBER
TIME
NUMBER OF BAG
1

Opposite: Change of address card for Actor/Director Simon Mcburney
"The necessary diversions of blessing tate", a work in progress

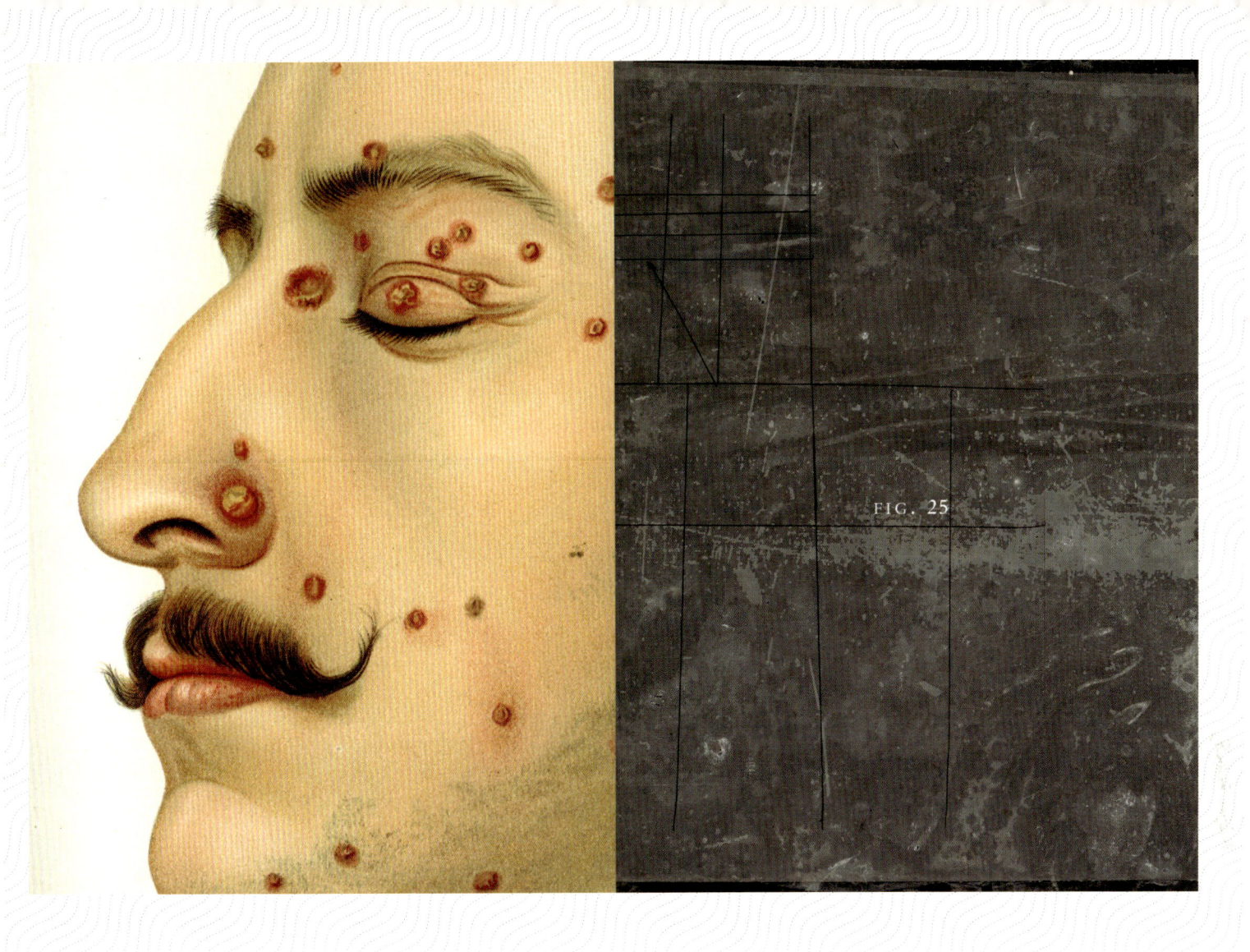

Promotional Theatre Poster for Complicite

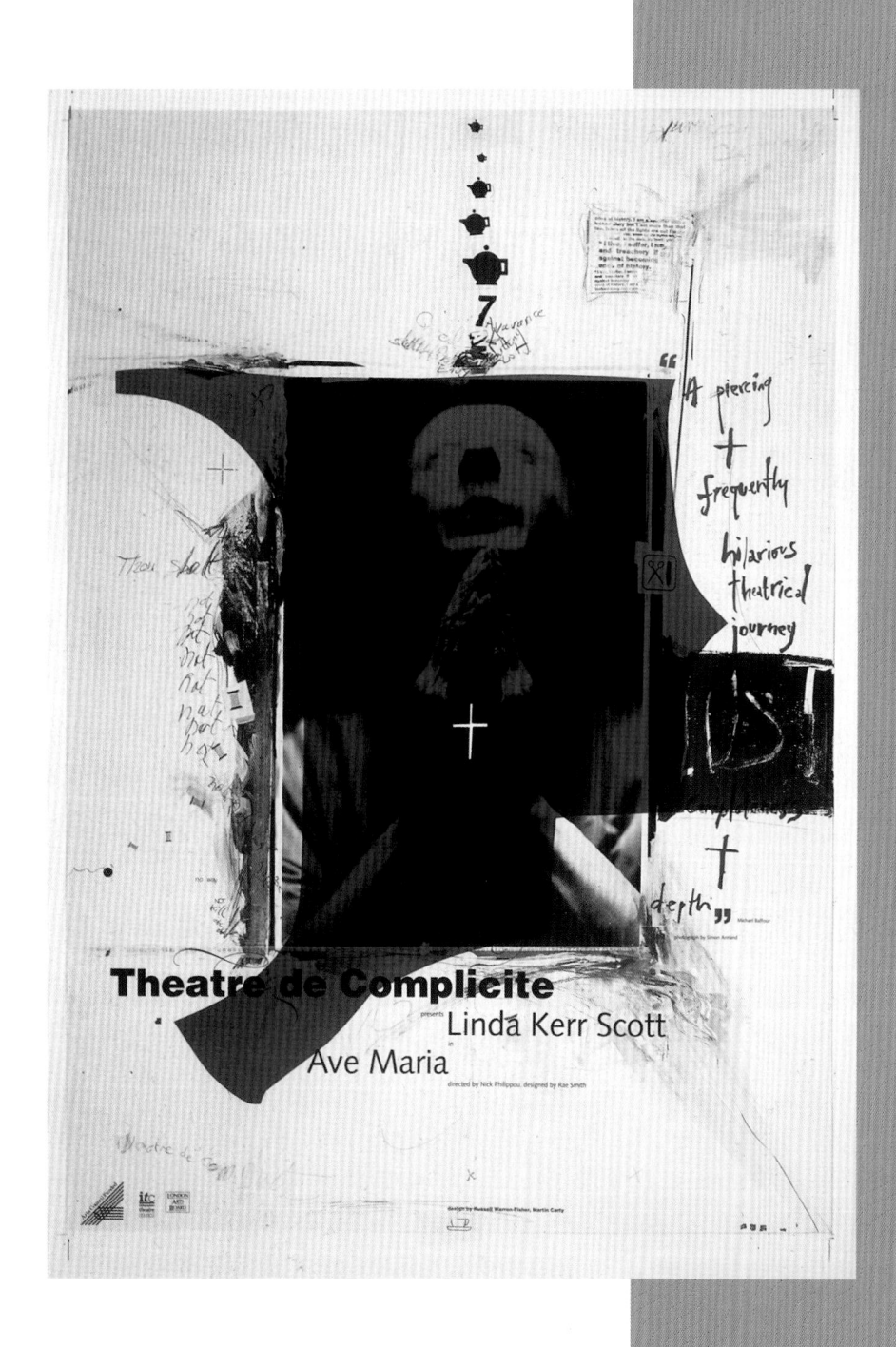

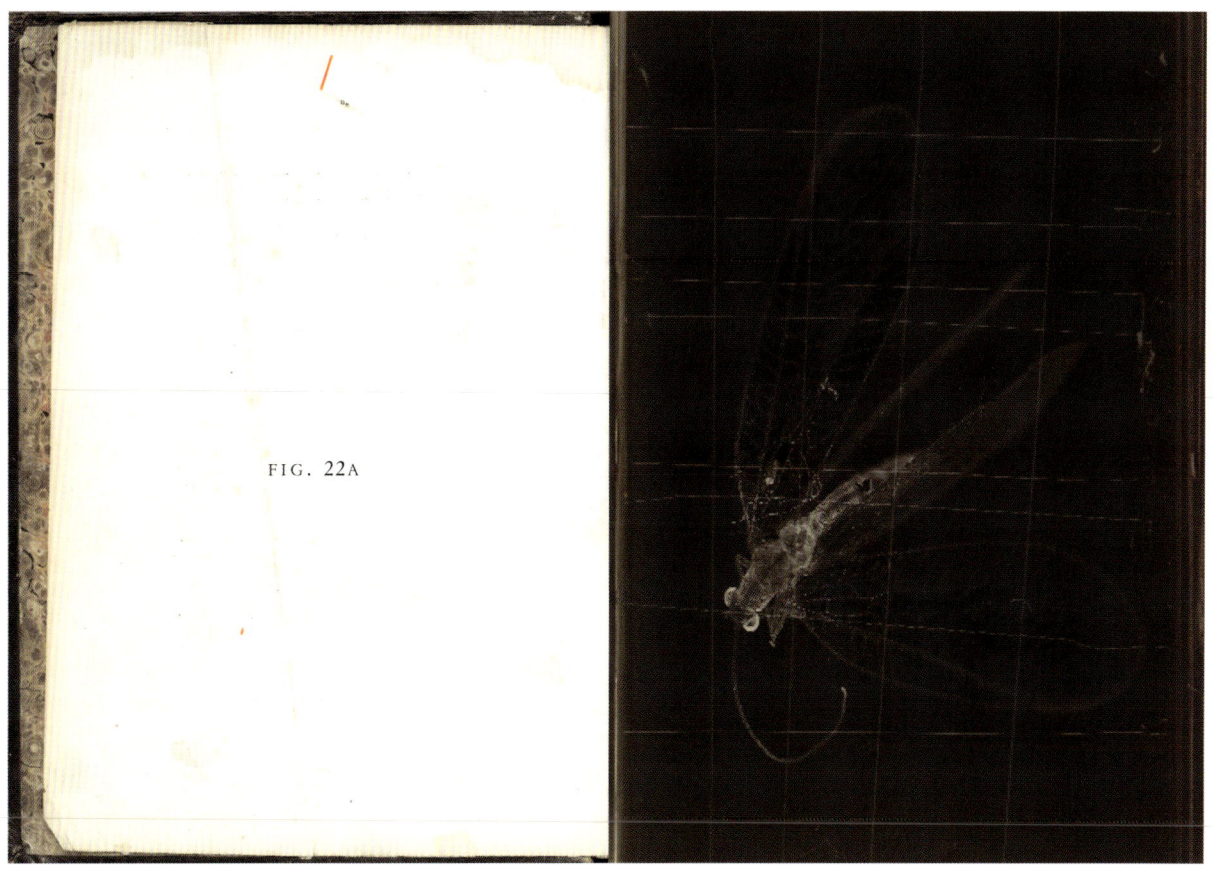

"The Necessary Diversions of Blessing Tate", a work in progress

Spreads: Pages from *the Orla Kiely Autumn & Winter Collection*, a combination of two dimensional patterns, textile designs and printing processes

219

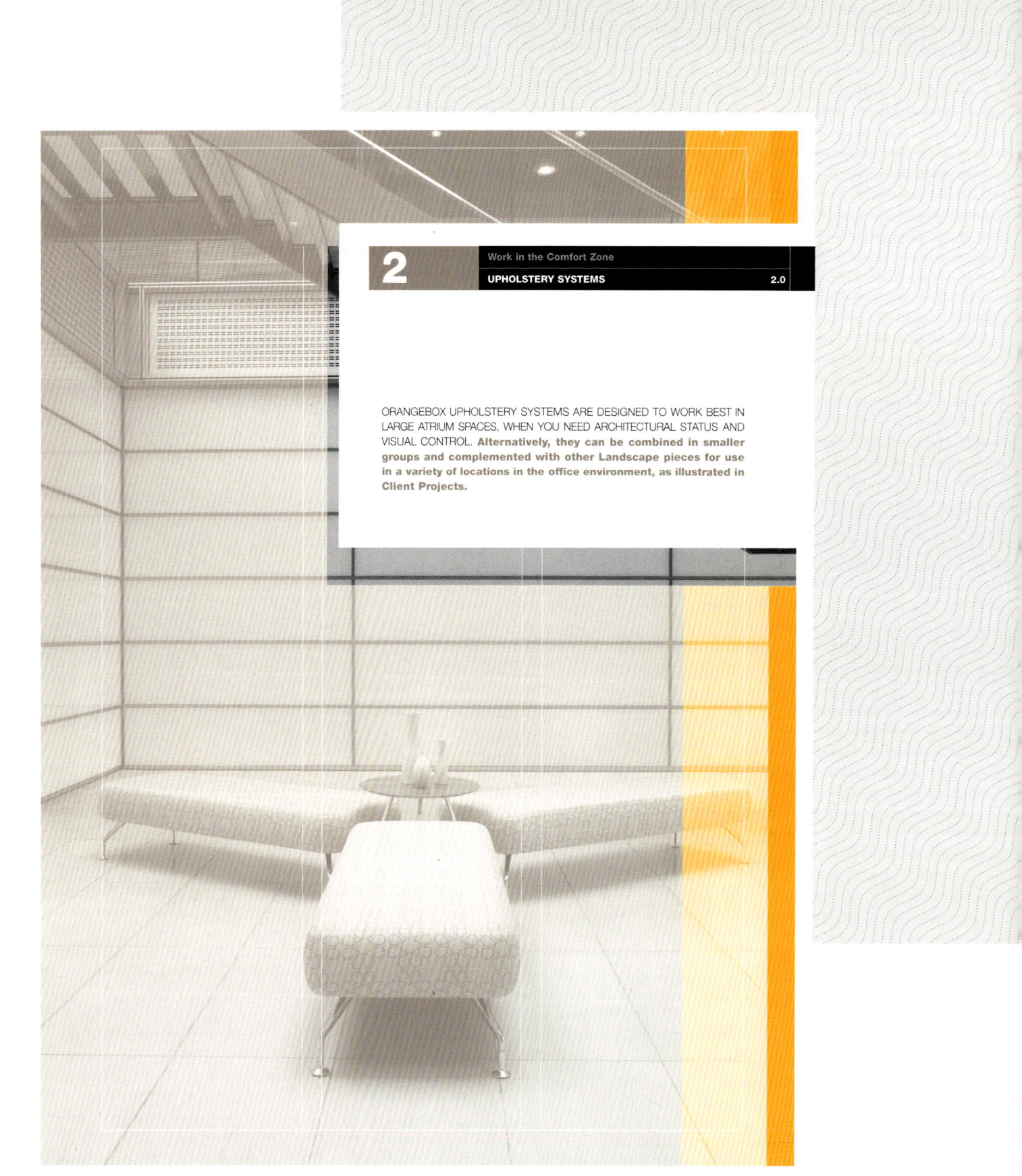

2 | Work in the Comfort Zone
UPHOLSTERY SYSTEMS — 2.0

ORANGEBOX UPHOLSTERY SYSTEMS ARE DESIGNED TO WORK BEST IN LARGE ATRIUM SPACES, WHEN YOU NEED ARCHITECTURAL STATUS AND VISUAL CONTROL. **Alternatively, they can be combined in smaller groups and complemented with other Landscape pieces for use in a variety of locations in the office environment, as illustrated in Client Projects.**

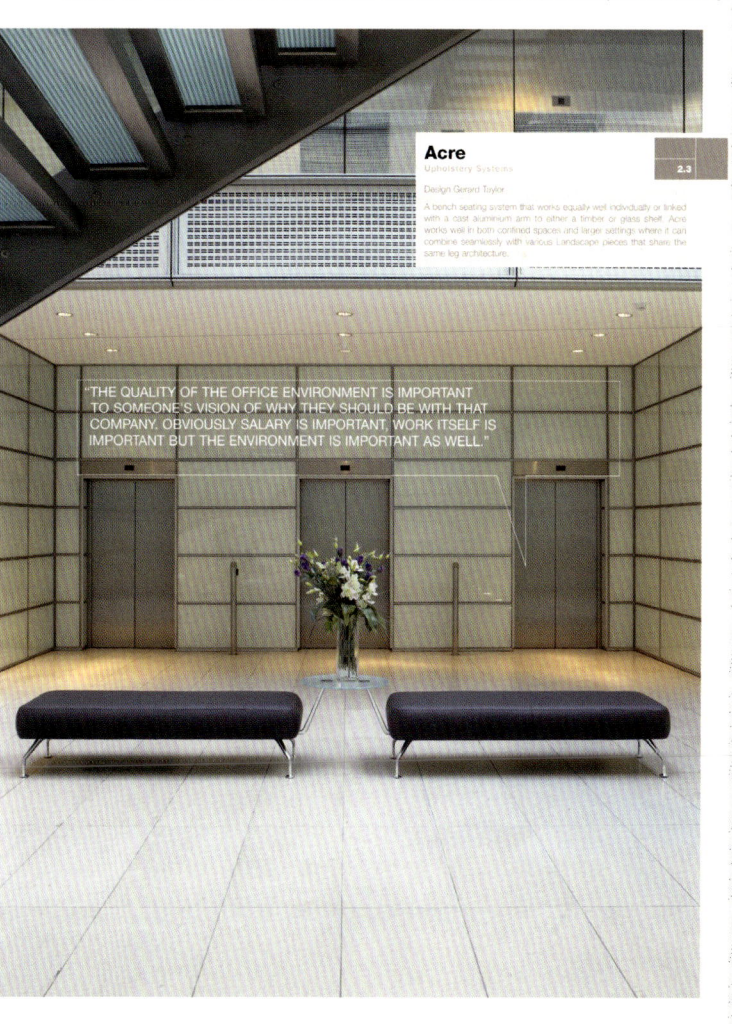

Spreads: Pages from a promotional brochure for Orangebox Limited

Boundary
Upholstery Systems

Design: Gerard Taylor

A modular upholstery system whose smart, simple components can be used individually or linked, depending on the requirements of the space. Boundary's low arm unit can also be specified, providing power for a laptop and a comfortable work surface.

Acre
Upholstery Systems

Design: Gerard Taylor

A bench seating system that works equally well individually or linked with a cast aluminium arm to either a timber or glass shelf. Acre works well in both confined spaces and larger settings where it can combine seamlessly with various Landscape pieces that share the same leg architecture.

"THE QUALITY OF THE OFFICE ENVIRONMENT IS IMPORTANT TO SOMEONE'S VISION OF WHY THEY SHOULD BE WITH THAT COMPANY. OBVIOUSLY SALARY IS IMPORTANT, WORK ITSELF IS IMPORTANT BUT THE ENVIRONMENT IS IMPORTANT AS WELL."

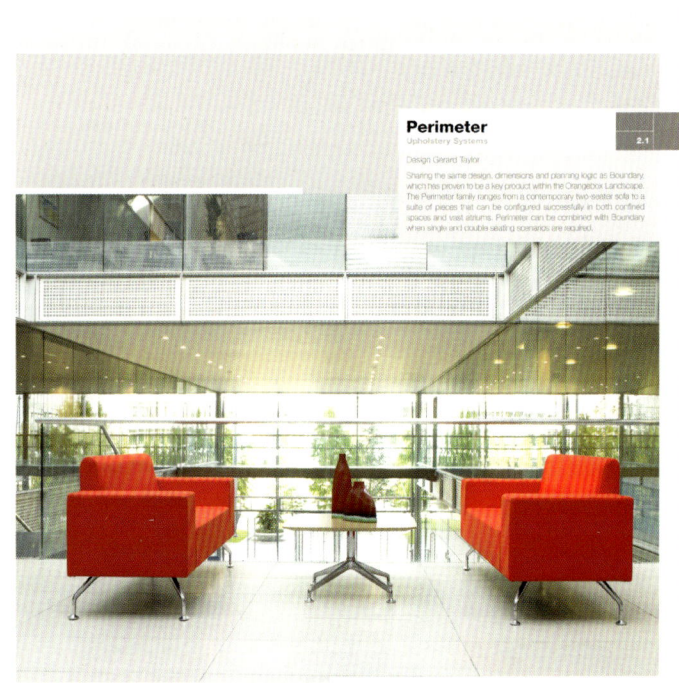

Spreads: Pages from a promotional brochure for Orangebox Limited

2.1 | Perimeter Upholstery Systems

"WE NEED THE ABILITY TO CHANGE IT IF SOMETHING DOES NOT WORK, we will probably have to take a higher degree of risk than we have in the past."

2.4 | Boundary Upholstery Systems

"ENERGY LEVELS FROM HUMAN BEINGS ARE VERY APPARENT. It's something you pick up instantaneously."

223

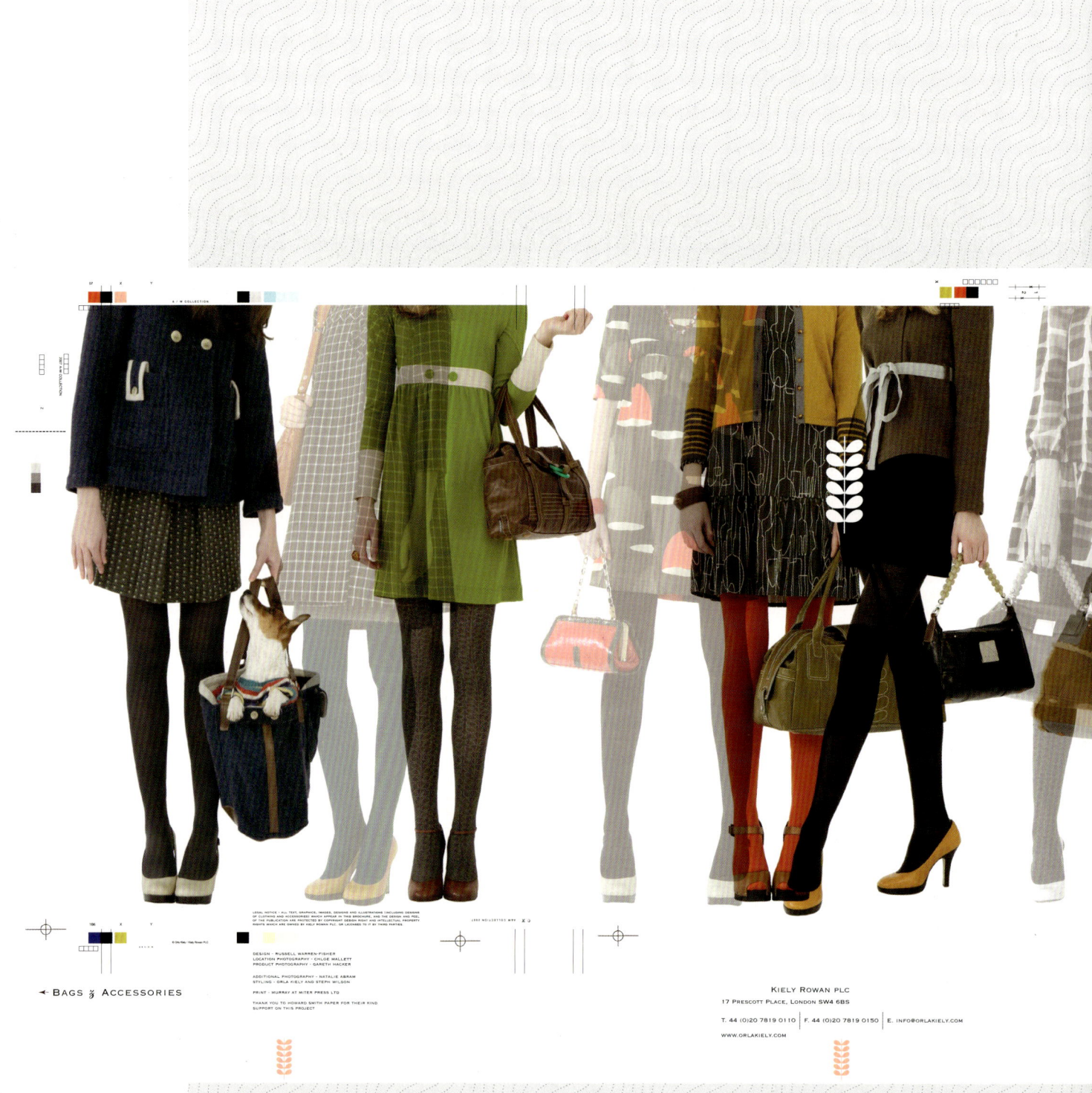

Spreads: Flat cover for *The Orla Kiely Autumn & Winter Collection*

Orla Kiely
Autumn & Winter '07

Ready to Wear

No. 1
GTUA7W/761 (long sleeve dress)
SJTA7K/923 (tights)
PATA7B/014 (handbag)

No. 2
GTHA7K/211 (cardigan)
GTUA7W/761 (long sleeve dress)
SJTA7K/923 (tights)
PATA7B/014 (handbag)

No. 3
DFWA7W/821 (coat)

No. 4
SSEA7K/224 (boat neck top)
VELA7W/552 (high waisted shorts)
PATA7B/022 (small shoulder bag)

No. 5
MOHA7K/852 (jacket)
SSEA7K/224 (boat neck top)
VELA7W/552 (high waisted shorts)
PATA7B/022 (small shoulder bag)

No. 6
GTUA7W/744 (short sleeve dress)
WSTA7K/923 (tights)
SLSA7B/021 (shopper)

No. 7
SPCA7K/212 (cropped cardigan)
GTUA7W/744 (short sleeve dress)
WSTA7K/923 (tights)
SLSA7B/021 (shopper)

No. 8
PNBA7W/742 (dress)
STPA7B/105 (clutch bag)

No. 9
MOHA7W/823 (coat)
STPA7B/014 (handbag)

No. 10
JCSA7W/824 (coat)
PNSA7W/744 (dress)
STPA7B/023 (shoulder bag)

No. 11
JCSA7W/824 (coat)
PNSA7W/744 (dress)
STPA7B/023 (shoulder bag)

No. 12
WSWA7J/753 (dress)
SSCA7K/221 (scoop neck sweater)
SHPA7B/025 (bag)

No. 13
WNSA7W/413 (blouse)
WINA7W/746 (dress)
PATA7B/014 (handbag)

No. 14
TBWA7W/823 (coat)
WNSA7W/413 (blouse)
WINA7W/746 (dress)
PATA7B/014 (handbag)

No. 15
TEAA7W/753 (dress)
SKRA7J/321 (t-shirt)
DFWA7B/021 (shopper)

No. 16
DFWA7W/843 (jacket)
DFWA7B/025 (tote)
TEAA7W/753 (dress)
SKRA7J/321 (t-shirt)

No. 17
CUTA7W/741 (dress)
SPFA7K/271 (scarf)
SPFA7K/294 (hat)

No. 18
CUTA7W/741 (dress)
SSCA7K/211 (cardigan)
SPFA7K/294 (hat)
SLSA7B/015 (holdall)

No. 19
WGCA7W/751 (dress)
PATA7B/035 (bucket bag)

No. 20
WLGA7W/746 (dress)
SJTA7K/923 (tights)
PATA7B/035 (bucket bag)

No. 21
WLGA7W/746 (dress)
SSEA7K/211 (cardigan)

No. 22
TSTA7J/344 (v-neck top)
VELA7/513 (slouchy trousers)
GTUA7B/021 (zip shopper)

No. 23
NDCA7W/754 (short sleeve dress)
SJTA7K/923 (tights)
PATA7B/041 (zip satchel)

No. 24
NDCA7W/741 (belted dress)
WSTA7K/923 (tights)
CLAA7B/014 (zip handbag)

No. 25
TBWA7W/853 (jacket)
NDCA7W/741 (belted dress)
WSTA7K/923 (tights)
CLAA7B/014 (zip handbag)

No. 26
WLJA7W/762 (dress)
LFOA7E/022 (mini sling bag)

No. 27
SSCA7K/221 (scoop neck sweater)
NDCA7W/653 (skirt)
BBEA7J/324 (t-shirt)
CLAA7B/041 (zip satchel)

No. 28
WLPA7W/741 (dress)
SJTA7K/923 (tights)
RELA7B/023 (shoulder bag)

No. 29
SSCA7K/221 (scoop neck sweater)
WSWA7J/632 (gathered skirt)
STPA7B/014 (handbag)

No. 30
SATA7W/511 (slim trousers)
CHAA7J/324 (t-shirt)

No. 31
PNSA7W/744 (dress)

No. 32
SCPA7W/744 (dress)
STWA7W/431 (roll neck top)

No. 33
WSWA7J/351 (long sleeve wrap)
CCTA7W/552 (shorts)
SPFA7K/294 (hat)
PATA7B/022 (shoulder bag)

No. 34
DFWA7W/821 (coat)
SPFA7K/291 (balaclava)
SLSA7B/015 (holdall)

No. 35
CUTA7W/423 (top)
VELA7W/552 (high waisted shorts)
SLSA7B/021 (shopper)

No. 36
SCPA7W/822 (laminated raincoat)
WPJA7K/271 (scarf)
RSLA7B/035 (bucket bag)

No. 37
PDIA7W/753 (dress)
WSTA7K/923 (tights)
RSLA7B/035 (bucket bag)

No. 38
WSWA7J/364 (smock top)
TTUA7J/291 (strappy vest & pants)

No. 39
SHPA7W/833 (coat)
SPFA7K/294 (hat)
SLSA7B/021 (bag)

No. 40
CBMA7K/221 (sweater)
SHPA7K/867 (gilet)
SHPA7W/963 (gloves)
TSTA7J/932 (leggings)

No. 41
CHAA7J/322 (3/4 sleeve t-shirt)
TSTA7J/741 (dress)
RTUA7K/211 (coat)
SHPA7B/025 (reversible tote)

No. 42
PNSA7W/421 (smock top)
JCSA7W/643 (skirt)
PATA7B/022 (small shoulder bag)

No. 43
SKRA7J/321 (t-shirt)
WPJA7K/224 (tank)
CCTA7W/552 (shorts)
SHPA7B/025 (reversible tote)

No. 44
BBEA7J/324 (t-shirt)
CCTA7W/512 (trousers)
RSLA7B/014 (handbag)

No. 45
WPJA7K/754 (dress)
CBMA7K/271 (scarf)
TTUA7J/322 (ls placket t-shirt)
SHPA7B/025 (reversible tote)

No. 46
SATA7W/742 (dress)
PATA7B/128 (big folded purse)

No. 47
CBMA7K/212 (cardigan)
TGTA7J/344 (v-neck top)
CCTA7W/552 (shorts)

No. 48
SPFA7K/761 (dress)

No. 49
CBMA7K/754 (dress)
PATA7B/041 (zip satchel)

No. 50
WINA7W/823 (coat)
CBMA7K/754 (dress)
PATA7B/041 (zip satchel)

225

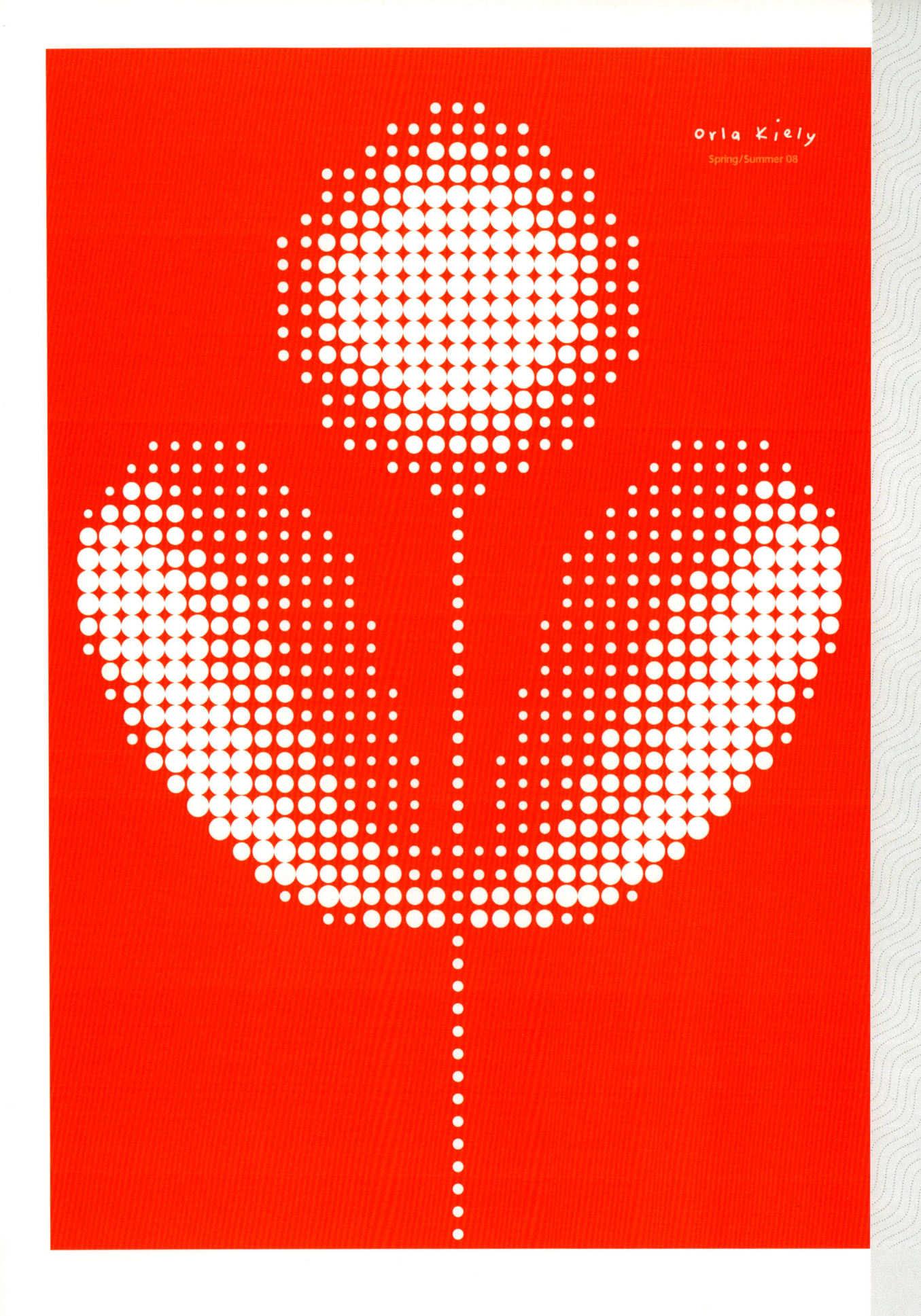

Spreads: Invitation for Orla Kiely Spring/Summer press night

Orla Kiely
Spring/Summer 08

Saed Meshki

Saed Meshki was born in 1964 in Iran. He started his artistic activities at the age of twenty four. During the fifteen years of his professional career, he has worked as a freelance in his personal studio on cultural projects. Saed studied graphic design in the Faculty of Fine Arts at Tehran University. He is now teaching at the same university.

Saed is a member of the AGI, an active member of the Iranian Graphic Design Society (IGDS) and a cofounder of *Neshan* (Iranian Graphic Design Magazine). He has been a member of the Selection Committee of the 7th Iranian Graphic Design Biennial, jury member of the first Iranian Self-promotional Posters Biennial and the 5th Exhibition of Children's Books' illustrator.

In 2001, he and three artists of his generation founded the 5th Colour Group with an objective to create a link between graphic design in Iran and the rest of the world. The group has organised several exhibitions both in Iran and abroad.

In the past few years, Saed has focused on book design. Currently he is art director and graphic designer of several publication houses. Saed has also been executing manager of *Sign* (Directory of Iranian Signs), project manager for the publication of *Iranian Contemporary Graphic Designers Series* (20 volumes, 2004) and art director and graphic designer of *Eye* collection.

In 2003, Saed founded "Meshki" publication house. Numerous books of illustration and literature are to appear soon. Moreover, Saed has been art director and graphic designer of several festivals. His artworks have been published in many books namely in *Area* and several other magazines. He has won numerous awards and prizes both at home and abroad, including First Prize of the first Biennial of Cover Design of Tehran (2003), Icograda Excellent Award in the 19th International Poster Biennial Warsaw (2004), and so on.

PROJECT: A PATHOLOGICAL SURVEY OF CONTEMPORARY IRANIAN CINEMA
TYPE: POSTER
CLIENT: FARABI FOUNDATION

"In the last two decades, Iranian cinema has received a lot of prizes at the international festivals. The criticizers have very good ideas about the Iranian cinema around the world. But nowadays the Iranian films do not have supporters in Iran. Therefore the economy of Iranian cinema is bankrupt! This poster is for the seminar about A Pathological Survey of Contemporary Iranian Cinema." – Saed Meshki

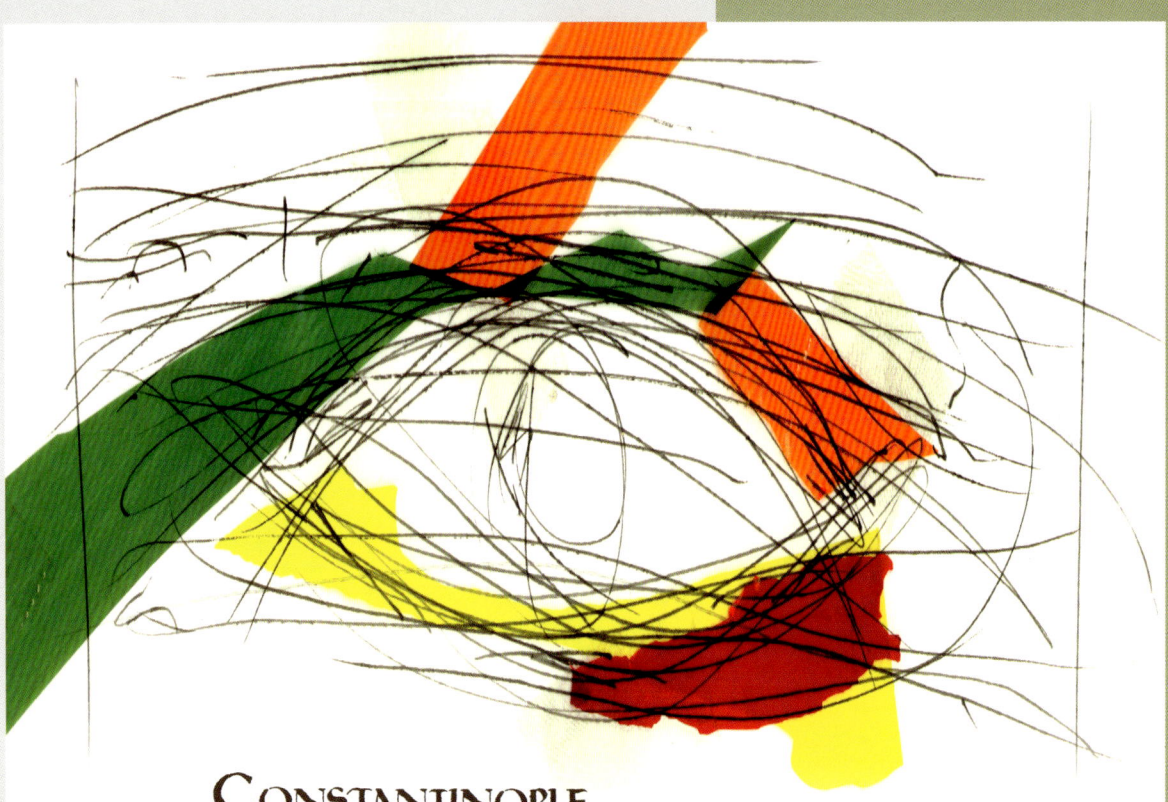

Constantinople

Jeudi, vendredi et samedi
3, 4 et 5 février 2005, 20 h
Théâtre La Chapelle
3700, rue St-Dominique

Constantinople :
Guy Ross, Ziya Tabassian, Elin Soderstrom
Matthew Jennejohn, Kiya Tabassian
www.constantinople.ca

Opposite: Concert Poster for Constantinople Group
Top Left: Poster for Self Exhibition in Shiraz, Iran
Bottom Left: Poster for Old Books Exhibition by International Theatre Festival of Iranzamin
Top Right: Poster for the 70th Birth Anniversary of Morteza Momayez

هفتادمین سال تولد مرتضی ممیز
نمایشگاه ۴۱ پوستر از ۴۱ طراح گرافیک جهان
The 70th Birth Anniversary of Morteza Momayez
Exhibition of 41 Posters by 41 International Graphic Designers

Top: Poster for News Exhibition
Bottom: Poster for the First Exhibition of IGDS
Student's Member by Iranian Graphic
Design Society

Top: Poster for the 23rd International Fajr Theatre Festival
Bottom: Poster for the 5th International Theatre Festival of Iranzamin

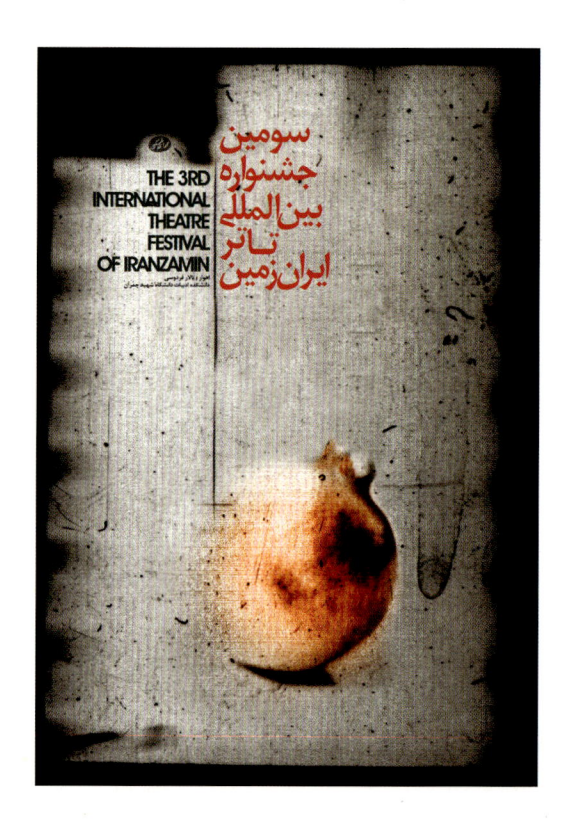

Top: Poster for Khozestan Great Book Exhibition
Bottom: Poster for the 3rd International Theatre Festival of Iranzamin

Top: Film Poster for A Little Kiss by Behnegar Co.
Bottom Left: Poster for Solidarity
Bottom Right: Poster for the 2nd International Festival of Comical Theatres

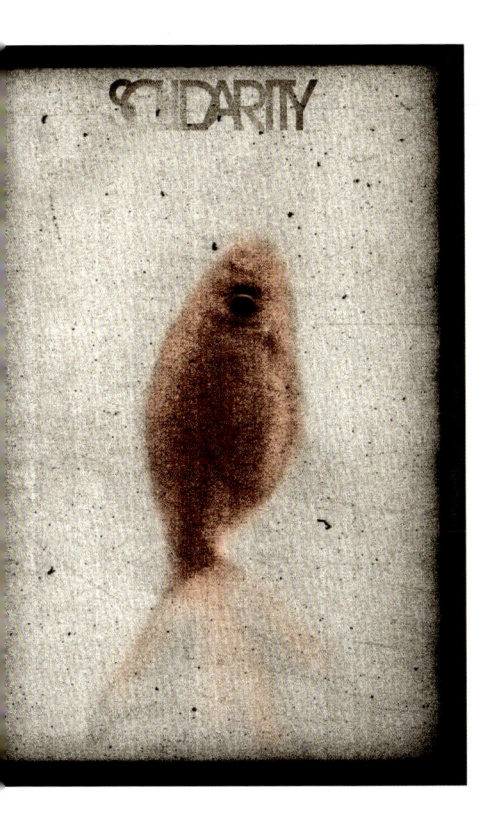

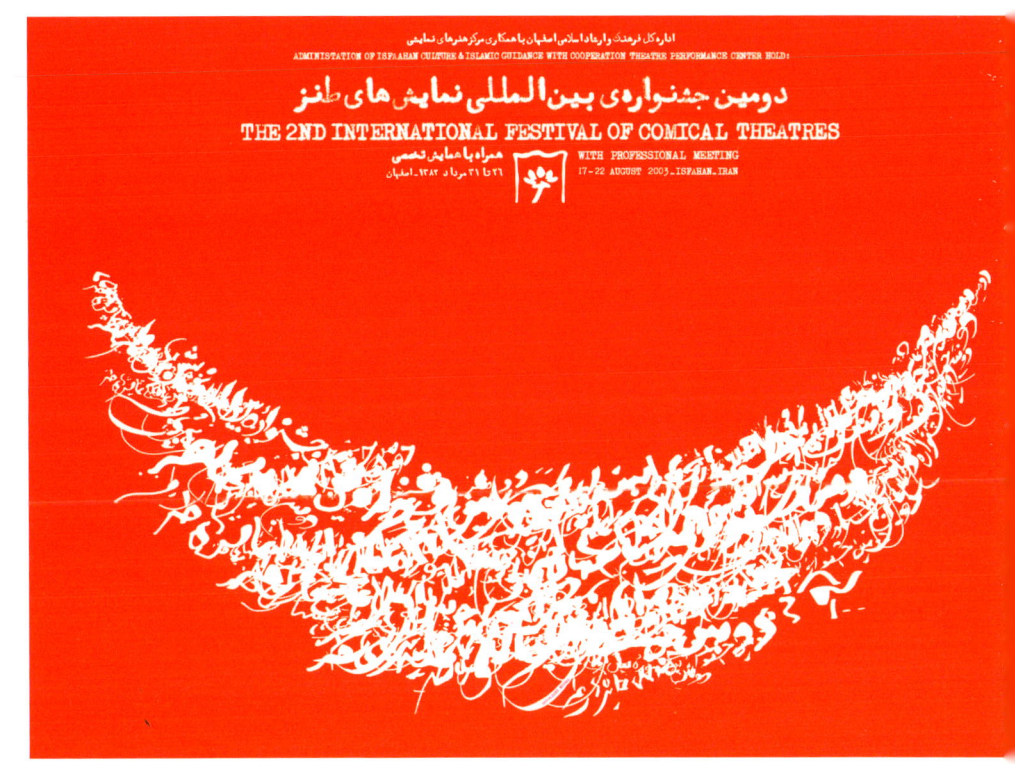

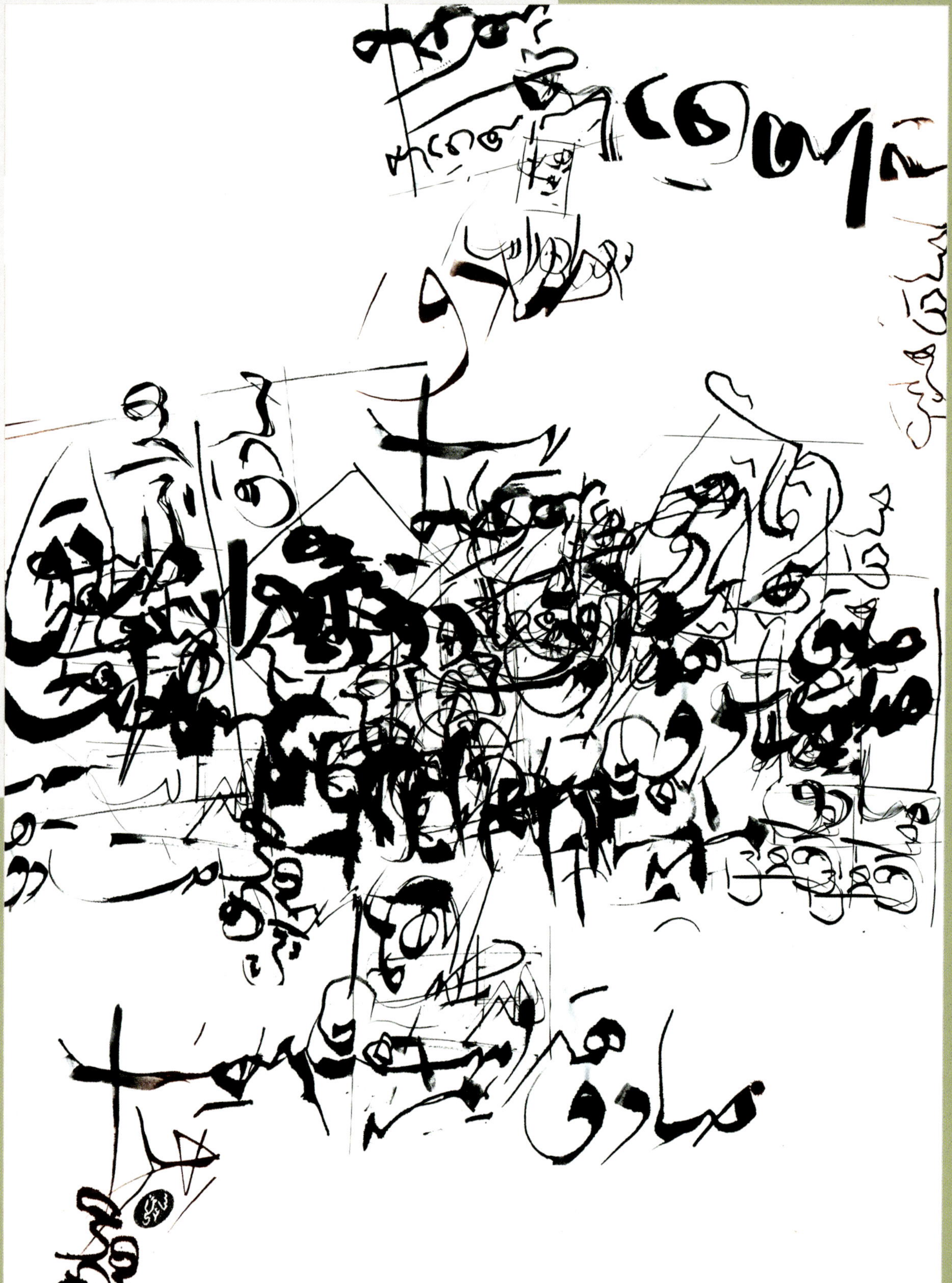

Opposite: Poster for the First Iranian Typography Exhibition
Poster for Assembly on Aesthetics of Religion by the Centre for Artistic Research and Studies

Assembly on Aesthetics of Religion

Tehran, December 26 and 27, 2005, The Museum of Contemporary Arts

نمایشگاه رنگ پنجم
پنجاه پنجم در ایتالیا

پنجاه پوستر از رنگ پنجم (بیژن صیفوری، مجید عباسی، سعید مشکی، علیرضا مصطفی زاده)
پنجاه پوستر برگزیده از نخستین و دومین نمایشگاه تایپوگرافی ایرانی
پالرمو، اردیبهشت ۱۳۸۴

Fifty-Fifty
The 5th Color Exhibition in Italy Palermo 2005

Fifty Posters by the 5th Color
(Majid Abbasi, Saed Meshki, Alireza Mostafazadeh, Bijan Seyfouri)
Fifty Posters of the First and Second Iranian Typography Exhibition

Opposite: Poster for Fifty-Fifty, the 5th colour Poster Exhibition in Italy
Poster for the 4th International Theatre Festival of Iranzamin

گزیده‌ی شعرهای شل سیلوراستاین

ترجمه‌ی احمد پوری

Book cover for *Contemporary Poem* published by Afkar Publication
Opposite: Book cover for *Contemporary Poem* published by Goftman Publication

اگر این ماهیِ کوچک رنگی نبود در

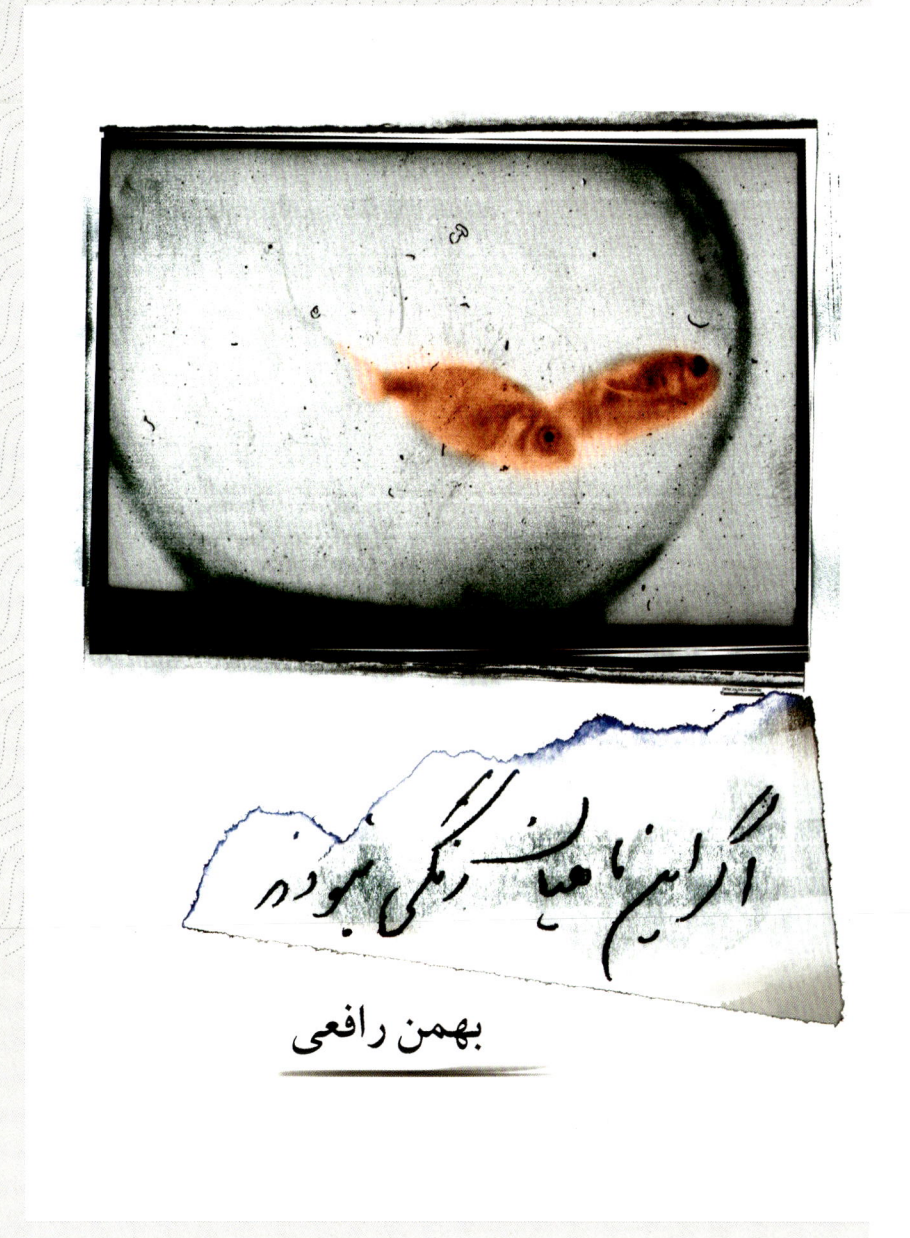

بهمن رافعی

Spreads: Book cover and layouts for *Asking Makes the Way Further* published by Mahriz Publication

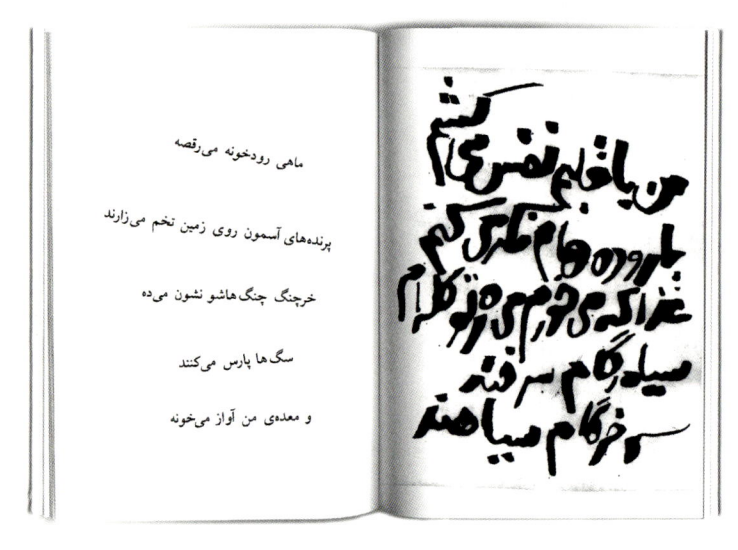

ابوالفضل ابراهیم‌شاهی
طراح کتاب ساعد مشکی

قدیم بی‌هوا می‌کشتن، امروز با هوا می‌کشن .

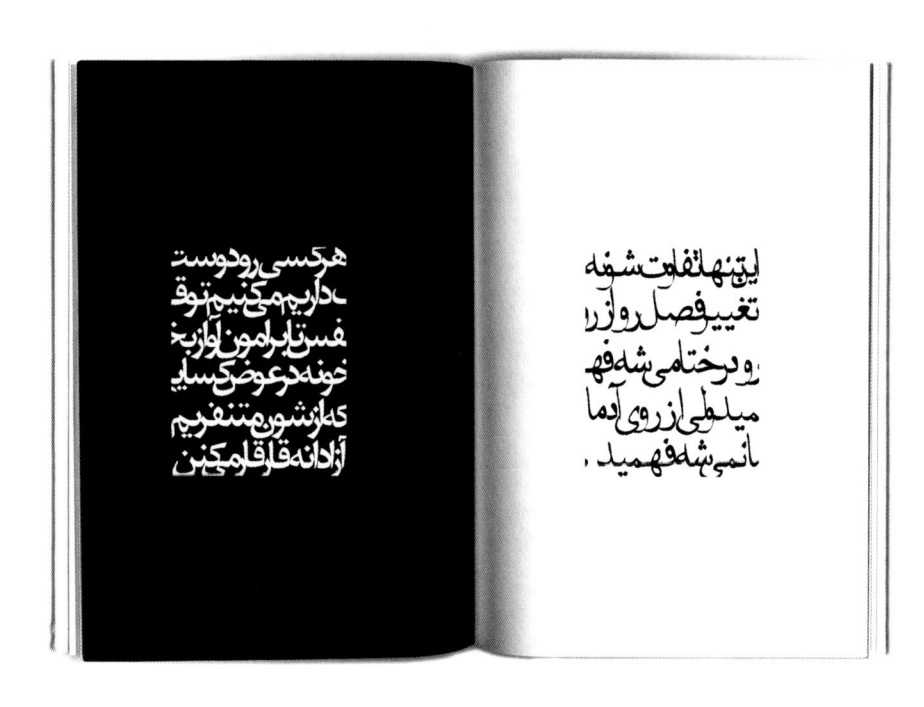

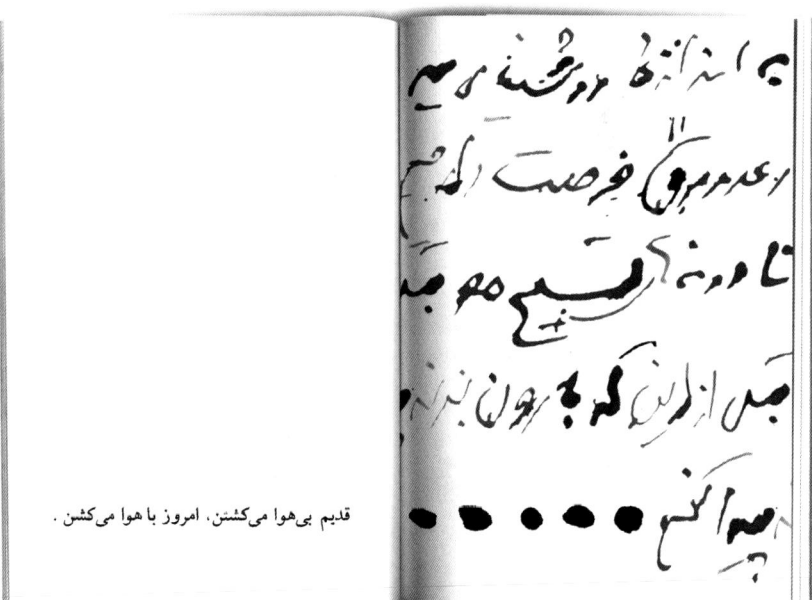

اونی که
عاشق آسمونه
حتمن
زمین می‌خوره .

CD Cover for In the Mirror of Sky by Avayedoost Co.
CD Cover for Green Shadows by Irangam Co.
CD Cover for Brief by Avayedoost Co.
CD Cover for Trio by Mahmehr Co.

244

CD Cover for Music of Film and Theatre by Avayedoost Co.
CD Cover for First Morning Meeting by Avayedoost Co.
CD Cover for Folk Music by Mahmehr Co.

Seymour Chwast

Seymour Chwast was born in New York and is a graduate of the Cooper Union, where he studied illustration and graphic design. He is a founding partner of the celebrated Push Pin Studios, whose distinct style has had a worldwide influence on contemporary visual communications. In 1985 the studio's name was changed to the Pushpin Group of which Mr. Chwast is the director.

Seymour Chwast works in a variety of styles. His work has been exhibited in major galleries and museums in the United States, Europe, Japan, Brazil and Russia, including a two-month retrospective exhibition, exhibition in the Kunstgewerbe Museum in Zurich, the Gutenberg Museum in Mainz, and the Museo de Arte in Sao Paulo, Brazil, and several one-man shows of his paintings, sculptures and prints in his country and abroad. His posters are in the permanent collection of New York's Museum of Modern Art, the Cooper-Hewitt Museum of the Smithsonian Institution, the Library of Congress, the Gutenberg Museum and the Israel Museum.

Mr. Chwast's work has been the subject of numerous magazine and newspaper articles. *IDEA*, Japan's leading graphic arts magazine, published a complete issue on his work. "Push Pin" was the subject of the *New York Times Magazine*. Harry N. Abrams published a book of his work titled *The Left Handed Designer*.

He is a recipient of the St. Gauden's Medal from the Cooper Union and the Gold Medalist of American Institute of Graphic Arts in 1985. In 1984, Mr. Chwast was inducted into the Art Director's Hall of Fame, and he received an honorary Doctor of Fine Arts degree from Parsons School of Design in 1992 and the Master Series Award from the School of Visual Arts in 1997. He has been a member of the faculty at the Cooper Union Art School and the School of Visual Arts and is a frequent guest lecturer to student and professional groups. His favorite skyscraper is the Chrysler Building.

PROJECT: WAR IS MADNESS
TYPE: POSTER
CLIENT: THE SHOSHIN SOCIETY

"War is Madness was one of several posters sponsored by the Shoshin Society which was dedicated to the exchange of ideas between Japanese and American designers. This poster commemorated the anniversary of the atomic bombing of Hiroshima." – Seymour Chwast

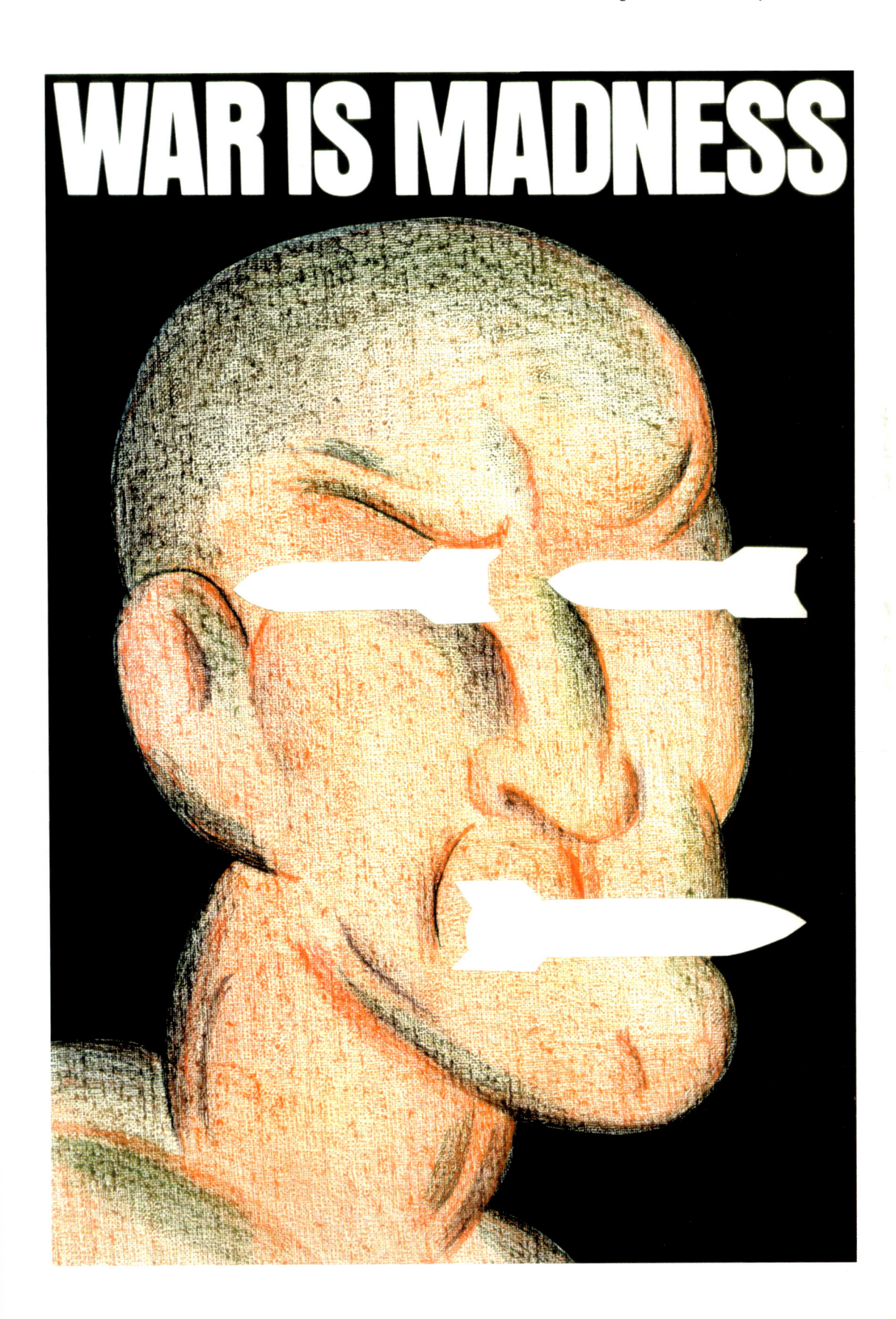

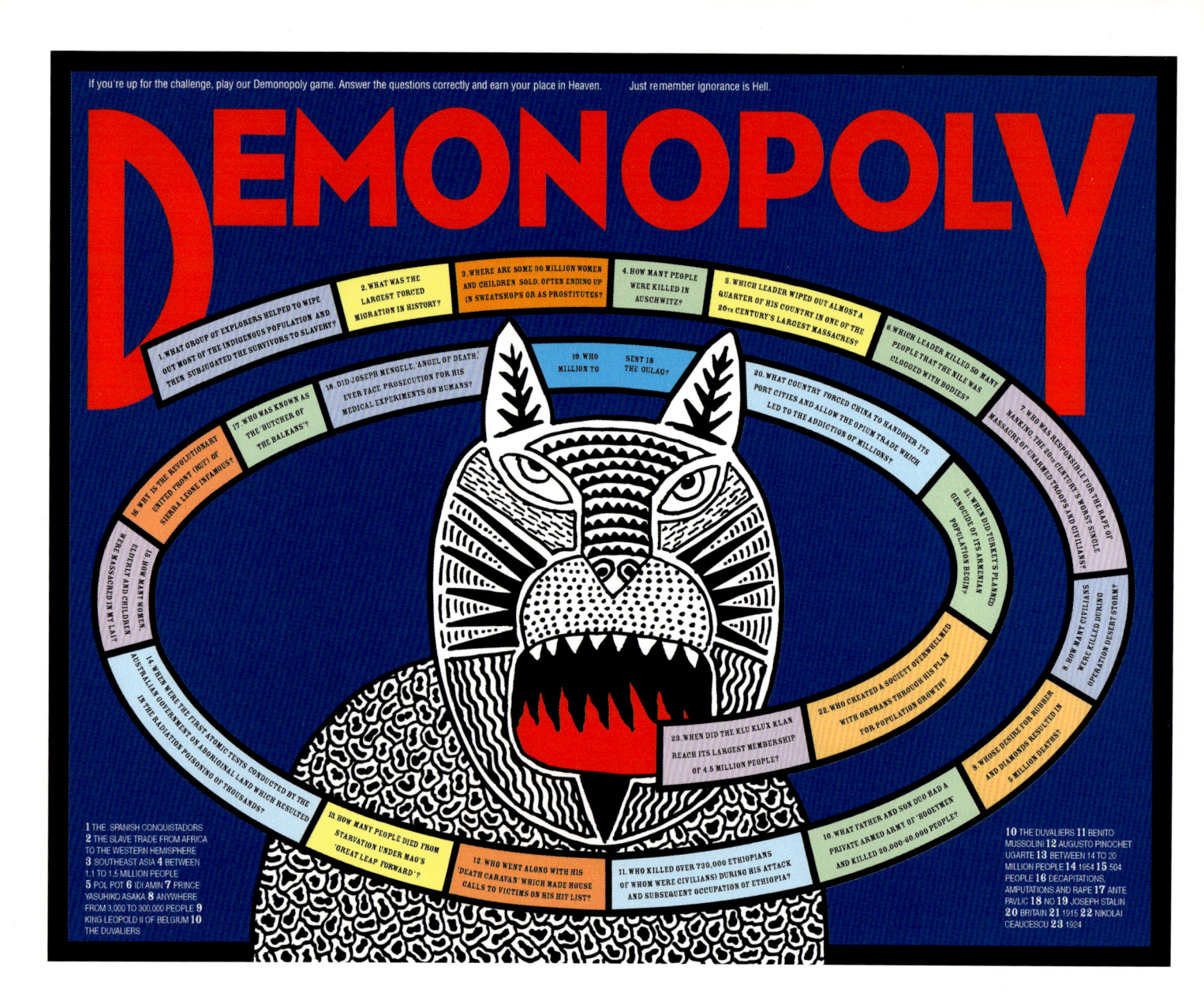

"Demonology", from *The Nose No. 10: Hell* for Self-Promotion

Top: Poster titled "What is Design?" for Cooper Hewitt National Design Museum
Bottom: Cover illustration for a self-promotion calendar

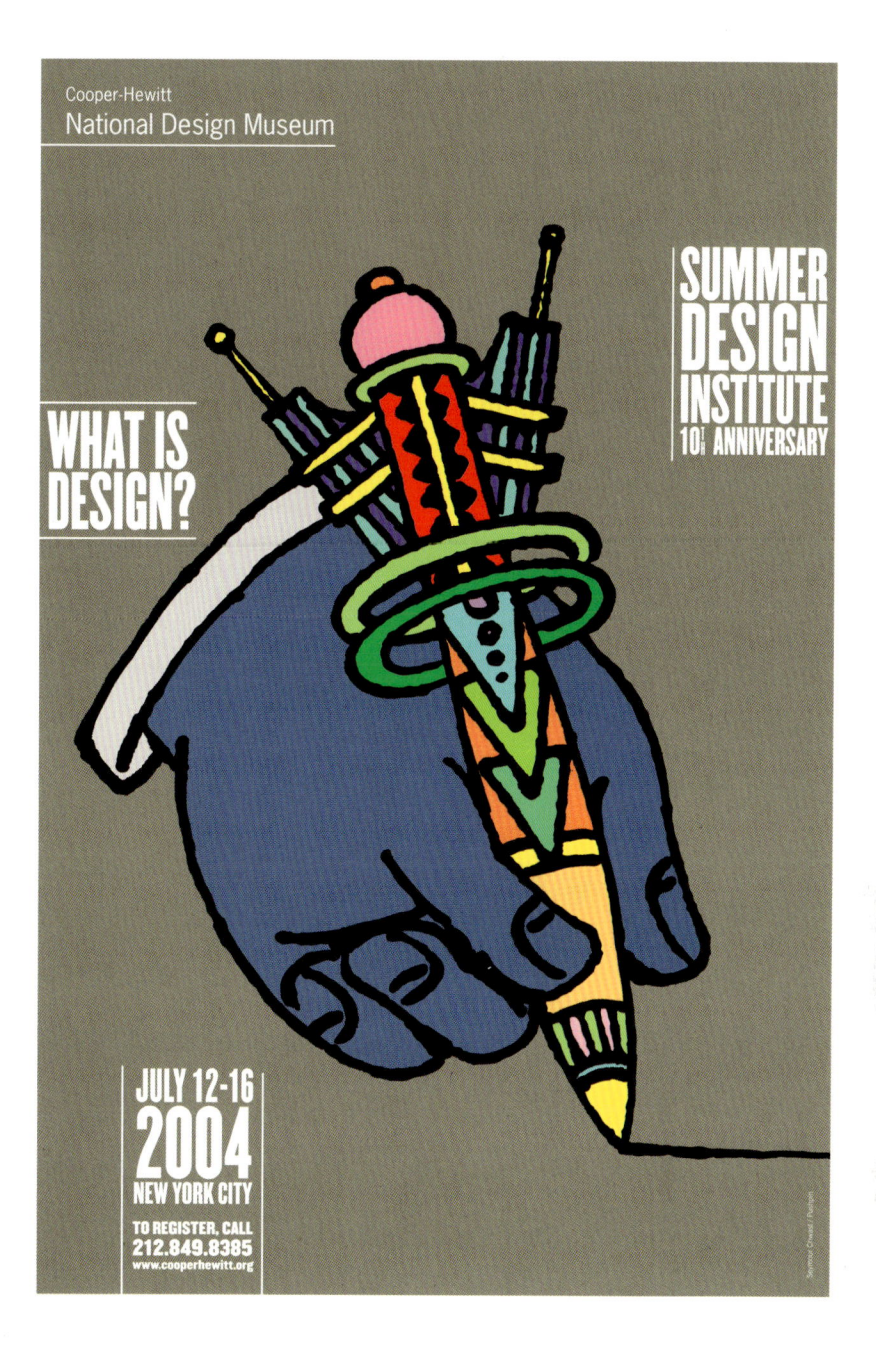

C U B A
HAVANA
Bahia Honda
Matanzas
Cardenas
Cienfuegos
Trinidad
Puerto Principe
Nuevitas
Santiago de Cuba
I. OF PINES
Broa B.
C. San Antonio

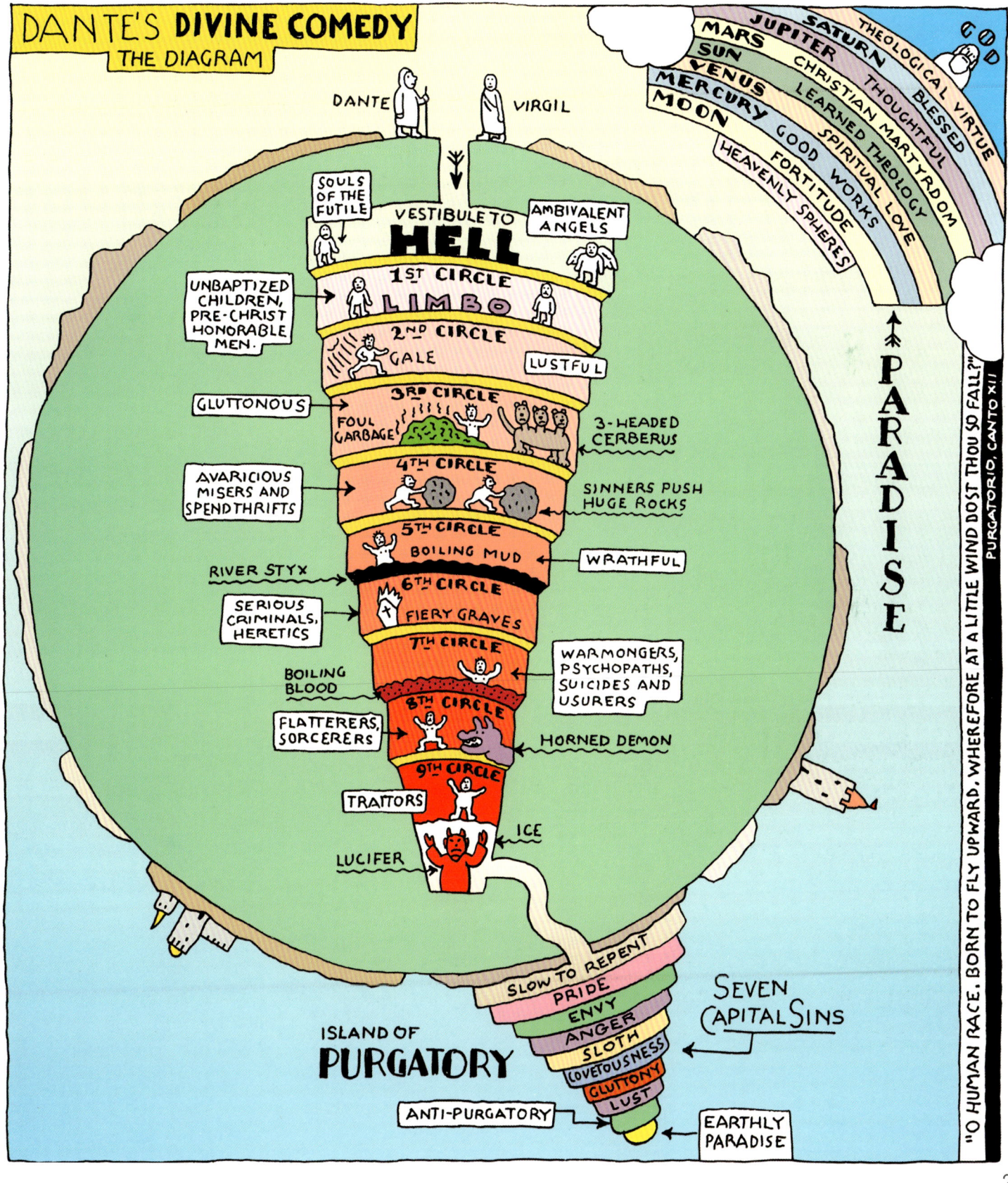

Opposite: Personal drawing titled "Fidel Castro"
Illustration titled "Dante Divine Comedy" for the *New York Times Book Review*

Illustration titled "Hi Rise Hell" from *The Nose No. 10: Hell* for Self-Promotion

Bottom Left: Illustration titled "Groucho"
Top Right: "The Kama Sutra of Reading", for the *New York Times Book Review*

Cover illustration for the magazine, *The New Yorker*

Design titled "End Bad Breath" for Personality Posters, Inc.,

Illustration titled "Crows" for *The New Yorker*
Opposite: Poster titled "No Go" for Peace Conference in the Netherlands

TIME TO ABOLISH WAR

HAGUE APPEAL FOR PEACE
MAY 11-15, 1999
THE HAGUE
OFFICE 777 UN PLAZA
NEW YORK, NY 10017
TEL: 212 687 2623
hap99@igc.apc.org
www.haguepeace.org
or, c/o IALANA, Anna Paulownastraat 103, 2518 BC The Hague, THE NETHERLANDS
tel +31 70 363 4484
ialana@antenna.nl

NO GO

THE HAGUE APPEAL FOR PEACE IS SUPPORTED IN PART BY GRANTS FROM THE MINISTRY OF FOREIGN AFFAIRS, HOLLAND, BARBARA M. WALKER, THE JOHN D. AND CATHERINE T. MACARTHUR FOUNDATION, LIFEBRIDGE FOUNDATION, PAUL AND DAISY SOROS FOUNDATION, SAMUEL RUBIN FOUNDATION, STEWART MOTT CHARITABLE TRUST

From Self-promotion publication, *The Nose No. 10: Hell*
Opposite: From Self-promotion publication, *The Nose No. 4: Electric Follies*

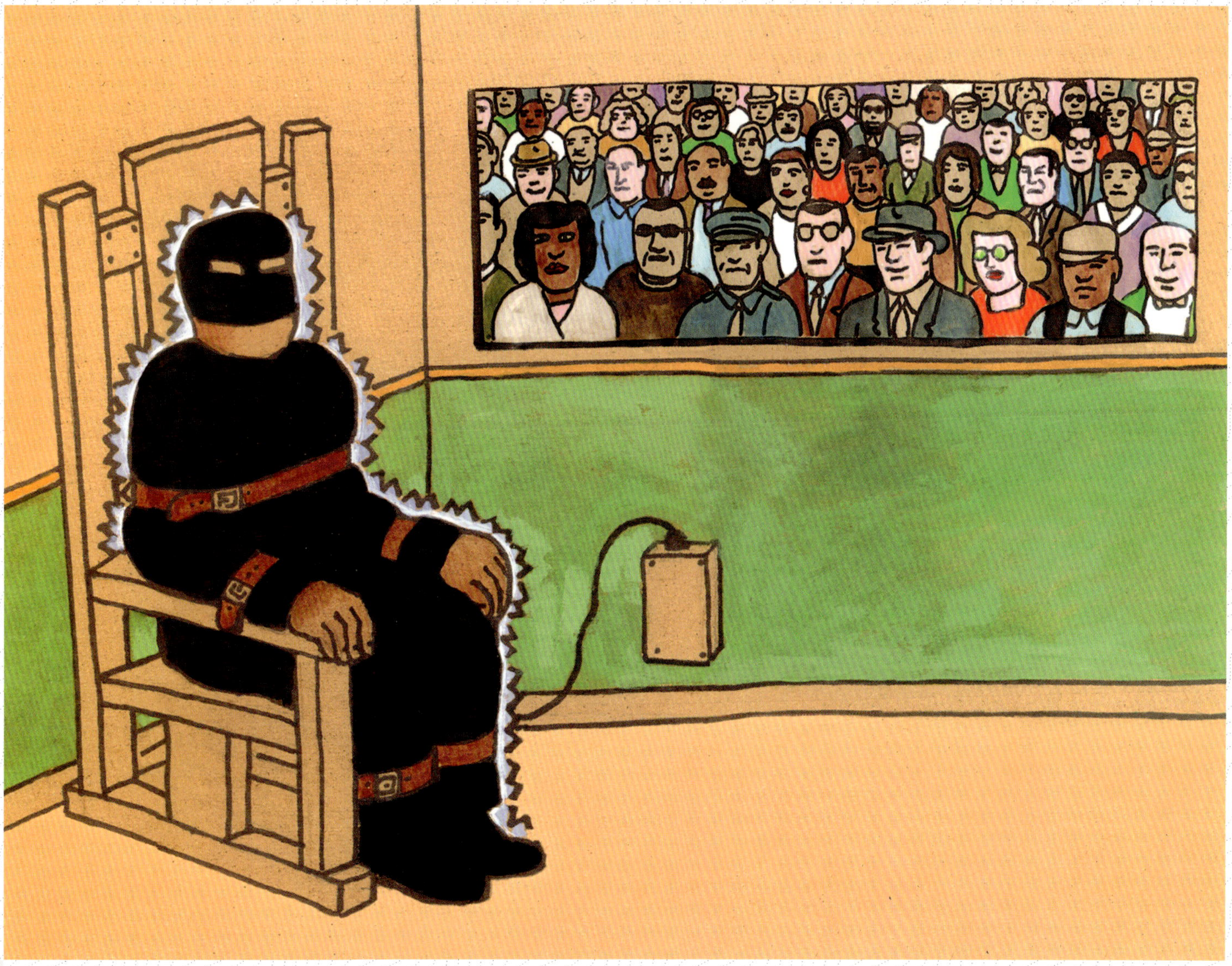

THE NOSE no. 11

TRICKS

Opposite: Cover for self-promotion publication, *The Nose No.11: Tricks*
Illustration for self-promotion calendar

Bottom Left: Poster for the anniversary of Toulouse-Lautrec's death
Top Right: Packaging for Serendipity 3, a restaurant in New York

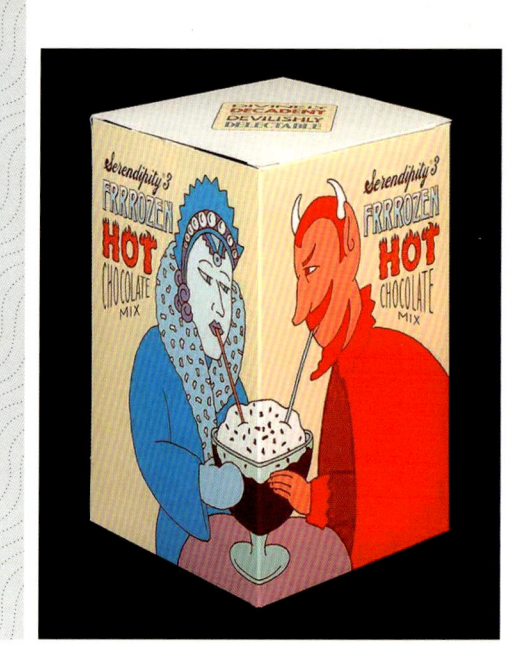

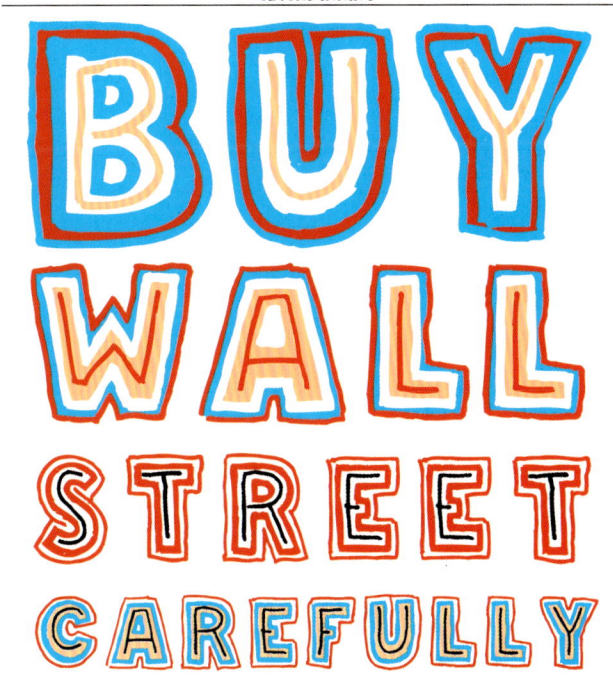

Layout design for Ultratype catalogue, alphabet design marketed by House Industries

Stefan Sagmeister

Stefan Sagmeister was born in 1962 in Austria. He now lives and works in New York.

Stefan sagmeister studied graphic design at the University of Applied Arts in Vienna. In 1987, Sagmeister won a Fulbright scholarship from the Pratt Institute in Brooklyn, New York. Here humour emerged as the dominant theme in his work. After three years in the US, Sagmeister returned to Austria for community service. He stayed in Austria working as a graphic designer before moving to Hong Kong in 1991 to join the advertising agency, Leo Burnett. In 1993 he returned to New York (via Sri Lanka) to work for Tibor Kalman at M&Co. When the studio closed at the same year, Sagmeister opened his own office "Sagmeister Inc.", and began to design branding, graphics and packaging for clients as diverse as the Rolling Stones, David Byrne, Lou Reed, Aerosmith and many others. Having been nominated five times for the Grammies, he finally won one for the Talking Heads boxed set. His list of clients includes the American Institute of Graphic Arts, Guggenheim Museum, HBO and Time Warner.

He has earned practically every important international design award. Solo shows of Sagmeister Inc.'s work have been mounted in Zurich, Vienna, New York City, Berlin, Tokyo, Osaka, Prague, Cologne and Seoul. He teaches in the graduate department of the School of Visual Art in New York, and lectures extensively on all continents. In 2001, a best-selling monograph about his work titled *Sagmeister Made You Look* was published by Booth-Clibborn editions.

Astonishingly, despite all these accomplishments, Stefan Sagmeister has only learned twenty or so things in his life so far. But he has managed to publish these personal maxims all over the world, in spaces normally occupied by advertisements and promotions such as billboards, projections, light-boxes, magazine spreads, annual report covers, fashion brochures, and, recently, on giant inflatable monkeys. In 2008 Abrams published these works, spanning the past seven years, in the book titled *Things I Have Learned In My Life So Far*.

PROJECT: DETROIT POSTER
TYPE: POSTER
CLIENT: AIGA DETROIT

"For this lecture poster for the AIGA Detroit in 1999, we tried to visualise the pain that seems to accompany most of our design projects. Our intern Martin cut all the type into my skin. Yes, it did hurt badly. Size: 27.5" x 39" (69cm x 99 cm), Photography: Tom Schierlitz." – Stefan Sagmeister

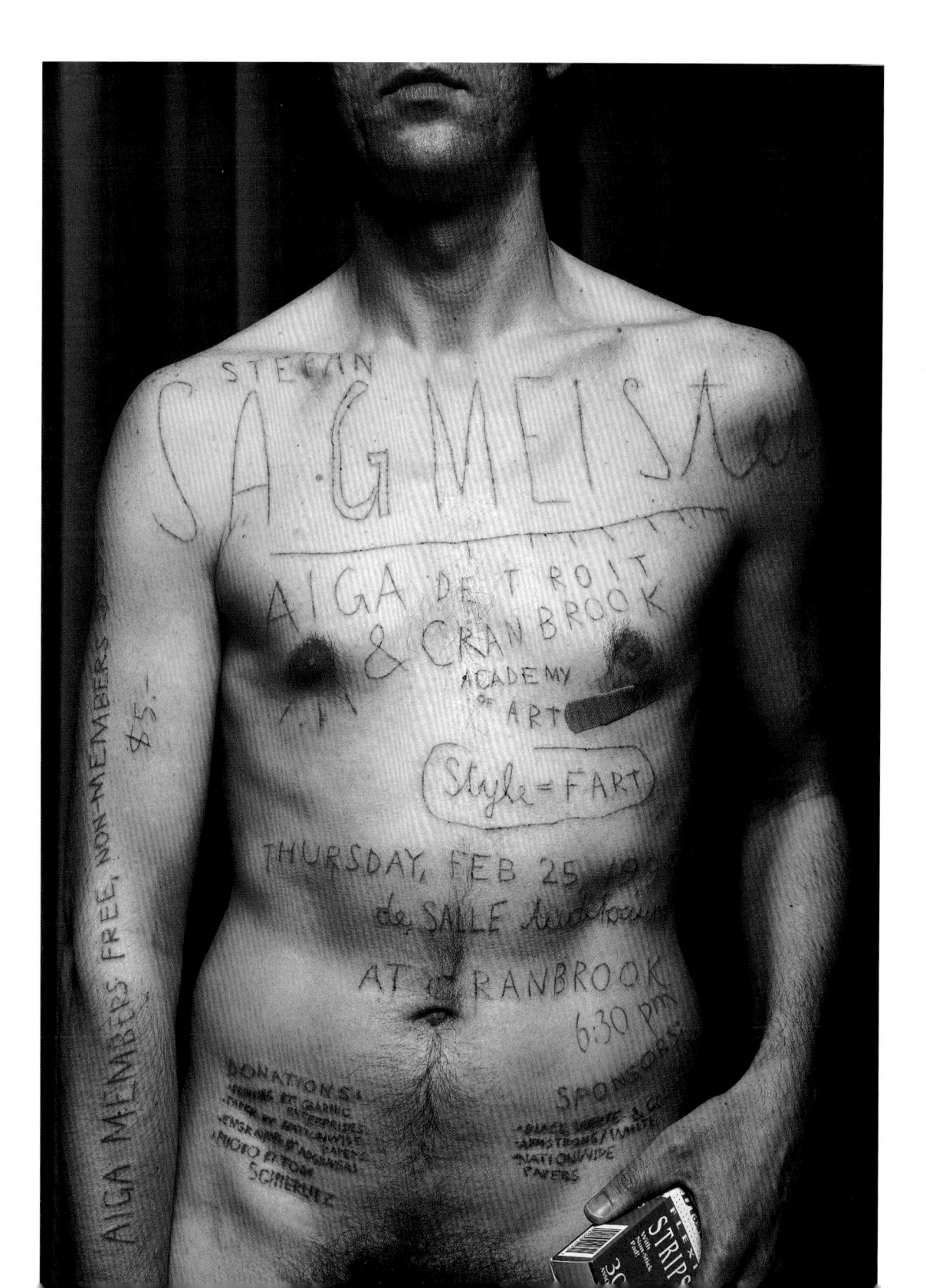

The letters "Trying to Look Good Limits My Life" are displayed in sequence as typographic billboards in Paris for Art Grandeur Nature, and they together work like a sentimental greeting card left in the park.
Opposite: Poster for Adobe Achievement Award

2003
Adobe
DESIGN ACHIEVEMENT AWARDS
CALL for ENTRIES.
GETTING AN "A"
ON THIS PROJECT
COULD GET YOU $5000
AND A TRIP TO CHICAGO.
Accepting entries
from APRIL 1
through
MAY 15, 2003.
Adobe
OPEN TO FULL TIME VISUAL ARTS STUDENTS
attending accredited U.S., U.K., and Canadian
(excluding the Province of Quebec)
institutions of higher education and who meet the eligibility
requirements described in the rules.
For more information on rules and submitting
Competition comprises of six individual categories in print, photography, illustration, web, video and experimental

Poster for announcing Lou Reed's new album "Set the Twilight Reeling"

Poster for the AIGA's Fresh Dialogue in New York

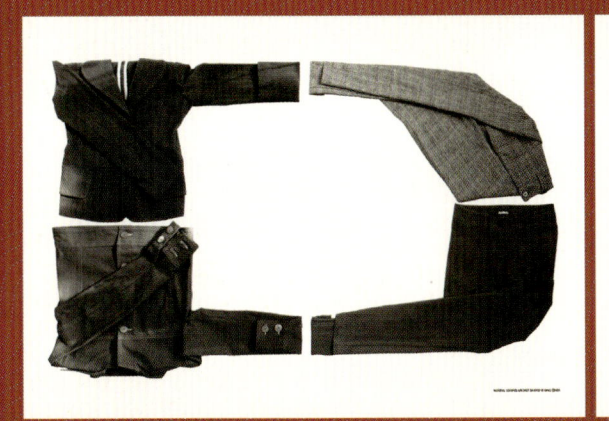

Spreads: Cover and layouts of catalogue spell out: "Material luxuries can be best enjoyed in small doses" for New York fashion designer Anni Kuan

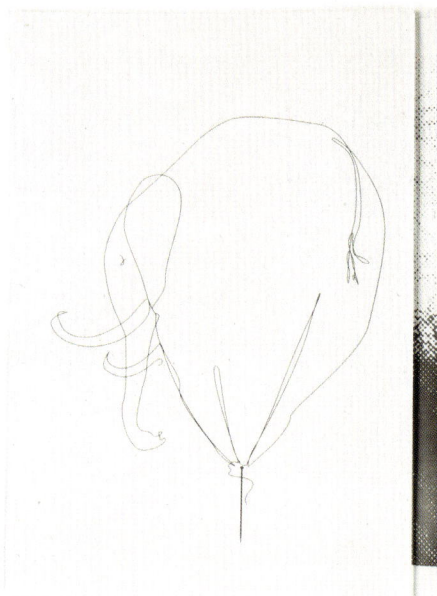

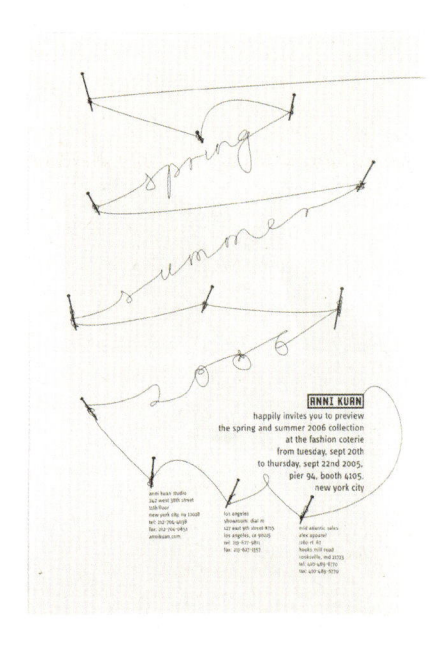

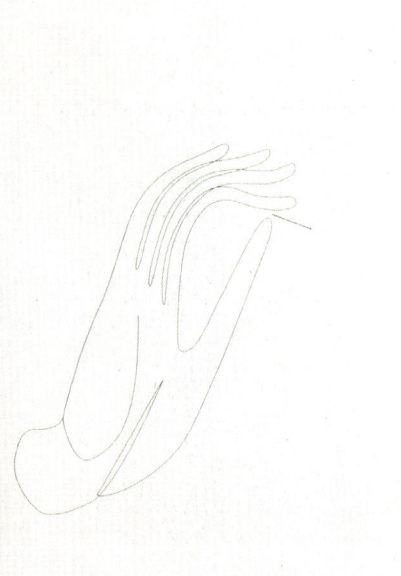

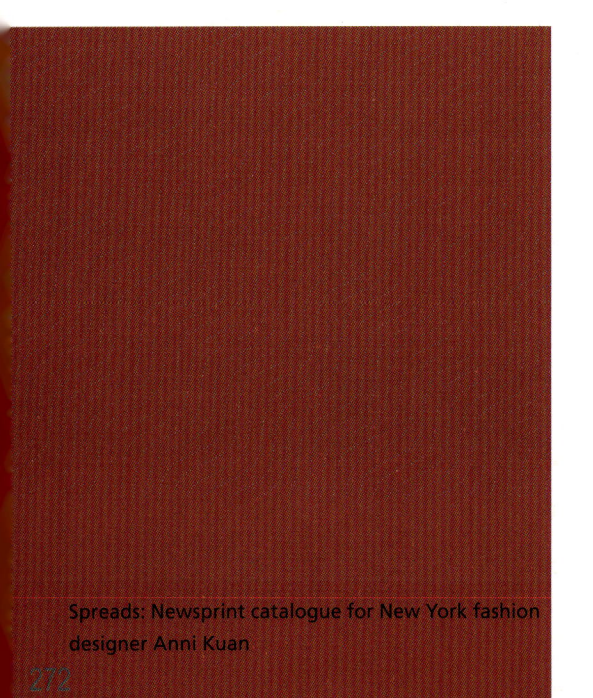

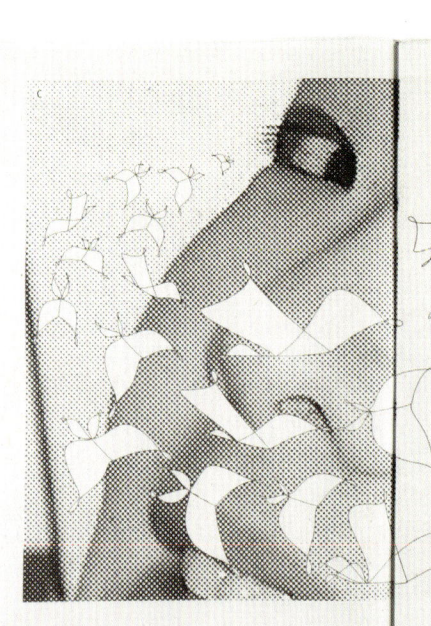

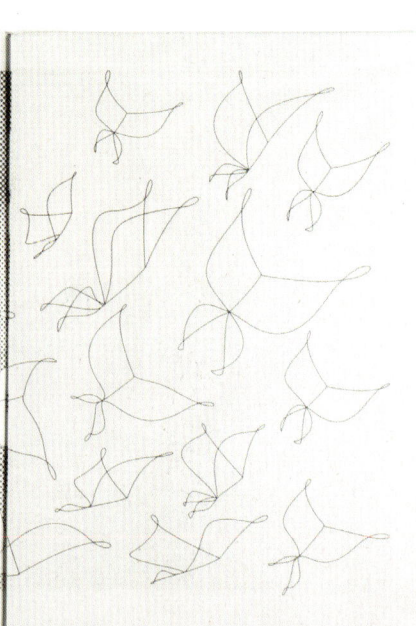

Spreads: Newsprint catalogue for New York fashion designer Anni Kuan

273

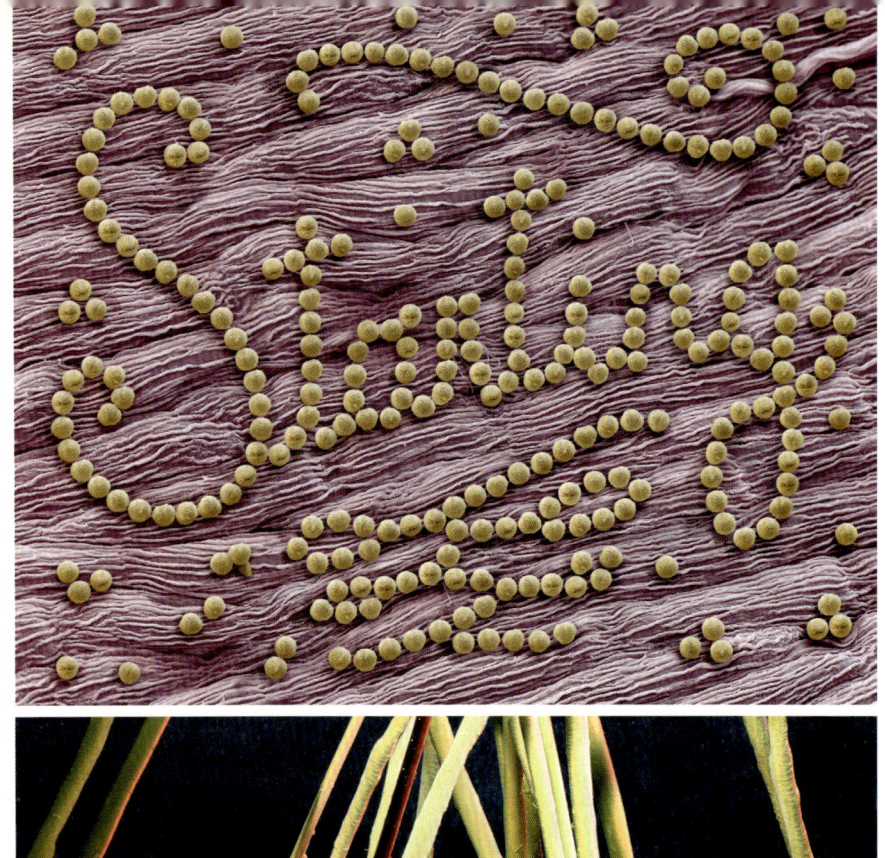

Spreads: An installment in the series of *Things I Have Learned in My Life So Far*, these dividing pages for *.Copy* magazine (Austria)

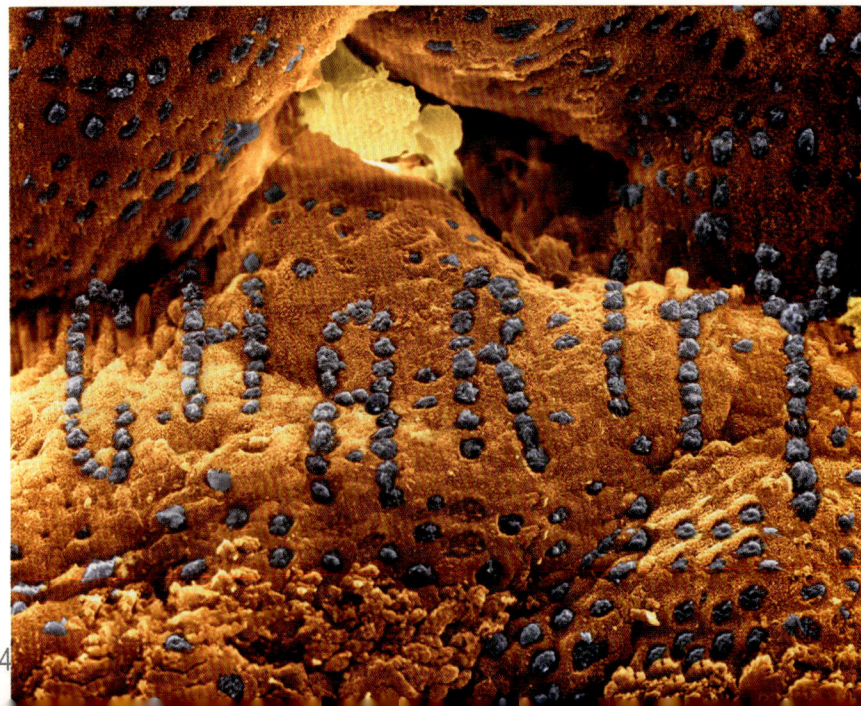

SURPRISINGLY EASY

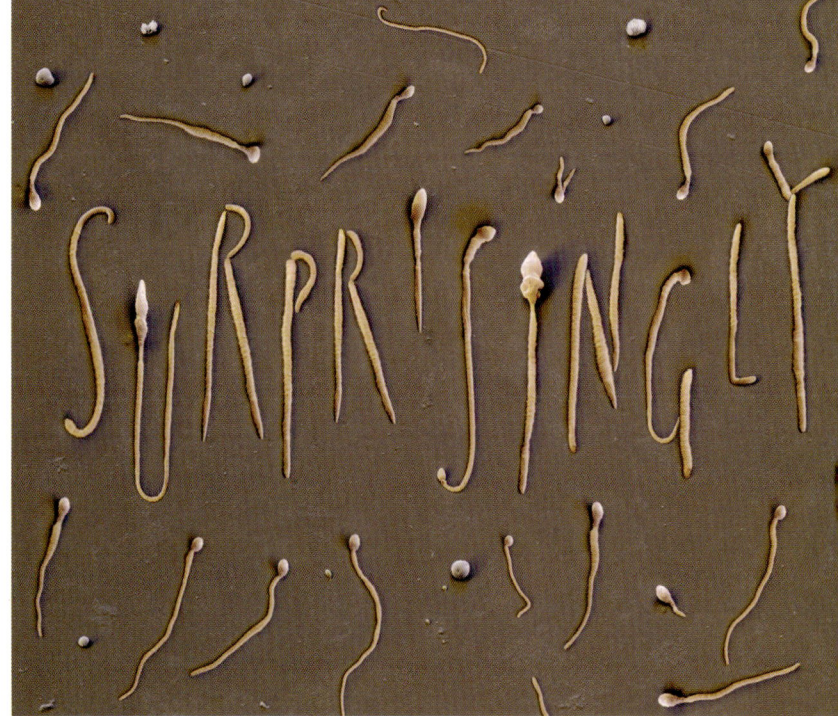

Spreads: CD Packaging design for Jamie Block

276

PRODUCED BY:
Mark HUTCHINS
& JAMIE Block
www.blocknyc.com
DPRO 7087 6 12893 2 9
www.blocknyc.com

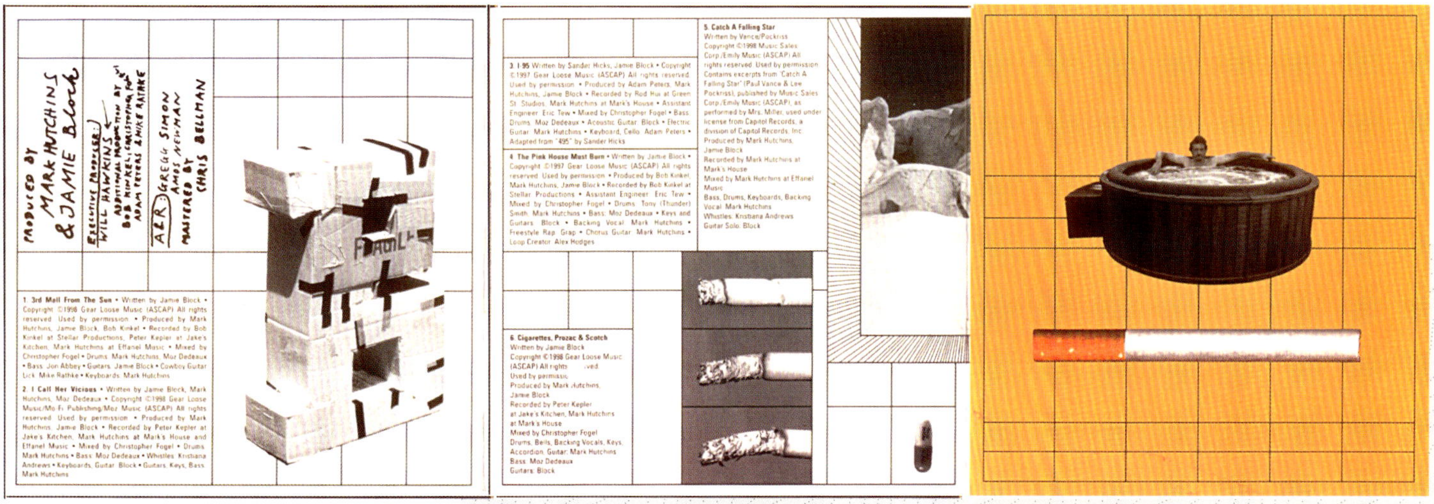
PRODUCED BY MARK HUTCHINS & JAMIE Block
EXECUTIVE PRODUCER: WILL HAWKINS
A&R: GREGG SIMON
AMOS NEWMAN
MASTERED BY CHRIS BELLMAN
1. 3rd Mall From The Sun • Written by Jamie Block • Copyright ©1998 Gear Loose Music (ASCAP) All rights reserved. Used by permission. • Produced by Mark Hutchins, Jamie Block, Bob Kinkel • Recorded by Bob Kinkel at Stellar Productions, Peter Kepler at Jake's Kitchen, Mark Hutchins at Effanel Music • Mixed by Christopher Fogel • Drums: Mark Hutchins, Moz Dedeaux • Bass: Jon Abbey • Guitars: Jamie Block • Cowboy Guitar Lick: Mike Rathke • Keyboards: Mark Hutchins
2. I Call Her Vicious • Written by Jamie Block, Mark Hutchins, Moz Dedeaux • Copyright ©1998 Gear Loose Music/Mo-Fi Publishing/Moz Music (ASCAP) All rights reserved. Used by permission. • Produced by Mark Hutchins, Jamie Block • Recorded by Peter Kepler at Jake's Kitchen, Mark Hutchins at Mark's House and Effanel Music • Mixed by Christopher Fogel • Drums: Mark Hutchins • Bass: Moz Dedeaux • Whistles: Kristiana Andrews • Keyboards, Guitar: Block • Guitars, Keys, Bass: Mark Hutchins
3. I-95 Written by Sander Hicks, Jamie Block • Copyright ©1997 Gear Loose Music (ASCAP) All rights reserved. Used by permission. • Produced by Adam Peters, Mark Hutchins, Jamie Block • Recorded by Rod Hui at Green St. Studios, Mark Hutchins at Mark's House • Assistant Engineer: Eric Tew • Mixed by Christopher Fogel • Bass, Drums: Moz Dedeaux • Acoustic Guitar: Block • Electric Guitar: Mark Hutchins • Keyboard, Cello: Adam Peters • Adapted from "495" by Sander Hicks
4. The Pink House Must Burn • Written by Jamie Block • Copyright ©1997 Gear Loose Music (ASCAP) All rights reserved. Used by permission. • Produced by Bob Kinkel, Mark Hutchins, Jamie Block • Recorded by Bob Kinkel at Stellar Productions • Assistant Engineer: Eric Tew • Mixed by Christopher Fogel • Drums: Tony (Thunder) Smith, Mark Hutchins • Bass: Moz Dedeaux • Keys and Guitars: Block • Backing Vocal: Mark Hutchins • Freestyle Rap: Grap • Chorus Guitar: Mark Hutchins • Loop Creator: Alex Hodges
5. Catch A Falling Star
Written by Vance/Pockriss
Copyright ©1998 Music Sales Corp./Emily Music (ASCAP) All rights reserved. Used by permission.
Contains excerpts from 'Catch A Falling Star' (Paul Vance & Lee Pockriss), published by Music Sales Corp./Emily Music (ASCAP), as performed by Mrs. Miller, used under license from Capitol Records, a division of Capitol Records, Inc.
Produced by Mark Hutchins, Jamie Block
Recorded by Mark Hutchins at Mark's House
Mixed by Mark Hutchins at Effanel Music
Bass, Drums, Keyboards, Backing Vocal: Mark Hutchins
Whistles: Kristiana Andrews
Guitar Solo: Block
6. Cigarettes, Prozac & Scotch
Written by Jamie Block
Copyright ©1998 Gear Loose Music (ASCAP) All rights …ved.
Used by permissic
Produced by Mark ‚lutchins, Jamie Block
Recorded by Peter Kepler at Jake's Kitchen, Mark Hutchins at Mark's House
Mixed by Christopher Fogel
Drums, Bells, Backing Vocals, Keys, Accordion, Guitar: Mark Hutchins
Bass: Moz Dedeaux
Guitars: Block

Spreads: Book Packaging design and layouts for David Byrne

Your Canceled Check Is Your Receipt. No Purchase Necessary. Employees And Their Families Are Not Eligible. Sanitized For Your Protection. Beware Of Dog. Contestants Have Been Briefed On Some Questions Before The Show. Limited Time Offer. Call Now To Ensure Prompt Delivery. You Must Be Present To Win. Slightly Higher West Of The Mississippi. Avoid Contact With Skin. Shading Within A Garment May Occur. Keep Away From Fire Or Flames. Replace With Same Type. Approved For Veterans. Price Does Not Include Taxes. No Solicitors. No Alcohol, Dogs Or Horses. Some Equipment Shown Is Optional. Reproduction Strictly Prohibited. Driver Does Not Carry Cash.

You are accosted in a dark alley by 3 armed youths who demand your wallet, but you are, unbeknown to them, carrying a powerful semi-automatic weapon.

Do you:
A. ☐ Administer justice. Shoot first and ask questions later, it's self defense.
B. ☐ Pull your weapon but leave the scene peacefully.
C. ☐ Give up your wallet and avoid the risk of violent confrontation.

279

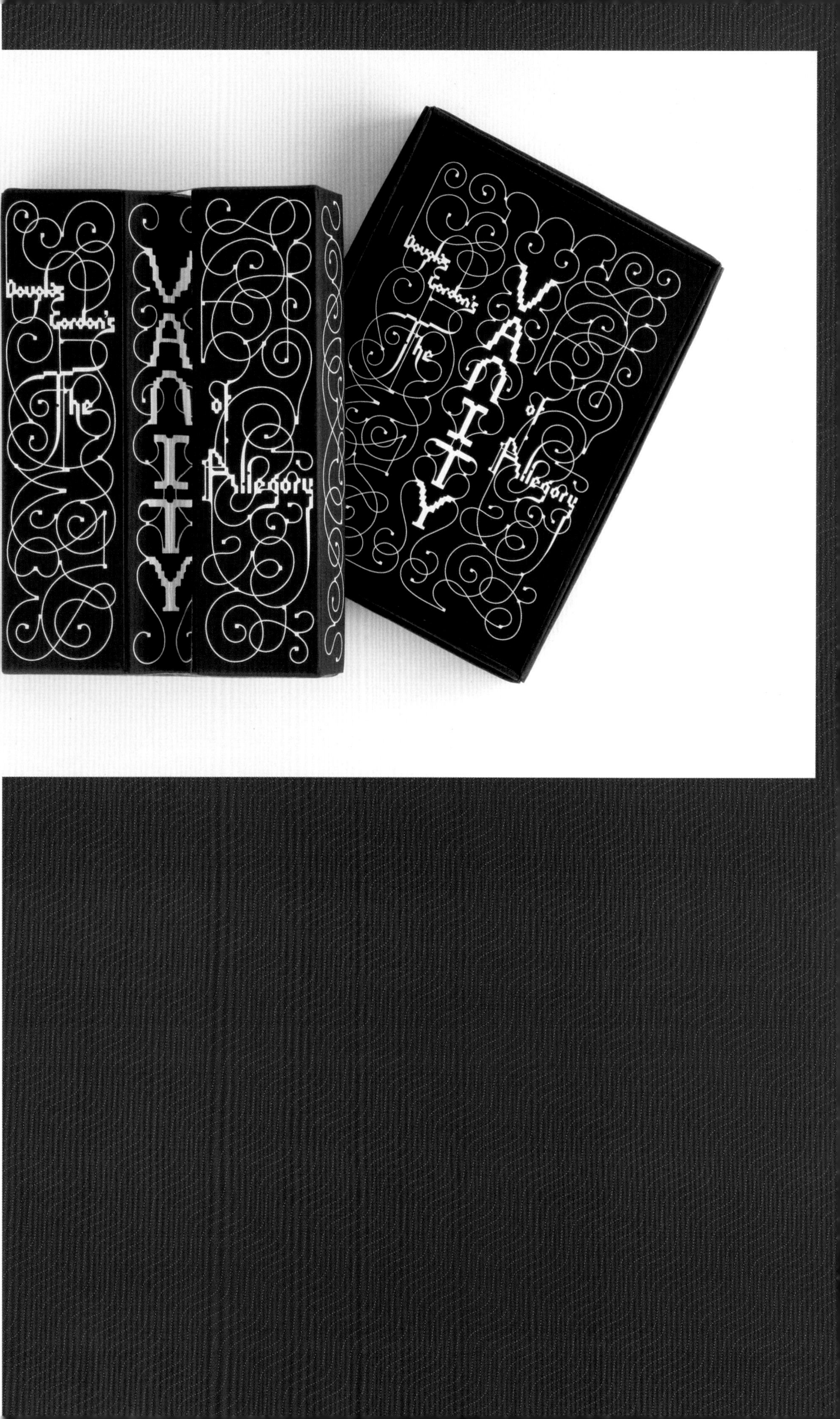
Douglas Gordon's
The
VANITY
of
Allegory

Spreads: Packaging design for Douglas Gordon's entire exhibition "The Vanity of Allegory" at the Guggenheim Museum, Berlin

Spreads: Billboard for the Experimenta in Lisbon, made out of newsprint paper

283

284

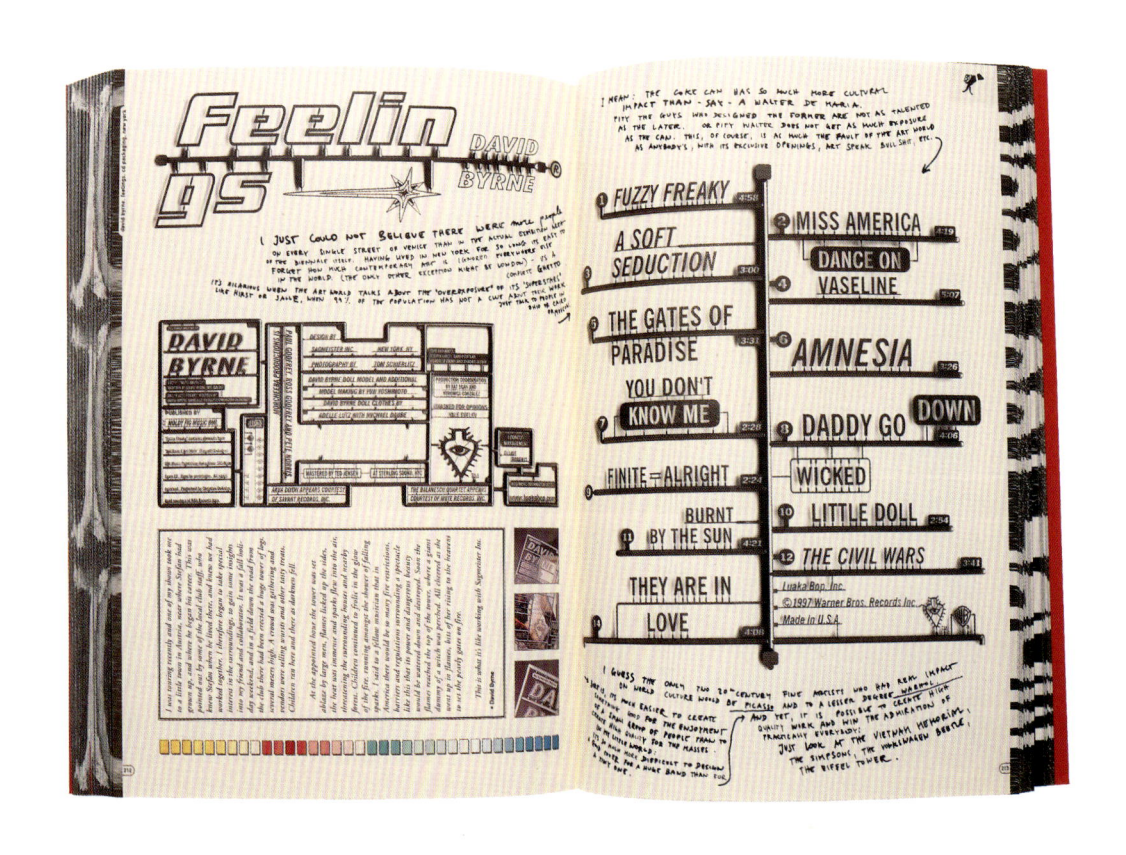

Book Design, paperback in a red transparent slip case

Spreads: Identity for Move Our Money

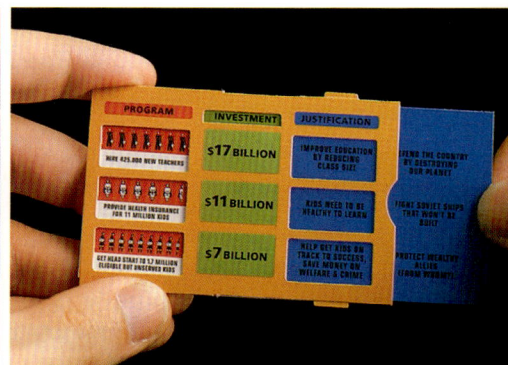

287

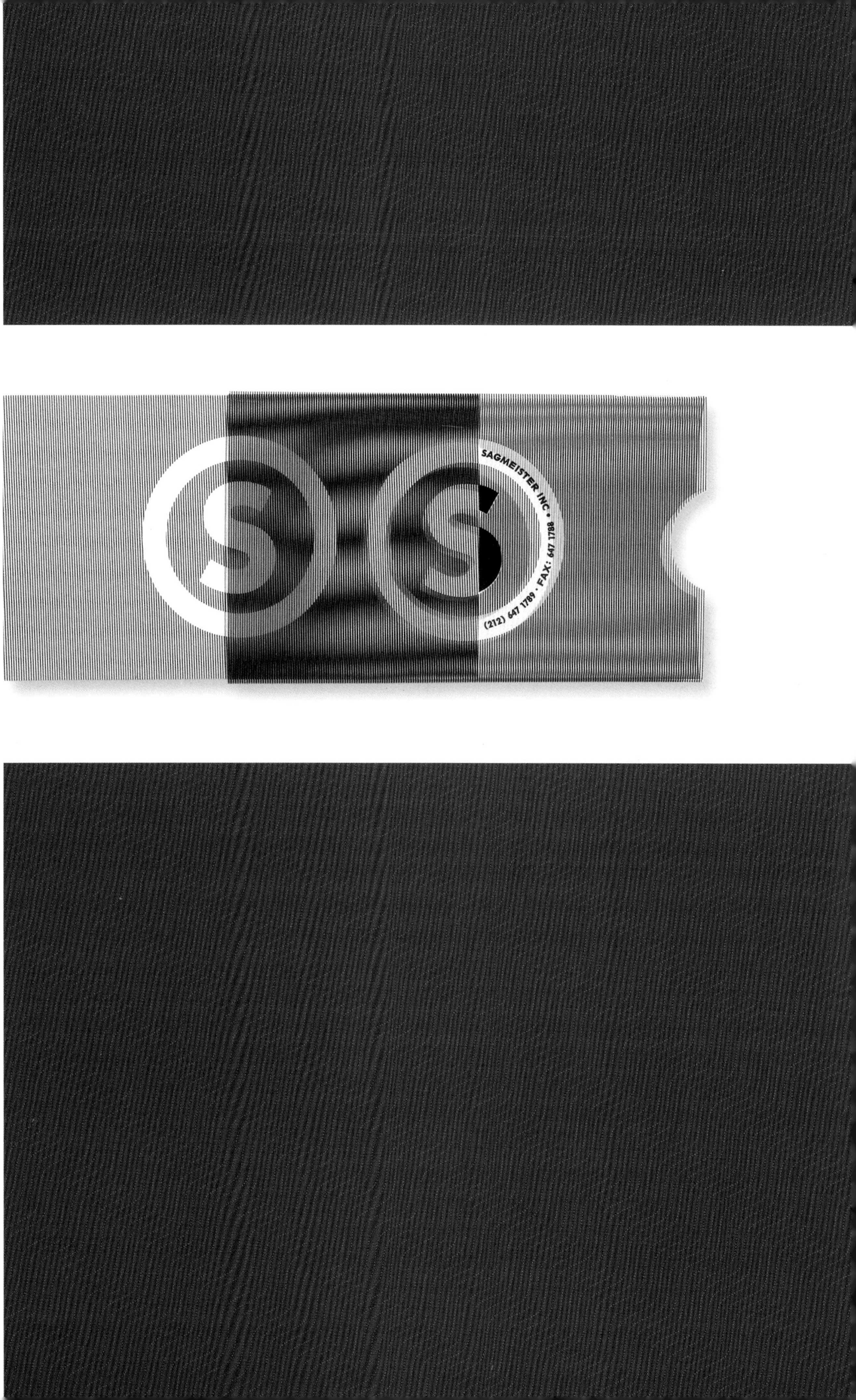
SAGMEISTER INC. •
(212) 647 1789 • FAX: 647 1788 •

Spreads: Card Design for Sagmeister Inc.

SAGMEISTER
Handarbeit
Museum für Gestaltung
Zürich
Ausstellungsstrasse 60
8005 Zürich
Ausstellung
3. Sept.–9. Nov.
2003
Öffnungszeiten:
Dienstag bis Donnerstag
10.00 bis 20.00 Uhr
Freitag bis Sonntag
11.00 bis 18.00 Uhr
Montag leider geschlossen.
Eine Ausstellung von
MAK, Wien
DIESE ANZÜGE SIND ein DIAGRAMM
Feelings
DAVID BYRNE
LOU REED
SAGMEISTER

Opposite: Poster for the exhibition of Sagmeister Inc. in Zurich
Poster for SVA

292

Spreads: Packaging design titled "Once in a Lifetime" contains 3 CDs and 1 DVD. This panoramic Talking Heads collection features cover paintings by the Russian contemporary artists Vladimir Dubossarsky and Alexander Vinogradov.

Spreads: Cover and images for Annual Report of Zumtobel AG, a leading
European manufacturer of lighting systems

295

Toni Traglia

Toni Traglia is an Italy-Swiss graphic designer and trained himself in Berna at the "Schule fuer Gestaltung". Since 1987 he has worked in the advertising field for the first five years of his working activity and then he specialised in the art direction, working for agencies located in Switzerland and Milan.

He has been entrusted with corporate design and packaging works. This is a sector of the visual communication of which he has always been fond, so he decided to work only with those companies, which needed his collaboration in this field.

When Toni Traglia begins a project, he follows ways to create functional and seductive design. Having worked with a lot of professionals in the brand and packaging design field, he tries to catch up with this objective by bearing in mind the different philosophies. Toni Traglia takes each job with a unique and personal approach. Essentially, his system of ideas is able to single out the different information of each job, in order to develop a project. It's necessary to understand and clearly analyse the client's needs and a correct understanding of his requirements will lead to the structure upon which one will construct creative concepts. However, this philosophy will mean nothing if the final result is not attractive. A sign should evoke fascination, which is also an essential function of visual communication as well as the role of the graphic designer.

PROJECT: CORPORATE IDENTITY
TYPE: LOGO
CLIENT: FUNKY JAZZ DANCE

"The target of the 'Funky Jazz Dance' graphic symbol was therefore to gain energy and lightness of this dance art. The research of spirituality and freedom through the body expression was the request of the customer." – Toni Traglia

Left: Cover of a dépliant for the tecnopolimers firm "Ga.Gi" S.p.A.
Right: Cover of a folder for technical files for the tecnopolimers firm "Ga.Gi" S.p.A.

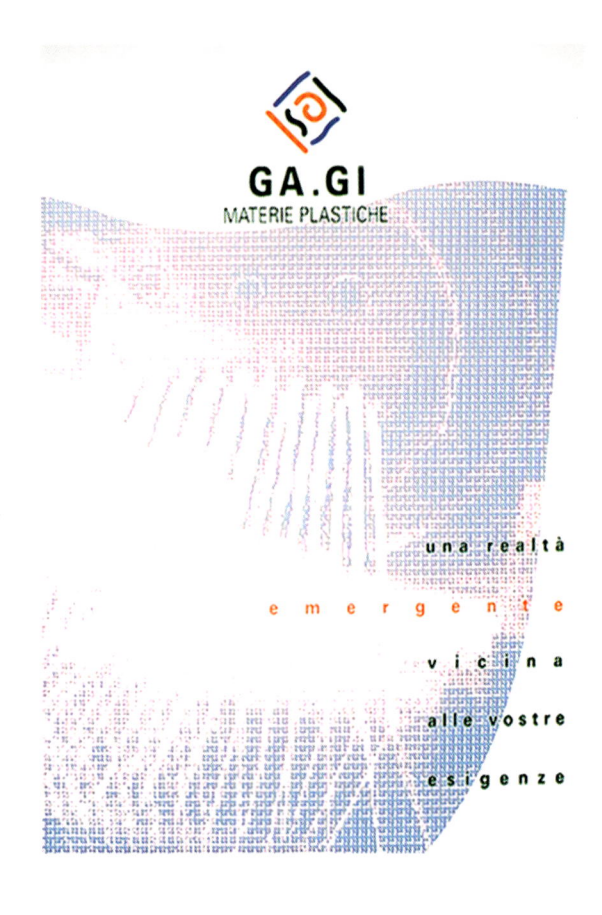

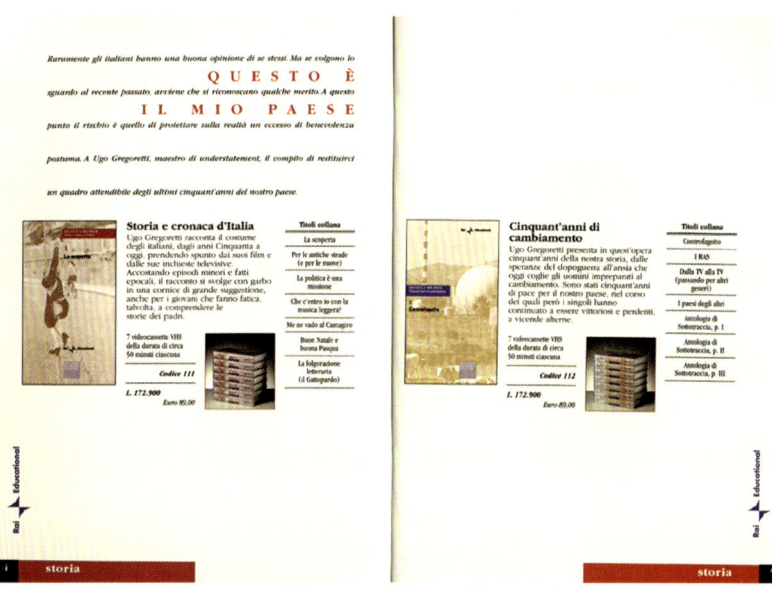

Bottom Left: Cover of a dépliant for the information firm Primenet
Top Right: In co-operation with and on behalf of the advertising agency Carcano &
Magnaghi-layout of a mail order selling catalogue for RAI Trade

Left: Project in brand and packaging design of "Vinò" for Cantine di Soave
Right: Project of structural design of the cosmetic trousse "Elegant" for Christian Ros's s.r.l.

Left: Project of a gadget with the application of the corporate identity "MilanOk" for Comune di Milano-Settore Turismo
Right: Restyling of the brand and packaging design "Blue Rose" and structural design for this new premium confection for the Icam S.p.A

The brand and packaging design "Virtù di Gola" for la Spiga Italia wants to reveal the love for naturalness.

Top: Brand and packaging design "Filabella" for Filab
Bottom: Brand and packaging design "Napolidea" for Agriovo

Top: Brand and packaging design for Vanini
Bottom: Restyling of brand and packaging design "Elegant" for Christian Ros's S.r.l.
Opposite: The brand and packaging design for Caffé Italiano interprets the nature of Italian taste and style

Caffé Italiano
creazioni dell'arte cioccolatiera italiana
Praline Assortite con Cremoso Ripieno al Caffè e al Liquore.
Assorted Pralines with Creamy Coffee and Liqueur Fillings
Espresso
Cappuccino
Corretto con Grappa
ICAM
Italian Chocolates by Agostoni da Morbegno
270g e
Caffé Italiano

Caffé Italiano
Espresso
Caffé Italiano
Cappuccino
Caffé Italiano
Corretto

Spreads: In co-operation with and on behalf of the advertising agency Carcano & Magnaghi restyling in brand and packaging design of "Wool Club"

WOOL
club

WOOL
club
la firma dei filati preziosi
MOZART · CHAINTECLAIR
WAGNER · CHAINTECLAIR
BRISBANE

U.G.Sato

U.G.Sato was born in Tokyo. After graduating from Kuwasawa Design School in 1960, he established Design Farm in 1975. Through the years he has held numerous solo exhibitions including "My Theory of Evolution" (1972 Tokyo), shows at the Lahti Art Museum (Finland), Print Gallery (Amsterdam), GGG (Tokyo), DDD (Osaka), Kawasaki City Gallery (Kawasaki), Taka-saki Art Museum (Takasaki), the Museum & Gallery in International Design Centre (Nagoya), Gallery Rambow (Güstrow), etc.

He has also participated in the following joint exhibitions: "Wood Boxes" (91 Gallery, New York); "Contemporary Humor" (Saitama Museum of Modern Art); "Art Is Fun" (Hara Art Museum); Poster Exhibition for Images International Pour les Droits de l' Homme et du citoyen (France and 39 other countries); "Beauty of Japanese Art" (Retretti Art Centre), etc.

Among the major awards, he has garnered to date including: Gold Prize at International Biennale of Graphic Design Brno (1978); Gold Prize at Poster Biennale in Lahti (1979); "Bulgarian Artists Federation Award in Sculpture" at Humor and Satire Biennale in Gabrovo (1989); Gold Prize at Warsaw International Poster Biennale (1996); Gold Bee at International Biennale of Graphic Design Moscow (1998); Gold Prize at International Eco Poster Exhibition (1998); Special Prize at Helsinki Poster Biennale (1997); Bronze Prize at International Triennial of Poster in Toyama (1997, 2000) and Gold Prize at Aosta International Ecological Poster Exhibition (2001).

His numerous publications include: *the World of Evolution of U.G.Sato* (Shisakusha), *U.G.Sato* (GGG Books No.36), *U.G.Sato* (Lingnan Art Publishing House), *Zoo*, *Red and Blue*, *Two-and Four-legged Animals*, *Rainy and Sunny*, *the Zebras Go Walking*, *Japanese Package*, *Poster*, and *Wood Boxes* (Rikuyo-sha, co-authored).

He is a member of AGI, JAGDA, TIS.

PROJECT: WHERE CAN NATURE GO?
TYPE: POSTER
CLIENT: NO COMMISSIONED POSTER

"This poster is one of ecological series on the theme of 'live and let live'. I appeal disappearing crisis of forests in the world through illusory expression of trees and birds formed." – U.G.Sato

U. G. Sato's Visual Structure of Humour, Illusion and Satire
The Museum & Gallery in International Design Center, Nagoya 11am-8pm. 18 July-3 August 2003

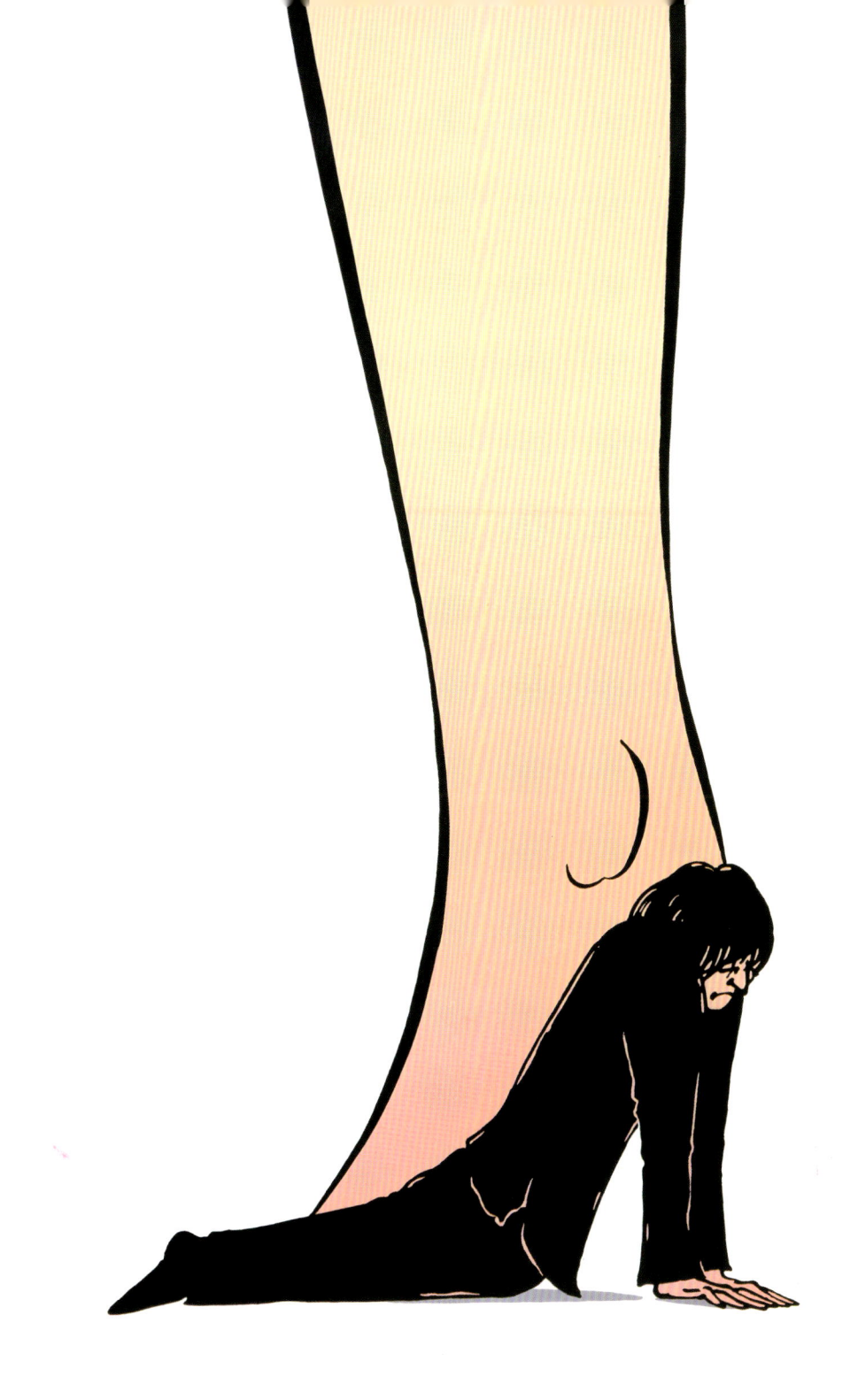

U.G. SATO'S STYLE OF EVOLUTION

Opposite: Poster titled "U.G.sato's Visual Structure of Humour, Illusion and Satire" for the museum in International Design Centre, Nagoya
Poster titled "U.g.sato's Style of Evolution" (No Commissioned poster)

Poster titled "Japanese Sake IPPIN" for Yoshikubo Brewery co., Ltd
Opposite: Poster titled "Face" (No Commissioned poster)

FACE by U.G. Sato
かお

Series No.1 : cool man

http://www.kt.rim.or.jp/~ugsato/

Left: Poster titled "Anti Nuclear Test by France" for Japan Graphic Designers Association
Right: Poster titled "Global Warming" for UNFCCC - COP3 - Kyoto

Top: Poster titled "FREEDOM" for ARTIS 89
Bottom: Poster titled "Preserve the Natural Heritage"
(No commissioned poster)

BREAK THROUGH TO **FREEDOM**

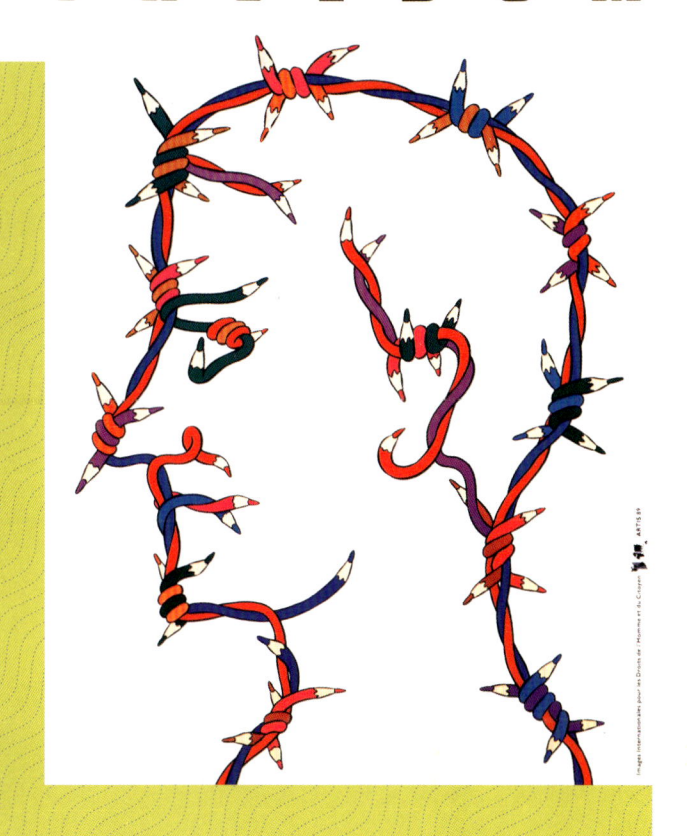

PRESERVE THE NATURAL HERITAGE

Poster titled "Where can Nature go?" (No commissioned poster)
Opposite: Poster titled "Henri de Toulouse LAUTREC" for Nouvean Salon des 100 Exposition International d'affiches, homage

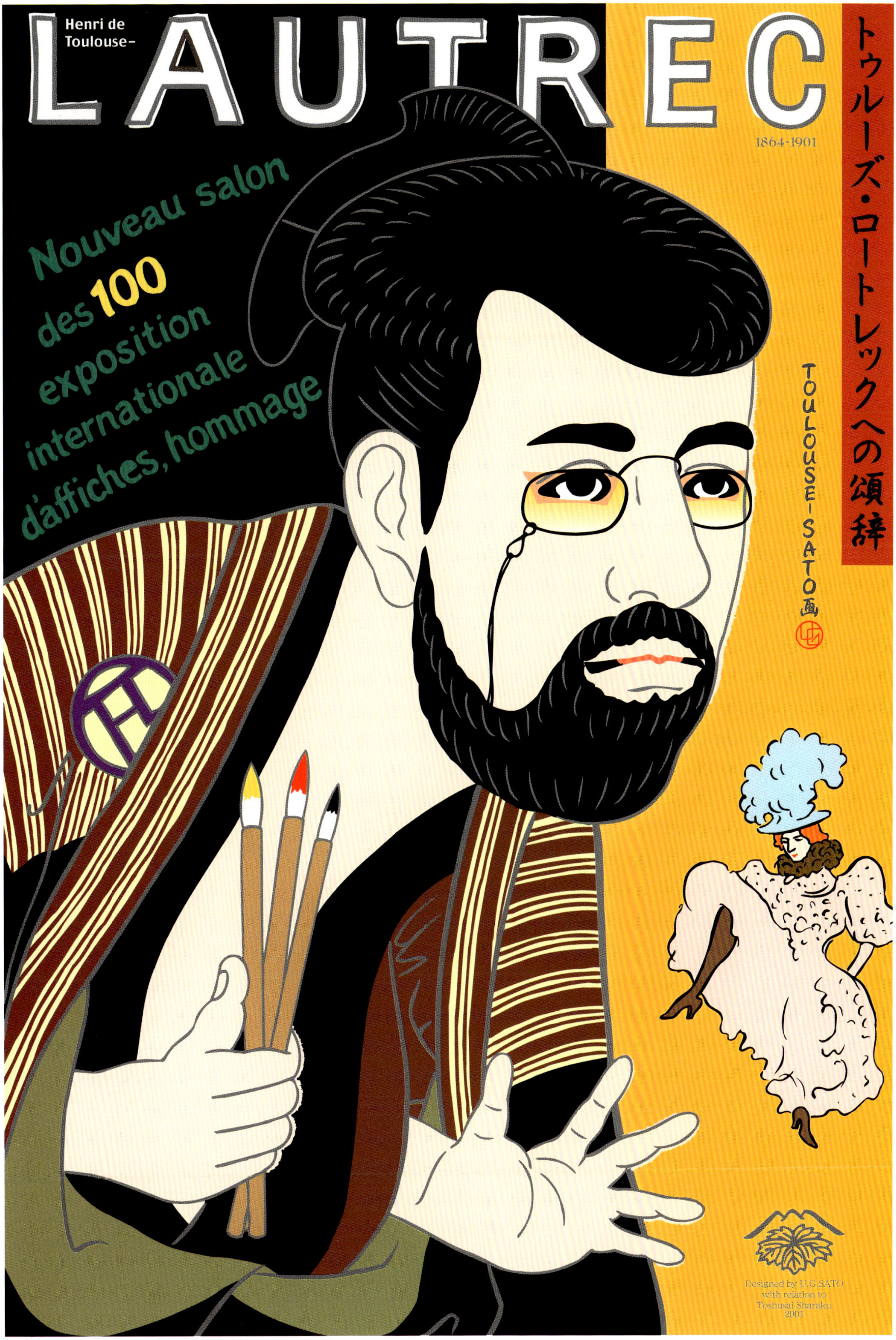
Henri de
Toulouse-
LAUTREC
1864-1901
トゥルーズ・ロートレックへの頌辞
Nouveau salon
des 100
exposition
internationale
d'affiches, hommage
TOULOUSE-SATO画
Designed by U.G.SATO
with relation to
Toshusai Sharaku
2001

WIND OF DESIGN EXHIBITION
The Museum in Tokyo National Fine Arts and Music
6 October–25 November 2001

Opposite: Poster titled "Wind of Design" for the museum in Tokyo Natural Fine Arts and Music
Poster titled "IGAS' 97" (International Graphic Arts Show) for Printing Arts Organisation Committee

Where
can
Nature
go?

Opposite: Poster titled "Save Green" for Japan Graphic Designers Association
Poster titled "Where can Nature go?" (No commissioned poster)

SAVE ENERGY

たくさんのふしぎ

Animals and Human Being—From Legs to Arms. Published by Fukuinkan-Shoten, Tokyo.

Opposite: Poster titled "Save Energy" (No commissioned poster)
Poster titled "Animals and Human Being" for Fukuinkan Shoten Publishers, Inc.

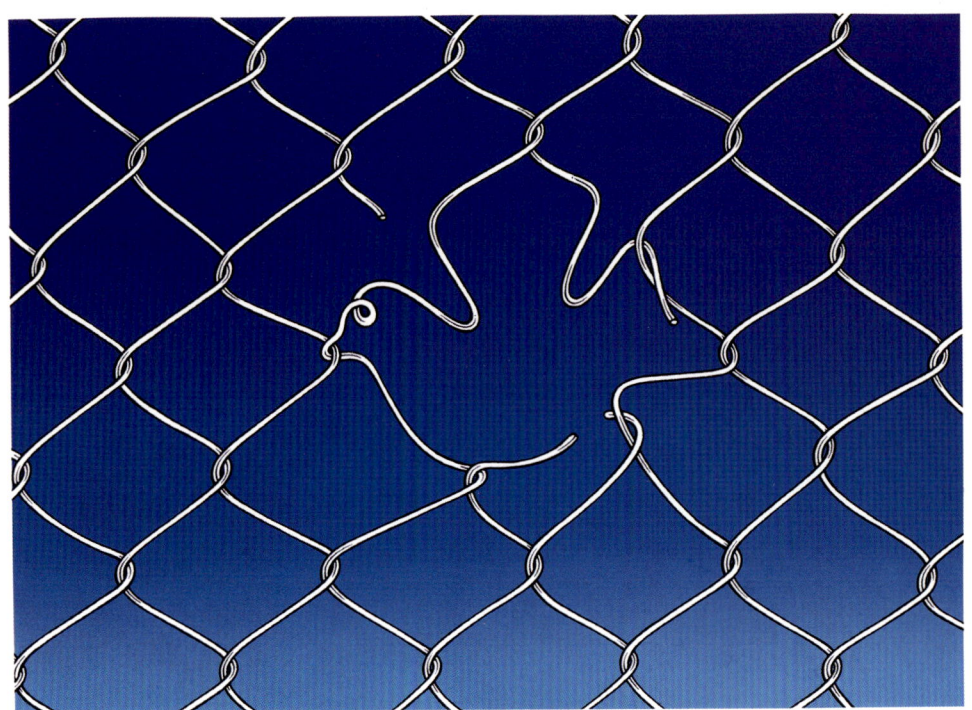

never-ceasing effort to remove its barrier shall we make
for PEACE

Top: Poster titled "Peace" (No commissioned poster)
Bottom: Poster titled "Family of Raccoon" (No commissioned Object)

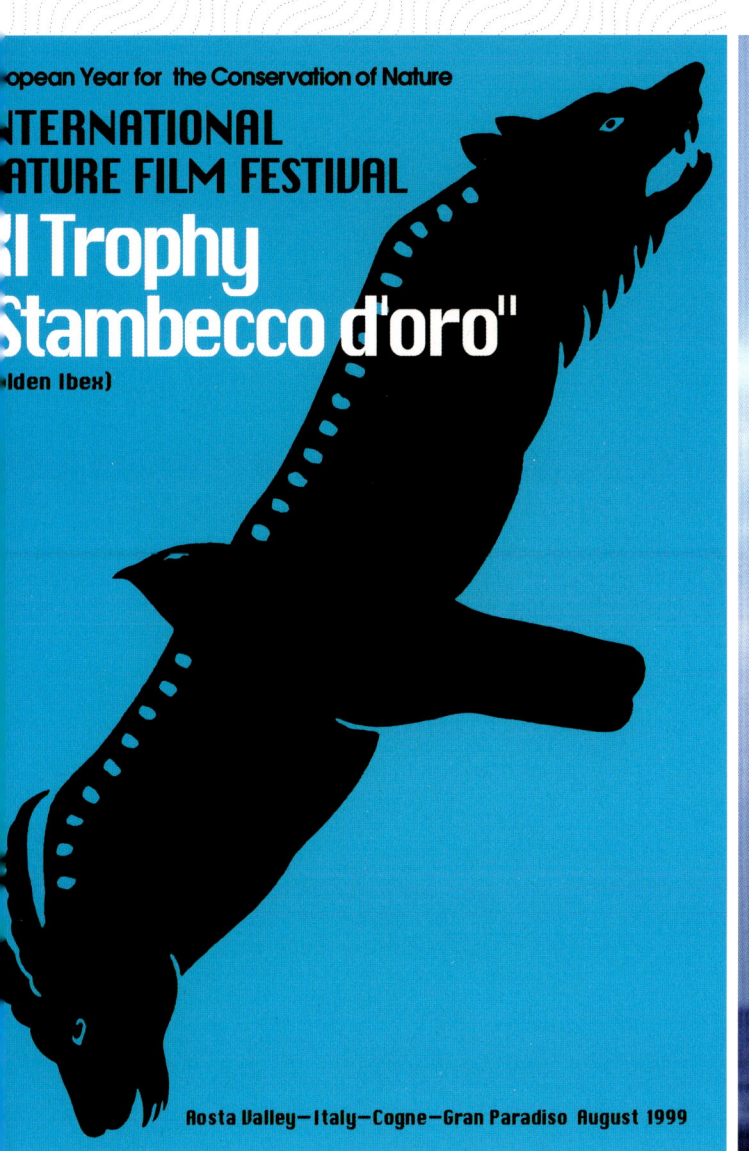

Left: Poster of International Nature Film Festival for AOSTA Valley
Right: Turning object titled "I want to fly!" (No commissioned object)

Poster titled "What's next for Gaia?" for Japan Graphic Designers Association

Top Right: Poster titled "The Tree Is Full of Life" (No commissioned poster)
Bottom Left: Poster titled "Water Is Life" for Japan Graphic Designers Association
Bottom Right: Poster titled "The 200th Anniversary of SHARAKU" for Mainichi Newspapers

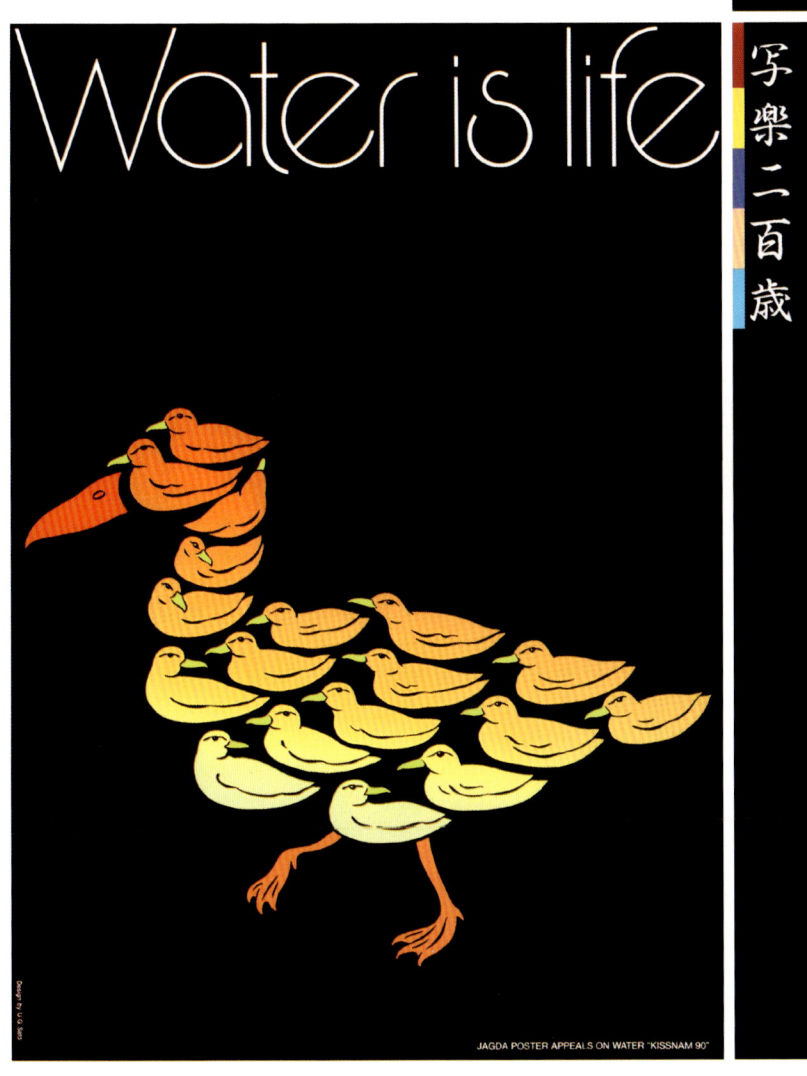

Vince Frost

A member of CSD, D&AD, ISTD, AGDA and AGI, Vince plays an active role in the world design community and often lectures at colleges and conferences. In the early 90s, he became Pentagram London's youngest associate director. After five years at the design industry's best finishing school, he set up Frost Design in 1994. Since then, many awards have come his way, including D&AD Silvers, Golds from the New York Society of Publication Designers and Golds from the New York and Tokyo Art Directors Clubs.

In 2004, Vince moved to Sydney where he continued to work for global clients and won international awards. Frost's approach is based on listening carefully to the needs of each client and then comes up with a solution making each project the very best it can be.

Vince's innovative use of photography and striking typography has been applied to a variety of work, including the award-winning literary magazine *Zembla*, stamps for the Royal Mail, advertising for ING Barings, TV advertising for BT, exhibitions at the V&A, and promotional campaigns for Nike. In 1996, he was awarded Designer of the Year at Chartered Society of Designers and shortlisted for the BBC design awards.

Since leaving London for Sydney Vince has been making his mark on the Australian design scene with a diverse range of projects from identities to magazines, and books.

Vince's work was the subject of a major retrospective: "Frost*bite: Graphic Ideas by Vince Frost" at the Sydney Opera House Exhibition Hall in January 2006. This comprehensive exhibition of Vince's work is accompanied by *Frost*(sorry trees)*, an inspirational book spanning more than a decade of award-winning work by one of the world's leading designers. His work is also currently featured in an exhibition about Australian graphic design at Sydney's Powerhouse Museum.

PROJECT: STRETCH MAGAZINE
TYPE: COVER
CLIENT: *POL OXYGEN*

"*POL Oxygen* approached Frost Design to do a special edition of the magazine with me as guest art director. The bronzed skeleton sculpture by Marc Quinn is used on the front cover, which reinforced the stretch theme. It unfolds to reveal a midget - a stretch on reality is only revealed once you open the cover." – Vince Frost

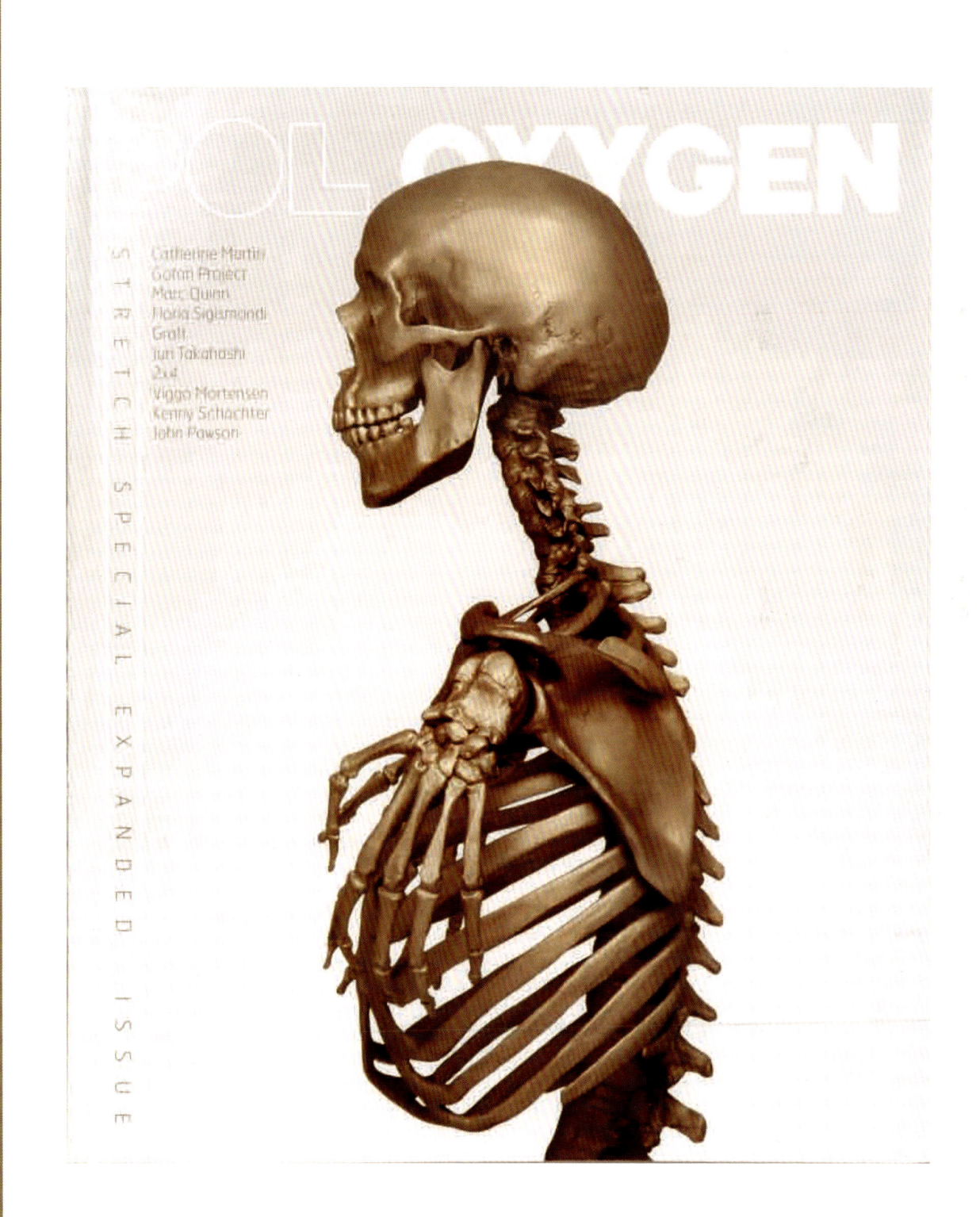

Spreads: Magazine design for *Ampersand*, D&AD's member magazine with content ranging from latest news and views, industry related features and profiles celebrating the world's most inspiring creativity

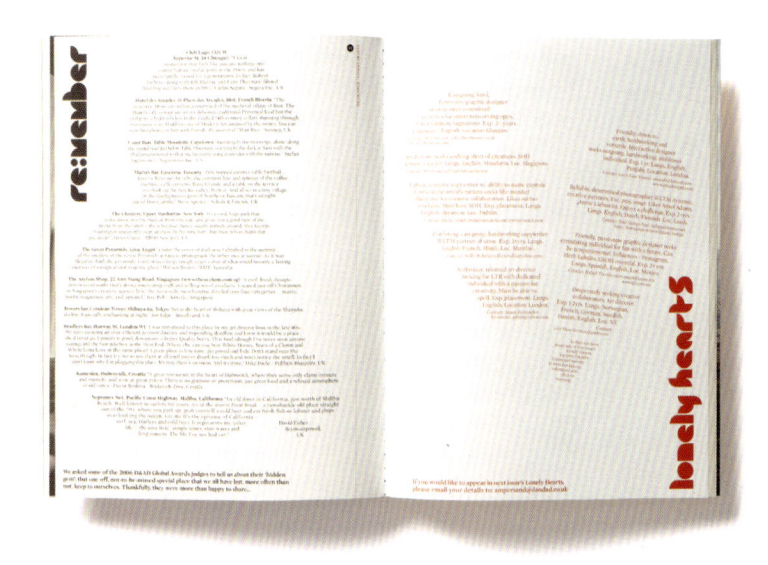

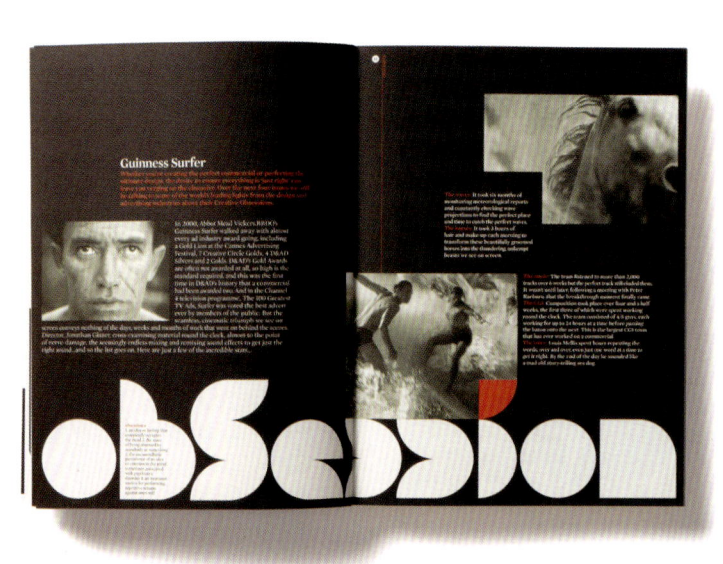

This spring sees D&AD gearing up for its annual celebration of creative excellence, during which many of the world's leading creatives will converge on London for Congress 2006. Sara Manuelli finds out more.
congreSS 06

FroStbite

welcome

To listen to his detractors you'd think he was responsible for heinous crimes against good taste
driving
Force

This spring sees D&AD gearing up for its annual celebration of creative excellence, during which many of the world's leading creatives will converge on London for Congress 2006. Sara Manuelli finds out more.
congreSS 06

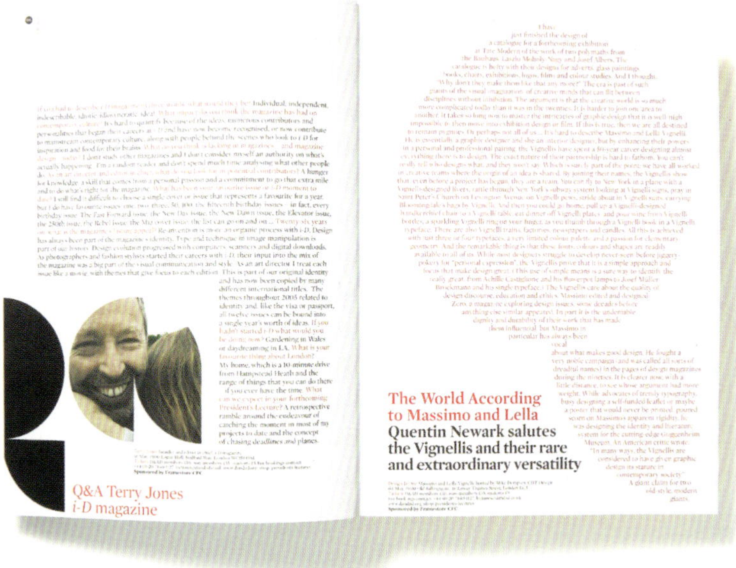

The World According to Massimo and Lella
Quentin Newark salutes the Vignellis and their rare and extraordinary versatility

Spreads: Magazine design for *Ampersand*, D&AD's member magazine with content ranging from latest news and views, industry related features and profiles celebrating the world's most inspiring creativity

334

Spreads: Magazine design for *Ampersand*, D&AD's member magazine with content ranging from latest news and views, industry related features and profiles celebrating the world's most inspiring creativity

335

Spreads: Exhibition on graphic design for Object Gallery

Frost*bite

Sydney Opera House and Object Gallery present Frost*bite: Graphic ideas by Vince Frost 7 January – 12 March 2006

Frost*
Frost*
Frost*

Super Cheap Auto
SUPER CHEAP
SUPER CHEAP
2004
35

Spreads: Book design for coinciding with an exhibition on Frost at the Sydney Opera House

339

SY D A N C E Y COMPANY

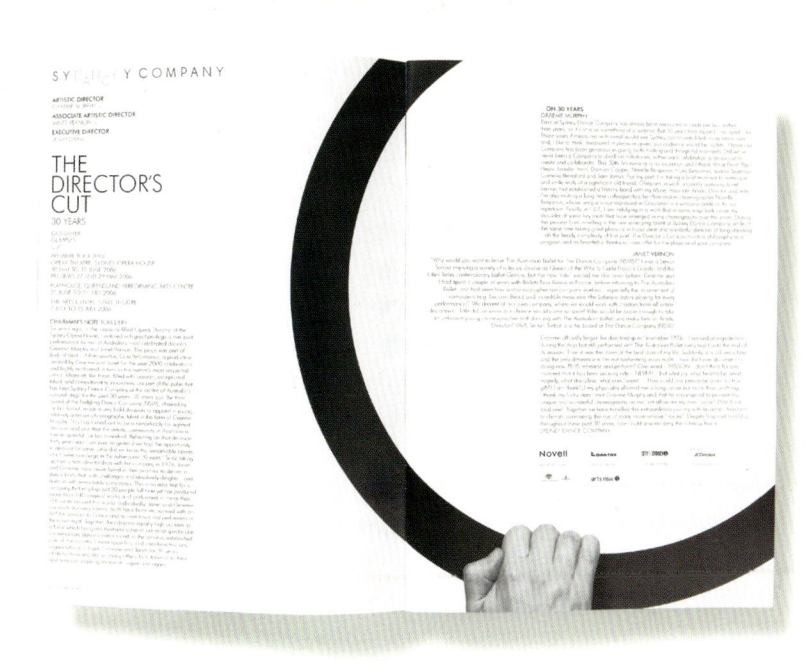

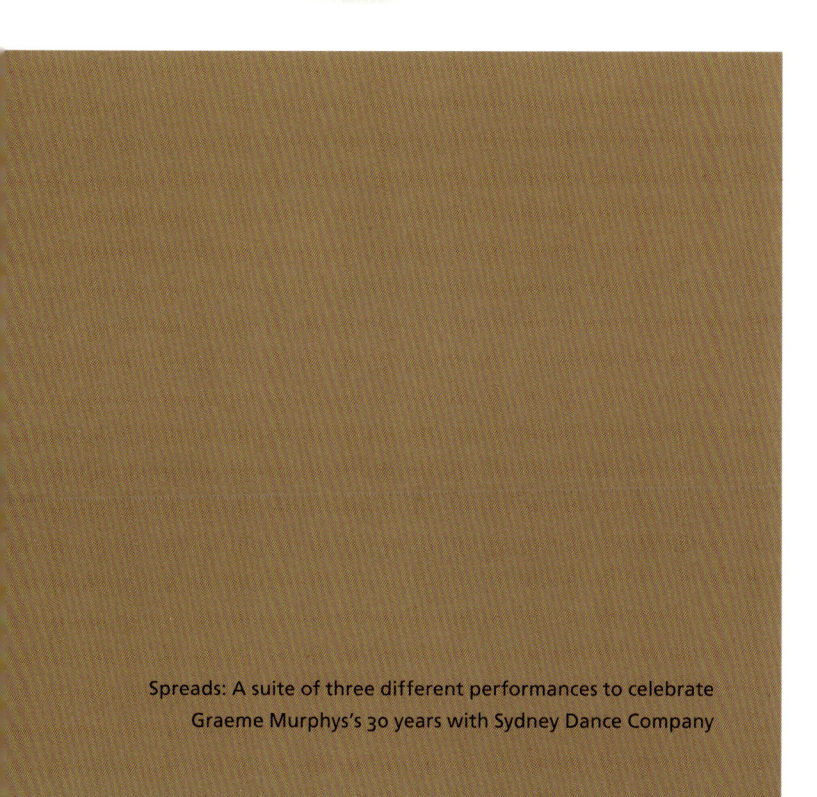

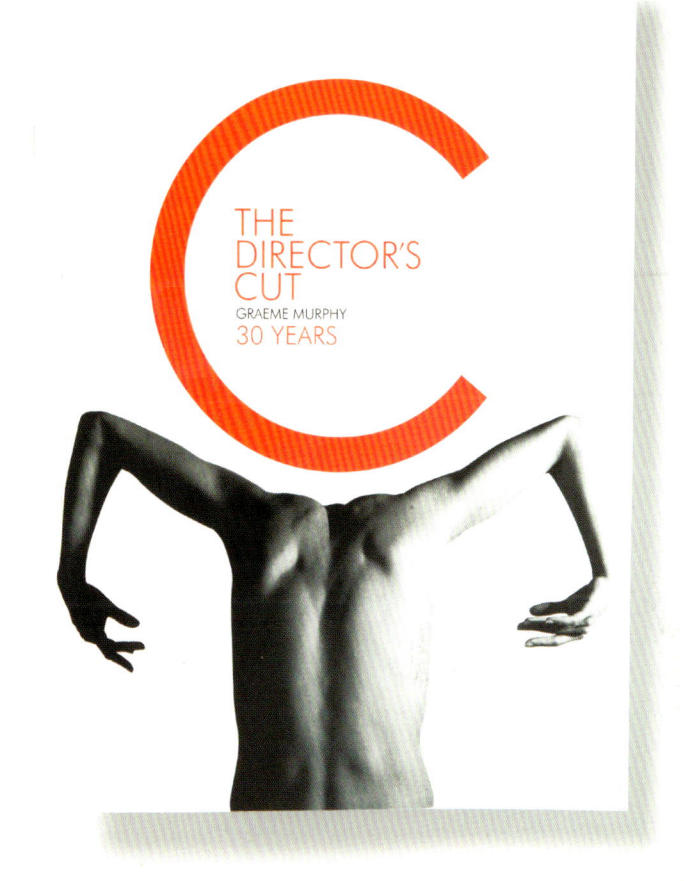

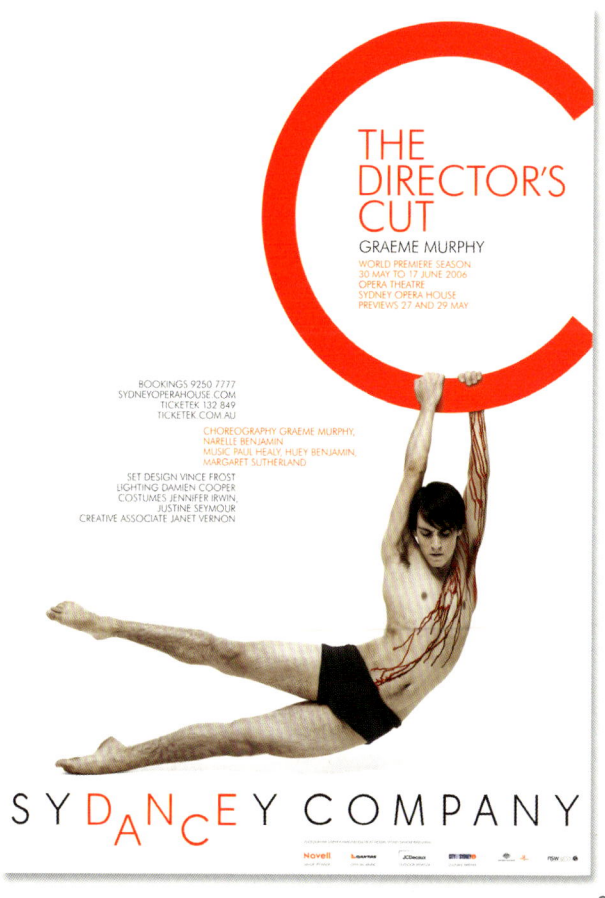

Spreads: A suite of three different performances to celebrate Graeme Murphys's 30 years with Sydney Dance Company

POL OXYGEN
Catherine Martin
Gotan Project
Marc Quinn
Floria Sigismondi
Graft
Jun Takahashi
2x4
Viggo Mortensen
Kenny Schachter
John Pawson
STRETCH
STRETCH SPECI
EXPANDED ISSUE
POL OXYGEN
STRETCH

Spreads: Magazine design for *Stretch* Magazine

Spreads: Cover and layout design for *Zembla*

344

345

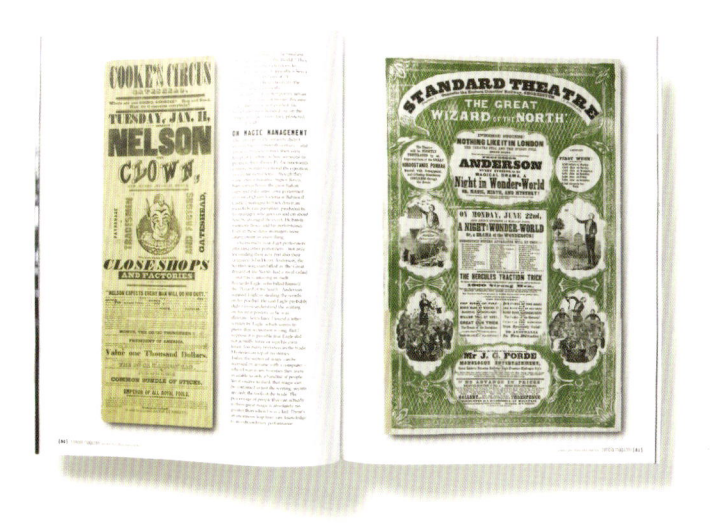

Woody Pirtle

Woody Pirtle established Pirtle Design in Dallas, Texas in 1978. In 1988, Woody merged Pirtle Design with Pentagram, the international design consultancy founded in London in 1972. For 18 years, Woody has been a partner in the New York office of Pentagram and worked on some of the firm's most prestigious projects for many of its A-list clients. Between 1988 and 2005, Woody and the office of Pentagram produced work for Brown-Forman, Bacardi Global Brands, Flying Fish Brewing Company, Watch City Brewing Company, Murray's Cheese, Really Cool Foods, IBM, Champion International Corporation, Fine Line Features, the Rockefeller Foundation, Nine West, Northern Telecom, Knoll International, Wellesley College, Princeton University, Brooklyn Law School, and Amnesty International, plus many others.

In 2005, Woody left Pentagram to re-establish Pirtle Design. Today, Pirtle Design continues to provide unparalleled design and consulting services that run the gamut of business and cultural endeavors, producing work for a diverse range of national and international clients. As a partner emeritus of Pentagram, Woody continues to access the staff and partners in the New York office, and is able to collaborate when larger projects require a greater depth of resources or inter-disciplinary support.

Woody's work has been exhibited worldwide and is in the permanent collections of the Museum of Modern Art , Cooper-Hewitt Museum in New York, the Victoria & Albert Museum in London, the Neue Sammlung Museum in Munich, and the Zurich Poster Museum. He has taught at the School of Visual Arts, lectured extensively.

As a member of the AGI, he has served on the board of *HOW* magazine, Sustainable Hudson Valley, and the American Institute of Graphic Arts. In October 2003, he was awarded the prestigious AIGA Medal for his career contribution to the design profession.

PROJECT: UCLA PALM TREE POSTER
TYPE: POSTER
CLIENT: UCLA EXTENSION

"The UCLA Palm Tree Poster was targeted at those contemplating registration in UCLA's extension program. By creating a palm tree composed of books placed on a beach, the poster very succinctly communicates the idea of learning from wherever one might live in the Los Angeles area – even on the beach." – Woody Pirtle

STOP ST. LAWRENCE CEMENT. SUPPORT HVPC.

Top Left: Poster "Stop the Plant" for Hudson Valley Preservation Commission and Scenic Hudson
Bottom Right: Commemorative poster for a Poughkeepsie Day School Annual Benefit

Top Left: Commemorative poster for the Brooklyn Ballet Company
Bottom Left: Initiative poster for Amnesty International
Bottom Right: Celebration of the Arts Poster for an annual Poughkeepsie Day School benefit event

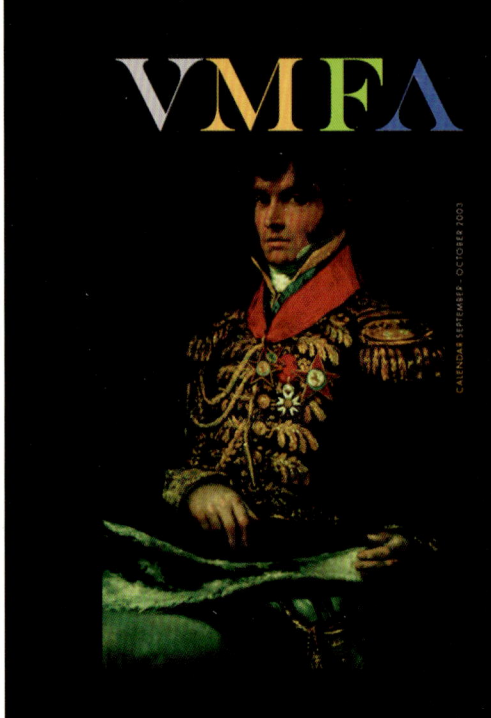

Spreads: Identity program for the Virginia Museum of Fine Arts

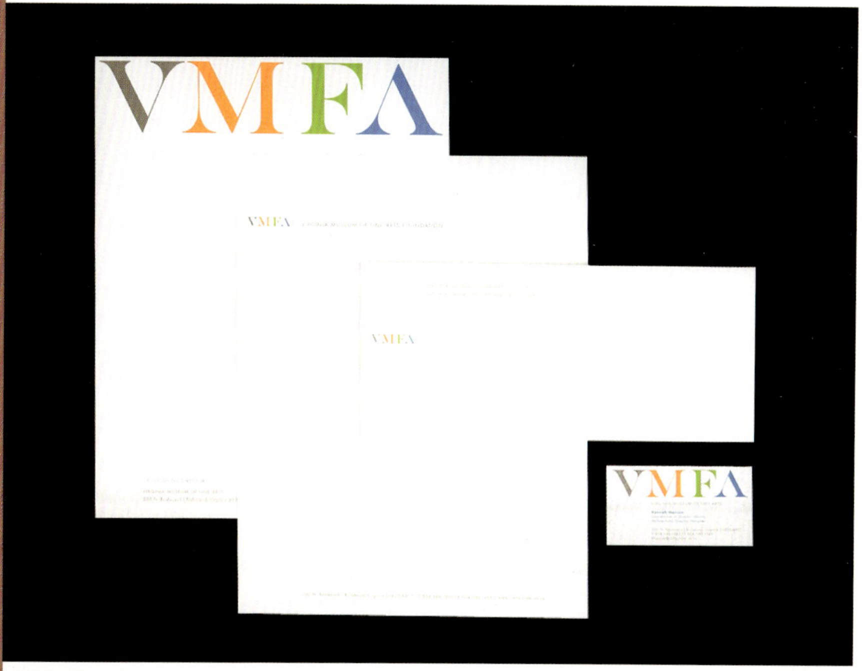
VMFA
VMFA
VMFA
VMFA

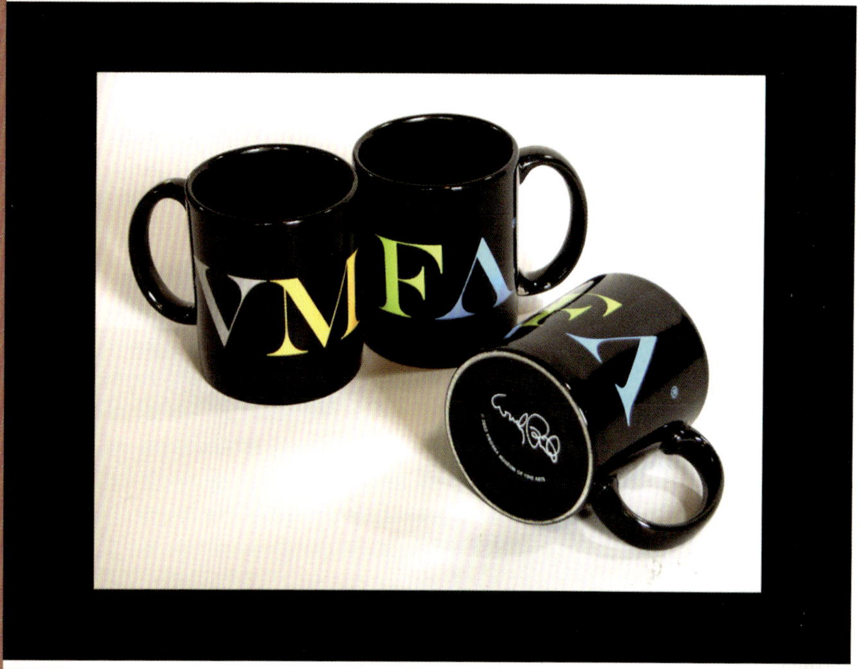
VMFA

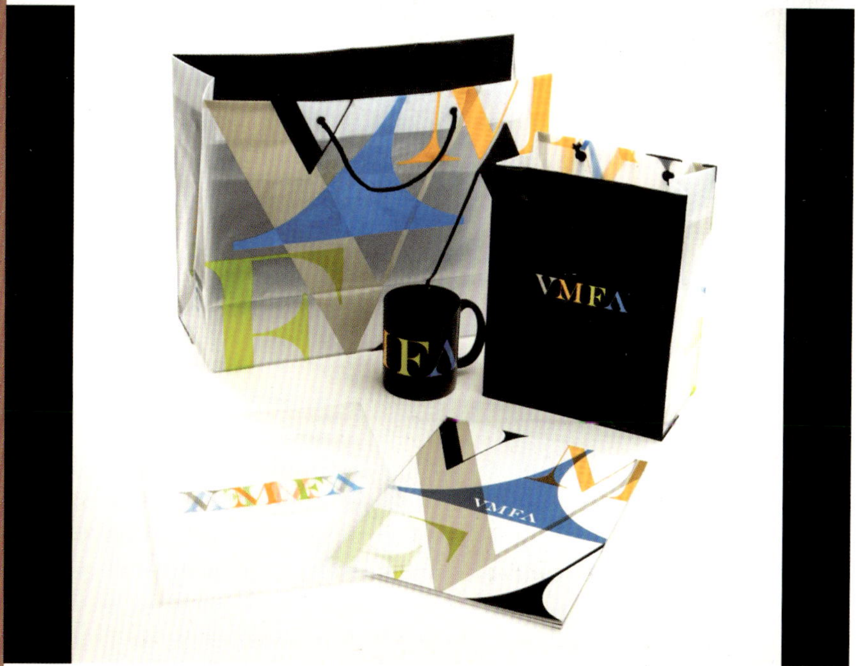
VMFA
VMFA

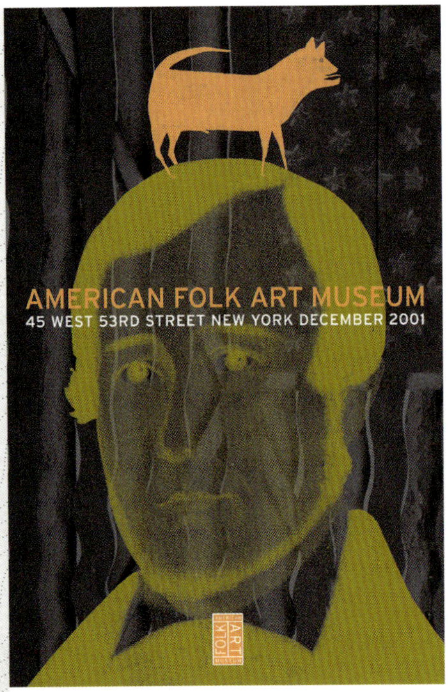
AMERICAN FOLK ART MUSEUM
45 WEST 53RD STREET NEW YORK DECEMBER 2001

Mr. & Mrs. Christopher Mayer
Ellin & Baron Gordon
Joe K. Kindig III
Alexis & George Contos
Cyril Irwin Nelson
The Andy Warhol Foundation for the Visual Arts
Nancy M. & Ben S. Greenberg
The Overbrook Foundation
Levy Charitable Trust
Jean S. & Frederic A. Sharf
Cordelia Hamilton
Didi & David Barrett
Elizabeth & Irwin Warren
John & Kathleen Ullmann
Arlene & Leonard Hochman
Furthermore, the publication program of The J. M. Kaplan Fund
Wendy & Mel Lavitt
Olde Hope Antiques, Inc.
Johnson and Johnson
Peter Tillou
Takashimaya Co., Ltd.
Skinner, Inc. Auctioneers and Appraisers of Antiques and Fine Art
Sanford L. & Patricia L. Smith
Su-Ellen Stern
Marion E. Greene
Mr. & Mrs. Charles M. Diker
Carol Peden Schatt
Jolie Kelter and Michael Malce
Tiffany & Co.
Mr. & Mrs. Edward James Brown

AMERICAN FOLK ART MUSEUM

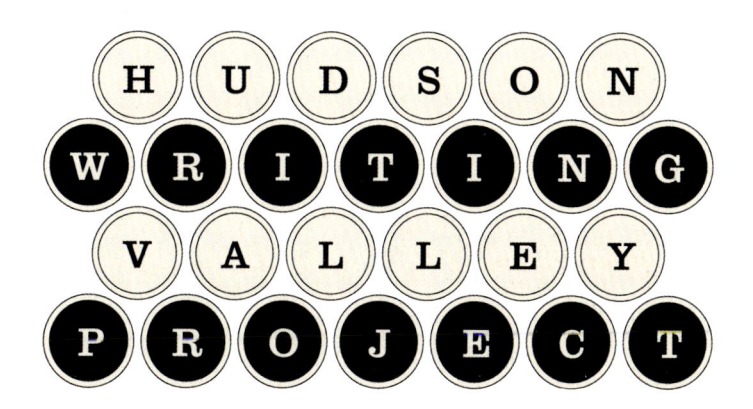

Opposite: Identity program for the American Folk Art Museum
Top: Symbol for Sustainable Hudson Valley
Bottom: Symbol for the Hudson Valley Writing Project

Wout De Vringer

Wout De Vringer was born in Rijswijk (1959).
He has been a member of the AGI since 2002.

From 1979 to 1984, he started his graphic design study at the Academia voor Kunst en Vormgeving Den Bosch. He was an apprentice at Samenwerkende Ontwerpers, Amsterdam and 2D3D, the Hague. From 1985 to 1986, he began to work as a freelance for Vorm Vijf, the Hague. He designed for PTT Telecommunication occasional print.

Together with Ben Faydherbe, he formed his own studio in the Hague in 1986. Thus he worked more for cultural institutions, such as NDT, the Hague Summerfestival and the Hague Movie house. He also created works for the semi-government: Centrum Beeldende Kunst, Dordrecht and Centrum Beeldende Kunst Provincie Utrecht.

He gave guest lectures and workshops at Yale University (New Haven), SUNY Purchase (New York State), CalArts (Los Angeles), the Art Institute of Chicago, University of the West of England (Bristol), St. Martins School of Art (London), Design skolen Kolding (Denmark) and College for Creative Studies (Detroit). He taught graphics at the Evening Academy in Rotterdam.

Dolly, A Book Typeface With Flourishes, was selected for the Best Book (2001) in the Netherlands and also for the "Schönste Bücher aller Welt", Leipzig.

PROJECT: HAAGSE ZOMER
TYPE: POSTER
CLIENT: HET GEBEUREN

"It is published in a book from the MoMA in New York (*Modern Contemporary - Art at MoMA since 1980*) and it was exhibited for many years in the 'Dutch Café' in the MoMA. The poster is part of their permanent collection."
– Wout De Vringer

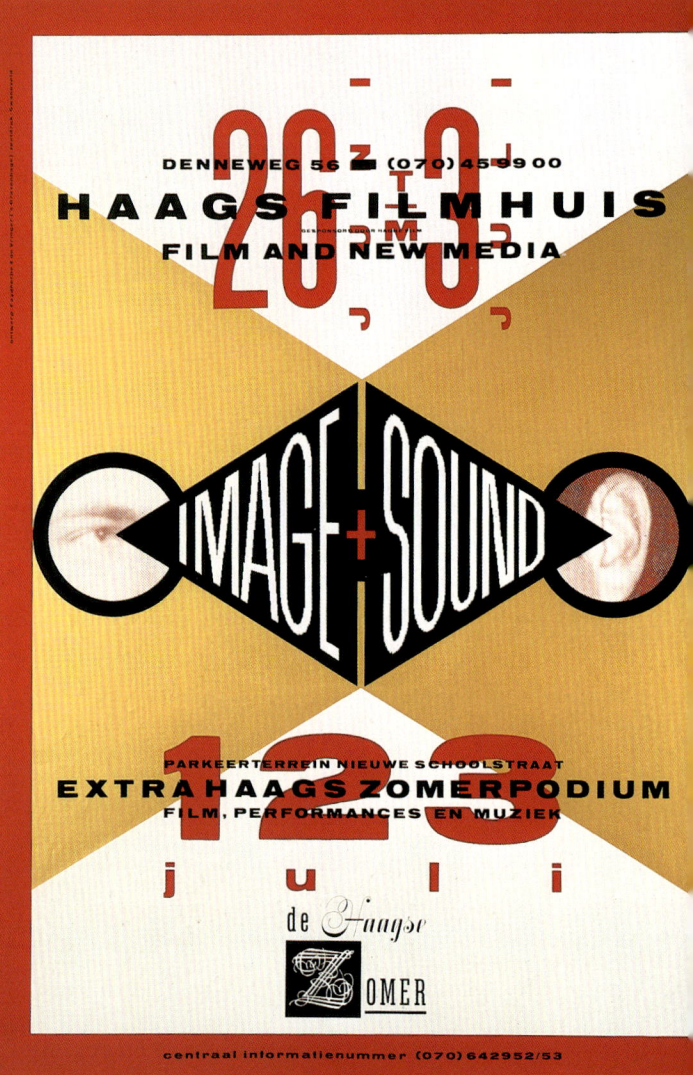

Spreads: Posters for haagse zomer (in collaboration with Ben Faydherbe)

357

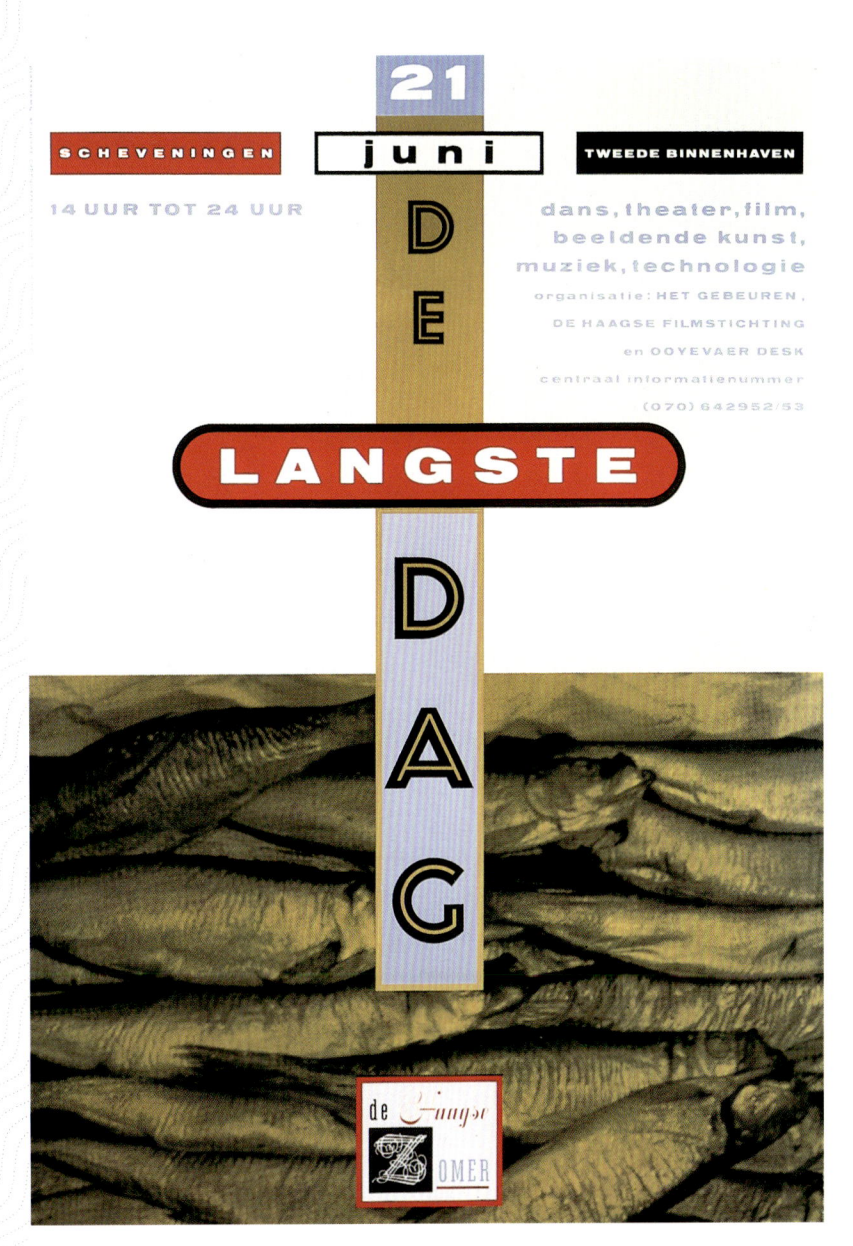

plein
de haagse zomer
92
5—14 juni
t/m
AMSTEL BIER
THEATER AAN DE HAVEN
VRAAG NAAR DE GRATIS FESTIVALKRANT 070 3543202

de Haagse
Zomer
88
10 T/M 19 JUNI Plein
10
14 T/M 19 JUNI Zeebelt WILLEMSTRAAT 7
t/m
11 T/M 19 JUNI Filmhuis DENNEWEG 56
25
25 JUNI Danstheater-Spui
juni

Spreads: Posters for Haagse Zomer. (in collaboration with Ben Faydherbe)

40 % AUTO

Oskar de Kiefte

Spreads: Cover and layout of catalogue for Centrum voor Beeldende Kunst, Provincie Utrecht

361

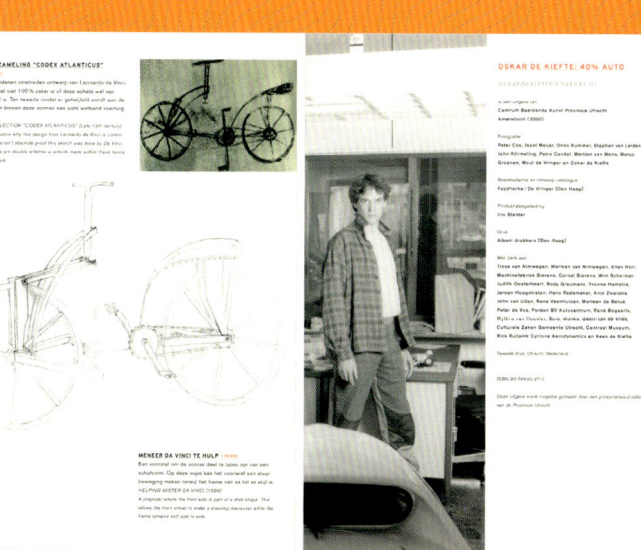

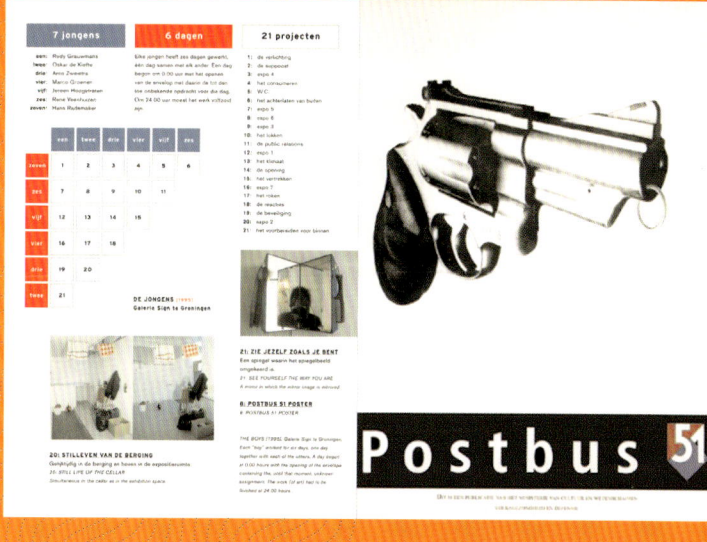

YOUNG DESIGNERS TRIGGER INDUSTRIES TRIGGER YOUNG DESIGNERS (1996)

Wedstrijd en conferentie door de Balie in samenwerking met het Sandberg Instituut en het Nederlands Vormgevings instituut.

Door FIAT CENTRO STILE (Italië) werd ik gekozen om te werken aan hun opdracht.

Met de zin PRODUCEREN WIJ EEN FOUT introduceerde Fiat het verzoek om fundamentele vragen te stellen bij de functie van de auto voor de nabije toekomst. Zij gaven aan dat een auto gemiddeld 2 uur per dag gebruikt wordt.

Ik heb gezocht naar mogelijkheden om de auto niet 22 uur zinloos langs de weg te laten staan. Dit resulteerde in een voorstel waarin openbare functies aan de auto toegevoegd worden, zodat de geparkeerde auto bruikbaar wordt en niet meer uit de stad geweerd hoeft te worden.

YOUNG DESIGNERS TRIGGER INDUSTRIES TRIGGER YOUNG DESIGNERS (1996)

Competition and conference organized by 'De Balie' in cooperation with the Sandberg Institute and the Netherlands Design Institute.

I was selected by FIAT CENTRO STILE (Italy) to work on their assignment. Fiat introduced their request, to ask fundamental questions about the function of the car of the near future, with the idea "Are we producing a mistake ?" They indicated that cars are used for only two hours a day, on average.

I have searched for solutions where the car can be used for more than just one purpose, so it can be useful throughout the whole day. This resulted in a proposal in which public functions are added to the car. So when parked, it can be used by the public and therefore it doesn't have to be excluded from the city center anymore.

FIAT PUBLIC (1996)

In de Salon te Utrecht

Een ontwerp voor een sociale auto.

Als deze auto geparkeerd wordt dan verspilt hij geen ruimte, omdat hij als bank bruikbaar is. Een ronde polyester bank met Kart-techniek.

Foto's A - F tonen de daadwerkelijke realisatie in 1996

THE FIAT PUBLIC (1996)

The Salon 1996, Utrecht

Design for a Social car

Public space is not wasted when this social car is parked, it can be used as a bench.

A round 6 seat polyester bench, Kart-technique.

Photos A - F show the process of constructing the actual car back in 1996.

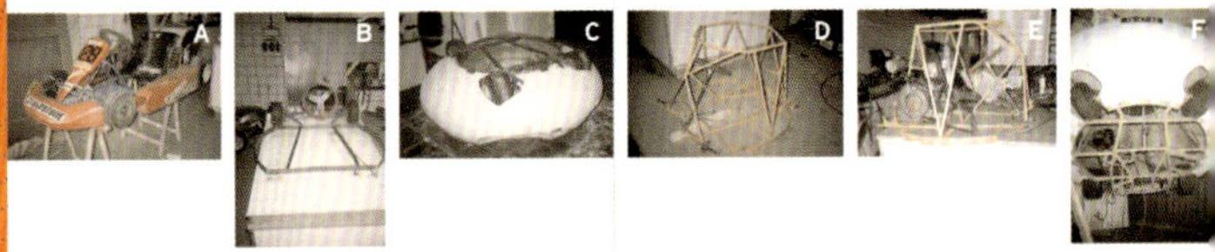

HEMA KLOK Ontwerpwedstrijd (1992)

De nummers van het 12 vel tellende wedstrijd-document vormde de tijdsaanduiding.

HEMA CLOCK. Design contest (1992)

The contest-document consists of 12 pages, each page used as one of the twelve time indications.

NEGENTIEN TWEEDUIZEND (2000)

Voorstel voor een nieuwe jaartelling.

NINETEEN TWO THOUSAND (2000)

Proposal for a new calendar-system

19 97

19 98

19 99

19 2000

19 2001

19 2002

VOORSTEL VOOR EEN LICHTRECLAME OP HET DAK VAN DE TU-EINDHOVEN (2000)

Een DAF-Truck die met de lichten aan rondjes rijdt op het dak.

PROPOSAL FOR A BILLBOARD ON TOP OF THE ROOF OF THE TECHNICAL UNIVERSITY OF EINDHOVEN (2000)

A Daf truck with the headlights switched on drives in circles on top of the roof.

CAMOUFLAGETENT (1997)

CAMOUFLAGE-TENT (1997)

ZEGEL VAN 65 CENT (2000)

148 jaar recycling 1852 - 2000

65 CENT STAMP FOR HOLLAND (2000)

148 YEARS OF RECYCLING 1852 - 2000

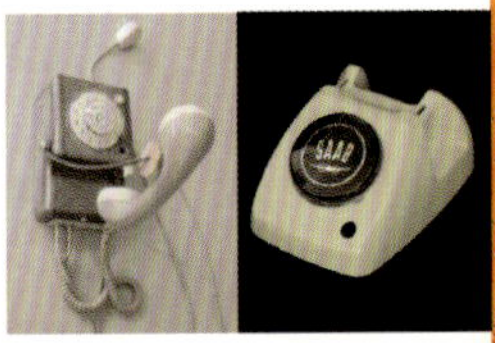

RESTYLED TELEFOONS (1992)

RESTYLED TELEPHONES (1992)

UNIVERSAL PRODUCT Shape 50 x 100 x 133,3

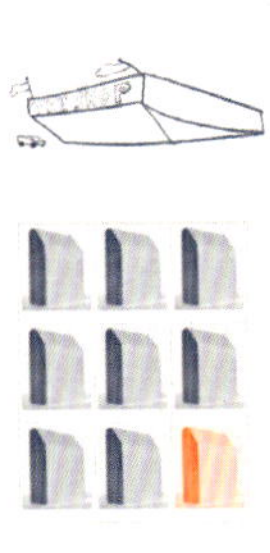

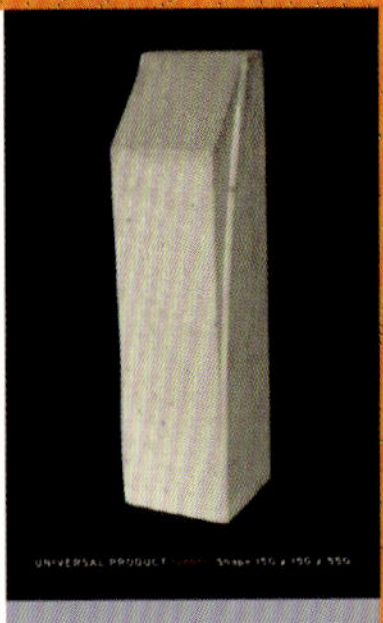

UNIVERSAL PRODUCT Shape 150 x 150 x 550

UNIVERSELE PRODUKTEN (1995-2000)

Een ontwerp voor een produktvorm. Bijna alle produkten kunnen hun vorm aan dit produkt ontlenen. Dit is mogelijk doordat is uitgegaan van een zo compleet mogelijk eisenpakket. De gebogen lijn op het produkt is puur esthetisch, het oog wil ook wat! Als je een gebouw wilt dan voeg je een deurkruk toe, wil je een rekenmachine... monteer een display!

UNIVERSAL PRODUCTS (1995-2000)

A design for a universal shape. This shape lends itself to almost any product.

I have been searching for the ultimate answer to the over all requirements of a product in general. The products' curved lines are merely there for aesthetic reasons: the eye wants something too! When we use the shape as a building we simply mount a doorhandle. Do you need a calculator? Add a display!

THE DIMENSIONS OF THE VOLUMES IN MM

5	x	10	x	13,3
50c	x	100	x	133,3
150	x	150	x	550
150	x	600	x	550
150	x	300	x	400
300	x	300	x	1250
600	x	600	x	1600
1500	x	1500	x	4000
6000	x	24000	x	34000

WILLENS EN WETENS

HERMAN

VERTIER EERST

TOT EN MET

LOTSBESCHIKKING

DANIE

BIJ NADER INZIEN

DE DRIE NICHTEN

BLIJVEND

VERVAL

HEDEN TEN DAGE

DE VERWEZENLIJKING

LANDZICHT

DE WANTROUWEN

VERVAL 2

AAN DE BEURT

TOT ZIENS

JEWELLERY (2000)

ZIJ HOUDT VAN HEM, HIJ HOUDT VAN HAAR (2000)

JAS VAN KNUFFELBONT (2000)

FUR COAT MADE FROM CUDDLY TOYS (2000)

NIEUWE SCHEEPSNAMEN VOOR DE BINNENVAART (2000)

NEW SHIPNAMES FOR THE DUTCH INLAND NAVIGATION (2000)

THE CONVERTED PORSCHE 928 SILVER AERO (1994)

Model 1:20

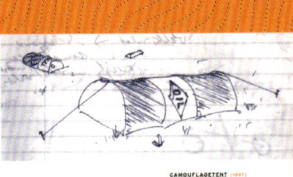

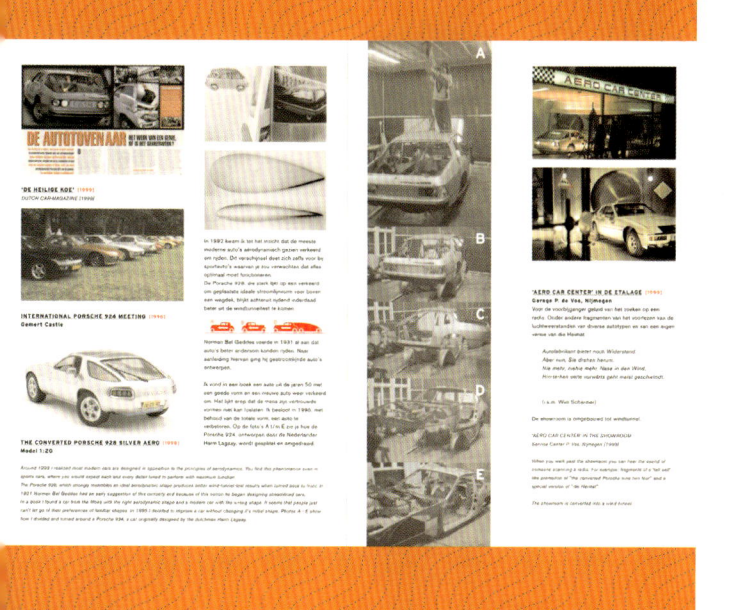

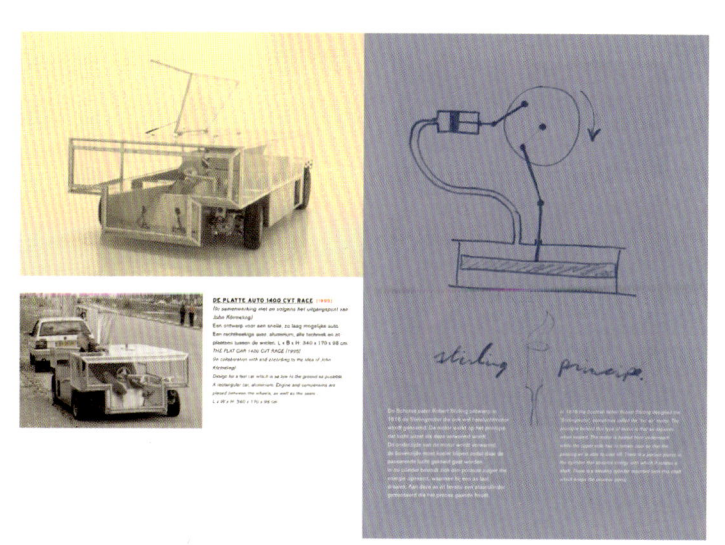

Spreads: Layout design of catalogue for Centrum voor Beeldende Kunst, Provincie Utrecht

363

merz: korte kalkhaven 1; dordrecht
Op woensdag 10 juni
organiseert De Stad een
avond over het thema:
de stad
Mirik Jung:
Nico Lamers:
Pictura

30 08 1991
1
de stad
In samenwerking met Teekengenootschap Pictura
organiseert werkgroep De Stad op vrijdag 30 augustus
een discussieavond over het thema:
Nieuwbouw in een oude stad
Twee inleidingen worden verzorgd door:
Wiek Röling
Hoogleraar architectuur TU Delft en voormalig
stadsarchitect van Haarlem
Rudger Smook
Architect en stedebouwkundige
Aanvang 20.00 uur Toegang fl. 5,- Pas 65/CJP fl. 2,50

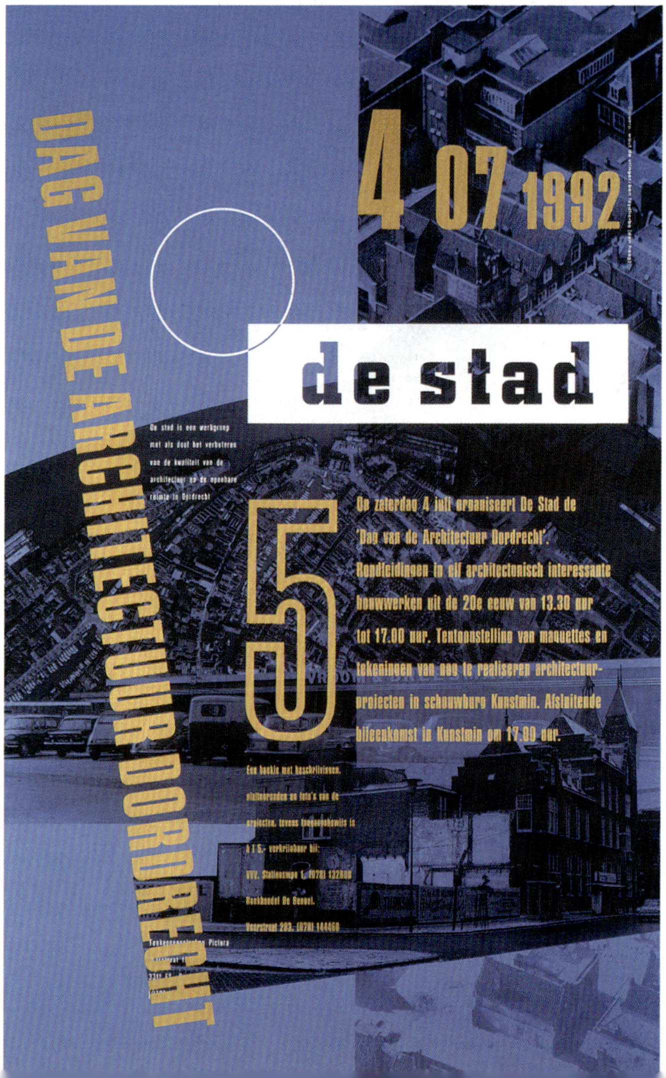
DAG VAN DE ARCHITECTUUR DORDRECHT
4 07 1992
de stad
5
Op zaterdag 4 juli organiseert De Stad de
'Dag van de Architectuur Dordrecht'.
Rondleidingen in elf architectonisch interessante
bouwwerken uit de 20e eeuw van 13.30 uur
tot 17.00 uur. Tentoonstelling van maquettes en
tekeningen van nog te realiseren architectuur-
projecten in schouwburg Kunstmin. Afsluitende
bijeenkomst in Kunstmin om 17.00 uur.

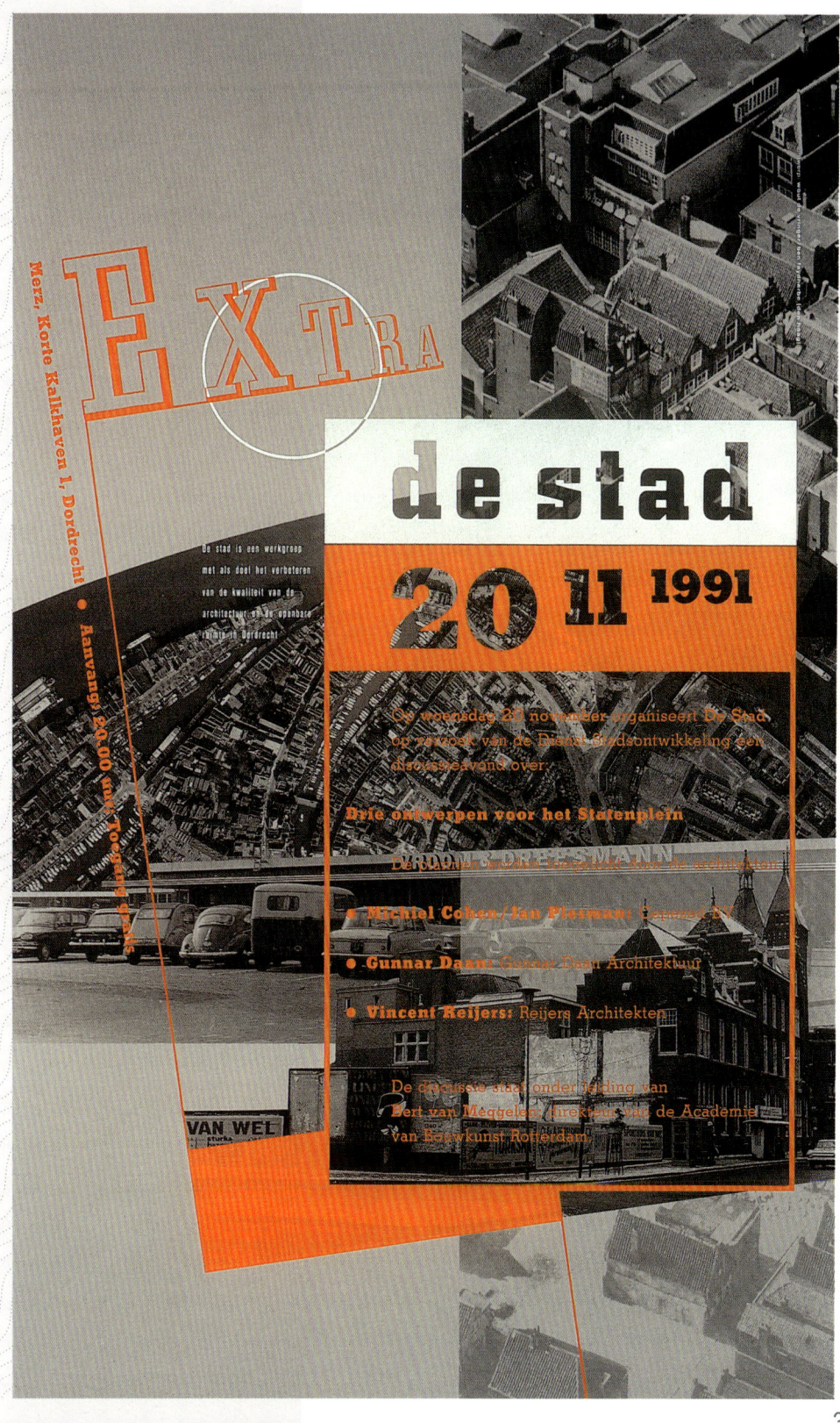

Spread: Posters for Centrum Beeldende Kunst Dordrecht

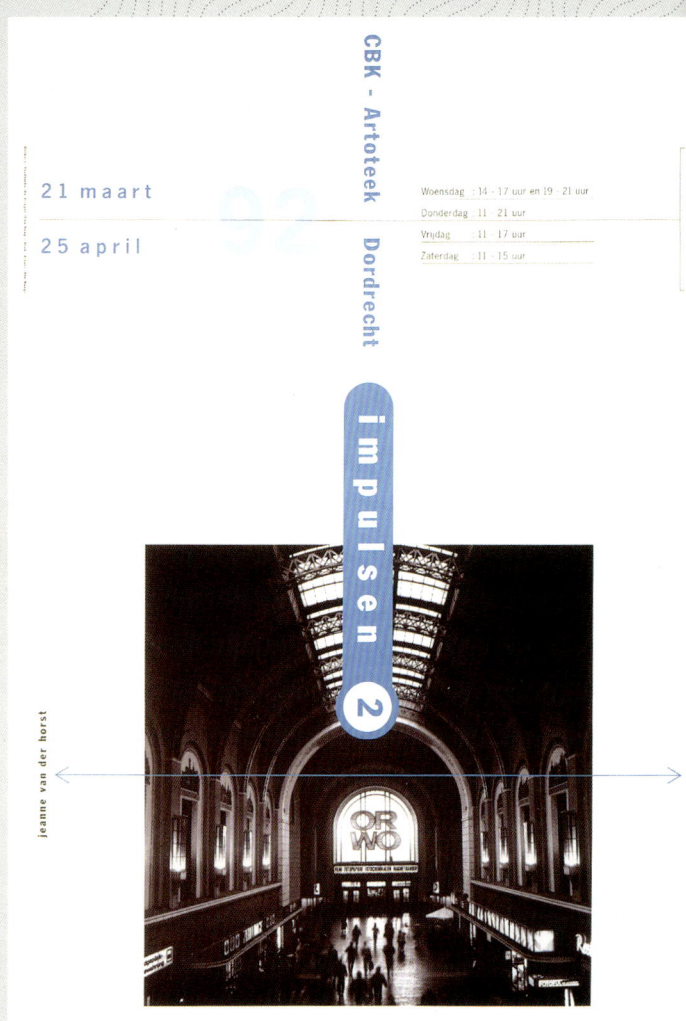

Left: Poster for group exhibition
Right: Poster for an exhibition of the work of two artists

Left: Poster for an exhibition on the work of bas maters
Right: Poster for a group exhibition

Poster for a group exhibition of artists from the Dordrecht area
Opposite: Poster for an exhibition of the work of two artists

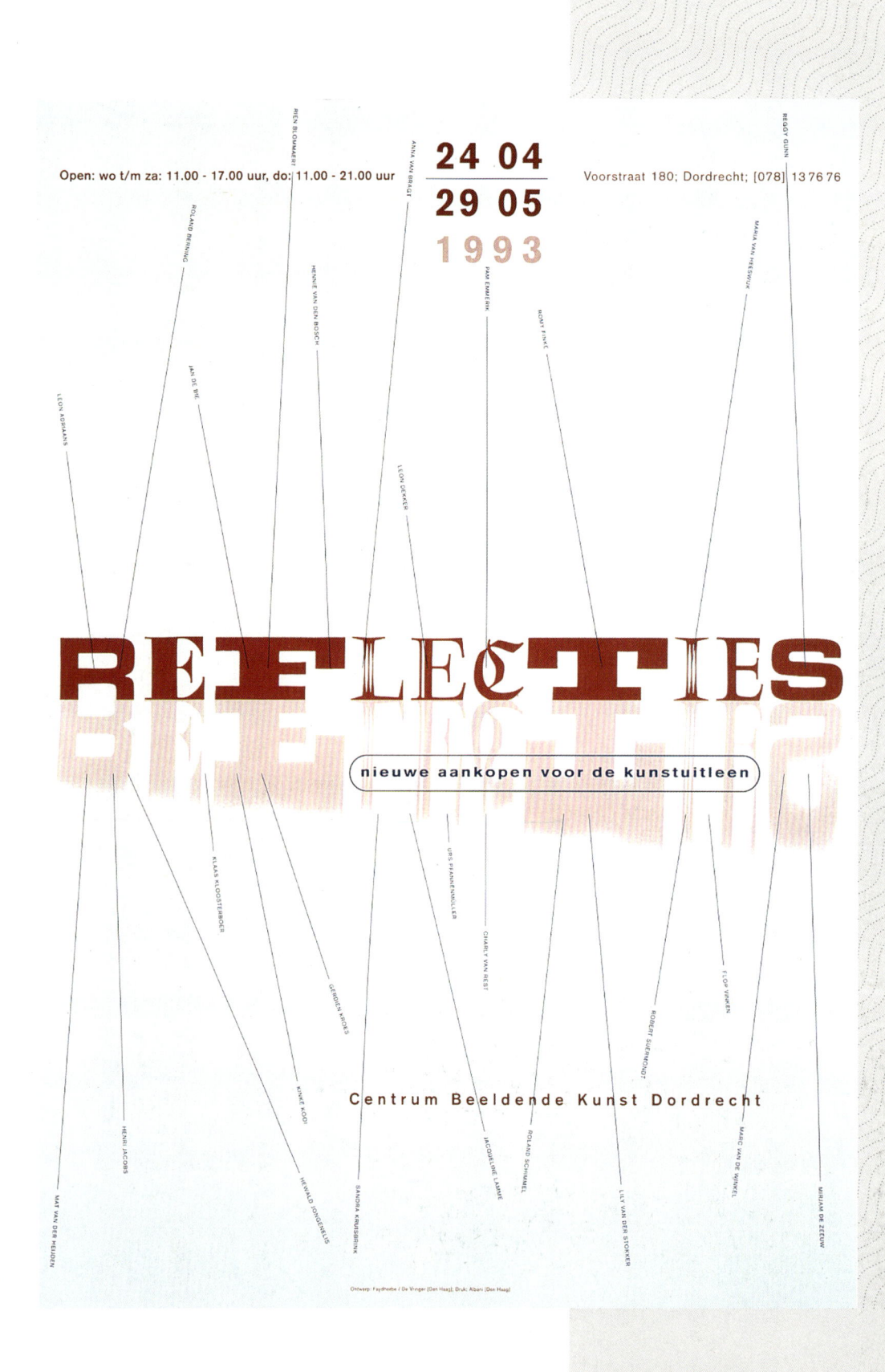

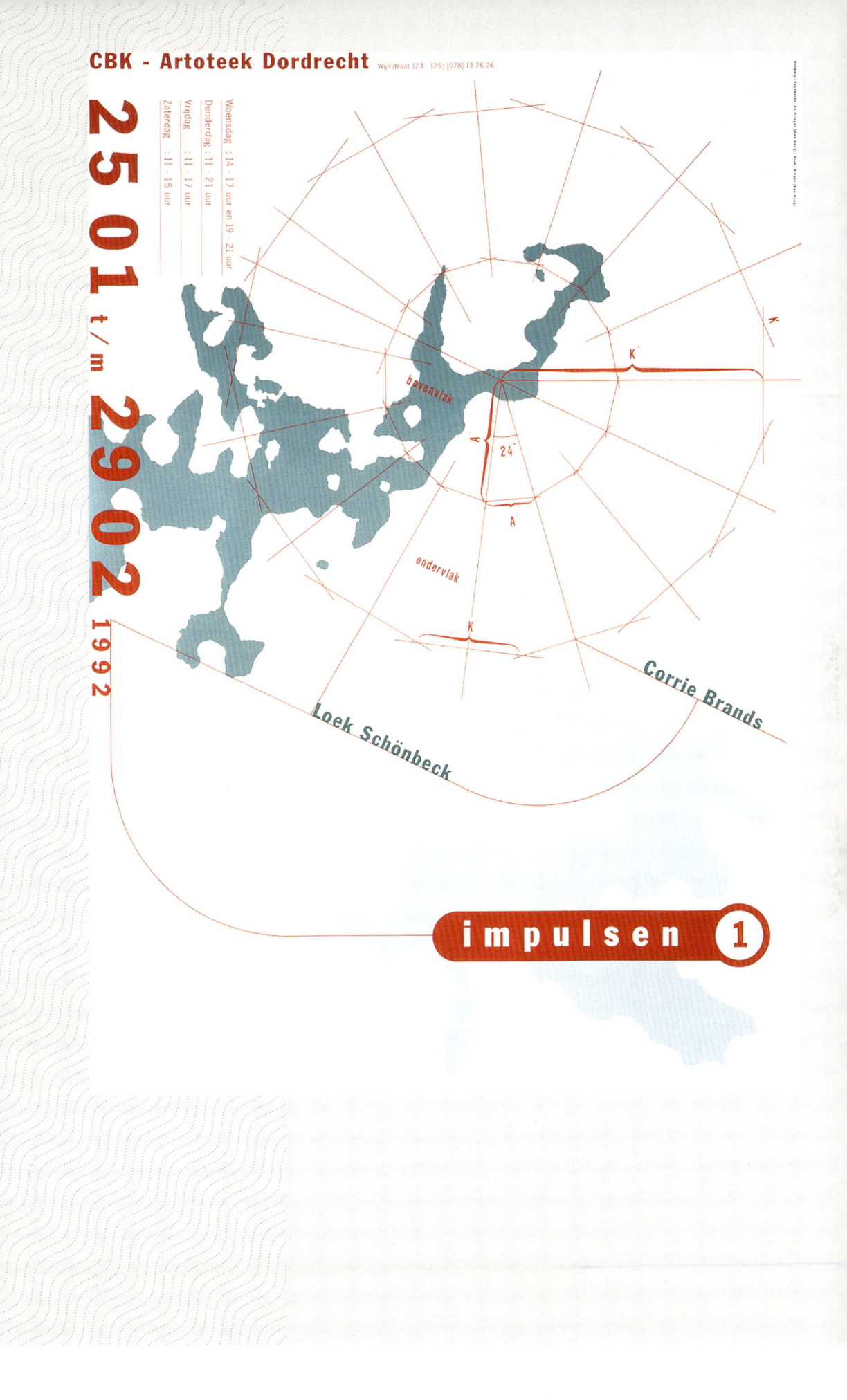

CBK - Artoteek Dordrecht Wijnstraat 123 - 125; [078] 13 76 76

Woensdag : 14 - 17 uur en 19 - 21 uur
Donderdag : 11 - 21 uur
Vrijdag : 11 - 17 uur
Zaterdag : 11 - 15 uur

25 0 1 t/m **29 0 2** 1992

Corrie Brands

Loek Schönbeck

impulsen 1

The design of the poster incorporates elements of a sketch made by the artist
for an exhibition of Piet Dirkx, a Dutch painter.

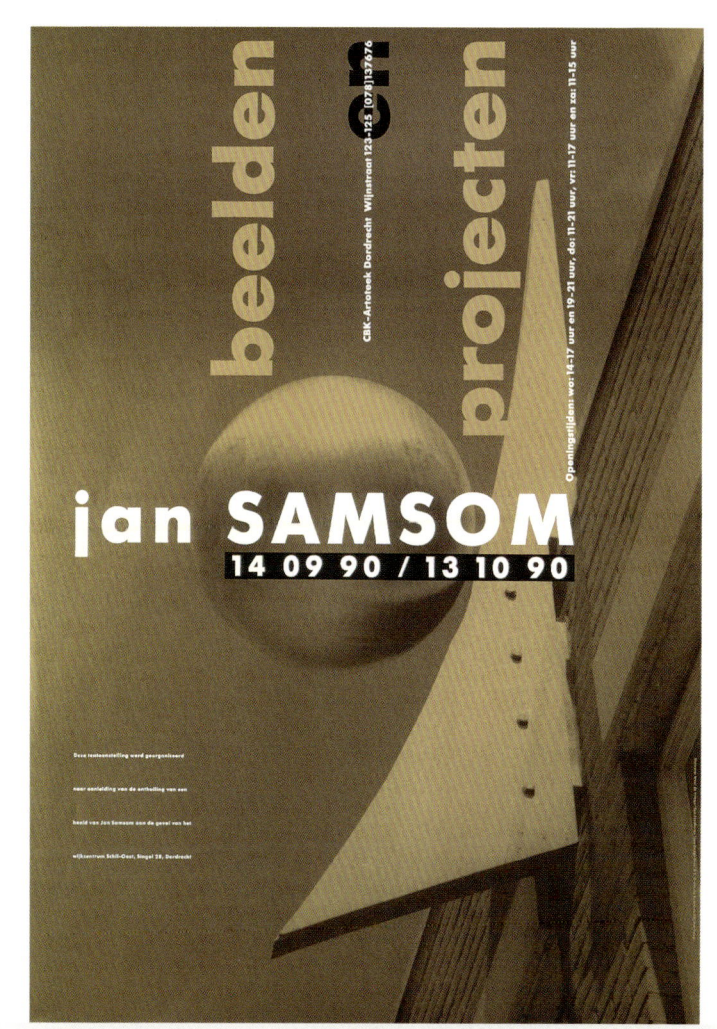

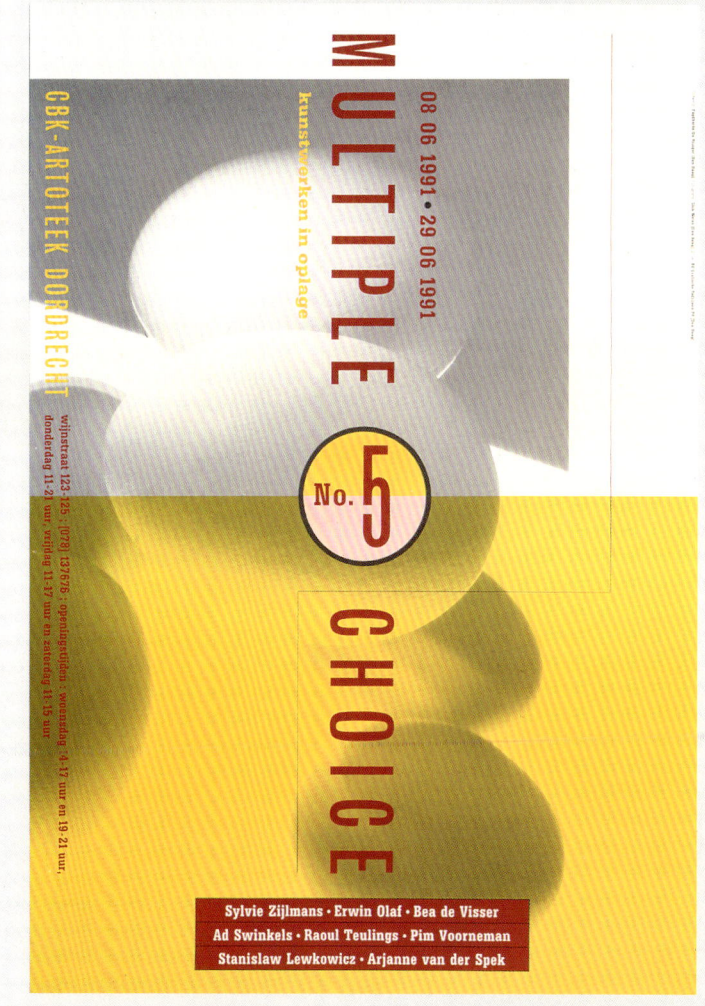

Posters for exhibitions by Centrum Beeldende Kunst Dordrecht

372

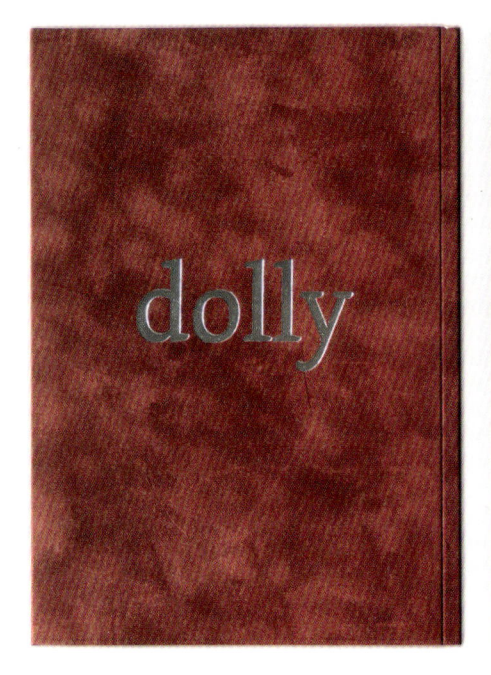

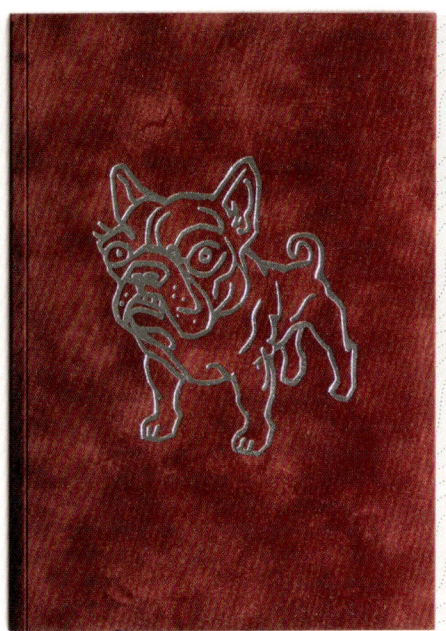

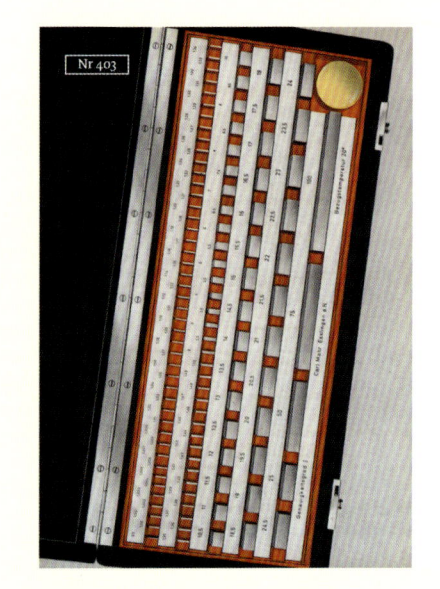

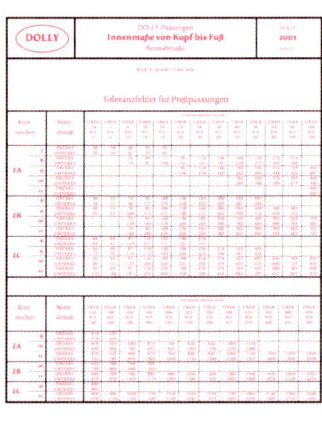

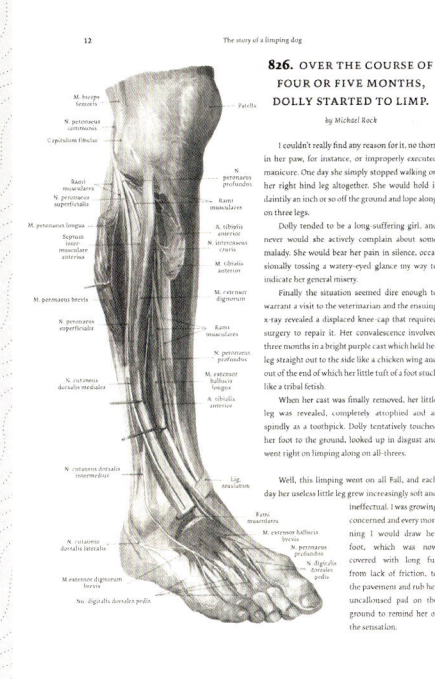

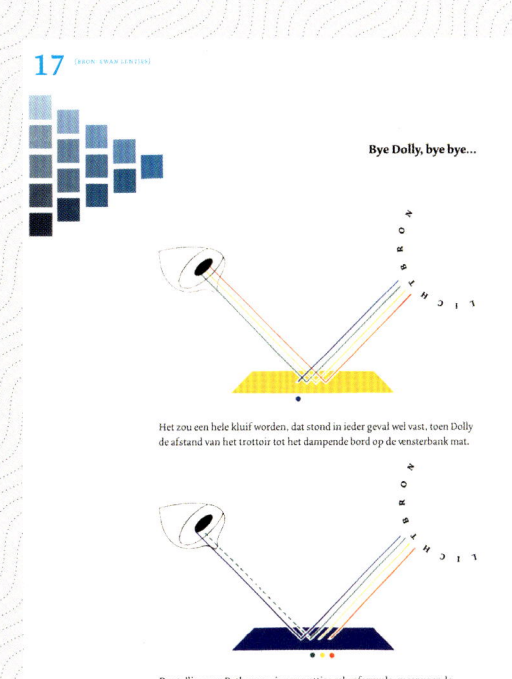

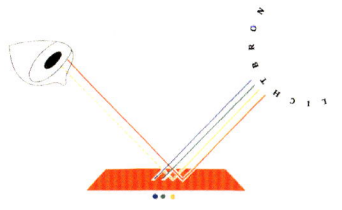

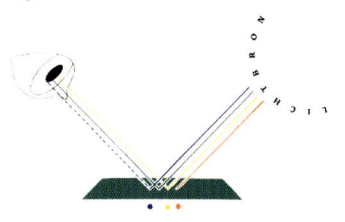

Spreads: the book is an alternative typeface-catalogue for a new typeface titled "Dolly" from Underware

373

Please send to:

PLEASE
FIX
STAMP
HERE

Underware

Schouwburgstraat 2

2511 VA Den Haag

The Netherlands

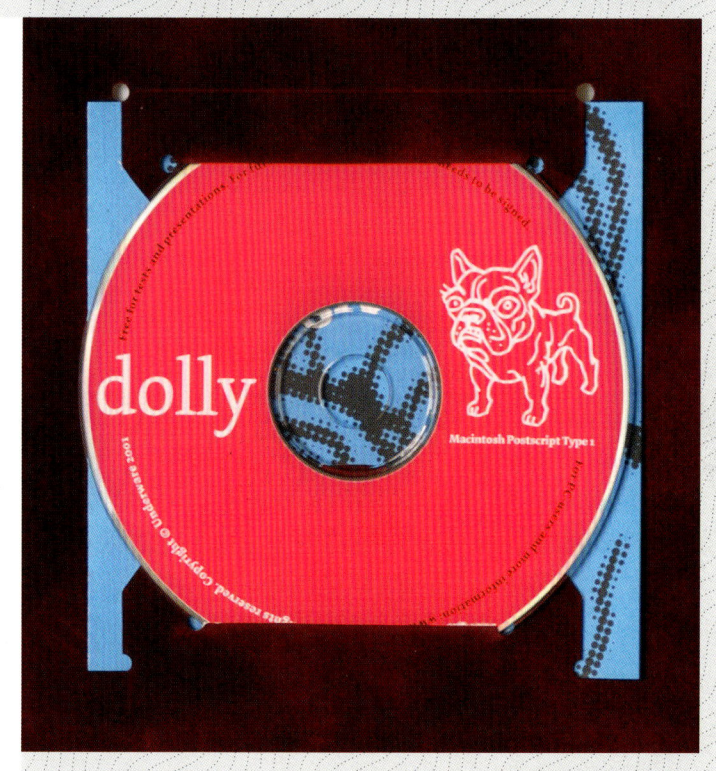

Europe

Get the license agreement!

What's this?
You already have the complete typeface in perfect condition on this CD-rom, together with a type specimen, and this order form. So you have the opportunity to use this typeface for tests and presentations.

Is this typeface free?
No. For further use a license agreement is needed. But you can use it privately without any problem.

What will it cost me? *
Dolly costs € 150,- for single-platform use. If you want to use it on two platforms, it costs € 200,-. On 3-5 platforms € 300,- And 6-10 platforms € 500,-. For further information about the multi-user scale, phone us at: +31–[0]70–4278117.

How do I get a license agreement?
Fill in this form and send it to:
Underware, Schouwburgstraat 2,
2511 VA Den Haag, The Netherlands.
If you want to order directly, you can fill in the form on our website www.underware.nl
or phone us: +31–[0]70–4278117.

And then?
After registration you will be informed about your license. Then you can use Dolly on as many platforms as you have registered for. For exact terms, see the license agreement.

I can't escape this?
No. The only exceptions are officially recognized places of education. A free license will be provided for educational users.

* Prizes per September 2001

I want to get the license agreement **now!**

COMPANY		
FIRST NAME	○ MALE	○ FEMALE
FAMILY NAME		
STREET ADDRESS		
CITY		
PROVINCE	POST CODE	
COUNTRY		
TELEPHONE		
FAX		
EMAIL		
VAT NUMBER		

○ MAC POSTSCRIPT TYPE 1   ○ PC POSTSCRIPT TYPE 1   ○ PC TRUETYPE
HOW MANY PLATFORMS? ○ 1 € 150 ○ 2 € 200 ○ 3-5 € 300 ○ 6-10 € 500 ○ OTHER
SIGNATURE

PHONE US FOR FURTHER INFORMATION ABOUT THE MULTI-USER SCALE ON +31–[0]70–4278117

Spreads: the book is an alternative typeface-catalogue for a new typeface titled "Dolly" from Underware

Spread: This is a jubilee book for an organisation, Dienst Weg-en Waterbouw, which is linked to the Dutch government.

Hoofdstuk 4
In een stroomversnelling, 1985-2000

Operatie Drieluik Het jaar 1985 bracht de dienst en haar medewerkers veel hectiek. Dat had alles te maken met het ingrijpende veranderingsproces dat Rijkswaterstaat sinds enkele jaren in haar greep hield. De maatregelen die de waterstaatsorganisatie nieuwe perspectieven moesten bieden, hadden van de plannenmakers een pakkende naam gekregen. Beeldend sprak men van een drieluik, daarbij verwijzend naar de drie belangrijke, nauw met elkaar in verband staande zaken die op dat moment speelden. Een speciaal in het leven geroepen projectorganisatie voerde 'Operatie Drieluik' uit. Het milieu vormde het eerste punt. Milieuonderzoek, dat bij Rijkswaterstaat vanaf de jaren zeventig op gang was gekomen als antwoord op de maatschappelijke kritiek en ter ondersteuning van wettelijke milieutaken (zoals de uitvoering van de Wet Verontreiniging Oppervlaktewateren), vond tot 1985 bij een aantal diensten plaats. Naast de Wegbouwkundige Dienst, hielden ook de Deltadienst, het Rijksinstituut voor Zuivering van Afvalwater en de directie Noordzee zich daarmee bezig. Operatie Drieluik moest aan de spreiding van inspanningen een einde maken en zorgen voor bundeling van het milieuonderzoek in een 'natte of aquatische' – Rijksinstituut voor Zoetwaterbeheer en Afvalwaterbehandeling — en een 'droge of terrestrische' – de Dienst Weg- en Waterbouwkunde — milieudienst.

Het tweede punt dat via Operatie Drieluik moest worden gerealiseerd, was de hergroepering van waterstaatstaken in het zee- en kustgebied, waarbij de directie Noordzee de beheerstaken en een nieuw te vormen specialistische dienst — Dienst Getijdewateren — de onderzoekstaken kreeg. De kwestie die bij velen binnen en buiten de Rijkswaterstaat voor de meeste commotie zorgde, was de voltooiing van de Deltawerken en de daarmee samenhangende opheffing van de Deltadienst. Operatie Drieluik moest als derde punt zorgen dat de kennis en kunde die bij de Deltadienst in de loop van de jaren was opgebouwd voor Rijkswaterstaat en Nederland behouden bleef.

Dienst Weg- en Waterbouwkunde Als uitvloeisel van Operatie Drieluik kreeg de Wegbouwkundige Dienst een nieuwe naam — Dienst Weg- en Waterbouwkunde (DWW) — en twee geheel nieuwe hoofdafdelingen, te weten Waterbouw (WB) en Milieu (MI). De hoofdafdeling Waterbouw was een samenvoeging van het Centrum Onderzoek Waterkeringen van de gelijktijdig opgeheven directie Waterhuishouding en Waterbeweging, de afdelingen Fysische Modellen en Grondmechanica van de eveneens gelijktijdig opgeheven Deltadienst en een deel van de afdeling Ontwikkeling Nieuwe Werkmethoden van de Deltadienst. De komst van de nieuwe hoofdafdeling bracht een verbreding van de waterbouwkundige taken van de dienst. De werkzaamheden van WB werden verspreid over twee (functionele) afdelingen, te weten Onderzoek en Ontwikkeling (WB/O) en Adviezen (WBA). WBO telde drie onderafdelingen, te weten Constructieve Hydraulica, Geotechniek en Praktijkonderzoek. Onder WBA vielen twee onderafdelingen, te weten Waterkeringen en Overige Waterbouwkundige Constructies.

Balans van 75 jaar

De twintigste eeuw ligt inmiddels achter ons. Het was een periode, waarin de mens in technologisch opzicht een grote sprong voorwaarts maakte. Hoewel we er niet altijd even goed gebruik van maakten, is er toch veel positiefs te melden. Dat geldt zeker voor de weg- en waterbouwkunde. We hoeven daarvoor alleen maar te kijken naar de manier, waarop wij Nederlanders met water hebben leren spelen. De groeiende kennis en kunde, maar vooral ook de durf van Nederlandse waterbouwkundigen maakten megaprojecten als Zuiderzeewerken en Deltawerken mogelijk, deed ons de grote rivieren die een keer in banen leiden, de andere keer de ruimte te geven en maakten het ons mogelijk de Noordzee de toegang tot ons laaggelegen land te ontzeggen.

Het is ook de eeuw waarin het personen- en goederenvervoer drastisch veranderde. Paard en wagen verdwenen voorgoed uit het straatbeeld. De belangrijke rol van het railvervoer aan het begin van de twintigste eeuw werd grotendeels overgenomen door de auto. Dat maakte een heel andere infrastructuur noodzakelijk. Het asfalt veroverde Nederland op de idyllisch ogende straat en zandwegen. Had de 'gewone man' in de jaren vijftig als summum van mobiliteit een Mobylette, in de jaren zestig en zeventig werd die op grote schaal vervangen door de auto. Het groeiend aantal voertuigen vroeg om steeds meer en bredere wegen. De toenemende kwaliteit van het wagenpark, de hogere snelheden en het verbeterde comfort voor de weggebruiker gaven het begrip bereikbaarheid nieuwe inhoud en leidden tot nog meer voertuigen en nog hogere eisen aan het wegennet. De toenemende mobiliteit stelde ons voor de uitdaging de gevolgen voor mens en milieu zo beperkt mogelijk te houden. Termen als 'ZOAB', 'ecoduct' en 'geluidsscherm' werden toegevoegd aan de Nederlandse taal.

Niet al onze problemen zijn opgelost. Recentelijk hielden we onze voeten niet droog en er staan nog steeds files. Toch mag de twintigste eeuw wat Nederland betreft in civieltechnisch opzicht zonder twijfel succesvol worden genoemd.

In de rol, omvang en het takenpakket van de 75-jarige Dienst Weg- en Waterbouwkunde is in de loop van de tijd nogal wat veranderd. Het Rijkswegenbouwlaboratorium werd opgericht om oplossingen te geven voor de nieuwe eisen van de toenemende mobiliteit aan het begin van de twintigste eeuw. Het takenpakket (kwaliteitscontrole van bouwstoffen, mengsels en constructies, materiaaltechnologie, wegenbouw- en meettechniek en advisering over wegverhardingen) veranderde gedurende meer dan een halve eeuw nauwelijks. Het laboratorium adresseerde zijn aanbevelingen en resultaten aan de Hoofddirectie van de Waterstaat, die daarmee de activiteiten van de regionale directies stuurde. Qua omvang groeide de organisatie uit tot ongeveer 180 medewerkers in 1980.

Met de komst van de Wegbouwkundige Dienst werd de eerste ingrijpende uitbreiding van het takenpakket een feit. De dienst ging zich vanaf 1985 bezig houden met het gehele wegontwerp, dus ook met de constructieve aspecten van de onderbouw, de vormgeving en de landschappelijke inpassing van de weg.

---

aantal werken in uitvoering en de opvoering van de dagproducties. Al in het begin van de jaren zestig bleek daardoor dat de traditionele keuringsprocedure op den duur niet meer was te handhaven. Tot omstreeks 1960 voerde het Rijkswegenbouwlaboratorium, zowel een steekproefsgewijze bedrijfscontrole uit op de productie en verwerking, als een opleveringscontrole bij bouwstoffen en (bitumineuze) mengsels. In het begin van de jaren zestig stegen het aantal en de omvang van de wegenbouwprojecten echter zodanig, dat het Rijkswegenbouwlaboratorium de bedrijfscontrole steeds meer overdroeg aan de aannemers. Om de zaken in de hand te kunnen houden, nam Rijkswaterstaat, met het oog op de zelfcontrole van de aannemers, bindende bepalingen in de wegenbestekken op. Als gevolg daarvan voldeed de traditionele kwaliteitscontrole als opleveringscontrole niet meer en moest daarom — in 1966 — plaats maken voor een kwaliteitscontrolesysteem met kortingsbepalingen. Sindsdien werden aannemers op hun aannemersom gekort, als uit onderzoek van asfaltmonsters (boorkernen met een diameter van 10 cm) uit wegverhardingen bleek, dat de eisen in het bestek met betrekking tot dikte en eigenschappen van wegverhardingen niet werden gehaald. De hoogte van de korting was afhankelijk van de grootte van de geconstateerde afwijking.

Opnieuw verhuizen In 1963 moesten de verhuisdozen weer worden ingepakt. Na veel en langdurig overleg werd enkele jaren eerder besloten tot nieuwbouw, waarbij werd gekozen voor vestiging in de TH-wijk van Delft in de Wippolder. Daarmee waren de andere mogelijke nieuwbouwlocaties in Scheveningen, Voorburg, de wijk Bohemen in Den Haag en het industriegebied Plaspoelpolder in Rijswijk, definitief van de baan. Het nieuwe kantoor van het Rijkswegenbouwlaboratorium was onder supervisie van de Rijksgebouwendienst ontworpen door het Rotterdamse architectenbureau Van den Broek en Bakema. De bouw werd opgedragen aan het aannemingsbedrijf NEDAM uit Den Haag. De eerste paal voor het nieuwe gebouw ging op 23 september 1960 de grond in. Op 1 april 1963 werd de verhuizing vanuit Scheveningen een feit, waarna het nog enige maanden duurde voordat alle werkzaamheden op de normale manier konden plaatsvinden. Het gebouw zal door latere generaties worden bestempeld als een typisch jaren zestig kantoorgebouw: zakelijk, sober en functioneel.

Pensionering ir. Van der Burgh Op 30 juni 1965 was het opnieuw tijd voor een wisseling van de wacht. Ir. Van der Burgh ging met pensioen en werd opgevolgd door ir. C. van de Fliert, sinds 1953 hoofd van de afdeling Cement en Beton. Ir. van der Burgh verdween met het aantreden van zijn opvolger overigens niet direct van het toneel, aangezien hij 'bovenformatief' als adviseur aan het laboratorium verbonden bleef. Hij zou tot in 1968 aanblijven om de relatief grote groep bij het Rijks wegenbouwlaboratorium werkzame jonge ingenieurs in de geheimen van het werk in te wijden.

Wisseling van de wacht, 1965 Met het vertrek van ir. Van der Burgh verdween de generatie, die niet alleen gedurende 40 jaar het laboratorium had geleid, maar ook wezenlijke invloed had uitgeoefend op de techniek en de materiaaltechnologie op het terrein van de wegenbouw. Zijn opvolger, ir. Van de Fliert, werd in zijn nieuwe functie per 1 januari 1966 tevens benoemd tot hoofd van de Dienst Straatklinkercontrole van de Rijkswaterstaat, en tot voorzitter van de Keuringscommissie Bestratingsmateriaal.

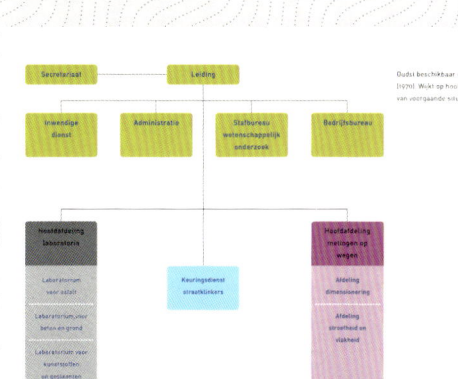

Yarom Vardimon

Born in Israel, and studying in England at the LCP (University of the Arts), Chelsea College of Art and the University of WestMinster, he has been a professor of visual communications since 1980. He was in charge of the submission of the undergraduate program. And presently, he is the vice president for Academic Affairs and dean of the Faculty of Design at the Shenkar College of Engineering and Design, Ramat Gan. His clients include leading Israeli industries, banks, medical centres, academic institutions and museums.

The distinctions he won in design include: Recipient of the Icograda Design Excellence Award; Fellow of the International Design Conference, Aspen, USA; Honorary Member of the Art Directors Club of New York; Recipient of the Design Excellence Award International; Design Conference, Mexico Design Year 2005.

He was elected to AGI in 1982. Besides, he was a Board Member and Director of New Media (2000-2003), past president of GDAI and past vice president of Icograda.

He has judged many international design events. His work is presented at major international exhibitions and permanent collections of museums in Europe, the United States, Japan and Israel.

PROJECT: YAD VASHEM MEMORIAL EMBLEM/SCULPTURE ON ITS 50TH ANNIVERSARY
TYPE: 3D IMAGE USED IN VARIOUS SIZES FROM A PIN TO A LARGE SCULPTURE
CLIENT: YAD VASHEM HOLOCAUST REMEMBRANCE MUSEUM

"The image was designed for the 50th Anniversary of Yad Vashem Holocaust Remembrance Museum in Jerusalem. 60 years after World War II, it is time to express a more optimistic approach of shaping the future along with the act of remembrance: Leaves emerging from barbed wire seemed like the right means for communicating a changing attitude. The assignment was an opportunity to explore a junction where our history and culture are reflected for creating a dialogue with anonymous people, on global, local and personal issues." – Yarom Vardimon

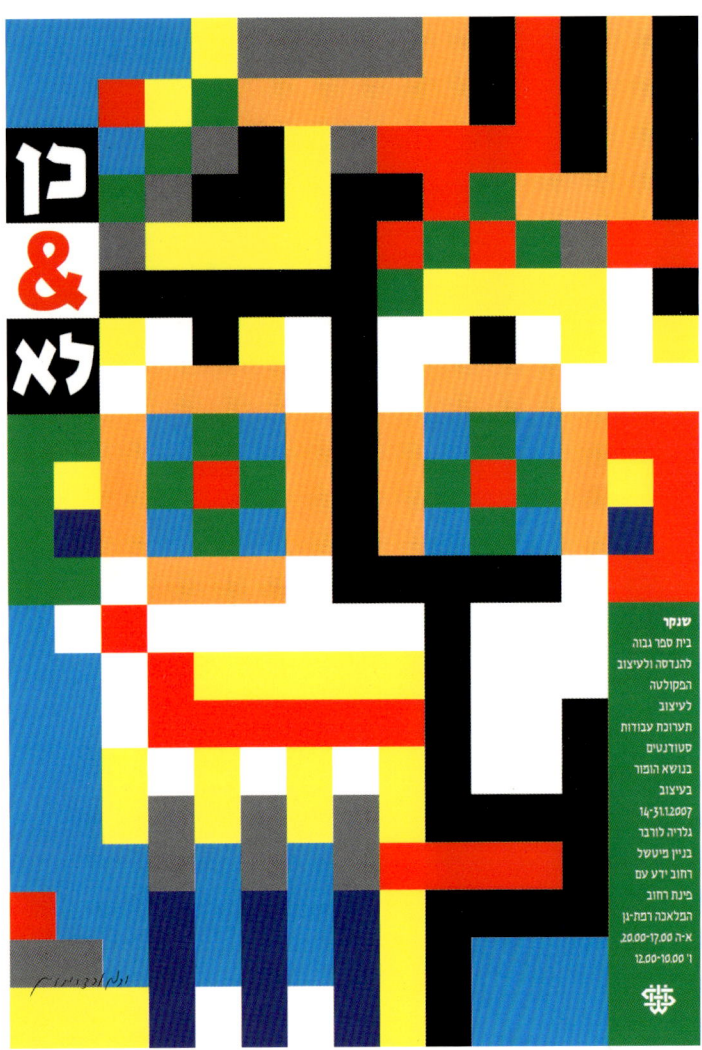

Top Left: Poster titled "Yes&No" for Shenkar College of Engineering and Design 2007
Bottom Right: Poster titled "The Right to A Dignified Standard of Living" (Supporting discussion groups in schools) for the Civil Rights Association 2006
Opposite: Poster titled "Separate Israel from Palestine" for ICU Publications

381

Mural (3x3 metres) for the Hadassah Medical Centre Mother and Child Pavilion 2007
Opposite: Children of the World - part of a wall at the Jerusalem Bi-Lingual (Hebrew-Arabic) School and images of boys and girls from 208 nations 2008

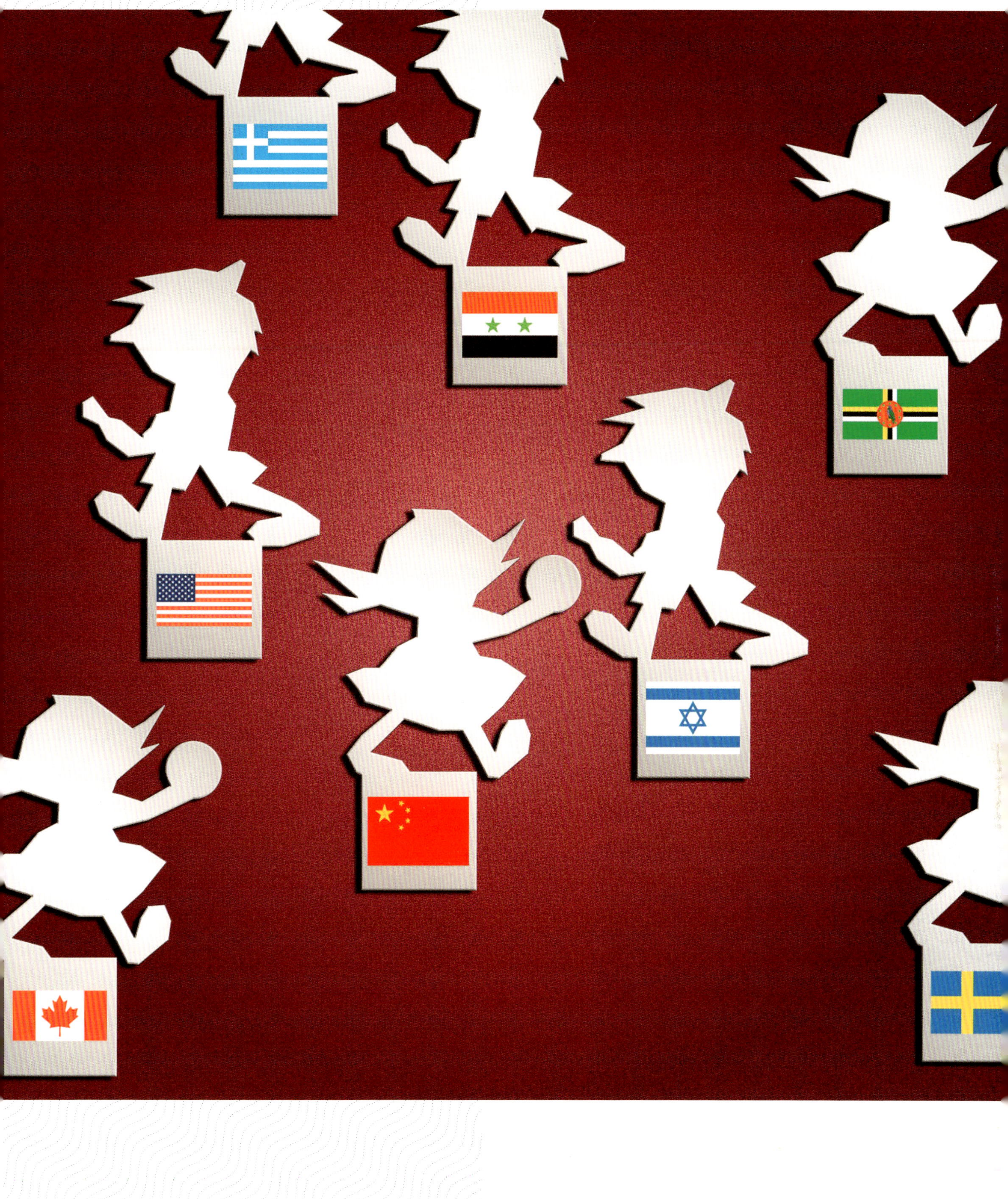

Spreads: Experimental development of visuals from deconstruction of work

PIG

Poster for Ceramic Market at the Bezalel Academy Jerusalem selling students' products

Top Left: Environment poster
Bottom Right: Society poster

387

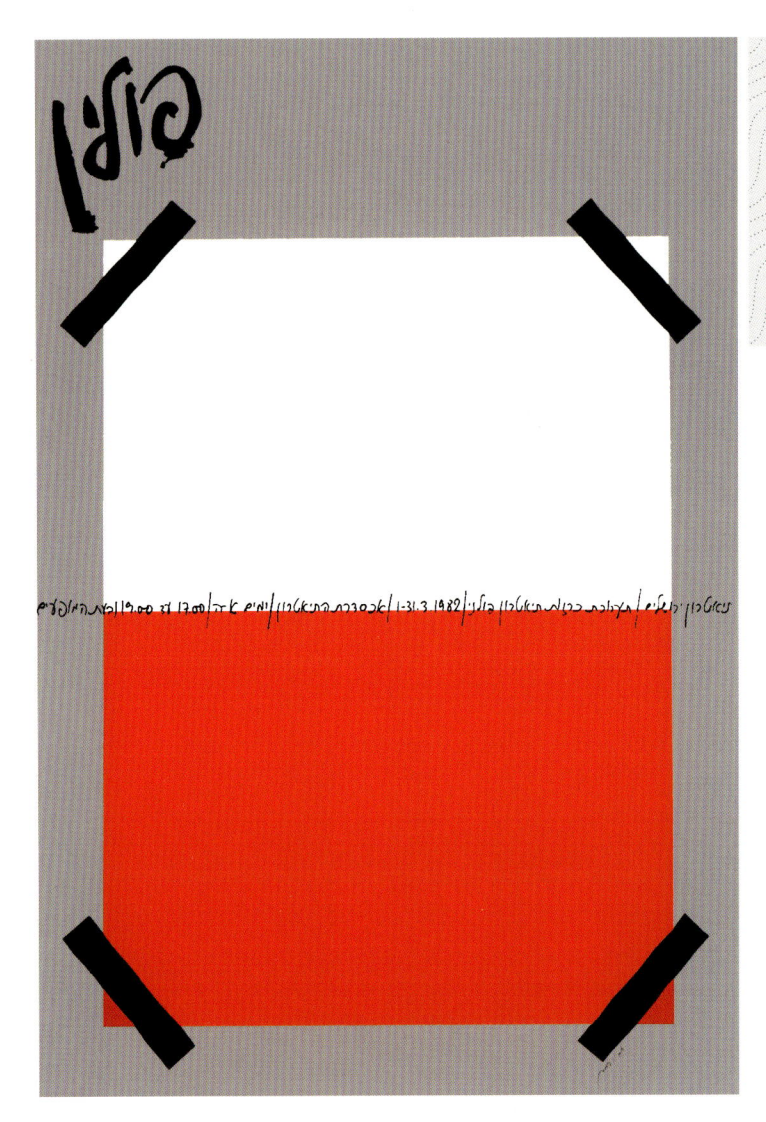

Left: Poster titled "Poland Exhibition of Polish Theater Posters" for the Jerusalem Theater
Right: Poster titled "370 Degrees" in the Shade Exhibition of Design for Shenkar College of Engineering and Design

Poster titled "Bezalel Lecturers Exhibition"

תערוכת
מרצי בצלאל
1970

אופק אברהם
אופיר אריה
אורון אשר
בקון יהודה
בייל ניון
בהט דניאל
גולדרייך ארטור
גרינסט אריה
דני אפרים
הירש יוסף
הופר דן
האוור אברהם
הדני ישראל
ורדימון ירום
ויינר ברני
זבצקי לידיה
טולקובסקי צבי
ימיני יחיאל
מווסי צילה
עשת פנחס
עפרוני יצחק
עונן נדולה
פינס יעקב
פוסק אבינדור
פלהיים מיכאל
ציזיק מילכה
קלדרון דוד
רווב יורם
רונן ורה
רפופורט משה
שטרן פרידל
שטרן יוסי
שנהב דודו

בית האמנים, רחוב שמואל הנגיד, 12 ירושלים 14.3-1.4.70

Environment poster titled "Green"

Left: Anniversary poster for Israel Graphic Designers Association
Right: Poster titled "Bezalel" for annual exhibitions at the Bezalel Academy Jerusalem

Top Left: Poster titled "Left-Right-Left-Right-Left-Right Boom!"
Bottom Right: Environment poster titled "Air" 2007

Left: Poster titled "Bezalel Academy Jerusalem Annual Exhibitions"
Right: Poster titled "Equality" for ICU Publications

393

Letter "U" image titled "You!" for Champion Industries USA
Opposite: Ambition image, letter "H" for Champion Industries USA

DAY DREAMING

Top to bottom:
Logo for cosmetic brand Ze
Logo for the Israeli Sinfonietta
Logo for Steel Industry Packer

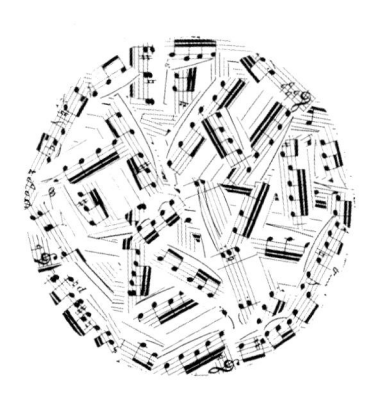

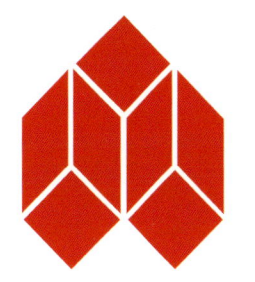

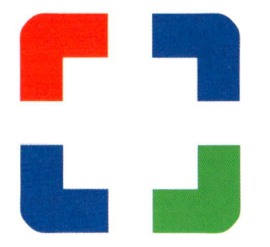

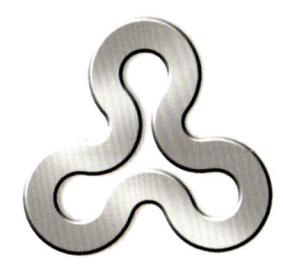

Top to bottom:
Logo for Gallery Sea-gull
Logo for Israel-Italy Design Forum
Logo for Electronics Company Miles
Logo for Weaving Company Shoham

Top to bottom:
Logo for Steel Industry PP
Logo for The Open University
Logo for Shenkar College
Logo for Emergency Heart Services Natali

Top to bottom:
Logo for Textile Industry Ouman
Logo for Medical Center Ramla
Logo for Gallery Or (Light)
Logo for bank Mizrahi (Eastern)

398

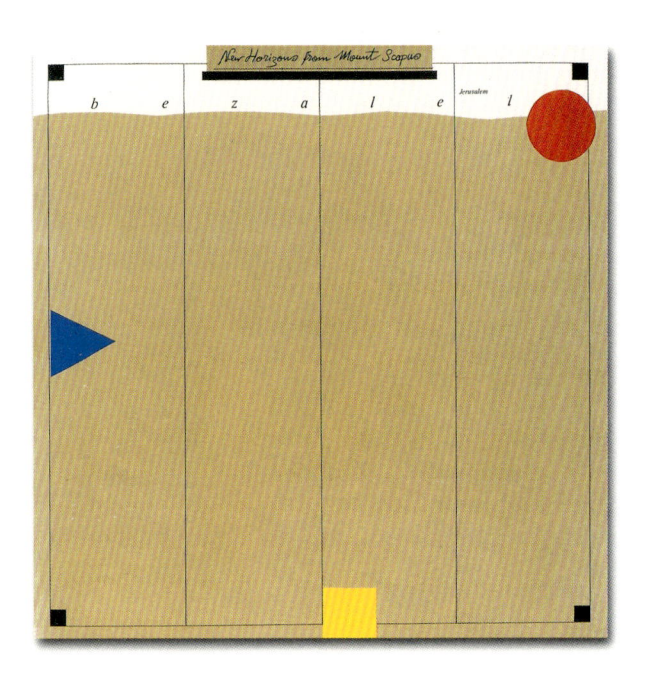

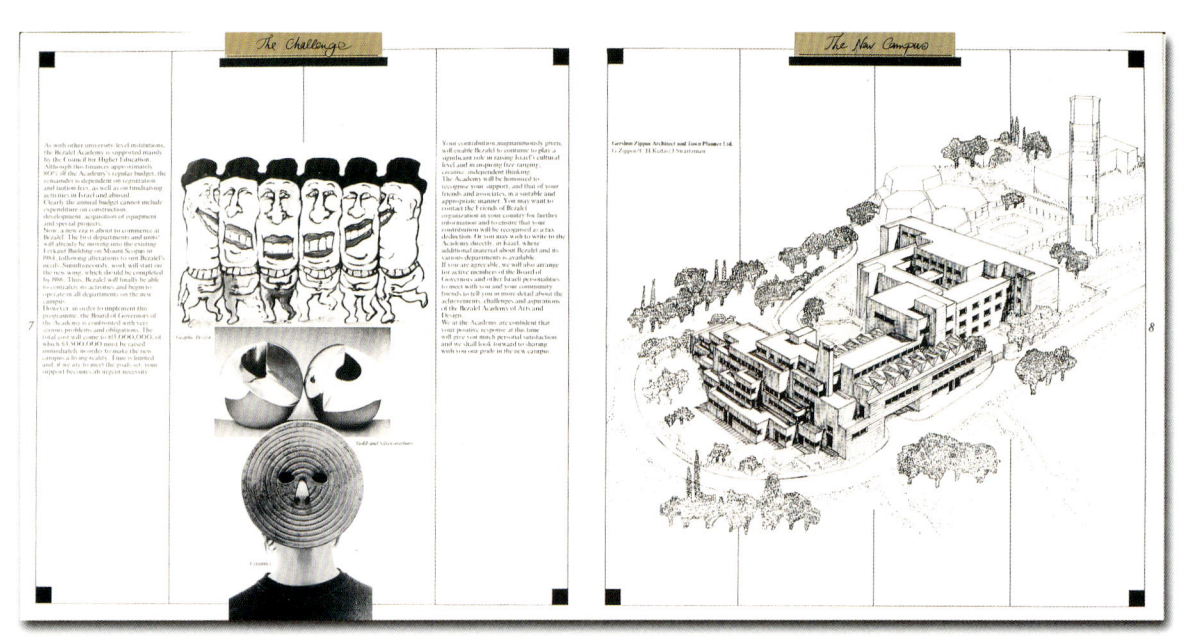

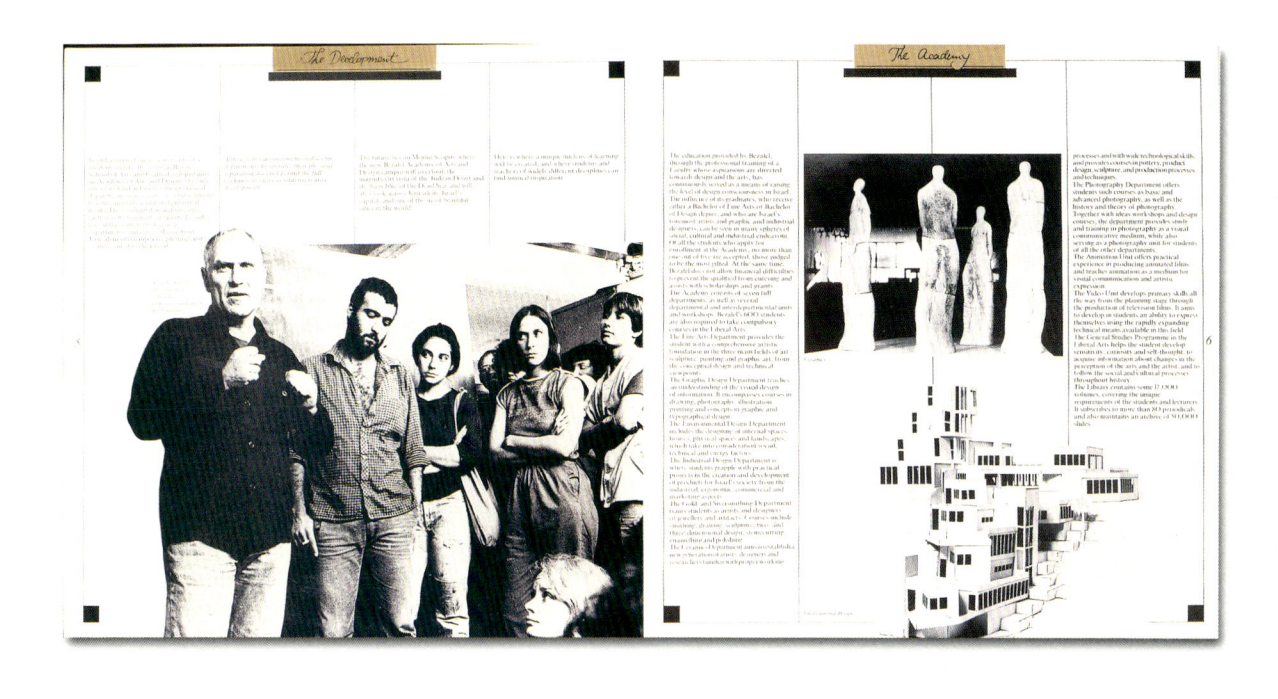

Spreads: Brochure Design promoting the Bezalel Academy new campus